Season of High Adventure

The Philip E. Lilienthal imprint
honors special books in commemoration of a
man whose work at the University of California Press from
1954 to 1979 was marked by dedication to young authors
and to high standards in the field of Asian Studies.
Friends, family, authors, and foundations have
together endowed the Lilienthal Fund, which
enables the Press to publish under this
imprint selected books in a way that
reflects the taste and judgment of
a great and beloved editor.

Season of High Adventure

Edgar Snow in China

S. Bernard Thomas

UNIVERSITY OF CALIFORNIA PRESS

Berkeley / Los Angeles / London

Except where otherwise acknowledged, photographs are courtesy of the Edgar Snow Papers, Edgar Snow Collection, University of Missouri—Kansas City, and are used with the permission of Lois Wheeler Snow.

University of California Press
Berkeley and Los Angeles, California

University of California Press, Ltd.
London, England
© 1996 by S. Bernard Thomas

Library of Congress Cataloging-in-Publication Data

Thomas, S. Bernard, 1921–
    Season of high adventure : Edgar Snow in China / S. Bernard
    Thomas.
        p.   cm.
    "A Philip E. Lilienthal book."
    Includes bibliographic references and index
    ISBN 0-520-20276-7
    1. Snow, Edgar, 1905–1972.   2. Foreign correspondents—China—
Biography.   3. Foreign correspondents—United States—
Biography.   4. China—History—1937–1945.   I. Title.
PN4874.S5715T46   1996
070'.92—dc20   95-21157
                                                            CIP

Printed in the United States of America
9   8   7   6   5   4   3   2   1

To the three generations of my family
Evelyn
Ira, John, Ruth, and Kathy
and Laura

Contents

Plates and Map

Plates (following p. 202)

1. Edgar Snow at age twenty-two, as he embarked from New York in 1928 for the Orient
2. Edgar Snow's mother, Anna Edelmann Snow. Date unknown
3. Edgar Snow and father, J. Edgar, in 1941
4. Edgar Snow and sister, Mildred Mackey, 1941
5. Mildred Mackey and Howard Snow, 1941
6. Chiang Kai-shek, J. B. Powell, and Edgar Snow, probably 1929 or 1930, in Nanking
7. Peking student marchers, December 9, 1935
8. Helen (Peg) Foster Snow, in Peking in the mid-1930s
9. Helen Snow in the Philippines, 1939
10. Agnes Smedley, 1940s
11. Edgar Snow on arrival in the Red district in the northwest, 1936
12. Mao's preserved cave dwelling in Bao'an
13. Mao and wife, He Zizhen, Bao'an, 1936
14. Hillside cave dwellings of Mao and other Red leaders outside Yan'an
15. George Hatem (Dr. Ma Haide) and wife, Sufei
16. Edgar Snow and Evans Carlson, in the Philippines, 1940
17. James Bertram in the Philippines, 1940
18. Edgar Snow and Soong Qingling (Madame Sun Yat-sen), in later 1930s
19. Edgar Snow as a war correspondent at Stalingrad, February 1943
20. Edgar and Lois Snow with children, Christopher and Sian, 1954
21. Edgar and Lois Snow with China group in Geneva, 1961
22. Rewi Alley outside his Peking home, 1960s

Map

Acknowledgments

The Edgar Snow Collection in the University Archives at the University of Missouri—Kansas City has been the indispensable resource for research on the life and career of Edgar Snow. The collection was initiated in 1972 through the Edgar Snow Memorial Fund, with the late Mary Clark Dimond as its guiding force. I have returned often to work in the lovely Edgar Snow Reading Room in the archives. The collection is based primarily but by no means solely on the Edgar Snow Papers donated by Lois Wheeler Snow. I am indebted to the university archivist, David Boutros, for his gracious help and his warm interest in my work, and to Marilyn Burlingame, who oversees the Snow collection, knows it thoroughly, and responds promptly and expertly to every request, no matter how arcane. She is a gem—for all researchers on Snow and his China.

The Smedley-Strong-Snow Society in Beijing was another invaluable resource. I am particularly beholden to its former secretary-general, Liu Liqun, for his help in all my China work, and for sharing with me his Snow expertise and the research holdings of the society, and for his good "connections" in gaining access for me to other Snow contacts and materials in China. An Wei, a fine Snow scholar from Xi'an, informatively shepherded my wife and me through "Snow country" in Yan'an and Bao'an. My research assistant, Liu Wei, was a well versed, most able, and delightful companion. I am grateful as well to the many individuals from "Snow times" that I met and interviewed in China. They are cited in the notes and are all listed in the bibliography. I was particularly fortunate to meet and talk with the doughty Rewi Alley in Beijing in what was the final year of his long life, and also to experience the ebullience of Indusco pioneer Lu Guangmian, still enthusiastically promoting the currently revived Gung Ho movement until his death in 1995. Israel Epstein gave me his keen observations and assessments on Snow's place in China's revolutionary history. Huang Hua, whose long relationship with Snow goes back to Yanjing University days in the mid-1930s, and who interpreted for Snow in the Red district in the northwest in 1936, graciously gave me much time in Beijing from his very busy official schedule.

In this country, many other library research collections have contributed significantly to this undertaking. I thank the staffs of the Rare Book and Manuscript Library and the Oral History Research Office, Columbia University; the Hoover Library, Stanford University; the Rare Books and Manuscripts Division, New York Public Library; the Tamiment Library, New York University; the Manuscript Division, Library of Congress; the Harvard University Archives; the Manuscript Section, University of Washington Library; the Hatcher Graduate Library, University of Michigan; the Kresge Library, Oakland University; the Woodruff Library, Emory University; and others. Also the Information and Privacy Staff, U.S. Department of State, and the following presidential libraries: Franklin D. Roosevelt Library, Harry S. Truman Library, Lyndon B. Johnson Library, and the Nixon Presidential Materials, National Archives, Washington, D.C. In China, the Beijing University Library was most helpful, and the State Library and the Labour Library of Foreign Literature in Moscow kindly answered my bibliographical queries and sent me copies of Snow-related Soviet materials.

I am grateful to the late John K. Fairbank for his early encouragement and counsel on this project, and to the late Owen Lattimore and O. Edmund Clubb for sharing their remembrances of Snow. The late Harry Davis warmly and knowledgeably guided us to the Snows' Hudson Valley homesteads of the 1950s, and to Ed Snow's American gravesite in a friend's garden overlooking the river. Dr. Charles and Nina Hogan opened their Snow correspondence files to me; Bertha Taube, John McDermott, and Paula Gerson made it possible for me to research the Grace and Max Granich Papers; Grant Harris, Senior Reference Librarian, Library of Congress, and Eugene Beshankovsky, Slavic Bibliographer, Lehman Library, Columbia University, gave me much help with Soviet sources on Snow. My colleague Helen Kovach-Tarakanov generously and expertly translated Russian language materials, and my former colleague Shih-chen Peng was always available and consulted often on

Chinese language items. Snow's brother-in-law, the late Claude Mackey, and Snow's nephew, John Snow, filled me in on much family history. The late James Bertram responded warmly and informatively from New Zealand to all my questions on those old Peking days and gave me access to the manuscript of his memoir before publication. Seiko and Reiko Matsuoka imparted their memories of Snow in Tokyo just after the war, including his friendship with the late Yoko Matsuoka, his literary agent and translator in Japan.

Oakland University was generous with research grants for my China trips, and the university and my department colleagues were always fully supportive of this project. Patricia Tucker did much typing, computer work, and other chores for me as our department secretary. Mary Sue Perria put the entire manuscript on those magical little computer disks and has patiently and skillfully handled all the seemingly endless revisions, additions, and stylistic changes. I owe her very special thanks. I am grateful to all the people at the University of California Press, especially Erika Büky, Valeurie Friedman, and Edith Gladstone, who have guided me and my manuscript through the publication process. And I am pleased to have this work designated a Philip E. Lilienthal book. I have the warmest memories of Phil's encouragement and support of my first writing ventures in the China field.

Lois Wheeler Snow has been unstinting in her support of my work. She very graciously provided me with transcripts of over sixty of Snow's diary books, ranging from 1928 to 1971, and with much personal information and photographs. I particularly appreciate her thoughtful gift of Ed Snow's much underlined copy of my work on the initial years of the People's Republic of China. Helen Foster Snow has been generous from the start with her vivid remembrances of the China years. I have had access to her voluminous unpublished writings and her personal correspondence files, as well as to her Nym Wales Collection at the Hoover Library. I thank her for this, and for her kind permission to use her unpublished manuscripts for this book.

The suggestions, criticisms, and comments of various China specialists (including anonymous readers) have benefited me enormously. I especially acknowledge Michael H. Hunt, William L. Holland, John S. Service, and Richard von Glahn. Naturally, I am finally responsible for the contents of this book.

Our children have contributed by an effective combination of patient forbearance at the interminable duration of this enterprise and subtle prodding for me to get on with it. I thank them on both counts, and for much more. My daughter, Ruth, was additionally helpful with the China map.

Finally, though truly first, is my wife, Evelyn. It is customary on these occasions to include a tribute to one's long-suffering, supportive spouse, who is almost always the first reader and critic of every draft. All this is true of Evelyn, but there is vastly more. She has been my invaluable partner and mainstay through almost a decade of Snow research and writing. She has accompanied me on all my Snow expeditions, in this country and abroad, and been with me in library research and interviews. She has typed all manuscript drafts and been the first to notice flaws in the writing. She has indeed been a full participant in every phase of the Snow story I have attempted to recount. It is my good fortune to have her as a partner in this work, and in my life. She has my deepest devotion and gratitude.

Note on Romanization of Chinese

I have essentially adhered to the *pinyin* system of romanization for Chinese proper names, places, terms and titles in this book. This system was introduced in the People's Republic of China in recent decades and is now also generally used in the West. I have made some important exceptions. Some major names from the Nationalist era appear in their familiar form: Sun Yat-sen, Chiang Kai-shek, and H. H. Kung. Also, I have kept the Soong family name (rather than the pinyin, Song) for the three Soong sisters and brother, T. V. Soong. And since Snow was of a pre-pinyin generation of China hands, I have retained his usages in direct quotations and citations from his published and unpublished writings (and from others of the time). It seemed appropriate as well to keep a few places and terms from the Nationalist period in their original forms. I list them here, with their current pinyin version in parentheses: Nanking (Nanjing), Canton (Guangzhou), Chungking (Chongqing), Yangtze (Yangzi) River, Kuomintang (Guomindang). In a number of other cases, I have included (in parentheses) the pre-pinyin version of places and names on first citation where that seemed useful to the reader. China's capital is a more exceptional case. Under the Kuomintang from 1928 to 1949 it was called Beiping (Peiping in pre-pinyin), meaning northern peace. The name reverted to Beijing (northern capital) when the city again became China's seat of government in 1949. But all through these changes, until fairly recently, "Peking" was the commonly preferred foreign appellation and was always Snow's name of choice. I have used it interchangeably with the two versions above.

Abbreviations

ALSP	Anna Louise Strong Papers
BFA	*Battle for Asia*
CHTP	Charles Hanson Towne Papers
CQ	*China Quarterly*
CWR	*China Weekly Review*
Diaries	Edgar Snow diaries, transcribed from the original notebooks
ES	Edgar Snow
ESC	Edgar Snow Collection
ESP	Edgar Snow Papers
FEF	*Far Eastern Front*
HFS	Helen Foster Snow
HSP	Howard Snow Papers
IPRP	Institute of Pacific Relations Papers
JBP	James Bertram Papers
JKFP	John King Fairbank Papers
JTTB	*Journey to the Beginning*
LC	*Living China*
MP	Mildred and Claude Mackey Papers
NTJP	Nelson T. Johnson Papers
NWC	Nym Wales Collection
POOS	*People on Our Side*
RAP	Rewi Alley Papers
RCT	*The Other Side of the River: Red China Today*
RHP	Random House Papers
RNORC	*Random Notes on Red China*
RSOC	*Red Star Over China*

SEP	*Saturday Evening Post*
SMHP	*Stalin Must Have Peace*
TLR	*The Long Revolution*
TPOSP	*The Pattern of Soviet Power*
3-S Society	Smedley-Strong-Snow Society

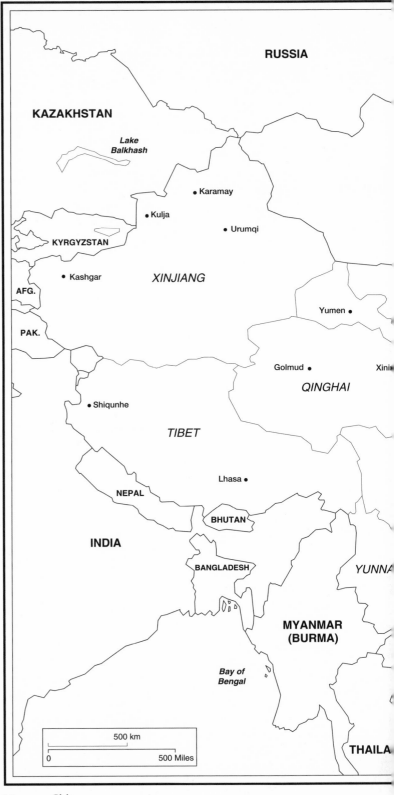

Map 1.   China

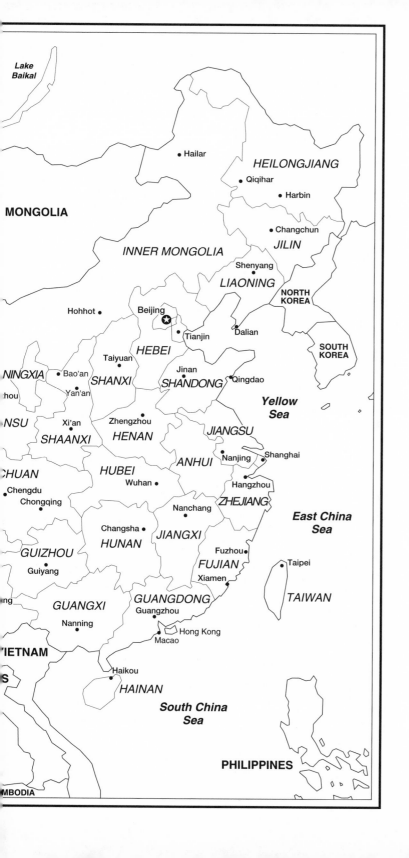

Introduction

I still vividly recall the high-school classroom in 1938 when my history teacher—a courtly silver-haired scholarly gentleman who was also the school dean—took the better part of a class hour extolling a new book he had just read called *Red Star Over China*. This was in the first year of Japan's total war on China, and a time of mounting fascist menace in Europe. To these dark and foreboding prospects, the China journalist Edgar Snow's uplifting firsthand account of the virtually unknown Chinese Reds cast a bright shaft of light and hope. His picture of these courageous young anti-Japanese revolutionaries and of their modern-minded, seemingly upright leaders gave promise of victory in war and a revitalized China to come.

Red Star not only had its own salutary impact on informed and influential American and British opinion but would become a generic model for later journalistic "Edgar Snows" in reporting on Red China over the next decade. (The noted journalist Theodore H. White, who came to China a decade after Snow, was told by an American general in Chungking in 1945 that the only power the Chinese Communist forces had was "what American newspapermen tell Americans about them. Guys like you and Edgar Snow, who talk about the Communist guerrillas and their areas—you guys are what makes their strength.") It would inspire and help activate a generation of educated Chinese youth, with noticeable effect on that nation's future. And Snow and his book would occupy a unique niche in the arcane internal political maneuverings and conflicts of international communism. Indeed, Snow's account was in many ways a harbinger of the national communisms (among which he acutely placed the Soviet variety) that eventually tore apart the Communist world. When the Chinese Red leaders again turned to Snow in 1960, after a hiatus of over two decades, they evidently hoped he could do for the People's Republic abroad what he had done for its revolutionary precursor. Snow himself then felt strongly that his earlier role placed a special burden on him to help bridge the troubled waters of Sino-American (non)-relations. The Russians, on their part, who from the first viewed Snow and *Red Star* with hostility, would begin openly to accuse him of using that book to spread the Maoist nationalist "anti-Soviet" heresy in America.

Red Star did its bit in steering my interest in history toward the Far East (as we then called East Asia) and especially China, a process further propelled by service in the Pacific in World War II. As a postwar graduate student, I spent over a year in Beijing (then Beiping) during the 1947–1948 climactic turning point of the Chinese civil war. The ancient capital we called Peking remained very much the one Ed and his first wife, Helen (Peg) Snow, had known in the mid-1930s—perhaps a mite more faded and down-at-the-heels, but still a beautiful and gracious old city. Its mix of the best qualities of China's classical past and of the youthful voices of its present and future was a spellbinding, exciting experience for young Americans beginning our immersion in China's history and culture. We foreigners were witnesses to the denouement of the revolutionary process Snow had so presciently forecast a decade earlier. A new wave of Chinese students yearned and demonstrated for an end to civil conflict, and for a democratized and renewed China, much as Snow's Yanjing (then, Yenching) University students had done in the famed anti-Japanese December Ninth Movement in 1935. Decades later in 1989, another generation of Beijing students would continue to be the spearhead for the still unfulfilled democratic aspirations that have infused China's twentieth-century revolutionary history.

I have been particularly drawn to the story of Snow's thirteen-year sojourn in China, a seminal period for that nation's stormy modern odyssey and for Snow's life and career. He arrived in Shanghai in 1928, the year of Nationalist ascendancy to power under Chiang Kai-shek, following the latter's break with the left, and massive suppression of his former Communist allies. It marked also the onset of organized Communist rural armed struggle against that regime and soon of Japanese military aggression against China that led to full-scale war in 1937 and the resumption of Nationalist-Communist collaboration. Snow left China in early 1941, at a time when this fragile wartime unity was rapidly eroding, presaging a reignited civil war after Japan's surrender, and Communist mastery by 1949. In the preface to their book on a 1982 conference of veteran China journalists, Stephen R. MacKinnon and Otis Friesen note as one of the major questions addressed at the gathering, "How did American journalists perceive and respond to one of the most momentous events of the century—war and revolution in China during the 1930s and 1940s?" I attempt here to give an account of how one such major and influential journalist-author of that time responded to these events. Included also is a substantial epilogue that begins with a brief overview of Snow's global wartime activities as a world correspondent for the *Saturday Evening Post* and then picks up the Snow story from the postwar years to his death in 1972. It deals with the 1950s—for him, professionally bleak—and the three return visits to China in the final decade of his life.

Snow, a middle-class youth from middle America, had come to China devoid of any political agenda or sinological background. He had had some journalistic training and copywriting experience and harbored larger literary ambitions. He wanted to see the world, with Shanghai a mere stopover, and to try his hand at producing travel accounts of his adventures along the way. He returned home a fully seasoned, politically astute "new" China hand and famed journalist-author. His is a saga of personal, political, and professional development in reaction to the momentous events he witnessed, participated in, and reported. His story tells us much about the China he came to know and alternately (or simultaneously) loved, was appalled by, despaired of, and finally saw redemptive hope for in the Red star he chronicled to the world.

Snow's initial return to the China of the People's Republic in 1960 seems, in retrospect, to be a futile attempt—by Snow and the Chinese leaders alike —to recreate the unique spirit, setting, and effect of an earlier time when Snow and the revolution were in their buoyant youth. And in 1970, it would finally be the realpolitik calculations Snow disdained that would give him the opportunity to bring another historic Mao message back to America.

Serious, in-depth research on Snow became possible and practical after his death in 1972, with the establishment of the massive and ever-expanding Edgar Snow Collection at the University of Missouri–Kansas City (Snow's hometown). At the same time, the Smedley-Strong-Snow Society in China (now replaced by the China Society for People's Friendship Studies) gathered together much additional primary material on Snow from China-based sources. Many other major library depositories of personal, institutional, and presidential papers, Freedom of Information Act materials, and the availability and cooperation of Snow family members, friends, and former colleagues, in this country and abroad, have all contributed to the data base.

John Maxwell Hamilton was the first to utilize such resources in his skillful groundbreaking biography of Snow published in 1988. In my own more concentrated focus on the China period and connection, I have had the benefit of the further strengthening of the Kansas City Snow collection. The Edgar Snow Papers are now fully catalogued and accessible. There are major additions to the holdings of Snow correspondence from his siblings, J. Howard Snow and Mildred Snow Mackey, and her husband, Claude. Mildred in particular lovingly and proudly preserved Snow's letters to the family from the time he left Kansas City until the end of his life. The collection now encompasses materials from many long-term Snow friends and co-workers. In two extended research trips to China, I had direct access to Snow files held by the Smedley-Strong-Snow Society and the Museum of the Chinese Revolution in Beijing. I also received materials from individuals interviewed in that city, and in Shanghai, Xi'an, and Yan'an. A trip by car to the original Red northwestern "capital" at Bao'an allowed me to retrace Snow's vastly more strenuous, and hazardous, 1936 trek to his rendezvous with Mao in the latter's still carefully maintained primitive cave dwelling. The fantastic configurations of the yellow-orange loess hillsides of northern Shaanxi remain as indelible an image for me as they were for Snow.

Newly available memoirs and personal papers of important participants in Snow's China life and work add more texture and background. Helen Foster Snow has provided personal correspondence and many other items not included in her Nym Wales Collection at Stanford University. Chinese and Russian sources have been especially revealing on the status and publishing history of *Red Star* in China and Russia, and on its political and polemical place in the Communist world from the book's publication to more recent times. Snow's massive published (and some unpublished) writings are, of course, the indispensable baseline on his work and thought for all Snow researchers.

In addition to his voluminous personal and professional lifelong correspondence, Snow kept a diary from the time he left America in 1928 to his last trip to China in 1970–1971. He accumulated about eighty diary notebooks during those years. He did not make entries systematically; there are gaps of months and apparently even of years. Lois Wheeler

Snow has supplied me with transcripts of over sixty of these handwritten books; most of the others evidently cannot be located. The missing ones are largely from the 1950s and 1960s and are somewhat less central to my present study. However, the diaries of his final six-month stay in China are available and are of inestimable value in documenting Snow's ambivalent reactions to the China of the Cultural Revolution. The diaries offer unique knowledge and insights on Snow's personal and working life, experiences, relationships, and thinking. They thereby yield a richer portrait of the more private man, one not always in harmony with his public persona. Snow best expressed the value and meaning of his diary-keeping. "As one gets older (say, 40?)," he noted in a November 1945 entry, "each day and its record of it, seems important—proof that such a person really lived, etc., slept, felt heat or cold, lonely or befriended, young or old, or hopeful or sad, or glad, or mad."*

But beyond even the evidentiary base, what must finally be the distinguishing feature of a work of this kind is the vantage point, and approach, the writer brings to the task. The emphases, analyses, and judgments in my account of Snow in China are necessarily products of my own background and experience as a historian and modern China specialist. Some of the major themes that thus emerge in this complex study of a complex man may be briefly summarized as follows.

Though China (and the sorry state of the world in the 1930s) radicalized Snow, the process did not displace but was rather an overlay on his innately liberal-humanistic, individualist impulses. The two "sides" never quite meshed, nor were they ever really resolved. It would lead to some soul-searching by him, usually confined to his diary, or occasionally mentioned in personal and confidential correspondence. As a friend of the left, Snow was concerned always to guard what he felt was his independent-minded personal integrity. He did not wish to "join the team," as he laconically put it in a diary entry during his last visit to China. And when Lois, in response to an invitation from their Chinese hosts during that trip, promised to return the following year with their

---

*Some twenty of the diary transcripts, from 1928 through 1933, and 1936, are now on deposit in the Edgar Snow Collection, as are the original diaries of his 1970–1971 China trip. Robert M. Farnsworth, professor emeritus of English at the University of Missouri–Kansas City, has cited the diaries of Snow's 1930–1931 travels through southwestern China, Formosa (Taiwan), Indochina, Burma, and India in the introductions to his useful compilation of the feature articles Snow wrote during that journey (for full details on all my sources I refer readers to the bibliography, acknowledgments, and notes). I deal with these travels in chapter 5, which is directly based on these diaries and articles, and much else.

children, Snow snapped, "Send me a postcard." Snow's independent ("honest") stance had admirably suited the political interests of the inherently maverick Mao-led Chinese Communists whose cause he so sympathetically reported in the late 1930s, and it would suit them again in the final decade of Snow's life as the Mao regime began probing the possibilities of an opening to America. "We do not expect you to agree with everything we say," Mao told Snow in 1970. "You have a right to your own opinion. It is better to keep your independent judgment." As recorded in his diary, Snow thanked the chairman "for his defense of independence of view." This exchange took place as Snow stood beside Mao on the Tiananmen rostrum on China's National Day celebration—the famed visual symbol of the imminent dramatic turn in Sino-American relations. The setting gave this conversation a particularly surrealist character. The two men were looking down, as Snow described it, at the masses of chanting youths, with Mao statues and the chairman's words in huge block letters flowing by. It was a vivid expression of the extremes of the Mao cult and the rigidly imposed ideological conformity for which Snow's diary entries at the time expressed great repugnance. It all epitomized the many contradictions and pressures of Snow's singular status (and usage) as Mao's American friend and symbol. On a visit to Beijing University a few days after the well publicized Tiananmen "photo opportunity," Snow irritably recorded his reaction to the greeting he received from a woman official there. "She made my position quite clear when she said, 'We welcome you as an old friend of Mao Tse-tung.' What a bitch, as if I would not exist otherwise."

These episodes demonstrated Snow's vulnerabilities in reforging his earlier relationship to Mao. Though "Integrity was the coin of [Snow's] realm," the late John K. Fairbank noted in 1989, "imagine being beguiled by the Great Helmsman in his Great Hall under the full blast of Chinese friendship!" How much more so, I would add, not only on Tiananmen, and in the Great Hall of the People, but in the aura of one-on-one dining and relaxed conversation in the intimate surroundings of the Red leader's private home.

But of considerably greater import and substance for an assessment of Snow's long-term links to Mao and the Chinese revolution were the convictions he came to hold in the 1930s in response to a China in deep distress and crisis. They were convictions he carried with him and further reinforced on his journey to the Red northwest in 1936. He firmly believed in the necessity for a revolutionary-style "people's war" against the Japanese invader, one that would simultaneously advance the twin goals of national and social liberation. He saw the Communists taking the lead in this. In fact, he privately worried at the time of the Communists' united front negotiations with the Chiang government in 1937 that the Reds were "throwing in the sponge." Early on he pinpointed the indigenously based character and nationalist perspectives of Mao-led Chinese communism and viewed the Reds as both Marxist-Leninist revolutionaries and Chinese patriots. Truly, Snow was something of a "Maoist" before there was a generally recognizable Maoism. His highly influential part in building up Mao's persona and prestige in China and the West were anathema to Moscow and the Stalin-controlled Comintern. Not even Snow's subsequent admiring wartime reporting from Russia could erase the Soviet's antipathy to him. Thus, while Snow's critical-minded, China-oriented leftism was well in tune with Mao's challenges to the Moscow-led world Communist establishment, in the 1930s and again in the 1960s, Snow's stance led to numerous collisions for him with the more orthodox Communist movement directed by the Kremlin. It would result in some curious episodes among his various encounters with its adherents.

Snow had a strong and abiding sense of responsibility as an engaged journalist whose work had a direct impact on the history he recorded. As Lois Snow said of him after his death, "his writing had taken on the nature of political action," and "as a writer, [he] had to be personally responsible for all he wrote." Yet Snow recognized that though he could not avoid "responsibility for power," he was not himself "a man of power." "It bothers me greatly," he privately brooded while in China in 1970, "that I have not solved this contradiction in my lifetime."

Snow was but one in a line of Westerners who sought to "change China" for the better. This could take a personally interventionist (and frustrating) direction; the remarkable story of the wartime Chinese industrial cooperatives (Indusco or Gung Ho) being a case in point. Initiated by Helen and Ed Snow and Rewi Alley, Indusco was a kind of parable on the pitfalls of efforts by Westerners to "reform" China. And as it played in America (with big publicity boosts from Snow), Indusco illustrated the altruistic-paternalistic American "helping hand" urges toward China. Did Snow fit the profile of the American "Sentimental Imperialists" delineated by James C. Thomson and coauthors in their book on the American experience in East Asia? Perhaps—though Snow always thought of himself as a thoroughgoing anti-imperialist, and he was almost as anxious to "reform" America as China.

Indusco was also a prime example of the exceptional partnership of the two Snows in their China work and causes, with Helen (who then wrote under the pen name Nym Wales) generally taking an "energizing" role. But they were also something of an odd couple in their sharply divergent styles, personalities, and temperaments. It made for an increasingly edgy relationship—an "eternal duel," Snow later rather bitterly (and perhaps unfairly) characterized the marriage. Divorce, and remarriage to the gifted actress Lois Wheeler, came in 1949 after lengthy legal and personal wrangling.

Snow wanted America as well to play an actively "progressive" international role, though he also had a "middle American" and strongly anticolonialist aversion to the nation being dragged into "foreign" wars to defend European empires. He had quickly understood that Western empire and privilege in Asia were doomed by the dual forces of Japanese expansionism and Asian nationalism. But despite his own warnings of the virtual inevitability of war in the Pacific, his personal conflicts over America's gradual involvement in global hostilities were not fully resolved—as was true for most of the American people—until Pearl Harbor. Snow's later disenchantment with cold war policies would put an end to his notions of "good" American interventionism—a still pertinent issue and dilemma as America seeks its appropriate and effective posture in a post–cold war but no less turbulent world. ("Oh, perhaps we have already intervened too much in the affairs of other peoples," Allen Dulles, head of the Central Intelligence Agency during the Eisenhower years, would later tell a young CIA recruit.) Beyond this, Snow understood that a proudly nationalist, unified, and developing new China could no longer be subordinated to the great powers, whether Russia or America.

As the United States edged toward war in Europe and the Pacific in 1941, Snow charted his vision of a new world—decolonialized, demilitarized, mutually cooperative, interdependent, and at peace. He expressed his Western-based faith in the boundless vistas for human progress offered by modern science and technology, and his liberal-radical belief in "rational" planning, and hope that a "higher" democracy, defined in social and economic as well as political terms, would ultimately prevail in America and elsewhere. The world that emerged from the war, however, failed to conform to Snow's scenario. Increasingly sidelined in his journalistic work, he viewed the developing picture with a jaundiced eye. (Snow, a charming and sociable man, was also often subject to pronounced downswings in mood.) As he wrote his old China friend Jim Bertram in 1952, "Events in Asia, Russian policy everywhere," along with American "blunders" and failure to offer "constructive" alternatives, "have depressed me over a long period, and seem to have left me merely old, cynical and disillusioned."

Snow's reconnection to China in his final decade lifted his spirits and put his derailed career at least partially back on track. But for him, to the end, the world remained very much out of joint. Ten years after Snow's death, Lois Snow acknowledged in a commemorative speech, ironically delivered in Beijing, "Despite the yearning for world peace, it seems outside our present grasp; despite the cry for democracy, it is still out of the reach of most of humanity."

Ultimately, the story of this complicated, fascinating, and influential man's "journey to the beginning" (as Snow called his autobiography) transcends the immediate China setting. It is a tale of personal and professional growth and achievement, of inner conflicts, and of bright hopes and somber realities. It is a narrative of one individual's remarkable efforts to improve the world in the face of daunting obstacles, shattered visions, and flawed redeemers. It holds as well a message on the necessity to keep trying.

I have been fortunate in the course of the eight arduous years of this project to meet, interview, and correspond with a great many good people who knew Ed Snow and shared those times, places, and endeavors with him. But above all, it has been an uncommon pleasure to spend this period in the vicarious company of this fine, often ambivalent, sanguine and despairing, very human, and engaging man. I trust the reader will find a similar pleasure.

Prologue

"You belong to the middle class don't you?" Mao asked. I said, "Many papers have called me a leftist." He laughed broadly.

Edgar Snow diary entry, July 1963,
referring to his meeting with Mao in 1960

CHAPTER 1

Setting

In the course of a grueling and hazardous overland trek from remote southwestern China to Burma in 1931, twenty-five-year-old Edgar Snow confided to his diary: "However well I readjust myself to life in America, my youth, the best part of it, lies ever in the Orient. This was the season of high adventure, experience, and unusual thrills." Snow, who had arrived in China three years earlier, would in fact not return to America for another ten years. His greatest "high adventure" was still to come with his famed pioneering journey to the Chinese Communist base in equally remote northwestern China. Not merely his youth, but a major portion of his life would be linked to China. After his death in 1972, some of his ashes would lie there forever.[1]

In his early twenties Snow sought out the more distant and untraveled frontiers of the world; in later life he viewed himself and his origins in American frontier terms. A "child of a rich, open, frontier civilization," he somewhat romantically characterized himself in his autobiographical *Journey to the Beginning* (hereafter *Journey*). Born in Kansas City, Missouri, July 19, 1905, Snow was a member of the first truly postfrontier generation in middle America. His life encompassed the unsettling transformations both of twentieth-century America and of the world outside. From its earlier, largely agrarian, small entrepreneur roots (epitomized in Snow's father's origins and career), the United States emerged as a corporate industrial and military giant playing an increasingly powerful and ultimately dominant role in a world battered by war and convulsed by revolution.[2]

In his work as an influential, and often involved, recorder of these turbulent times in Asia and Europe, Snow took with him the democratic individualist values and outlook, as well as some parochial remains, of his quintessentially American family background. After 1928 in China, and elsewhere in Asia, he developed a growing awareness of—an "awakening," as he later described it—and an empathy for the miserable plight of the peoples of these lands. During the 1930s in China he became convinced of the necessity for radical (revolutionary) social and political change there, and for determined resistance to Japanese aggression—the two being interrelated. While he put his primary faith for this in the Chinese Communist revolutionaries, he did not discard his bedrock "American" convictions (which included strong aversion to imperialism) but instead linked them to the vastly different circumstances and imperatives of the struggle for human betterment and national survival he found in China and in colonial Asia. His own ingrained sense of compassion and social justice served often as the cementing factor. Writing to his father in 1933 of his outrage and discouragement at the depressing state of affairs in China, he observed, "Perhaps this country is too much for anybody with a background of passionate faith in the idea of Justice and fair-play for every man as the keystone of the conduct of human affairs."[3]

In sharp contrast to the corruption, greed, and demoralization he had witnessed in most of China, Snow found the Chinese Communists he first encountered in 1936 to be "men of probity and selflessness." The "plain fact was that the Reds *were* 'better' people than their enemies." For their part, China's Communist leaders regarded Snow (in the sense of the attributes and reactions noted above) as a trustworthy "honest bourgeois" journalist. Yet the exigencies of later Chinese Communist politics and policies could cause them to set aside the special relationship when Snow's independent views did not suit them. The 1950s decade of China's Soviet alignment and the xenophobia of the late 1960s Cultural Revolution were two such examples. In any case, it is probably fair to say that Snow, who arrived in China with neither a missionary zeal to save it nor a revolutionary passion to change it, had a greater impact on that country than any other nonofficial Westerner active there in the critical years of revolutionary and anti-Japanese conflict.[4]

Through the 1930s and most of the 1940s, as Snow wrote of war and revolution in Asia and Europe, of Japanese and Nazi aggression, of Chinese and Soviet communism, and of the collapse of colonial empires, his viewpoint and sympathies, communicated in compelling and evocative human terms, would find an influential place in "mainstream" America. This was best exemplified by the great influence of his classic pathbreaking account of Chinese Communism, *Red Star,* and by his subsequent decade-long role as a major wartime correspondent and associate editor of that most "American" of mass-circulation magazines, the *Saturday Evening Post* (hereafter, the *Post*). Snow tended to view himself as a kind of intermediary between his American homeland and the revolutionary forces he felt he had come to know and understand. His American-style idealism and Asian-style radicalism proved a strong combination in this regard.

In the sharply changed situation of the 1950s, the linkages Snow symbolized were torn apart by the pressures of the new world of cold war. (As the China historian John Fairbank put it, Snow was "mugged" by the cold war.) Snow was turned off by, and isolated from, the zealously anti-Communist and illiberal American political-ideological climate prevailing in those years. He had been "professionally destroyed" by his "refusal to climb onto the cold war bandwagon all these years," he wrote Jim Bertram, his New Zealander friend from the China days. He was equally separated from a revolutionary new China now closely aligned with the Soviet-led "socialist camp." Not only were Snow's non–cold warrior views distinctly out of fashion in America; his "honest bourgeois" role was now also unwelcome in the seemingly monolithic and anti-imperialist Communist world. The fact that Snow early on could perceive the nationalist (or Titoist) potential of the Chinese revolution did not endear him to either contending side, and he saw himself becoming "persona non grata in all camps." Snow, in fact, continued throughout the postwar years to stress the long-term American national interest in a mutually beneficial relationship with a unified, independent, and modernizing China. He saw the new China as the logical culmination of the extended revolutionary process there. "It is a pity," he wrote his old friend in China, Rewi Alley, in 1955, "that so much unnecessary bitterness has prospered between China and the U.S. due largely to ignorance and monumental miscalculations on both sides." While the interplay of Snow's American and Chinese "sides" had made him a highly effective communicator of the Chinese revolutionary cause to his American audience in the 1930s and into the war years, this would be a much more daunting task in the dramatically changed setting of his return to China in 1960. And even the apparent validation of his Sino-American bridge-building efforts in the final year of his life would have its ironies for him.[5]

For much of the 1950s Snow, in the domesticity of a fulfilling new marriage and family, occupied himself in his Hudson Valley home north of New York City writing his "me-moirs" as he called it. It "ended up as a kind of personal view of history more than personal history," he noted. "I putter around a great deal with such prosaic deeds as gardening and carpentering, read books, play with our two infants, and enjoy the company of ma femme, Lois," he informed Bertram. "Now I seem to be content," he wrote a boyhood friend in 1954, "to study the globe in an illuminated Rand-McNally version on my desk." In this more introspective mood, he investigated and pondered his family roots and an America that now seemed lost forever. As he did so, the effect of the frontier on those roots and on that America took on a special meaning for him.[6]

Writing to his brother in 1954, Ed noted that his research into the "frontier land" history of the Snow family, plus a recent reading of the historian Walter Prescott Webb's *Great Frontier,* "has given me a new conception of the Snow line of thinking as passed on by the old man." Its spirit of self-reliance and individual enterprise still had its impact and carryover "down to our own generation," he explained to Howard. It held its own despite the rise of a big-business-dominated America in which "the individual no longer really count[s] for much." Snow clearly felt all this most keenly in terms of his own situation in those years: one in which his nonconforming stance had cut him off from the establishment media and its sources of comfortable livelihood. "We are well but not prosperous," he informed Jim Bertram in 1958. "We live by our wits and our wits are in short demand."[7]

Snow's vision of an earlier frontier America of enterprising, self-made citizens applied most convincingly to the history of his own pioneer forebears. The Snows had found opportunity and success in the settlement and development of the agrarian Midwest. But for many others, as recent revisionist historians of the American West have emphasized, there was a darker and seamier side of exploitation, injustice, and discrimination, and also often of personal failure. Nevertheless, it was through his own family background that Snow could find the verities and values he sought.[8]

The Snow family went back to a founding ancestor of English stock, William Snow. Originally from North Carolina, he had settled in the Cumberland region of Kentucky, then still part of Virginia, in the late eighteenth century. It was there that Ed's grandfather, Horace Parks Snow, was born in 1849. By then the family owned a fine farm with pasture, orchards, and stables—but no slaves. Snow's great-great-grandfather had freed his slaves, and the Snows were antisecessionist and pro-Union during the Civil War. There were some family claims of connection with a more distant forebear who had supposedly come to New England on the second voyage of "that capacious tub, the 'Mayflower,'" Ed wryly observed. Snow himself was tempted to lean on this tenuous claim when, in the early 1950s, he was apprised of a Captain Samuel Snow from Salem, Massachusetts, who had been appointed the first American merchant consul for the Canton trade in 1799. Though Ed was unable to find any evidence of a direct family link, the possible China connection seemed too intriguing to ignore. In *Journey*, he thus somewhat ambiguously, though not inaccurately, wrote of Samuel Snow as "another Snow who had preceded me" to China.[9]

After the Civil War Horace Parks Snow ("H. P.") moved west with the frontier to settle near Winfield, Kansas, in the 1880s, with his wife, Louisa (of an English-Irish Virginia family), and seven children. He farmed and also ran a general store and ultimately acquired extensive holdings in Kansas, Missouri, and Texas. His boast, as Ed was careful to emphasize, was that he had never worked for another man a single day in his life. H. P. was an egocentric and colorful character; a widower at the time of his death in 1933 at age eighty-four, he had a breach of promise suit on his hands, according to Ed, "which ate up quite a lot of a considerable estate." Ed remembered him as "a splendidly robust and picturesque old man, lord of the world he surveyed." Ed's middle name, Parks, which he never used as an adult, derived from H. P. (It was so unfamiliar that when his native Kansas City decided to recognize him posthumously with a day in his honor, the occasion was erroneously proclaimed as "Edgar A. Snow Day.")[10]

Snow likened these westward migrations to his own youthful urge to see the world—"the pull of some frontier dream, some nameless beckoning freedom, . . . beyond the sunset." In a less lyrical vein Helen, his first wife, had quipped, "his family have been moving west for generations; when [Ed] Snow began migrating he moved so far West he arrived in the Far East."[11]

Snow's father, James Edgar (J. Edgar), was born in 1873 and was raised on the farm in Kentucky and then in Kansas. In 1899 he married Anna Catherine Edelmann, originally from Columbus, Ohio, a devout Catholic of mixed Irish-German immigrant background. Her mother, Mary Ann Fogarty, had come to this country with her parents from Ireland, and her father with his parents from Silesia. Snow later noted that though his grandfather Snow had been a wealthy landowner, his mother's father had worked all his life as a bricklayer (although later establishing a small family construction business) and her grandfather was an Irish immigrant who had worked as a common laborer.[12]

The Snows, Methodists and firmly anti-Papist, found this first Catholic connection most upsetting. J. Edgar, in marrying the lovely Anna, had agreed to study Catholic doctrine with a view to conversion and to have their children baptized and sent to parochial schools. He himself had attended Southwestern Methodist College in Winfield, Kansas, for two years and had come to Kansas City in 1893. He was a thoughtful, well read person of strongly independent mind, "a man of integrity and high principles," a sister described him. Versed in the literary classics, he was fond of reciting favorite passages. Snow remembered his father, apparently lost in his own thoughts, going about the house "muttering lines of Shakespeare to himself, or quoting from Dante." J. Edgar declaimed in similar fashion as he worked in his print shop on Cherry Street in Kansas City.[13]

After editing a trade journal, J. Edgar had purchased a small printing business. This suited both his independent spirit and his love for the printed word. He operated this enterprise for over thirty years, content with a modest livelihood, and with pride in the quality and uprightness of his Snow Printing Company. "We were a middle class family with more respectability than money," Ed would recall, "though we had enough to eat and wear always and a comfortable home." His dad, Ed had earlier observed, "was a genius at making ends meet through thirty years of practice." J. Edgar "was not a hard-nosed businessman," remembered a close Kansas City friend of Ed's, but rather "a man of ideals and dreams, a thinker with "a soft but distant" personality.[14]

Both Howard and Ed were often impatient at their father's lack of a strong money-making instinct. (The two youths went with "an upper middle-class crowd," according to their brother-in-law, Claude Mackey, and had talked their father into buying a Cadillac. Writing from the Orient in 1931, Ed reminisced to his sister about the "old days" and of "Dad driving the old Cadillac.") Howard, followed by Ed, left for New York in the mid-1920s, in part when it became clear that J. Edgar was unwilling and unable to finance expansion of his business. Later, in China, Ed would remain skeptical of his father's desire to modernize, even if money should come his way through inheritance from Horace Parks.[15]

J. Edgar exemplified the ideals of the pioneer-agrarian life and culture that had nurtured him. In this, he reflected as well some of the themes of early twentieth-century rural midwestern progressivism. Very much his own man, he distrusted the rising forces of big business and big government. As an insular, nativist American, he was also estranged from the country's burgeoning metropolises with their mix of new immigrant populations. Howard (who continued to live in New York until the mid-1930s) and Ed, on the other hand, found their life in New York exciting. To J. Edgar, however, New York seemed "a bunch of Jews and foreigners." It had "swept you fellows off your feet," and "you imagine it is America," he wrote to Ed in 1930. "When you get back to the United States, I suggest that you see America first." As the depression deepened in the early 1930s, he inveighed against Wall Street and bloated millionaires. Although a Republican, he was for a time rather taken with the ideas of Huey Long, though he called him "a sort of political brigand." His suspicion of the high-living temptations of places like New York surfaced when he was preparing to come east in 1941 (for the first and only time) with his daughter, Mildred, and her husband. They were to visit Ed, just back from the Orient and living in New York, and Howard in Boston. J. Edgar cautioned his sons not "to take us to expensive places to entertain us or buy us expensive meals or suggest costly hotels. . . . You know that we are not used to extravagance and I shall feel uneasy if you wasted any money."[16]

Yet middle American insularity could be matched by a "sophisticated" New York provincialism. Famed Missouri-born regionalist artist Thomas Hart Benton pointed to the latter phenomenon when leaving New York in 1935 to live and work in Kansas City. In terms not very different from J. Edgar's, he wrote, "New York, stacked up against the rest of America, is a highly provincial place. It has such a tremendously concentrated life of its own," he added, "that it absorbs all the attention of its inhabitants and makes them forget that their city is, after all, only an appendage to the great aggregation of states to the north, south, and west."[17]

In contrast to Ed's father's somewhat unbending qualities were the loving warmth and devotion of his mother, a woman of sweet and gentle nature infused by a strong religious faith. J. Edgar soon decided against conversion to Catholicism, a stance that grew into overt opposition. This became a major strain on family harmony, even taking such needling forms as J. Edgar's insistence on eating meat on Fridays while the rest of the family ate fish. Though he acquiesced in a parochial education for Mildred and Howard (who were five and three years old when Ed was born), he insisted on public school for his younger son. Ed, however, did receive full religious instruction after school and went through the rituals from first communion to confirmation. As a running counterpoint to this, J. Edgar subjected Ed to Sunday afternoon "sermons" of his own—usually carefully selected readings from such authors as the celebrated orator and agnostic Robert Ingersoll. (In a letter to his father from China in 1929, in which he "went on at length on things Chinese and otherwise," Ed good-humoredly reminded J. Edgar of "all the verbosity to which you were wont to treat me when I was a young and helpless unsophisticate.")[18]

While his father's views left their mark, it was equally Ed's naturally skeptical "from Missouri" temperament that kept him from adherence to any organized system of proclaimed truth and faith, religious or secular. (During his last, often troubling trip to China in 1970, Snow observed in his diary that the all-pervasive "Little Red Book" of Mao quotations was "like the cross and the rosary.") Out of devotion to his mother he attended mass while he lived at home; by the time he entered college, he later wrote, "I was indifferent to sectarian religion of any kind." He would occasionally allude to an attraction for the ancient Chinese philosophy of Taoism, presumably for its focus on the individual, its paradoxical-whimsical view of human experience, and its skeptical rejection of conventional beliefs. In a 1948 article on Gandhi's assassination, Snow characterized himself as "an agnostic and pragmatist, an ex-Catholic turned Taoist, a Hegelian fallen among materialists"—the last presumably referring to his bent for a Marxist-influenced dialectical approach to world affairs. In any event, while Mildred and Howard remained "fairly good" Catholics, he would be regarded on the maternal side of the family as "the lost black sheep."[19]

Ed's mother's death in 1930, and the poignant circumstances surrounding it, ended any remaining links to the church for him. Hospitalized for surgery in the Catholic-run Evangelical Hospital in Kansas City, Anna contracted peritonitis after some three weeks there, went into a coma, and died. As his father wrote of these sad events to Ed in China, it seemed there may have been some neglect and incompetence by her doctors and nurses, compounded by the callous insensitivity of one of the nuns in dunning the family for payment of the hospital bill in the presence of the sick woman. In voicing his sorrow and bitterness at all this, Ed's father inevitably saw it as further vindication of his views. Anna had taught Ed to respect "all priests and nuns as good and kind," he wrote. Now "Fate chose a cruel and tragic time to disillusion her." Rereading this old letter in 1951, Ed found himself crying and still outraged at what had happened. With his mother's death, Ed was never again to attend a mass. Her passing severed his closest bond to home and made an early return to America less urgent.[20]

Snow continued to maintain an affectionate correspondence with his widowed father. Particularly in the earlier China years, he would write of his appreciation to J. Edgar for "the early shaping of my mind and habit under your tutelage," and for J. Edgar's "splendid qualities" as a father. The latter, on his part, took great pride in his son's writing accomplishments. He and Mildred kept a scrapbook of Ed's articles, and J. Edgar would often carry clippings around with him. Nevertheless, their worlds of experience and outlook grew increasingly far apart. As Ed's stay in Asia lengthened to almost thirteen years, followed by wartime and early postwar assignments abroad, he saw his father again only rarely.[21]

Meanwhile, J. Edgar's predictable failure to keep up with the times was his eventual undoing as a businessman. "New machines and methods of production have nearly eliminated me," he wrote to Ed in November 1941. His major accounts, including the *Kansas City Star,* were shifting to cheaper providers. Business was bad, and he had neither "the strength or spirit to build it up again." It was now "too late to expand or get a modern shop." Embittered and dispirited, as his world of the independent small businessman and its values seemed to slip away, he went into a long decline with frequent mental lapses, until his death in 1958 at age eighty-five. Largely dependent in the final fifteen years of his life on the care and solicitude of his daughter and her husband, his sole source of income came from a 120-acre Butler, Missouri, farm property he had inherited from Horace Parks. Rented out to a tenant farmer, it provided the meager sum of $1,000 to $1,500 annually. On J. Edgar's death, Ed received a one-third share of the income of this property. Remarking in his diary in 1963 that this slim legacy was the only inheritance he had ever received in his life, Snow thought back on his own self-reliant Missouri boyhood.[22]

CHAPTER 2

Kansas City

"I could claim to be a farmer, worker, businessman, intellectual," Snow summarized his background, which, aside from the final category, related to his youthful work experiences in early twentieth-century Kansas City. He worked first as an errand boy and "printer's devil" in his father's print shop after school hours and in summer vacations. The *Kansas City Star* was one of his father's customers, and he spent time "hanging around" the press room there. In his father's shop he learned to set type and feed a press, and "to like the smell of ink and freshly cut paper." Before entering college he "had determined to be a writer." Many good writers at the turn of the century started by working as apprentices in printing shops; according to the literary critic Malcolm Cowley, that was "sounder training" than any professor of creative writing could offer. In high school Snow published a paper ("The Delt") for his fraternity, of which he was president.[1]

Snow later recalled, perhaps half-facetiously, that when his father refused to give him a raise from ten to fifteen cents an hour, he went into "business for myself" selling subscriptions to the *Post*. He was also able to ride free on the streetcar while soliciting sales, thus saving himself the one-mile walk to school (his father did not provide the nickel for the fare). All this seemed quite in keeping with J. Edgar's lifetime code. His own much more affluent father had always insisted on his children making their own way; J. Edgar, for example, had repaid the money advanced him by his father for his college stint. Ed's other odd jobs during the school years included drugstore soda clerk, stock boy for a pump company, mail clerk for a railway company, farmhand at harvest time, and a salesman of printing for his father. Money thus earned helped defray later college expenses. It was essentially the typical boyhood experiences of middle-class life in mid-America of that era. For a fuller flavor of the setting in which the Snow family functioned, it is useful to look briefly at Kansas City's history and development in those times.[2]

Kansas City is situated in the center of the United States on both an east-west and north-south axis. Located on the great bend of the Missouri River, at the edge of the Great Plains and at the head of the Santa Fe Trail, it was the jumping-off place for the great westward migrations of the nineteenth century. In the latter half of that century, Kansas City became a major crossroads and rail hub and emerged as a leading grain storage and milling center; in the extent of its stockyards and meat packing operations, it was second only to Chicago. Though meat and bread made Kansas City, it developed into much more than a cow town. By the mid-1920s the total value of its factory production (steel, clothing, paints, food processing, auto assembly plants) was close behind that of Pittsburgh.[3]

Kansas City's population grew from some fifty-five thousand in 1880 to just under two hundred fifty thousand in 1910, and four hundred thousand by 1940. The city became primarily a mercantile and financial center with a large middle class. It contained a greater proportion of native-born Americans than any other metropolitan center in the nation. Its small but diverse foreign-born population, mostly Irish, German, and Italian, were concentrated in poorer districts of the city, principally the West Bottoms and the North End. African Americans numbered under 10 percent of the population in the 1920s and lived mostly in the eastern section of the West Bottoms, with Irish, German, and native-born white laborers in the remaining portions. The West Bottoms (and later also the North End) was the original base and political stronghold of the Pendergast Democratic political machine that dominated the city until Boss Tom Pendergast's federal prosecution in 1939, a prison term, and his death in 1945. Harry Truman was the most notable example of a politician who emerged from the machine, though Truman himself was untainted by its corruption.[4]

The machine-dominated politics of Kansas City further exacerbated the tensions already present in the Snow household over the religious issue. The Democratic party was identified primarily with its Irish Catholic base, and indeed some of Snow's relatives on that side of the family had links to the machine. An uncle served in the municipal administration and was caught up in the scandals that later erupted. Ed himself, as a boy, had met Tom Pendergast through this uncle. While Snow's mother, Anna, was a Democrat, J. Edgar gave his support to the independent (and also Republican-backed) reform forces, and viewed the Catholic connections of the machine politicians as still another mark against the church.[5]

In looking to the outside world in the early twentieth century, Kansas City and Missouri reflected the insularity of most of America. The nation's entry into World War I intensified the antiforeignism of native Americans. Though focused on German-Americans, it was felt and expressed more generally. The superintendent of schools in Missouri, for example, urged local boards of education to hire only native-born teachers. The postwar Red Scare in 1919–1920 both mirrored and reinforced these attitudes by targeting the foreign-born as sources of "bolshevism." The early postwar years also witnessed a revival of the Ku Klux Klan, which, on a "100 percent American" platform of hostility to Jews, Catholics, and foreigners, in addition to African Americans, mushroomed into a powerful force. It garnered some 100,000 members in Missouri before its sharp decline there and elsewhere by the mid-1920s.[6]

Many of the above currents provided fertile ground for those battling against Senate ratification of the Treaty of Versailles with its Wilsonian provisions for a League of Nations. Anti-League views were also popular in various ethnic groups, including the Irish, who with their animus toward Britain were disturbed at the power the League structure would give to the British empire with its dominions. (Snow's always strong suspicion of that empire, as well as his more general and deeply felt anticolonialism, may have gained an early start from the Irish side of the family.) Missouri's Senator James Reed, a former Democratic mayor of Kansas City and a politician of considerable oratorical skills, was a leading and effective opponent of the League who found backing among ethnic Democrats and isolationist Republicans alike. In a rousing speech in September 1919 he expressed the prevailing mood. "The man who is willing to give any nation or assemblage of nations the right to mind the business of the American people ought to disclaim American citizenship and emigrate to the country he is willing to have mind America's business."[7]

Snow grew up in Kansas City in the two decades from 1905 to 1925 that witnessed many of the developments and patterns described above. The family lived in solidly middle-class neighborhoods of pleasant, tree-lined streets and neatly maintained homes. These were in one of the early southern Kansas City residential districts developed by real estate planners early in the century. The Snows lived in comfortable homes first on Mercier Street, then on nearby Charlotte Street, the last and most important family residence. Though Snow had many warm memories of those years, and of Kansas City, he could also be negative. In later life, for example, he referred to a boyhood California summer adventure as "running away from home," and in a letter to Mildred in 1932 he talked of that "depressing Charlotte Street maison," adding that one of his "chief motives" for leaving Kansas City "was perhaps to get away from that house." Still he could at times be quite sentimental and nostalgic about the "homestead" and, particularly before his mother's death, wrote home frequently, always in the warmest and most loving terms.[8]

Snow attended the local public schools—Norman Grade School and Westport High School, graduating from the latter in 1923. After a year at the Junior College of Kansas City, and still unsure of his ultimate career goals, he left school for a year and followed Howard to New York. Ed also seems to have had a connection with a Kansas City advertising executive and friend of the family (B. G. "Bunny" McGuire) who was transferring to New York. Snow apparently worked for him as his secretary for a year and gained some acquaintance with the advertising copywriting field.[9]

Snow returned to Missouri in the fall of 1925 and entered the University of Missouri's noted school of journalism. Despite its interior Columbia, Missouri, setting, the school had an international reputation under its founder and dean, Walter Williams. The latter had especially good connections in the Far East, and by 1928 there was an influential network of some fifty Missouri journalism graduates working in the Orient, the majority of them in China. Williams, later president of the University of Missouri, developed special links between his institution and American-sponsored Yanjing University on the outskirts of Peking and helped in establishing its journalism department. In welcoming Williams on a visit in 1934, the *Yenching [Yanjing] News* wrote that "people in the Far East have come to ask all American journalists stationed in this part of the world, 'What year did you graduate from Missouri?'" Although Snow spent only a year at the Missouri campus before returning again to New York, a letter from Dean Williams he carried with him when he reached Shanghai in 1928 would serve him well in launching his journalistic career there.[10]

While at Missouri, Snow held his first newspaper job as a part-time campus correspondent for the *Star*. He mostly paid his own way in college, receiving little financial help from his father. Lukewarm toward formal education, he was never to complete college, in Missouri or elsewhere, though he took some evening extension courses at Columbia University after his return to New York. It was only "when I took Asia for a classroom" he wrote years later, that he began to discover "the joyful rewards of solid accomplishment based on hard study."[11]

In the summer of 1919, at age fourteen, Snow had already experienced the great travel adventure of his youth. He and his slightly older pal, Charlie White, had been working for a week in the wheat fields of Kansas and each had earned $50. A third friend, Bob Long, was driving his 1917 Model T Ford to California to join his parents there, and the two boys decided to go along—without first informing their parents. It was an example of the new mobility and greater freedom of young people in the emerging age of the automobile. After many harrowing adventures and near calamities on the two-week trip over the mostly unpaved Santa Fe Trail, the inexperienced travelers arrived in southern California. With Bob Long and his car now gone, the other two were left to fend for themselves with $5 between them. The boys rode freights to San Francisco, earned some money serving meals to railroad workers, scrounged other meals, and bummed their way back home riding the rails.[12]

Their many experiences hopping freight trains included a few nights in local jails and contact with migrant workers as well as with bums and hoboes. Snow's several brushes with accidental death through the years helped breed in him a fatalism often displayed in the chances he took and the dangers he accepted in the course of his work. "I have had such close calls," he wrote a young friend in 1968, "that I think fate has most to do with our survival." He liked to cite a Chinese proverb, "A man's life is a candle in the wind." Snow's fatalism, though, was never of the passive, accepting variety he so strongly deplored of the Orient; on the contrary, it was the kind that suited his activist, risk-taking nature. "Many materials formed the fabric of his character," Lois Snow remembered of Ed; "daring-to-do is noticeable in the weave." As Snow wrote to Charlie White thirty-five years after their California escapade, "I have never forgotten the adventurous summer we spent together—which probably profoundly influenced my life, as it gave me a travel itch which eventually took me all over the world and around it a number of times."[13]

In his boyhood years in Kansas City Snow conformed to the conventional patterns and standards of his social and economic milieu. He was a Boy Scout (reaching Eagle Scout rank), an active fraternity member in high school and college, and a saxophonist in a jazz band he formed with his friends. (Kansas City in the 1920s, with its proliferation of prohibition-era clubs, had become a leading center of the new Jazz Age.)

Generally described as "nice looking," he was a soft-spoken "well-bred, natural kind of person," with a good-humored likableness Helen Snow called his "Irish charm." That Ed Snow was a member of the "right crowd" (the "better families," as his friend Charlie White phrased it) seemed reflected in his high-school yearbook characterization. Under the rubric Can You Imagine it supposed, "Edgar Snow mingling with vulgar mob."[14]

All Snow's fellow students in grade school and high school, he later recalled, were white, and with rare exceptions were from native-born "upper-middle" and "middle-middle class" families. Segregation was taken for granted in both school and social life and applied to Mexicans and Asians as well as African Americans. Desegregation had never arisen for Snow as a "controversial question" before he reached college. His early contact with the Chinese was limited to a local laundryman whom he and the other neighborhood boys delighted in taunting. In high school, though Snow had one Jewish schoolmate as a "crony," he was apparently undisturbed at the exclusion of this youth, and of all others of "his kind," from the fraternities in which Ed was a prominent figure.[15]

All in all, the America that Snow took with him when leaving Kansas City permanently in 1926 to begin to work at the (copy-) writer's trade was a mixed bag. Its elements included a self-reliant spirit, individualist values, a strong urge to succeed materially and otherwise, and a background (aside from his brief California lark) that left him still largely unaware of and uninvolved with the diversity of peoples not of his own kind. Years later he would write in his diary, apropos of a private meeting he had with President Truman in 1947, that "My own background had been the same as his. I knew nothing of foreign peoples. I didn't know a communist from a Catholic when I went to China."[16]

Yet, perhaps above all, Snow also took with him special attributes of his own: a zest for travel and adventure, and a deep curiosity about and interest in people as individuals. His reading of books such as Hugo's *Les Miserables* had already awakened an innate empathy with the underdog. In the "great classroom" of the outside world, he would begin to sort all this out.

CHAPTER 3

New York and Beyond

"After all," Calvin Coolidge pronounced in 1924, "the chief business of the American people is business," expressing in this oft-quoted and typically laconic remark the prevailing mood of mid-1920s America. "Under the beneficent influence of Coolidge Prosperity," Frederick Lewis Allen wrote in 1931, "business had become almost the national religion of America." And the high-pressure salesman and the advertising agency were its evangelists. Again in Coolidge's words, "advertising ministers to the spiritual side of trade." The soaring Wall Street bull market of the later 1920s seemed to offer unlimited vistas for riches to all who participated, including the growing multitude of smaller investors. New York, the nation's business and financial fulcrum and its publishing and advertising center, was the mecca for ambitious bright young men from the provinces seeking their fortunes. Howard and Ed Snow neatly fitted this description.[1]

Howard, who had preceded Ed to New York, reflected both the spirit and the opportunities of the time. In New York, and then in Boston, Howard worked in public relations–promotional jobs with the American Bankers Association and later the National Association of Manufacturers. The two brothers were much alike in looks and personality. Howard, perhaps the handsomer, earned extra money in the earlier New York days by posing for ads, including a full-page one in the *Post* for Spur ties. He symbolized in key respects the business ethic and outlook of the Coolidge-Hoover era and retained much of this standpoint through the New Deal years. He believed firmly in business success and enjoyed the aura of being part of the big business world. While Ed would move on for the next two decades to a vastly different, highly adventurous and eventful life and career, almost all of it overseas in the storm centers of the world, Howard would build a secure family-centered life in the Boston suburbs. In sharp contrast to Ed's wanderlust, Howard stayed put; in fact, he never in the course of a very long life (he died at ninety-two) ventured west of Kansas City.[2]

Ed, on returning to New York in the summer of 1926, went back to work, now as a copywriter, for Medley Scovil and Company, a small advertising agency specializing in accounts with financial houses. Ed was very close to Howard, whom he looked to as something of a mentor. In New York they shared an apartment in mid-Manhattan, together with Bert Ord, a Kansas City friend. Another such friend, Buddy (Charles) Rogers, stayed with them for a time before going off to Hollywood to play the lead in the famous Paramount film *Wings*. Rogers was then on his way to stardom, and later to marriage with "America's Sweetheart," Mary Pickford. "Proximity to such grandiose success" could at times be discouraging, Ed wrote his sister, but he recognized that Buddy's case was indeed exceptional and that he (Snow) should be able to make "a milder success of my own." (Actually, before he left New York in early 1928, Snow for a time had been in the running for a lucrative position with MGM studios in California as a film scriptwriter and reader.) Though Ed had aspirations for success similar to Howard's, he saw it in literary as well as material terms. "I went to New York with the firm intention of making a hundred thousand dollars before I was thirty," Snow told a radio interviewer in 1946. With that amount in hand, he added, he could set himself up "to produce great masterpieces for which I felt the literary world was waiting." It seemed that easy then.[3]

For the time being, however, the possibilities at Scovil's were much more modest. His income in the early months of 1927 ($60 per week) was adequate for the shared expenses of his living arrangements. He informed his father at that time that his weekly expenses (including tailor and entertainment) came to $41. He was also paying off debts to his parents and Howard and managing to save money. Such savings (which by then totaled a few hundred dollars), he told his father, "you may call for should an emergency present itself." Though careful in all his expenditures, he made an exception for clothing, "as I find this is an important asset both commercially and socially." And while life in New York was "no bed of roses," "I will succeed. I am determined to raise my head above the crowd and to amount to something in a larger way than at present seems possible in Kansas City." Even earlier in 1926, when he still talked of "dear old K.C." as the place in the world he considered to be "home," he quickly added, "But how is one to be sure of it, until one has tried the other places?"[4]

The Snow brothers, as attractive and eligible young men, had some entrée to New York's young social set. But with their limited monetary resources and careful spending habits, it was a restricted access at best. Mother naturally kept warning them of the "pitfalls of sin, gin, [and] actresses," Ed complained to Mildred, adding that even were he to be tempted by "the drumbeat of night life, tinsel and jade," his financial situation would make indulgence impossible. In like vein, Ed assured his mother that the two youths avoided dates with girls of "extravagant taste," preferring instead those of the "better sort" who appreciated the " 'intelligent comraderie' of youth with youth." This approach, Ed somewhat tongue-in-cheek acknowledged, brought more rejections than acceptances. Yet as the holiday season neared in December 1927, the two had invitations to a series of parties extending well into the new year; all at little expense to themselves, Ed was quick to inform his father. "You see," he explained impishly, "attractive, intelligent young men are in great demand just now on the New York debutante market. Pooh-pooh and tish-tish." On quite a different level, Ed spent evenings as a member of the New York National Guard "manicuring a horse over in Brooklyn."[5]

New York, for young Snow, was an overwhelming experience. There "is about this town," he told Mildred in the inflated "literary" prose style he was then cultivating, "a power which asserts itself over all within its confines, that punctuates the lives of the millions that breathe its clamorous air, and controls the spirits and souls of its constituents." His inherently skeptical, humanistic outlook was also coming through. With Lent approaching, even should he try "to avoid all gaiety," he gently teased his devout sister, "who is there to stifle the joy of the skylark?" He wondered "why men should shut out the light of God, the better to love him."[6]

Snow at first found his work at Scovil's interesting and reasonably challenging. He wrote ad copy for banks, was involved in the production end of the business, and garnered a few new accounts for the firm. He entered and won a promotional letter-writing contest sponsored by the *Savings Bank Journal*. The award was a Remington portable he had been "yearning" to own. He continued to think of a business career as the path to financial success and for a time considered enrolling in night law school, which would provide the most practical professional supplement "to one's business pursuit." Snow had brought in as one of his accounts a Jersey City bank whose young and dynamic president, Kelley Graham, had also become a friend and counselor. Graham later strongly encouraged Snow in his 1928 travel and writing plans. (Throughout Ed's years in the Orient and after, he kept much of his funds in Graham's bank.) Snow was already exhibiting his ability to develop lasting friendships with many of the prominent, well placed people he met. They responded to his agreeable personality, quick intelligence, and adventurous spirit and were ready to befriend and help him.

But by the beginning of 1928, Snow was becoming increasingly restless and dissatisfied with his job. For one thing, a promised raise from Mr. Scovil had been deferred because of Snow's habitual tardiness (a lifetime tendency). Besides, he felt he was worth much more than Scovil would ever pay him and planned to move on in a couple of months to another ad agency, or to become advertising manager in a large corporation. (The fact that Howard was advancing rapidly probably played a part in these plans.) Beyond this, Snow was directing more and more of his thoughts toward broader horizons and a more creative writing career. "The truth is," he recalled (perhaps more from the perspective of a decade or two), "that I had learned to hate the money-grubbers of Wall Street." In the Manhattan apartment, he set up a "quiet nook" for his reading and writing and submitted occasional squibs to two literary contacts he had made, Charles Hanson Towne, editor of *Harper's Bazaar,* and Mrs. William Brown (Marie Mattingly) Meloney, editor of the *New York Herald-Tribune* Sunday magazine. Both would be of much help in advancing his writing career.[7]

By the next month, Snow had taken dramatic steps that would alter the entire course of his life. His ad agency office was not only near Wall Street but looked out onto the docks and ships of the lower tip of Manhattan. Pursuing his dream to "see the world," he resigned from Scovil's and secured a job as a deck boy on the SS *Radnor,* a merchant ship operating under the Roosevelt Shipping Lines. Characteristically, he got the job through a personal contact with Kermit Roosevelt, president of the company and the son of Theodore Roosevelt. Roosevelt also gave Snow a personal letter of introduction to the various American consulates overseas and cautioned him to keep it confidential from the ship's captain and officers. Snow was indeed a very special deckhand! The "money-grubbers of Wall Street" also played a bit part in this unfolding scenario. With advice from his financial-banking contacts, Snow made a small "killing" in the overheated stock market in the months before he left, coming out with an $800 windfall that would, he calculated, provide the necessary cushion for a year of world travel and of travel writing.[8]

Snow had acted with typical independence reminiscent of his boyhood California adventure almost ten years earlier. By the time his detailed letter outlining his plans and actions reached home, he was already on his way. His wages on the *Radnor* would be the "prodigious sum" of $25 per month, he informed his parents; he planned to stay with the ship until it reached Shanghai by way of the Panama Canal. Then he would leave the *Radnor,* and "vagabonding and tramping" in whatever way "most happily offers itself," he would complete his "odyssey." All told, he expected to be away nine months, perhaps more. His round-the-world expectations were reflected in his request for addresses and letters of introduction to relatives in Ireland. The *Radnor*'s itinerary included Panama, Hawaii, the Philippines, China, and possibly India. Ed had prevailed on a Kansas City fraternity friend, Alvin Joslin, to sign on with him as deck boy. Thus, he assured his parents, he would have the companionship of "a boy of my own Class." He had been inoculated against "all diseases of the Orient" and was "civilized enough to escape any corrosions of a venereal nature."

Snow's trip was hardly undertaken in a reckless manner; there had been careful thought and painstaking preparations. He had accumulated what he felt to be minimally necessary funds, had consulted with and received the enthusiastic endorsement of older friends and advisers such as Kelley Graham and Charles Towne, and had worked out arrangements with editors in Kansas City and New York to do travel pieces. He had made an agreement with the Kansas City *Journal-Post* to be their "roving correspondent" and had been encouraged by Marie Meloney to submit stories for the *Herald-Tribune* magazine—"the finest newspaper magazine published in the United States," Ed felt. Dean Walter Williams and others at the University of Missouri had provided him with names and addresses of their journalism graduates around the world, particularly in the Orient. He took with him also letters of introduction to "important people" in Asia, the Middle East, and Europe, and "blanket" letters of introduction to American consuls along the way. Keep in mind that Snow was then all of twenty-two![9]

The *Herald-Tribune* and *Harper's Bazaar* were useful early outlets for Snow articles. Charlie Towne in particular, almost thirty years Ed's senior, proved to be an invaluable friend and informal literary agent. *Far Eastern Front,* Snow's first book, was dedicated to him. Towne was a prolific author, columnist, and editor, and even an actor in his later years. When Ed eventually saw him again in 1941, he observed in his diary that Towne "is of the Oscar Wilde period of literature, and already and inevitably anachronistic." A "histrionic" figure, but "a grand person" and "a handsome old man with blue eyes, friendly, popping from his head."[10]

In exuberantly romantic prose, Snow gave his parents the reasons for all these moves. He spoke of his "intense eagerness to visit the more interesting countries of the world . . . before the imagination and spirit of my youth had dimmed. . . . Happiness at the moment meant but one thing. And that was travel!! Adventure! Experience!" In an affirmation of his lifetime "free lance" spirit, he declared that he would not settle for a "monotonous existence" as a "cog in a gargantuan machine." "How could I labor over the lifeless little duties spread before me when this song of cities was beating in my brain!" In like manner, he wrote the editor of the *Journal-Post* that his purpose was " 'a footloose, carefree ramble round the world.' I shall go where, when and as I choose." Surely here was a classic example of what the philosopher Joseph Campbell calls "following your bliss." (On a less rapturous level, the distinguished *New York Times* China correspondent Tillman Durdin later had much the same experience in getting to the Orient. He left a Houston, Texas, newspaper job in the early 1930s, took a deckhand job on an American ship that ultimately reached Shanghai, where he jumped ship to take a job with the American-run *Shanghai Evening Post and Mercury*.)[11]

Snow, however, was not burning all his bridges behind him. He had been assured of a place with another advertising agency on his return; but first, he promised his folks, would come a visit to the family in Kansas City. It would be thirteen years before Snow was back in New York, and even longer for Kansas City. He was never to see his mother again.

Travel-adventure books, and world travel, were much in vogue in the United States in the 1920s. Snow had read Richard Halliburton's best-selling accounts of his spectacular and exotic travel feats. Interestingly, both of Snow's earlier California travel companions, Bob Long and Charlie White, also traveled to the Orient in the late 1920s. Bob Long visited China during a nine-month overseas college group trip; White, on summer vacation from medical school, toured the Far East as a member of a band playing aboard ship in the same summer that Snow arrived in Shanghai. Snow was well suited for travel writing. In the opening sentence of *Journey,* he described himself in 1928 as a youth "full of curiosity and wide open to the world." He had a flair for vividly detailed description, though there were some callow tendencies toward purple prose to overcome. His people-centered writing was already infused with a warmly good-humored style and personality. As Snow moved on to the broader field of political reporting, he remained an appealing companion for the reader in an age of personal journalism.[12]

As the *Radnor* pulled out to sea from Newport News in the predawn hours of February 26, two days after leaving its Brooklyn pier, young Snow stood on deck, tired and sleepy in the chill wind, anxious to see his first sunrise at sea. As he watched the now fully exposed sun, "looking like a great golden button," "I had a sensation of thrilling poignancy. This was the dawn of another life for me," he wrote in the diary he now began and kept up fairly consistently until the final year of his life. Though feeling slightly apprehensive, he was buoyed "at the thought of what new friends and new delights for my senses awaited me." A friend had remarked to Snow on an earlier occasion that perhaps it took "a certain kind of genius" to be able to know and feel "the drama" of one's life experiences. "If I had nothing else," Snow declared, "I have the kind of genius he speaks about! For I am always awake to the stimulus of the unusual things that do haply occur to one who looks for them." Indeed, Snow had this genius.[13]

As a word-conscious budding writer, Snow was alert to the speech patterns of his crewmates. He found it a specialized and limited lingo that he estimated to contain around one thousand words, some four hundred of them expletives, with two ("fuck" and "bastard") appearing in at least eight of every ten sentences. But, he soon discovered, when it came to the work at hand, that they, not he, were the "intelligent" ones. He came to appreciate the special skills and physical strength required by the demanding manual labor, as well as the satisfaction in a job well done. He euphorically noted that one could take the same pride in "a good job of sweeping" the deck that "one accords to any other business."[14]

With his characteristic interest in people, he noted of his shipmates that "Each of them is an interesting study in himself," and for each he would always retain "vivid recollections." To Howard, he wrote of the "carefree blithesome spirits" and "utter content" of the crew, an "unselfish, generous, and simple-souled" lot. In contrast to this youthfully romanticized image, Snow later recollected that after sailing around Central America, about half the crew jumped ship, a reflection of the "wretched" morale and personnel of the American merchant fleet at that time. Under these circumstances, he found himself promoted first to ordinary and then to able-bodied seaman, "though still scarcely knowing a winch from a wench."[15]

Snow spent his free time reading travel accounts of the East and working on Adventure Bound articles he sent to Charles Towne. He induced the ship's mate to let him steer the ship partway through the Panama Canal "for the thrill of it." Panama City, he wrote Towne with a touch of young masculine bravado, was "a town of infinite wetness." After a few beers (his first legal drinks), only "my dread of disease saved me" from the attractive young Spanish prostitutes lining the streets. In truth, he was much more taken with the city's lush tropical jungle setting.[16]

The *Radnor* finally pulled into Honolulu with its boilers leaking and needing six weeks of repair. Now it was Ed and Al Joslin's turn to jump ship for an idyllic three months of loafing in Hawaii. It also gave Snow his first writing success, "In Hula Land," which Towne published in *Harper's Bazaar,* and for which he paid Snow the princely sum of three hundred dollars. Towne thought the "Hula Land" piece "a splendid article" and found it to be a "90%" improvement over the first three manuscripts Snow had sent him. "You have found your literary stride," he wrote Snow. "Hitherto, you have been feeling your way, working somewhat in the dark and now you have emerged into the light." From such praise, Snow told his mother, "my ears now resemble two boxes of over-ripe strawberries." He worried that he would be unable to repeat this success without the inspiration of "unearthly beautiful" Hawaii.[17]

Snow's Hawaiian article was on the frolicsome side, befitting the subject matter and presumably well suited to the *Harper's Bazaar* audience. Yet it already exhibited the qualities that helped give broad appeal to his later work: a warmly engaging personal style and sharply observant descriptive powers. Additionally, Snow showed a sensitivity to and sympathy for an indigenous people and culture (the native Hawaiians) submerged under foreign intrusion. This became a dominant motif in Snow's outlook as he reacted to Western colonialism and Japanese expansionism in Asia. At any rate, Snow had made a breakthrough as a promising travel writer.[18]

Stimulated by this triumph, Snow found material for another successful article in the unorthodox manner in which he proceeded to Asia. Despite the beauty and pleasures of Hawaii, Snow was eager to continue to the Orient. But his attempt to find work on a ship headed that way proved fruitless, while his money began to run out. (He and Al Joslin apparently set up a pineapple stand to eke out some income.) Joslin decided not to go on to Asia with Snow. He lingered on a while in Hawaii before returning to Kansas City for a successful career in the advertising business. Thirty-five years later, retired and on a European tour, he called Snow at the latter's home in Switzerland, and the two arranged to meet for a day or two in Nice. But just before Snow was leaving for the airport, Al phoned to say he had decided to cut his tour short and fly home immediately. As Snow recorded it in his diary, "It was too comical a repetition of our parting in Honolulu at that last moment 35 years ago to be believable." "That night I remembered 100 things about the 20's and early 30's. The intensity of life's appeal, the excitement of small pleasures, the thrill of strange sights and smells, sounds and people. I thought of men and women I had known then with a sudden vividness that astonished me."[19]

Dan Crabb, a young American friend Snow had made in Honolulu, was leaving for Japan as a first-class passenger on a Japanese liner, the *Shinyo Maru*. With Crabb's enthusiastic cooperation, Snow decided to stow away by joining Crabb in his cabin, and staying on when the ship sailed. He fully expected to be discovered by the purser, in which case, as he later wrote Towne, "I intended to let him in on the joke." One surmises that Ed already had an "adventure" article in mind. His first break into print, with its $300 windfall, had put him in a euphoric state in which anything and everything seemed possible. "I've been treading with winged sandals on clouds of pink bliss!" Add to this Snow's fascination always with the excitement of a risk-taking venture, particularly if it could be parlayed into a good story.[20]

In fact, fortune continued on Snow's side, aided by his own resourcefulness. The "joke" incredibly lasted the entire nine-day trip to Yokohama. This was all the more remarkable since there were just seven American passengers in first class, only two of whom had come aboard in Honolulu. Further, the ship swarmed with security men, since the Japanese ambassador to the United States, Tsuneo Matsudaira, his wife, and daughter (betrothed to the Japanese crown prince) were also on board. While all these factors added greatly to Snow's tension, they also helped ensure an exciting story. Snow subsisted on breakfasts served in Crabb's cabin; he mingled with the passengers during the day, even playing bridge with the ambassador's wife and daughter, and wolfed ham sandwiches with his drinks at the ship's bar in the evenings. Special tips to the cabin boy and bartender helped keep the secret.

In Yokohama on June 22, the problems of disembarking and getting through customs seemed insuperable, but again fate was kind to Snow. The VIP media treatment of the ambassadorial party's arrival provided the necessary cover. With the connivance of an English journalist, Snow was able nonchalantly to leave the ship, passing himself off as one of the local foreign reporters. Snow and Dan Crabb accompanied the newsmen to Tokyo, where the two were feted at the American Club. Ed's coup had made him something of a minor celebrity among the Western journalists in Japan. "There must be an odd streak in human nature," Ed wrote Towne, "which delights in seeing anyone defraud a public-service institution." Ed was even offered a job (politely refused) by the managing editor of the English-language *Japan Advertiser*. The newsmen agreed to delay breaking the story (as already written by Snow) until he and Crabb had left Japan. As a youthful American's rare adventure, with built-in ingredients of suspense and excitement in a somewhat exotic setting, it was the right stuff for the *Herald-Tribune*'s magazine. Skillfully composed by Snow, with a focus on his own amusing and attractive persona, it appeared under the title, "A *First Class* Stowaway." A version was also published in the *Kansas City Journal-Post,* highlighting the "Kansas City boy" angle.[21]

After being questioned by a Japanese foreign affairs investigator, the two youths felt it expedient hurriedly to leave Tokyo. They traveled through central Japan (which Snow worked up into a Japan travel piece) and sailed from Kobe to the southern Japanese port of Nagasaki, and from there by ship to Shanghai, where they arrived in the steamy heat of early July. Crabb, in the spirit of the times for well-heeled American college youth, was continuing on to Port Said and a "darkest Africa" trek. Snow wrote Mildred that the stowaway "ordeal" had "destroyed much of the 'daredeviltry' spirit with which I had embarked from New York," and that it was "probably the most sensational thing I shall ever do." In this instance Snow proved a poor prophet.[22]

Snow planned to stay in Shanghai no more than a few weeks or months or to leave immediately if he could find work on a ship bound for the Philippines or India. Attractive journalistic opportunities in Shanghai, and growing involvement in the China scene, kept postponing a departure date. "I could scarcely have chosen a more interesting period in which to arrive in China," he wrote home after less than a month in Shanghai. The onset of the Great Depression in 1929 greatly diminished the opportunities for business success back home. His mother's death in 1930 and Howard's marriage by the end of that year cut off his closest family ties. His own marriage on Christmas Day, 1932, to Utah-born Helen Foster, a talented and spirited young woman determined to make her own mark as a writer in China, completed the pattern. Snow stayed on, in time becoming the most notable American journalist in Asia.[23]

PART 1

Initial China Years

CHAPTER 4

"New Influences and Ideas That Have Streamed into Me"

Truly, Snow had arrived in China at a momentous juncture in that nation's tempestuous modern history. The final imperial dynasty, the Qing (Manchu), had been toppled in 1911 and a republic proclaimed in 1912. Although the Cantonese revolutionary Sun Yat-sen had been the leading figure in the anti-Manchu movement, he and his new Nationalist party, the Kuomintang (KMT), were soon cast aside. China descended into a decade of dictatorships, warlordism, political fragmentation, and constant warfare among contending (and often foreign-backed) militarists. It was a bitter parody of Sun's "Three People's Principles" for China—nationalism, democracy, and people's welfare.

While in political exile in Japan, the middle-aged Sun married twenty-two-year-old Soong Qingling (Ching Ling) in 1915. She was one of the three famed Soong sisters, daughters of the Shanghai tycoon Charlie Soong. She had been educated at Wesleyan College for Women in Macon, Georgia, and after returning to China had gone on to Japan to work with Sun in his revolutionary cause. From 1918 through the early 1920s Sun ineffectually attempted to build a secure political and military base in southern China centered on Canton, in preparation for a campaign against the militarists to the north. In 1923, at a low ebb in his political fortunes, and spurned in his earlier efforts to gain support from the West, Sun turned to Soviet Russia for help. He agreed to an alliance with the Russians, to collaboration with the fledgling Chinese Communist party (CCP) organized in Shanghai in 1921, and to a radicalized program of mass mobilization of labor and the peasantry. The Soviets in turn provided Sun's movement with military and political advisers and assistance and helped reorganize the Kuomintang and build a revolutionary army. The reinvigorated and immensely strengthened Nationalist movement, with effective input from dedicated young Chinese Communists, was soon poised in southern China for a northern expedition to unify China.

Sun died of cancer in March 1925, leaving a legacy of unfinished revolution to successors split into left- and right-wing camps. The new National Revolutionary Army, commanded by Chiang Kai-shek, swept through southern and central China in 1926–1927, aided by a massive upsurge of the peasant and labor movements led largely by Communist cadres. (The Hunanese Mao Zedong was a central figure in organizing the peasantry.) But by the spring of 1927 the now anti-Communist Chiang had broken with the left wing of the Kuomintang and turned on his erstwhile Communist allies to massacre thousands of Communists and leftists in Chinese-ruled Shanghai. Spearheaded by gunmen of Shanghai's potent Green Gang, the coup crushed the powerful Communist-led labor movement in control there. Following the coup came a violent purge of Red elements throughout China, the suppression of radical peasant and labor organizations, and a total break with Soviet Russia.

After some futile and costly insurrectionary efforts, at the end of 1927 and in early 1928 the remnant Communist military forces took refuge in the hinterland of southcentral China. There, under the command of Mao Zedong and Zhu De, they would regroup, organize so-called soviet areas and a large Red Army, and wage a peasant-based mobile-guerrilla-style revolutionary armed struggle. Meanwhile, Chiang Kai-shek consolidated his power, based primarily on his military ascendancy and foreign support. He dominated the mercantile-industrial heartland of the lower Yangtze Valley and effected a series of uneasy and unstable accommodations with regional militarists in the rest of China. A national government was formed in October 1928 with its capital in Nanking. Chiang was president and also in command of the army and leader of a purged Kuomintang. His new links and status had been further enhanced by marriage in December 1927 to the younger sister of Madame Sun Yat-sen, the attractive Soong Meiling. The "Soong dynasty" connection was clearly a propitious one for Chiang. (The third Soong sister, Ailing, was the wife of China's wealthiest banker, H. H. Kung; a brother, Harvard-educated T. V. Soong, was a key Kuomintang financial and political figure.) Chiang had also embraced the Soongs' Methodist faith with his new marriage. As reported in the *Shanghai Times,* the wedding "was a brilliant affair and the outstanding

Chinese marriage ceremony of recent years." Held in the ballroom of Shanghai's plush Majestic Hotel, with some 1,300 invited guests, it followed by only eight months the April coup and massacre in the same city.[1]

Soong Qingling (Madame Sun) remained fiercely loyal to her husband's memory, and to the policies he espoused in the years immediately preceding his death. She left for Europe (initially for Moscow) after the collapse of the left in China, in the summer of 1927. She returned briefly in 1929 for Sun's belated state funeral and the entombment of his remains in the newly constructed mausoleum on Purple Mountain in Nanking—symbol of the Nationalist government's proclaimed continuity with Sun as its founding father. In 1931 Madame Sun came back to live in her home in the French Concession in Shanghai. There she continued her determined and courageous opposition to Chiang's government, which she regarded as a counterrevolutionary reversal of Sun's goals and principles. In those Shanghai years until the Japanese attack in 1937, she would be a major influence in educating the young Snow on all the above matters from her own political perspective.

The city of Shanghai was then the most visible, and important, center of the foreign economic and political presence in China. Through the extraterritorial and other rights granted the foreign powers and their citizens under the unequal treaty system beginning in 1842, a Western-created city had sprung up adjacent to the original Chinese walled town. In time a greater Shanghai municipality emerged as a hybrid Sino-Western metropolis and the largest city in Asia. A "fascinating old Sodom and Gomorrah," Snow called the Shanghai he knew in the early 1930s.[2]

The city was situated along the banks of the Huangpu (then, Whangpoo) River, which converged with the great Yangtze as it emptied into the sea. Shanghai was divided in three parts: an International Settlement, an adjoining French Concession, and, extending in a semicircle around these two, a much larger Chinese-administered area. The International Settlement was governed by a municipal council controlled by the foreign business oligarchy. In 1928 the council comprised British, American, and Japanese members, with the British predominating, while the French were in charge of their own concession. Though technically Chinese territory, these two areas were outside Chinese jurisdiction and were guarded by foreign naval, marine, and police forces. When the Japanese attacked Chinese Shanghai in 1932, they used the "neutral" International Settlement as a base for their operations. In his *Far Eastern Front* (1933), Snow sardonically remarked that the settlement's "'neutrality' was completely smashed not from outside, whence foreigners had long feared Chinese invasion, but from the inside, and by one of the major powers pledged to uphold it." Both at that time, and in the greater battle for Shanghai in 1937, Snow and other foreign correspondents could follow and report on the course of the fighting from this foreign-controlled sanctuary. "From the border of the International Settlement," Snow recalled of the 1932 action, "you could watch the fullscale battle, seeing the front lines of both sides." Snow was also able, at some risk, to visit the two sides, sometimes in the course of a single day.[3]

About half of greater Shanghai's Chinese population of some three million lived in the International Settlement and French Concession, as did some fifty thousand foreign nationals, in addition to large numbers of stateless Russians. This area was the principal center of modern banking, commerce, and industry in China, symbolized by the imposing Bund, and was the port for most of China's foreign trade. Its opulent and gracious foreign residential districts, clubs, and racecourses were worlds apart from the teeming streets and overcrowded tenements and shanties where the balance of the Chinese population lived. In foreign and Chinese-owned factories and workshops alike, the Chinese labor force worked under exploitative conditions of long hours, subsistence wages, and deplorable working conditions. Young women and children from the poverty-stricken countryside made up a substantial part of the workforce. Theodore H. White recalled his first tour of Shanghai industry in 1938 in the company of a young Danish municipal factory inspector. At a textile mill, the inspector "poked with his toe to show a cylinder of bamboo mat in the dump of factory garbage by the canal. In the mat was wrapped the body of a little girl, a factory worker; two or three such mats were put out each night to be collected with the garbage." Shanghai held the bulk of modern industry in China, foreign and Chinese, and over half of its industrial workers. The city was also the center of China's gambling, opium, prostitution, and labor rackets. It was, in White's words, a "city of monsters and missionaries, of light and laughter, of gangsters and gardens," where "the despair at the bottom was as inconceivable to a poor boy from Boston as the delights of depravity at the top were inconceivable to Brahmins of Boston."[4]

To some, Shanghai loomed as an alien entity divorced from the "real" China of the vast interior. It was also very much a center of key forces that had played and continued to play (albeit often underground) significant roles in the pressures for change and modernization in that nation.

Apart from its preeminence in industry and commerce, Shanghai was the focus of liberal and radical political and cultural currents (generally Western-influenced), and the heart of China's literary and media publications activity. The greater protections afforded by extraterritoriality contributed significantly to all these activities. In this Shanghai setting Snow began his education in "things Chinese, and otherwise."

On arriving, Snow contacted J. B. (John Benjamin) Powell, a Missouri journalism alumnus who was editor and publisher of the widely read and influential English-language *China Weekly Review* (hereafter *Review*). When Powell offered Snow a job on the *Review,* Ed decided to stay on in Shanghai for the while. He liked Powell with "his warm friendliness, imported corncob pipe, [and] his wonderful knack of storytelling"; also, the salary seemed "princely" (400 Shanghai dollars per month), particularly in Snow's impecunious state. ("I was flat as your Aunt Alice's hips," he told Mildred.) It was a sum, he exuberantly informed his mother, on which "one can become simply filthy with luxury out here on the fringes of the world." Nevertheless, he assured her, his world travel plans remained in place, and he expected to be back in New York by the following May "at the latest."[5]

Snow's entrée into his journalistic career was not unlike most other American China journalists of the time. "Most reporters came to East Asia 'by accident'—as wire-service people, freelancers, or student travelers prior to 1937," the historian James Thomson notes; many belonged to the "Missouri mafia," and "virtually none" had studied Chinese. Shanghai, an international city with a cosmopolitan and "sinful" reputation, served as a magnet. It was "an interesting place to be stationed," the China journalist A. T. Steele later remembered, where life "was comfortable, news plentiful, and communications good." Shanghai was then "the news capital of China," where the foreign press corps was based.[6]

The *Review* had been founded in 1917 by another Missouri alumnus, Thomas F. F. Millard, with Powell, then thirty, sent by Dean Walter Williams from Missouri to assist Millard in the project. Millard and Powell held similar convictions on the Far East, but the two differed widely in style and personality. In contrast to Powell's comfortably down-home qualities, the older silver-haired Millard cut a worldly, charming, and impeccably tailored figure. Powell's son, Bill, remembered Millard as still elegant and charismatic in his late years, "belting down martinis, and chasing and being chased." By 1923 Powell had bought out Millard and changed the name of *Millard's Review of the Far East* to the new title. The *Review* appeared continuously up to its pre–Pacific War issue of December 6, 1941. For most of this period, Powell served also as correspondent for the *Chicago Tribune*. Both Millard and Powell had become early champions of Sun Yat-sen's Nationalist cause, a stand highly unpopular with the British-dominated foreign community in Shanghai. Powell maintained his strong support of the Nationalists both before and after Sun Yat-sen's death in 1925 and viewed the emerging Nanking regime under Chiang Kai-shek as the auspicious birth of a "New China."[7]

Powell's deep interest in Chinese history and culture, and his good relations with local Chinese intellectuals and business leaders further separated him from most of the expatriate community. Advertisements for Chinese businesses appeared in the *Review,* and English-speaking Chinese students became avid readers and subscribers. The Nationalist regime, for its part, valued Powell's support. In the 1930s, according to Randall Gould, then editor of the American-owned *Shanghai Evening Post and Mercury,* the Nanking government bought up considerable quantities of each issue and mailed them out to various people, mostly overseas. Consistently pro-Nationalist and anti-Communist, Powell was also a vigorous opponent of Japan's aggressive policies in China. Though Snow came to differ sharply with Powell on the Nationalist-Communist issue, the two retained friendly personal relations, reinforced by their common support for an independent and strong China, and for firm resistance to Japan. In actuality, the growing menace of aggressive Japanese militarism posed the greatest threat to Chinese nationalist aims and, ultimately, to the Western position in China itself. It was a point Snow quickly came to understand. In the mid-1930s Ed's wife, Peg, reported on the Peking anti-Japanese student movement for the *Review,* and portions of Ed Snow's 1936 interviews with Mao on the CCP's anti-Japanese united front policies and proposals appeared first in the pages of the *Review.* Even so passionately dedicated and emotionally charged a supporter of the Chinese Communist cause as the writer-journalist Agnes Smedley maintained an affectionate friendship with Powell despite their frequently explosive and expletive-sprinkled political arguments. Powell courageously continued publishing the *Review* until the eve of Pearl Harbor and suffered incarceration and torture by the Japanese following their occupation of the International Settlement. Repatriated in October 1942 (weighing only seventy pounds), he had had most of both feet amputated and remained hospitalized for years. He died of a heart attack in 1947, immediately after delivering an impassioned speech on Far Eastern affairs at a University of Missouri alumni luncheon in Washington, D.C.[8]

Under Powell's expert tutelage Snow began his China journalistic career. Impressed by Powell's integrity and experience and his staunch defense of China's sovereign rights, Snow was quickly in accord with Powell's pro-Nationalist views, seen essentially as simply a "pro-China" position. Ed wrote admiringly of Powell to Mildred for "his fierce and courageous fight for fair-play and equality to the Chinese" against the opposition of the local foreigners. Snow later observed that his feelings at that time reflected also "latent sentiments" he shared with fellow-midwesterners Powell and Millard of identification "with the underdog in any struggle with the still mighty British Empire." He would finally conclude, however, that "the Kuomintang leaders were not so much dissatisfied with the way people in Shanghai were being 'eaten,' as by the fact that it was the foreign devil who was doing the eating."[9]

But meanwhile Powell put Snow to work helping prepare a special "New China" issue of the *Review,* to appear in time for the inauguration of the Nanking regime in October 1928. Powell also assigned Snow to the thankless job of drumming up foreign business advertising for that issue. For this task, at least, Snow could call on his New York ad agency experience, and the personal qualities that had won him accounts and friends there. Typically interested in new settings and people, he learned quickly. For the China portion of the work, he had the help of Chinese assistants and of Powell's large China library of several thousand volumes. It was "one of the best newspaper libraries in the Far East," Powell's son, Bill, later recounted. "The *Review* office became a gathering place for foreign newsmen and writers, partly because it was a good place 'to look something up.'"[10]

In pursuing advertising accounts, Snow's "hard-nosed" business sense collided with his more idealistic regard for Powell's championing of the Chinese cause. "I have the humorless task of trying to convince American and English business men to advertise in a medium which upon numerous occasions has incurred their displeasure," he wrote his father a few weeks after beginning work at the *Review.* Powell's stance "seriously endangered the business future of his magazine, a thing which, unfortunately, so many idealists are apt to neglect in promoting their noble ambitions." Wealthy Chinese merchants' advertising support almost made up for the withdrawal of foreign support, though Snow ruefully noted that credit for the latter accounts went to the *Review's* Chinese advertising manager. Snow managed to secure a goodly number of important foreign accounts (many of them deemed unlikely prospects) for the special issue.[11]

Snow still viewed himself as a transient observer of a mostly unappealing scene. He was also just a bit put off by his return to the "prosaic" business world. He remained determined to be on his way once he had amassed a few hundred dollars. Dean Williams, coming through Shanghai, pressed for Ed to apply for a newspaper slot in Singapore, where Williams had as yet not placed one of his Missourians. Snow had the offer of a lucrative editor's job on a new English-language paper upriver in Hankou; but, he confided to his mother in perhaps another facet of "latent" midwestern sentiments, he "had no fancy for being buried in a god-forsaken dump controlled by the slant-eyes." Yet Snow's ingrained sense of humanity was coming through as well. In a fairly early Shanghai diary entry, he remarked on the foreigners' practice of calling their rickshaw men "coolies." And they did have names—"one would not keep even a cow for a year and continue merely to call her 'cow.' It is stupid to do so, and the Chinese concludes the foreigner is stupid when he does the same with him."[12]

The attractions of China that Snow did discover at this early stage were still largely those of the privileged foreigner with an income in U.S. dollars, who could buy all the amenities (and many luxuries) of life for a pittance. "One can live in such style over here on so little," he informed his mother. "For instance, I can have a rickshaw available day or night for $24 a month—$12 in our money. . . . Such are the allurements of the Orient." While Snow's China outlook, sympathies, and involvement were destined for very radical change, the fact that he (and his wife) could live comfortably and even in style (especially later in old Peking) on a very modest and uncertain dollar income would play its part in keeping him in China. It allowed him to function much more flexibly as a writer-journalist, mostly avoiding the daily routine and demands of a permanent full-time newspaper connection. As always in his career, he preferred such less confining and more independent—even if less secure—work and writing arrangements.[13]

By the fall Ed was in a mellow mood. His advertising sales were going extremely well, removing any earlier "business" constraint on his now unalloyed enthusiasm for Powell's role as the nemesis of the "diehard" local British and Japanese, and "the American money-grabbers as well." He was also becoming better acquainted with the impressive list of Missouri-bred newspapermen in China, all of them "goddam good journalists!" He was proud of his part in the enlarged special issue of the *Review*. His name appeared both as assistant advertising manager and author of a well-researched article on road construction in China. "Thus your brother enters into the field of Far Eastern journalism. Huzzahs and banzais!" he chortled to Howard.[14]

Snow continued to work on articles he sent on to Towne, including one stemming from his Shanghai advertising experience that Towne placed with a marketing journal back home. Pursuing his penchant for freshly eyed "people-places" writing, Snow churned out shorter pieces on topics ranging from the silk and porcelain industries to fortune-tellers, and "China's Woolworth," and "Nanking Today," among others. These he sold to the Associated Press through their correspondent in Shanghai (a Missouri man, naturally), who found them "splendid" and "most interestingly handled," and asked for more. Ed was writing "like a house afire" and had developed "a remarkable style," Towne reported to Howard.[15]

In an initial foray into the China political scene, Snow visited the Nationalist capital at Nanking in mid-October. With the special entrée afforded him by the Powell-*Review* connection, he met Chiang Kai-shek and other top officials and interviewed Sun Fo, Sun Yat-sen's son, who was the new minister of railways. This occasioned some thoughts on Snow's part about Sun Yat-sen, now "ambitiously" referred to as "the George Washington of China." Though probably a great man who had immeasurably benefited China, Sun was also, Snow judged, "a dreamer and an idealist, as well as a dangerous radical" who "strongly tended toward Communism."[16]

At the beginning of 1929 Snow, substituting for the busy Powell, represented the *Review* (and also Powell's commitments to the *Chicago Tribune* and the British *Manchester Guardian*) on a Nanking-sponsored select press expedition to the northern China rail junction of Jinan in Shandong (then, Shantung). Japanese military forces had moved in there in May 1928 in an effort to thwart the Nationalist advance on Peking. It was an expression of Tokyo's "strong China policy," a reaction to the potential unification of China, perceived as a threat to Japan's "special position" and further ambitions in Manchuria. Clashes had occurred, and the Japanese had occupied and continued to hold Jinan and to block rail traffic, while negotiations to settle the matter dragged on. An agreement on Japanese withdrawal was reached in April, though it involved also much backtracking by the Chinese on the terms of settlement.[17]

Snow's Jinan reports spotlighted Japanese obstructionism and spurious versions of the prevailing situation. He focused as well on the human miseries and economic dislocations, and on the groundswell of anti-Japanese sentiment it evoked among the Chinese. Snow raised the crucial question for Japan's China policy at this critical juncture in East Asian affairs: would Tokyo continue to "hold the mailed fist over the *miserables* of Shantung" in pursuit of its China interests, or would it renounce this approach "and make an effort to recapture the trade and goodwill which she has lost as a result of her actions here?" Though Japan ultimately retreated somewhat in the Jinan affair, a militarist-dominated Japan in the coming decade would opt for the "mailed fist" in China, with tragic consequences for both the Chinese and the Japanese peoples.[18]

The Jinan trip turned out to be more exciting than anticipated, at least in print. Based on inaccurate reports that Ed and others in the press party had been detained by the Japanese, Powell cabled the news to the U.S., where it was carried by the Associated Press, the *New York Herald-Tribune,* and the *Chicago Tribune,* among others, as well as being widely circulated in China. "It was an extraordinarily lucky adventure for me," Ed wrote Howard, and "as a result of the jaunt I was No. 1 news in the Far East for several days." For his part, Howard typically remarked to the family, "I can't say I could go much for that sort of thing—I guess Ed has all the 'yen' for adventure in our family."[19]

Again through Powell's connections, another "once-in-a-lifetime" opportunity came Snow's way, once more postponing his China leave-taking. This was to be a trip over the restored eight-thousand-mile national railway system. The venture, organized by the ministry of railways (a leading advertiser in the *Review*), was meant to publicize and promote the idea that such travel for tourists was now possible, safe, and comfortable. Snow's descriptive articles would appear in the *Review* and then as tourist informational brochures of the ministry and perhaps result in a small travel book as well. It seemed an ironic juxtaposition to Snow's just-completed experience with Japanese railway interference in Shandong. Actually, the proposed trip was delayed until mid-April by renewed infighting among Kuomintang factions in the south, and by warlord rumblings in the north.

In recounting these matters to his father, Snow included some of his developing thoughts on China's deep and seemingly intractable problems. (The ten-page missive was a prime example of Snow's letter-writing style to the family in these youthful years: unrestrained accounts of his work and personal activities, contemplations of life in general and China in particular, and unabashedly sentimental yearnings for home and family.) China, he wrote, was in "a pitiable condition," lacked inspired leadership, and needed a "crusader," a "practical idealist," Ed felt. The "stench and decay, the misery and sufferings and national agonies" cried out for a "Great Redeemer" to lead China "into the salvation of a spiritual materialism." This last had echoes of Coolidge-era rhetoric, and indeed Snow contrasted America's material progress with the "dimness of medievalism" in societies such as China and India. The conservative Confucian tradition had stifled initiative and innovation. Snow held up the Promethean model of the dynamic, nature-conquering civilizations of the West against China's centuries-long dreamlike passivity. Science, machines, industrialization—they were China's principal needs, he declared.[20]

Snow would cast off much in these early formulations. Nevertheless, they contained seeds of his later responsiveness to *revolutionary* activism, in the form of the Chinese Communist movement, as the dynamic for China's revival. Marxism, of European origin, incorporated Western concepts of historical progression and unbounded material advancement based on ever-higher levels of productive forces and social organization. As Kenneth E. Shewmaker notes, Americans such as Snow were attracted by the Chinese Communists' untraditional ("un-Chinese") qualities of youthful idealism, optimism, and their "modern" rational-scientific approach to transforming China. These traits, as Snow observed in *Journey*, were in sharp contrast to the "inert fatalism of old China" and appealed strongly to him "as a Westerner." And while in *Red Star* he dismissed the "saviour" thesis for China, he immediately added that he nevertheless felt in Mao Zedong "a certain force of destiny." Conversely, when Snow met the extremely un-Western Mahatma Gandhi in India in 1931, he found him "a considerable bore" who "does not appeal to me." Much more on these matters later.[21]

Prior to the start of his China railway journey, Snow was offered an associate editor post on the *Review* by Powell, as well as the opportunity to replace Millard as the Shanghai correspondent for the *New York Herald-Tribune*. But, as he told his father, he refused to be "harnessed" to, or "sidetracked" by such permanent commitments, "luscious" as they might be. He now hoped, following the railway assignment, to continue toward home via Russia and central Asia. In April he began the railway trip that he looked back on as a vital turning point in his growing awareness of and response to the searing realities of Chinese life.[22]

The four-month journey took Snow on "the grand tour" of China, from the scenic spots of the verdant lower Yangtze Valley, into central China, then north to Peking, and beyond the Great Wall to Manchuria and Korea. It was mostly pleasant and comfortable, and with opportunities for good gift shopping for the family. Ed turned out the required travel pieces, appearing as special supplements in the *Review,* and later as booklets of the Chinese Tourist Bureau. He was accompanied as guide, interpreter, and coauthor by a forty-year-old recently returned student from Harvard named S. Y. Livingston Hu. Though the latter sported the title of technical expert of the ministry of railways, Hu's position was, as was often the case with the educated elite, a sinecure obtained through good connections. Devoid of railway expertise, Hu was a haughty individual who concentrated on the comforts and pleasures he considered his due as an official. Missouri-educated Snow chose to regard Hu's attributes as primarily the product of his Harvard background.[23]

From Peking in June, Snow and his companion traveled west on the Peking-Suiyuan line to Zhangjiakou (then, Kalgan). Beyond that city in China's northwest lay a vast area then experiencing devastating drought and famine. At Snow's insistence they continued on into the famine zone, with their special car hooked to a freight-passenger train. Coincidentally Rewi Alley, a New Zealander who was a factory inspector for the Shanghai municipal council, was on that train, squatting on the floor of one of the wagons with the mass of Chinese famine refugees. A powerful, squarely built man, he was a twice wounded veteran of the western front in the great war and had come to Shanghai from New Zealand in 1927. He was now on his way to the famine zone to spend his vacation time helping to build an irrigation canal under the auspices of the International Famine Relief Commission. The project, directed by the legendary American engineer and China road-builder O. J. Todd ("Todd Almighty"), served also to provide work and grain for famine victims. Alley would spend the remainder of his long life in China; at his death in 1987 at age ninety he was an honored figure in the People's Republic. He worked tirelessly among China's laboring masses in the decades of war and civil war. Snow and Alley would later become fast lifetime friends and partners in their wartime efforts to aid China and its people. But it was here that Snow first met Alley fleetingly and as yet from different worlds.

When Snow and Alley first encountered each other on the crowded station platform along the famine route, the contrast in appearance of the two foreigners could hardly have been greater. Alley had developed a badly suppurating red eye, was dressed in crumpled khakis, and was dusty and bedraggled from rain pouring through the broken roof of his car. Snow, riding in his private VIP carriage, was attired in an immacu-

late white linen jacket, shirt, and shorts with long white stockings. To
Snow, Alley seemed "a queer duck, but interesting." Hu superciliously
refused Snow's request to allow Alley to share their comfortable accommodations. Alley cheerfully returned to his peasant companions and the
two apparently had no further direct contact as the train moved on to
the end of the line at Salaqi (Saratsi), south of the Gobi Desert in what
is now Inner Mongolia.[24]

Large areas of northwestern China had suffered drought and famine
throughout the 1920s, in addition to the normal ravages of such human
plagues as bandits, militarists, extortionate tax collectors, landlords,
grain merchants, and moneylenders. But the great famine of 1929–1930,
witnessed by Alley and Snow in Suiyuan, was the most calamitous of all
and took at least two million lives. Salaqi, Alley later wrote, "was altogether a very shocking place," with its population swelled by famine victims who had walked there from faraway villages. As Alley described the
scene, "Deserted villages were ransacked of timber, animals stolen or
killed, and women sold to dealers who would ship them south, while the
men, old women and boys existed on the charity of the soup kitchen
until most died and were thrown into the city moat. These were scenes
hard to forget."[25]

This experience of horror, death, and inhumanity would haunt Snow
the remainder of his life. It was a further jolt in the "consciousness-
raising" process he was undergoing in China. From this ordeal, he subsequently recalled, he "began to doubt that the real revolution [in China]
had begun." Yet Snow's reaction was still largely on the compassionate
rather than the political level. He expressed it in an article he did on the
famine. His graphic description of the scene focused on the Famine Relief Commission's canal-building project that could immediately save
perhaps a quarter million lives by providing grain for work and solve the
famine problem in the future. Snow placed blame for the tragedy on the
drought, warlord battlings, and inadequate transport facilities. Aside
from a brief questioning of the Chinese government's willingness to cooperate with international aid efforts (absent from the version published
in the pro-Nationalist *Review*), Snow's animus was directed more at the
foreigners in Shanghai who spoke of "the so-called famine" and who
even counseled their friends back home "not to be taken in by all this
'starvation propaganda.'" (An excerpt from Snow's article was included
in a fund-raising appeal in America for China famine relief.)[26]

In Shenyang (then, Mukden) on his railway trip, Snow interviewed
Zhang Xueliang, the "Young Marshal" who had succeeded his warlord

father (assassinated by Japanese agents in 1928) as the military-political overlord of Manchuria—China's northeast (Dongbei). This proved to be Snow's only encounter with a man who was to have a special role in the destinies of both Snow and China. The interview, which Snow wrote up as a *Herald-Tribune* piece, came as a crisis was building in Sino-Soviet relations. The Young Marshal was attempting to oust the Russians from their management role in the jointly owned and operated Chinese Eastern Railway, the czarist-built line that ran across northern Manchuria from the Siberian frontier east to a junction point above the Russian port of Vladivostok on the Pacific. Zhang Xueliang had hitched his star to Chiang Kai-shek's Nanking regime, and the move against the Russians had both a nationalist and an anti-Communist connotation. It was also an indirect challenge to Japan's much more dominant and powerful "special position" in southern Manchuria. The Soviets responded vigorously, sending their troops across the frontier. A negotiated settlement followed the defeat of the Chinese forces, fully restoring the Russian presence on the railway.[27]

Snow's talk with the Young Marshal touched on all of the above points. Despite the impending confrontation with the Russians, Zhang declared Japan to be the primary enemy and affirmed his patriotic support for a united China (including Manchuria) under a strong central government. Snow was impressed by Zhang's candor and forthright, confident defiance of Japan. Discounting the "rumors" (truthful) of Zhang's opium habit, Snow found the youthful warlord to be an appealing and popular figure, whether in mingling with the students on the large modern campus of Northeastern University in Mukden, or playing golf in his stylish plus-fours. However, in another article from Manchuria, Snow voiced skepticism at the probabilities of Chinese success in breaking Japan's stranglehold on southern Manchuria. The odds in the coming contest were "greatly in favor of the Japanese," and the chances of China "retaining, or rather regaining," control of her Manchurian provinces were "exceedingly remote."[28]

The 1929 Sino-Russian conflict led to still another extended postponement in Snow's homebound plans, probably the critical one in his gradual abandonment of these intentions. Powell had wired him in Peking to cut short the railway project and return to Shanghai to take over the *Review* while he rushed up to Manchuria to cover the breaking story for the *Chicago Tribune*. Powell's absence stretched on to include a trip to the Soviet Union, and Snow remained in charge for some six months. Listed on the *Review's* masthead as assistant editor, he retained this connection until the end of March 1930. He also took on Powell's chores as Shanghai correspondent for the *Chicago Tribune* and *Manchester Guardian*. Being "an editor and correspondent for two major world newspapers leaves little time for writing letters home," he rather grandly informed the family—in the course of writing just such an affectionate nine-page letter! Though impatient for Powell to return so that he (Snow) could be on his way, Ed was increasingly caught up in his budding China journalistic career. Never before had he been so well-informed on all current happenings, he wrote home. He was "enjoying the prestige" of his new jobs. "See my stories in the Chicago Tribune?" Ed wondered what that eminent paper (then ruled by the autocratic Colonel McCormick) would say "if they knew their Shanghai correspondent had never worked on a copy desk in his life and was still a little damp behind the ears?" Snow's task was eased by the friendly advice of Millard and other veterans in the Shanghai press corps. His growing fund of information and insight on China did not as yet extend to the Communists, whom he referred to as "numerous bands of Chinese Communist-bandits, who still exercise control of remote sections of the country." Hard, firsthand intelligence on the Reds was lacking, and Western journalists in Shanghai were dependent on government handouts that dismissed the Reds as "bandits." Snow himself would once and for all dispel the "bandit" myth in his *Red Star*.[29]

In Shanghai, Snow participated in another government-sponsored public relations travel stint—this time in the air. He was a passenger in October 1929 on the trial run for the start of amphibian air service from Shanghai to Hankou. Operated by an American aviation firm under contract to the Chinese government, it marked the inauguration of Nationalist China's commercial air service under its official airline, China National Aviation Corporation. Snow wrote up the flight as a promotional piece for the *Review* in his now well honed travelogue style. The eight-hundred-mile trip, wonder of wonders, took only seven hours each way—"was such a feat possible except by the aid of that mysterious and fantastic creature of Chinese imagination, the omnipotent Dragon?"[30]

During his tenure editing the *Review,* Snow made local waves over the practice in many foreign buildings in Shanghai of barring Chinese from using front elevators and entrances reserved for Caucasians. He targeted the British-owned building in which the *Review* had its offices and excoriated such "ridiculous regulations humiliating to the Chinese." Snow's editorial provoked a "die-hard" reaction from the British-run *North China Daily News*. But the discriminatory policies were quietly dropped, though the *Review*'s lease was not renewed. Actually, Snow's views were in complete accord with the *Review*'s policies under Powell and undoubtedly further enhanced its standing among its many Chinese subscribers and advertisers. According to Powell's son, "the incident later became one of [J. B.'s] favorite stories and he would jokingly claim that he got back just as the British were throwing Ed and his typewriter into the street."[31]

Snow followed up his anti-segregationist mini-crusade with a piece in the *New York Sun* the next year noting with satisfaction the ending of discriminatory policies in Shanghai's foreign shops and hotels. Faced with growing competition from Chinese-owned enterprises in the more assertive Chinese Nationalist political climate, foreign investors and shopowners could no longer ignore the buying power of the Chinese customer. Catering to this clientele had become a matter of economic survival. "The policy of exclusionism reigns no more," Snow declared, "except in foreign clubs where the white-haired die-hards still gather to lament the passing of days 'When these yellow men knew their betters and acted accordingly.' "[32]

Howard and Ed missed each other dreadfully, with Ed nostalgically recalling their life together in New York, and Howard constantly importuning his brother to come home. At the same time they took pride and interest in each other's accomplishments in New York and Shanghai respectively. "Ed has certainly made the most of his travels," Howard wrote his mother in July 1929, and "is proving himself to be a cracker-jack reporter." That he has been able to do all this at age twenty-four and in less than a year "is almost unbelievable!" But "while proud of what Ed has done," he observed to the family in October, "I do wish he would come home. It would make us all so much happier and a little closer together." A few months later Howard was evincing understandable skepticism at Ed's constantly reiterated pledges to return home. "It doesn't phase me any more to read this in his letters," Howard commented to his mother on one such pledge. "He has written it so often that I begin to suspect him of putting it down for lack of any other news."[33]

At the same time Howard fully supported Ed's writing career and, through his advertising-publications connections, was instrumental in getting some of Ed's early pieces into print. Yet as Howard continued to move up to ever better positions and salaries in the business world, Ed felt further left behind and apart from that particular road to success. And while Ed was becoming more and more attuned to Chinese sensitivities and aspirations, Howard retained a stereotypical view of the "slant-eyes," and a belief that "the climate there is not good for white people." As Ed's horizons broadened, Howard's focused more narrowly on his New York–based business career. Juxtaposed to the brothers' strong and enduring mutual affection was the widening gulf in their material and occupational goals and circumstances. Their dialogue through the succeeding decades was in many ways a fascinating paradigm of America itself, where traditional modes of thinking would be constantly challenged by a vast range of new problems and forces, domestic and foreign.[34]

As Powell's absence stretched on through the final months of 1929, Snow resigned himself to another winter in Shanghai. (The chilly dampness did not help his chronic problem with sinus-related head colds, aggravated, he often felt, by his "inordinate" desire for cigarettes.) The decline in silver prices in the mounting world depression had its effect on Ed's plans. He had kept his money in silver (Mex) dollars; with the sharp drop in the exchange rate for gold (U.S. currency), he was "practically on my uppers," he morosely informed his mother. "What will happen when I have to buy gold before I start travelling I do not know."[35]

Yet in a number of ways, Snow was sinking deeper roots in Shanghai. Together with a young American friend, he rented a small well-furnished apartment and took on an "excellent" cook-housekeeper-valet. Lodging, food, and servant cost each of the two Americans a total of thirty dollars gold per month. Still longing for "the sparkling streets of New York," Ed could appreciate the fact that "a treasure" such as his new cook, even if available in New York, would have to be paid ten times more than the ten-dollar-a-month Shanghai wage.[36]

Snow was also building a cosmopolitan circle of friends in Shanghai. "They include members of every race that is found in any numbers in the Orient," he told his mother, describing them in his usual colorful way:

There is a German newspaper man and a woman author of Deutschland; a Soviet Russian whose Polish wife has a voice like a bell; a Chinese who loves English poetry; an American marine officer [Evans Carlson] whose wife is a lovely southern girl whose specialty is tea with raisin crumpets; a Georgian from the Caucasus, and Georgians are the most entrancing of all women; a young Chinese couple who are my favorites, though they live like mice on a government salary that wouldn't buy your lettuce; a Japanese girl with gold teeth and a brain—a rare combination in Nihon—who is teaching me something of her language in exchange for my criticism of her English and applause for her divine sukiyaki; an Indian poet married to a Japanese, who together own a garden that is a miniature Arcadia; and an American Jewess who looks like an Irish girl—"all these," as Rupert Brooke would say, "have been my loves." Figuratively speaking, of course.[37]

In December Snow accepted an offer to be the Shanghai correspondent for the Washington-based Consolidated Press Association (Con Press), a newly organized service representing a number of American newspapers, including the *New York Sun* and *Chicago Daily News*. The job called for Snow to send in mainly "mailers" (rather than routine spot cable dispatches) on interesting background stories he came across. Essentially part-time, at a modest monthly salary of eighty dollars, it suited Snow's footloose temperament, seemed a good stop-gap while he thought out his longer-term plans, and allowed time for other writing. As a "roving correspondent," he hoped to do stories for Con Press during a trip into Soviet Central Asia and beyond, which he planned to take in the spring of 1930. But his application for a Soviet visa was denied, presumably for his ties (severed at the end of March 1930) with the anti-Soviet *Review*. Ed turned instead to an alternate plan through southern China and Southeast Asia, to begin in the fall. Con Press approved the project, with Snow to receive three hundred dollars monthly for feature stories and pictures.[38]

The heartrending death of his mother in March 1930 further reduced the pressure for an early return home. Ed continued to play with the idea of going back to New York in the fall, but his interest seemed half-hearted. The impact of the depression, and of his long absence, on job opportunities worried him. "Anxiously" he inquired of Howard on the possibilities of "a good advertising or publication job" in New York. A month later, June 1930, still voicing his intention to return, he aired his anxieties at the prospect—the dearth of good jobs in depression America, and his distaste at the thought of the "old 9 to 5 routine" after two years of "personal management freedom."[39]

There was sadness in Ed's yearning to rekindle the old carefree times with Howard. "We will know many happy days again, many of them," he told Howard, "and recapture an old scent for living." But the past could not and would not live again. Howard's marriage in December 1930, closely followed by Mildred's, dashed any such illusions. Now almost all his close, and to him supremely important, family ties in Kansas City and New York were broken. ("Old faces, old times are forever haunting my waking hours," and "you never need fear that I shall not return," he had written his mother a few months before her death.) Ed summed this up to Mildred from remote Kunming (Yunnanfu) in January 1931. "Since you and Howard are both tied up in marriage and domesticity, I see no reason for my early return now. . . . What a gap has been left in things for me, now that Howard has started a new life!!"[40]

With the pull of his warm youthful family memories and connections now set aside, a maturing and more worldly-wise Snow affirmed the independence that would be the credo of his life. Writing to Howard from Shanghai at the end of 1931, after yearlong travel in southern China, Southeast Asia, and India, Ed felt that he preferred to stay on in China because "I do not wish at present to be confined to a desk job." Though only on a modest reporter's salary, "I have great freedom and no one can make so bold as to order me here or there," he added. "One has to make certain sacrifices in the world to be able to thumb one's nose at it."[41]

In the longer term, Snow's changing perspectives were probably even more critical in loosening his ties to family and home. He had come to appreciate the people and culture of China, while gaining deeper insight into that nation's problems, politics, and aims. After two years away, by the early months of 1930, his views were beginning to clash with the conventional insularity, racism, and paternalism that most Americans (including his family) directed toward the non-Caucasian and "backward" regions of the earth. Additionally, a gap was now developing between his new thinking and experiences, and the culture of material success he had been part of in Kansas City and New York.

Given his sympathies for China's national cause and distaste for the Shanghai "die-hards," Snow voiced his hostility to the entire system of extraterritoriality, which gave legal sanction to foreign economic interests and privileges in the treaty ports and concession areas of China. In the spring of 1930 he wrote an apparently unpublished piece condemning the presence of American marines in Shanghai. He sent it on to Howard to place for publication, though he doubted its acceptability: a publisher "might be accused of being anti-marine, which is a cardinal sin in America I'm told." Howard himself, in what was often to be a contentious (though not unfriendly) dialogue between the two, found Ed's comments on the marines to be "critical, sarcastic." Ed rejoined that "Americans at home ought to know, or be reminded of, this offensive organization's presence on Chinese soil. To talk of Sino-American 'understanding' while they are still here is to talk nonsense." Ed twitted Howard on the "color" issue as well. He hadn't seen "a good-looking American girl for months," he wrote his brother in June 1930. "You see, I draw the color line; I haven't been out with a white girl since last December."[42]

Snow distanced himself further and more openly from Shanghai's foreign establishment in a mid-1930 article for H. L. Mencken's influential and iconoclastic *American Mercury*. He targeted the American businessmen and missionaries and gave evidence of his growing estrangement from the American milieu that spawned them. He took a caustic and telling look at the realities of the International Settlement ("a poorly camouflaged British colony"), focusing on the seamy and "wicked" side of Shanghai life. In the best debunking fashion, Snow zeroed in on the Americans' transplanted country club existence, their naughty dalliances and naïveté in their Shanghai world of Russian mistresses, exclusive brothels, and cabarets. In the process, they brought glitter to the settlement's night life—"it is American money and American laughter that enables all the joints to function profitably." Snow typically saved his sharpest barbs for the missionaries—not very successful in saving souls but doing very well in all other respects. Though written mostly in an irreverent and amusing style suited to Mencken's journal, Snow's article had a more serious point to make. It was the theme of the foreigners' isolation from, ignorance of, and lack of interest in the Chinese people around them, whom they saw as "so much background— necessary for trade and industry, but isn't it—ah—unfortunate that they couldn't all be like us?" Their knowledge of the Chinese, Snow commented, came principally from "solemn, pidgin-English conversations with their houseboys."

Snow also sensitively captured the empty sadness of such foreigners. In the green-lawned environs of the country club, he wrote, "the Shanghai American can sit in cloistered tranquility. Far from the sickly Orient, he lolls in cushioned ease, sips amber drinks, dreams lazily under a sky of deep velvet and misty chrome, hears Rudy Vallee come out of the orthophonic, feels the warm breath of the parched earth against his temples, and believes he is back in Evanston—and perhaps wishes to God he were."[43]

Ed's article did not amuse the Shanghailanders, among whom he soon found himself in the doghouse, at least temporarily. According to Helen Snow, even Millard and Powell were unhappy with the piece. In *Journey,* Snow wrote that his comments on Christianity in the article had evoked a sharp response from the "town elders" to the effect that "Christianity had made Shanghai what it was." Personally, Ed added sardonically, "I would never have gone that far." To his father, who took a dim view of Mencken, Ed defended the latter as "the Knighted adversary of ballyhoo, of which our American life is the credulous minion." "For every line of satire he writes, a hundred are written in the pompous bourgeois publications to the effect that God's in his heaven and all's right with America. . . . We are afraid of the truth."[44]

The hostility Snow engendered, particularly among the British, in championing Chinese rights probably contributed to the compilation of a dossier on him by the British-run settlement police. Apparently based on "information" supplied by a White Russian informer, it painted a lurid past for Snow as a clandestine and dangerous agent of the Third International. This, before young Snow had the opportunity even to discover the left, in China or elsewhere. But as always, the radicalism really at issue was the more substantive and threatening one of Snow's challenge to smug notions of white superiority and supremacy. He would find himself on further blacklists through the years for defying other powerful interests, imperial or political, including the Japanese, the Kuomintang, and the Soviets. The Shanghai files would crop up in various places and times, including American FBI files in the 1950s.[45]

Snow was becoming disenchanted with the Nanking regime as the harbinger of an invigorated China, and of its capacity to unify the country under an effective and stable central government. The continuous and inconclusive conflicts between Chiang Kai-shek's forces and his many and varied military and political opponents throughout the country reinforced this view. Commenting to his father in December 1929, Snow marveled at Chiang's ability to "hang on." Largely uneducated, "personally unimpressive, and a man of narrow vision and with few scruples," Chiang remained in power because his enemies could not make common cause against him.[46]

In a subsequent *Herald-Tribune* article, Snow criticized the Kuomintang for deifying Sun Yat-sen and building a cult around the man and his doctrines. It was blind idolatry that served the political purpose of the Nanking government. Sun's concept of "political tutelage," for example, was being used to avoid genuine steps toward constitutionalism and democracy. Snow quoted the prestigious Western-educated liberal scholar Hu Shih on this point: "Who are these men that head the government and would lead us through the gates of self-government? . . . Do Chiang Kai-shek, Feng Yu-hsiang, and Yen Hsi-shan and other militarists have any conception of what a democratic government is? I think not." Sun, now no longer the "dangerous radical" of Snow's first months in China, emerged as an enlightened though far from infallible leader whose words had been twisted and who would have been the first to reject such worship. Sun had in fact sought to awaken the Chinese from age-old superstition and intellectual passivity, Snow declared. Defending his criticisms of the National government to his father, Ed compared the Kuomintang's use of the Sun cult to Spain's use of "the incense and idolatry" of Catholicism to enslave the Americas centuries before. "Spain betrayed Christ; the Kuomintang may yet betray Sun Yat-sen."[47]

Snow's growing aversion to the Kuomintang posed dilemmas for him on the subject of extraterritoriality and the restoration of full Chinese sovereignty. A simplistic "pro-China" position begged many questions. As Snow turned more sharply against the Nationalist regime and grew openly sympathetic to its liberal and leftist opponents, the protections of extraterritoriality became crucial to his own freedom to act and write as he did. "We couldn't have done anything if we'd been under Chinese law," Helen Snow later observed. "A Chinese would have been executed for even messing with such things as we did." (Nor could such Chinese even depend on the protection of the International Settlement. Alleged Communists among them were picked up by the settlement police and routinely turned over to Kuomintang authorities.) Nevertheless the larger issue remained. Extraterritoriality *was* the legal underpinning for imperialism in China, and a barrier to a fully independent China. It was interesting that Snow's article on Sun Yat-sen itself revealed some of these difficulties and contradictions. He noted that Hu Shih's critiques had appeared in the British *North China Daily News,* an organ bitterly opposed to the Nationalist government and its aspirations to end extraterritoriality. Publishing Hu Shih's articles obviously served the paper's ulterior political motives, but, as Snow made clear, such articles could not be printed in Kuomintang-ruled China. The extraterritoriality issue vis-à-vis the Western powers would ultimately be subsumed by the much more menacing Japanese threat and would be ended only in the course of the Pacific War. Indeed, extraterritoriality also protected American journalists like Snow (and Powell) from the Japanese—until Pearl Harbor. All in all, life in old China for American partisans of a new China had its anomalies.[48]

Two years away from New York and almost four from Kansas City, Snow wrestled with his growing disaffection with American norms of success generally, and his brother's in particular. According to the "American credo," he propounded to his father in February 1930, money rather than intellectual or cultural attainment, was "the sole end of life" and the measure of success. Those who questioned this were thrust aside as violators of "the American duty of making more money than one really needs." (Snow had the advantage of living quite comfortably in

China on a very modest dollar income.) Applying these thoughts to Howard and himself, Ed underscored their differing perspectives but still harbored hopes of coming back to New York and the brother he adored. Howard's ambition, Ed observed, was to amass a fortune through business as rapidly as possible and only thereafter turn to the finer things of life. But Howard had an "artistic, sensitive heart," an impediment in "the American struggle for success." As a result, Ed felt, the odds were against Howard's "attaining the status he desires as quickly as he desires."[49]

Continuing in this vein, Ed declared that he too had "suppressed the fires of other loves" in pursuing aims similar to Howard's. But he had rejected status and had "fled New York." When he sailed out of Manhattan harbor, he had sworn "to forget the necessity of emulating" the American "princes of business" he had been taught to worship. "An older pantheism beckoned to me from across sunlit seas, and I wished to investigate it." That Ed had exhibited a daring élan in leaving New York in 1928 is unquestionable; that he had turned his back on the possibilities of a later financially successful New York career (albeit as a writer) is much less clear. Recall that such "mini-princes" of the business and media world as the banker Kelley Graham and the author-editor Charlie Towne had enthusiastically spurred him on his way, on the assumption of the one-year jaunt Ed had planned. (Both in fact were importuning him to return, a year or so later.) Ed was looking back to 1928 with 1930 hindsight. Yet as he discarded old verities and goals, "The new influences and ideas that have streamed into me do not fuse coherently; . . . nothing orderly, definite, dependable evolves."[50]

The buoyant, romantic youth who dallied on Waikiki and stowed away to Japan had become a more burdened and seasoned adult of twenty-five. His optimistic confidence and faith in the world he had known, and the comfortable assurance of his place in it, had been battered by traumas back home and the impact of a "pitiable" China. He had already proved himself an able journalist and talented writer and was poised for an adventurous journey to colonial Asia and remote Yunnan— China at its most scenic and medieval. Thus far, he had been introduced to an ancient world where human misery and poverty were endemic, and injustice and greed seemed the norm. He had become sensitized to people of color and aware of cultures and histories he had once thought of only vaguely as backdrops for colorful travel accounts. He had aligned himself with the national cause of China and the Chinese, but with shaken faith in the Nationalists as champions of that cause.

An anecdotal parable Snow recorded in his diary seemed apropos to his own quest. An American railroad builder in northern China sits with Chinese to discuss where railways should be built. "Each point he suggests is turned down because it is a 'sphere of influence' of either Russia, Japan, France or Great Britain. Exasperated, he finally emits, 'Then where in hell is China!'" In the years just ahead, new influences and ideas would continue to stream into Snow, further changing and radicalizing his image of China, and of the world.[51]

In short, he was becoming Edgar Snow.

CHAPTER 5

Travel Is Broadening

As Snow prepared for his travels south in September 1930, he envisioned it as a first stage in his long-postponed journey home. From India he would go on to the Middle East, then Europe, and finally New York. But these vague plans hinged on his financial resources. In his arrangements with Con Press, it was apparently assumed that at some point he would return to Shanghai as part-time correspondent for the wire service, but Snow had no clear idea of the time required to complete the itinerary or the total expenses involved. During the project he was to receive three hundred dollars monthly plus very limited expenses and was to restrict himself to mail copy for his stories and to avoid expensive cable charges. Depression-era newspaper budgets were extremely lean, with foreign coverage, particularly from Asia, a low priority. "All the newspapers are tight," the general manager of Con Press, Horace Epes, wrote Snow the following year, "and a minimum of foreign news is crowding its way into print over protests from the city editors, sports editors and others fighting for their departments."[1]

As it turned out, Snow's proposed five-month trip, originally to include Persia and Arabia, had already stretched to nine months while he was still in India. And it became a much more costly venture than he had expected; since leaving Shanghai, he wrote Epes from Simla, India, in May 1931, he had been forced to spend some twelve hundred dollars of his own money. With the expenses of the projected Persia-Arabia leg of the trip still to come, "I shall be done for financially when I reach New York." Epes, for his part, replied that Snow's journey had already cost Con Press twice the budgeted amount (though Ed's copy had been "worth the cost") and instructed him to abandon the Persia-Arabia plan. Ed then decided against going on to New York at his own expense and returned directly to Shanghai. He was back by the end of July 1931, ten months after his departure, and resumed his work for Con Press. Interestingly, if he had been able to continue on from India, Epes had considered asking him to join their European staff and go into Russia. Snow was "much agitated" to learn of this lost opportunity and felt it "ironic that, principally because the prospect at home was so unpromising, I had turned back from Bombay." China was thus destined to be the making of Snow as a journalist and author. Russia would wait until the momentous wartime year of 1942.[2]

It had been an extraordinary year, surely all that Snow could have anticipated of adventurous travel and writing. He had traversed roadless areas of China that were bandit-ridden, opium-growing, and malaria-infested, encountered enchanting romance in Burma, and witnessed colonial rule and the growing resistance to it in Indochina, Burma, and India. The China portion of his travels dispelled any remaining notions that a genuinely progressive China might emerge under the Kuomintang, and his look at the Asian empires of France and Britain reinforced his strong anti-imperialist convictions. Though he returned to Shanghai debilitated and broke, "On the whole," he wrote Epes before leaving India, "I have enjoyed myself and have accumulated much of that item which constitutes the fortune of newspaper folk—experience." The East "holds few surprises for me now," he wrote Towne, "but its interest somehow deepens."[3]

Snow's trip at least partially fulfilled his 1928 plans, though the goal of travel round the world and back to New York eluded him once again. But he now traveled as a sophisticated and hardheaded observer and reporter; he noted in his diary at about this time, "A newspaper correspondent in China is a doctor required to issue daily bulletins on the condition of a man with the seven year itch!" His skills as a travel writer were now enhanced by a deepening and critical political perception. The quality of his copy was soon recognized by editors back home, and the *New York Sun* asked for longer pieces for its syndicated travel feature, The World Today. Ed became a regular contributor to it during most of 1931, with articles on Formosa (Taiwan), the coastal cities of southern China, Indochina, Yunnan, Burma, and India. (The book Snow planned to do on his trek through Yunnan province—"South of the Clouds"— remained unfinished business in the press of work on his return, starting with Japan's Manchurian aggression in September 1931.)[4]

As his ship steamed south through the China Sea after leaving Shanghai on September 25, 1930, Snow mused longingly over a romantic attachment in Shanghai. "I thought long of Chigeko," he recorded, "recalled our first days together on Scott Road, the sweetness and innocence of her, and I loved her very, very much." He pictured her "orange-like lips, her small flat nose and faint eyebrows, her rough, long hair, and her small neat hands." But he was soon caught up in the novel sights and encounters of his journey. His first extended stop was Formosa, under Japanese rule since 1895. He found the fertile semitropical island to be scenic, seemingly peaceful, clean, and efficiently run. Public services, education, and living standards were superior to anything he had seen on the China mainland. Under tight Japanese control, the Chinese population was being thoroughly "Japanized," he wrote. The Chinese were being treated essentially as subjects of the emperor, were taxed heavily, and compelled to send their children to Japanese-language schools. Perhaps a hundred thousand were engaged in the opium traffic, and prostitution was legalized and widespread. The Chinese Snow talked with felt they should be ruling the island themselves. They had had their chance, Snow observed in his diary, but had made a "mess" of it, as was now the case with China itself. Snow cynically noted that "one obvious explanation" for the absence of any signs of approaching rebellion in Formosa was that "there are no Chinese warlords there. No warlords, no revolution."[5]

Snow visited a reservation area of aboriginal tribespeople in central Formosa. It appeared a tranquil scene, with Ed treated to a concert of sorts on "instruments" of poles and stones. A week after his visit it was the site of a bloody aboriginal uprising against the Japanese. "Appearances are on brief acquaintance with a land deceptive," Snow later remarked. Yet his overall 1930 impressions were relevant to an understanding of the problems and tragedies associated with the Kuomintang takeover of the island in 1945, and of the persistence of an independence movement there.[6]

Running short of cash, Snow took second-class passage from Formosa to the southern China coast, sharing a small cabin with six Japanese and Chinese men and women. (This made a good story for the World Today column.) "It's nice to be back in China," he noted in appreciation of Chinese culinary skills on arriving in Swatow on the China coast. In Canton, southern China's metropolis and the base of the Nationalist revolutionary movement of the 1920s, Snow found a bustling prosperous city—"the most up-to-date" one in China. It was also one of the most corrupt. The major city services and tax collection were farmed out to private syndicates, with bribery, profiteering, and a squeeze on taxpayers and businesses the order of the day. (Snow was shocked to learn that Sun Fo, former mayor of the city, had been one of the most corrupt of all. In Nanking Sun had taken Snow under his wing, and Ed had liked and respected him.) There were no elections, nor much due process of law for accused prisoners, political or otherwise. Snow was particularly, and characteristically, struck by the plight of young women prisoners who had been the reluctant and unhappy brides or concubines of much older men, and who were accused of liaisons with young lovers. Thus while Canton appeared to be Chinese-ruled China at its best, it was far indeed from Sun Yat-sen's democratic vision that his Kuomintang successors claimed as their goal. Snow visited Sun's former home and shrine in Portuguese-ruled Macao ("the poor man's Monte Carlo"), and meditated that if Sun had lived on, "he certainly would have broken with the present government long ere now."[7]

Proceeding on to Indochina, Snow observed the French-proclaimed *mission civilisatrice* in action. He recorded his "memory of French customs officials whipping and beating natives when our boat arrived at Haiphong. And of the natives slinking off like whipped dogs, only without a whimper or word of protest." He thought the Vietnamese to be mostly "a sorry looking lot," while the French merchants were all fat, "with sometimes fatter wives." As to why all colonial Frenchmen developed "large girths," he noted, "the very obvious answer [is] that they eat ten course dinners and drink wines freely without anything but carnal exercise to wear it off." Cautioned not to pay more than ten cents per ricksha ride, he noted, "Why is it that men who think nothing of being charged $1.40 for a whiskey soda worth ten cents are always careful never to overpay a ricksha themselves and warn others in the matter?" Physical mistreatment by the French seemed commonplace, whether of hotel employees by managers or train passengers by conductors. "Later I concluded," Snow commented in *Journey*, "that it was the triumph of the method and the system over the human personality that was degrading about colonial doctrine; few men could resist it."[8]

Snow's visit to what is now northern Vietnam coincided with an abortive rebellion against the French, involving a native troop mutiny, scattered peasant uprisings, and student militancy and ending in massive reprisals and executions. Snow's "meagre" reports (smuggled out past the censors to Hong Kong) probably provided the only press coverage in America. The Vietnamese would inevitably be waiting for a later and more propitious opportunity—the next world war, for example, Snow concluded. It all gave him a long head start in appreciating the revolutionary potential in that French domain. Burma and India would provide further illustrations. But first came the high tension (and colorful copy) of Snow's Yunnan expedition. He had determined to enter Burma through the virtually untracked overland "back door" passage from China into upper Burma, a route to be made famous with the wartime construction of the Burma Road.[9]

With no rail or motor road connections to the rest of China, the most feasible entry into Yunnan was by way of the French-built railway from Haiphong to the Yunnan capital of Kunming. The train journey took three days and passed through some two hundred tunnels to reach Kunming, situated on the elevated Yunnan plateau, 6,400 feet above sea level. The rickety rolling stock on this unprofitable line added to the "scenic thrills" of the steep upward climb, as recounted by Snow for The World Today. Burma lay four hundred miles to the southwest, over trails and across mountains accessible only on foot or by mule and horse. Such an expedition, over bandit-infested and tribal country, required well organized, provisioned, and guarded caravans under skilled and experienced leaders. Snow quickly realized he lacked both the expertise and resources to mount such an enterprise on his own.[10]

Yunnan, a region of spectacular natural beauty, was mired in abysmal poverty. It was in the grip of militarist chieftains enriching themselves from the widespread opium cultivation and traffic, and from the province's finances and valuable tin-mining operations. The colorful and outspoken salt commissioner explained to Snow that in Yunnan "the only difference between a bandit and an official was that the official was a successful bandit." As for the new political dispensation under the Kuomintang, "it's just a new flag under old warlords." Numbing poverty led peasants to sell their daughters and even sons as slave labor, some twenty thousand children in Kunming alone. They worked in homes, workshops, and stores; boys labored under the most inhumane conditions of all, in the primitive tin mines.[11]

Snow was fortunate (up to a point) to meet up with Dr. Joseph F. Rock, a famed naturalist-explorer who had already shown Yunnan to be a botanical paradise of hundreds of plant varieties unknown elsewhere. Rock, then organizing a new expedition sponsored by *National Geographic,* the U.S. Department of Agriculture, and various scientific organizations, invited Snow to come along as far as Tali in western Yunnan. An Austrian-born naturalized American of fifty, Rock was a rather vain and misanthropic man, contemptuous of missionary "soul-savers" and Chinese officialdom. While he could be a charmingly urbane and delightful companion, his mood swings could transform him into an abusive and altogether unpleasant person. Snow's relationship with him was stormy and unpredictable. He kept Snow waiting for over a month, until the end of January 1931, before finally deciding to start the journey. At one point he rescinded his invitation to Snow and then once again persuaded Ed to join him. All this proved a wearing ordeal for Snow, who worried that the long wait in Kunming for Rock to make a start might compromise his arrangements with Con Press. An "odd genius— or an idiot," Snow privately remarked of Rock. It was particularly galling for one of Snow's temperament to find himself subject to his partner's every whim. "I am thoroughly disgusted with being dependent upon someone else's movements; never again for me," he bitterly recorded. "I ought to have got beyond that stage in life, anyway."[12]

Rock comported himself as a foreign potentate, traveling with a large retinue of retainers that included well-armed guards, cooks, and other housekeeping personnel, as well as muleteers, and occasional sedanchair bearers. The caravan had sixty mules and horses, supplies to last for a year "in the wilds," scientific instruments, and a complete medical kit. The nightly stops were occasions for well-prepared meals served on a linen-covered portable table, complete with china and silver service. Temples, thoroughly scrubbed by Rock's staff, were frequent overnight layovers. Local magistrates along the way provided contingents of soldiers whom Rock paid well. He carried ten thousand dollars in silver; once near the end of their journey Rock expressed suspicion (soon retracted) that Snow might have attempted to steal from him. This was the last straw for Ed. "I knew that from this moment I could never regard him with sincere friendliness, and I was glad only that tomorrow was our last day together." Yet Rock in his own way had compassion for the Chinese and often shared his medicines with diseased villagers along the way.[13]

After a three-week journey, Snow parted with Rock in Tali and turned south to Burma. He formed his own small caravan of mules and ponies, a cook, and a couple of muleteers. Attaching himself to a larger merchant caravan, Snow's entourage reached Bhamo on the upper Burma frontier after two more weeks of even more spectacularly scenic and fascinating travel. He had been one of a very few Westerners ever to "walk" from China to Burma. A decade or so later he would fly the same route by military plane in two hours. The forty-day Yunnan trip had more than satisfied Snow's taste for novel "travel adventures." Perhaps of special interest was the diversity of minority nationalities and cultures in the mountains and valleys, plains and forests of the China-Burma border areas. In the region of the Kachins, a warlike border people, Snow had a harrowing movie-script experience, complete with a last-minute rescue. He had ventured into a jungle area in advance of his caravan and suddenly came upon a band of Kachins, armed with swords and apparently intent on disposing of him. He held them off with a couple of "demonstration" shots from his revolver until two soldiers from his party who had heard the firing appeared.[14]

Less exciting but equally memorable was the exhilarating beauty of the unspoiled natural surroundings. "There is joy in this life; I understand Rock's love for it now," Snow noted in the early stages of the journey. "Today, as I rode over the mountain tops, with the azure sky an infinite ribbon over the rough horizon of sky-rubbing peaks, some of them snow-covered, I thanked God that I was doing this trip, as I had wanted, as I had planned." For Ed it was both justification and culmination of his three years abroad. Though cash in hand was low, "I would not have missed any of the things I've blundered into for the best advertising man's job in New York!" he exulted. "I *have* lived during these three years, and I have known many cities, felt often the tremulous touch of unexpected wonder and sweetness in strange places and faces few men I know can have understood."[15]

But a darker side to the experience also left its mark (including chronic bouts with malarial fever). Snow's immersion in the daily life of this backwater region of China, far from the amenities of the treaty ports, resulted in ambivalent feelings of sympathy and angry contempt toward its inhabitants. The filthy rat-infested inns, the ravages of diseases such as leprosy and syphilis, the universal opium habit, the poverty, sloth, and apathy appalled and repelled Snow. Above all, they violated his Western notions of energetic self-help and action to change intolerable conditions. "I say there is something fundamentally wrong with people who can live, year after year, in the midst of such squalor," he noted after a night in a typical inn. "I have seen pigstys kept far cleaner than some of the rotten holes into which these men climb for their opium pipe and dream bed." He was irritated at the people "who revel in the filth and discomfort in which they live." No beggar in America would sleep in the "mud dumps the people call their homes." He thought them "too lazy" to make the effort to improve these conditions. And in a final thrust, he summed up, "If anyone fancies that man has lost his capacity to live without the benefits of modern science and invention, let him travel through Yunnan." Snow had yet to meet a new breed of young Chinese, in whom he found the qualities lacking among the people he had thus far encountered in Yunnan and elsewhere in China. For the moment, as Snow disbanded his caravan and moved on to a sharply contrasting experience in Burma, he recapped his recent adventure: "A long, interesting, wearing, unforgettable journey."[16]

Before leaving Yunnan, Snow had learned of Howard's marriage; "e[t] tu Brute!," he wrote back to his brother. "Now all my friends, and all my family tied up in new circlets of gold." In a poignant, remarkably frank, and amusing letter to his new sister-in-law, Dorothy, written from Rangoon three months later, Ed underlined the anchor role Howard had played in his life, the sole exception to his distrust of binding ties, marital or otherwise. "The truth is I did not write to you [sooner] because I was not glad that you were Mrs. Snow." There was no personal malice in this, only that Dorothy was "something which had upset the regular flow of my plans. . . . I was suddenly depressed and for a great many days I felt much older than I am." He had always thought of Howard "as an entity which figured more or less constantly, directly in my life." The future he had envisioned in New York "would be a life with Howard." They would "know girls," but "nothing that would outlast its own first rapture." Ed, of course, was careful to add all the correct and gracious sentiments, in his most charming manner. ("Madame, I understand why my brother was weak.") In Burma, Ed found several nonbinding moments of rapture.[17]

Bhamo, along the Irrawaddy River in upper Burma, became the setting of a delightful interlude for Snow, with a lovely young Burmese woman named Malami. He met her through a local Englishman whose hobby was photographing Burmese girls in the nude. Snow's few days in Bhamo were spent mostly with Malami, who ministered to Ed's badly inflamed knee where he had been kicked by one of his caravan mules. "She is like something in burnished copper, only softened, animated by some divine and mysterious power," he rhapsodized in his diary. Though she offered to accompany Ed to Rangoon, he felt it prudent not to risk "a fearful row" with the British officers and passengers on the Irrawaddy steamer. "As it was their noses were up at a high slant because Malami walked to the gangplank and kissed me."[18]

In Rangoon, where he stayed for over a month, Snow met another Burmese girl, whom he described in equally alluring terms ("fragile and dainty," an "exquisitely modelled" face, "lustrous hair," etc.). In *Journey*,

Snow combined the elements of his Burmese encounters into a much more pristine but no less spellbinding nurse named Batalà. In this version, Batalà treated his knee and fever in Bhamo and again in Rangoon. "Batalà and I had shared an hour or two 'saved from that eternal silence' and that was enough," Snow reminisced. Not surprisingly, both at the time and later Snow waxed enthusiastic about Burmese women in general. He found them to be "among the most charming and emancipated in the world," with "a degree of social grace and freedom then unknown in China or India or anywhere in the Asia I had seen."[19]

Snow extended his Burma stay primarily to report on a rebellion of landless peasants and their leader, Saya San, who was killed in the suppression of the uprising. More violent and bloodier than the Tonkin uprising against the French, the revolt voiced the discontent of the mass of Burmese peasants whose rice lands had been bought up largely by Chettyars, an Indian banking caste there. (By the mid-1930s, almost half the paddy land in lower Burma was owned outright or mortgaged to Indian landlords.) Young intellectuals in Rangoon were calling for separation from India and longing for full independence from Britain. As in Indochina, Snow filed the only detailed reports to appear in America.[20]

With his already strong animus toward the pompous superiority of the British residents of Shanghai, Snow got more than his fill of this mentality in Burma and India. The condescension directed at Americans galled him almost as much as the racism toward "natives." At theater performances in Rangoon the playing of the British anthem always officially ended the proceedings. "It annoys the British extremely to see a white man walk out before this inevitable finale is played; for that reason I took exceeding delight in doing so," Snow snidely recorded. From the beginning Snow fully appreciated the critical importance of the color issue in arousing the nationalist sensitivities and bitter resentment of Asian intellectuals and other middle- and upper-class elements against white colonial rulers.[21]

Snow arrived in Calcutta in April with dour preconceptions of India. In part they reflected his distaste for the business-minded Indians who had descended en masse on Burma and undercut the livelihood of the less competitive and laid-back Burmese—"easy prey" for the Indians, Snow thought. The Burmese could gradually be drawn into India's "vicious, uncivilized caste system," making them "the same slaves as [the Indians'] own women." Still, India would contribute significantly to Snow's ongoing political education.[22]

In his four months in India Snow traveled the length and breadth of that vast and varied subcontinent. He met Gandhi (fleetingly) and had in-depth interviews with Jawaharlal Nehru, the president of the Indian National Congress, and other Indian nationalist leaders. He arrived in the aftermath of Gandhi's famous 1930 salt march to the sea, in defiance of the British colonial government's monopoly and tax on Indian salt production and distribution. The march sparked a nationwide nonviolent civil disobedience movement, and a boycott of British goods, all part of the struggle for independence led by the Congress. Shortly before Snow's advent, Gandhi reached an agreement with the viceroy calling off the campaign. The accord called for formal negotiations at a London roundtable conference to chart a new status for India. This truce aroused much controversy and dismay among younger Congress leaders such as Nehru, who felt the Mahatma had given up too much for too little, in terms of the goal of full independence. Snow, too, felt Gandhi had "surrendered" to the viceroy on "the very edge of success."[23]

Beyond the question of Gandhi's political judgment (though linked to it), was Snow's unsympathetic reaction to the Indian leader's methods and beliefs. He disliked the "passivity" of Gandhi's nonviolent philosophy, and his promotion of religiously based moral and ethical precepts as panaceas for India's ills and injustices. Nor did Snow think much of the Mahatma's "retrogressive" emphasis on self-sufficient homespun village industry, and seeming exaltation of asceticism and poverty—all symbolized by the Indian's spinning wheel, loincloth, simple diet, and spare living arrangements. Gandhi's vow (at age thirty-seven) of sexual abstinence likewise had no appeal for young Snow, perhaps most especially in the context of his Burma idyll. All in all, Snow considered Gandhi to be "the most enigmatic personality I have met in the Orient," and someone who "seems a ridiculous little showman who has hypnotized a nation with an epigram." Yet Snow could also see in him a "man of supremely fair and just mind—must be admired for wonderful power over men which derives from his kind of life." And in truth, Snow's personal values had much in common with those of the saintly Mahatma, though Ed saw his own as stemming from a "rational-scientific" base. "Truth, sincerity, devotion, and kindliness appeal to me as the standards by which men and their actions should be judged," Ed wrote his father from India in June 1931. Did these differ markedly from Gandhi's vision of truth, love, brotherhood, and "soul-force"?[24]

In his last meeting with Gandhi in New Delhi in January 1948, shortly before the latter's assassination, Snow would make the connection. The shock of the subsequent tragedy, and Snow's presence at the cremation and ceremony added a further emotional element. In a moving testamentary article that William L. Shirer calls "one of the classics of American journalism," Snow wrote of the profound truths and revolutionary character of Gandhi's teachings: nonviolence for a world of war, cold war, and nuclear weapons; social and economic justice; religious tolerance; personal purity and morality; and the fundamental axiom that only good means lead to good ends. "For years I had felt out of sympathy for him," Snow wrote, "yet even in this dull clod, the avatar had finally struck a spark before he died, when, in my last visit, I became conscious of my size in the mirror of him, and I saw him as a giant."[25]

Snow paid even more glowing tribute to Gandhi a decade later in *Journey*. As the concluding theme of that work, he pointed to Gandhi's "truth and message of brotherhood" as the indispensable beacon for the planet's survival. Nevertheless, Snow's "conversion" was hardly a complete and consistent one. He never, for example, abandoned his defense of armed *revolutionary* struggle as the ultimate recourse for an oppressed people. In *Journey,* he deftly left himself an "out" on the issue of violence when describing the Gandhi cremation scene. It had required police force to restrain the mass of people pressing against the funeral pyre. "Thus I saw Gandhi depart in a paradox as he had lived in one," Snow remarked, always himself aware of the Taoist inconsistencies and ironies of life.[26]

It was Jawaharlal Nehru, the young, handsome, urbane Oxford-educated intellectual, whom Snow immediately took to in 1931 and thereafter. Nehru's democratic, modern-minded ("Western"), and socialist approach to India's problems and future development struck a responsive chord in Ed. Nehru was refreshingly free of the pervasive religiosity of other Indian leaders and was committed to the thoroughgoing reform of India's caste-ridden society. Snow was also meeting his first "live" Communists and reading for the first time some basic Marxist and Leninist texts. He had already observed imperialism in action in Asia and noted that it benefited foreign business interests first and foremost. Nationals of the mother countries enjoyed a privileged and profitable life in the colonies, while the mass of the indigenous population endured abject poverty and exploitation. Native capitalists and landlords were no better, and often worse, than their imperial counterparts. In Calcutta, Snow observed, "nine-tenths of the population live wretchedly and seldom with enough to eat; one-tenth lives comfortably or in wanton luxury."[27]

The Leninist thesis that Asia needed both a national and a social (class) revolution seemed justified by what Snow had seen in China, and in the French and British colonies. In Bombay Snow inspected tenements occupied by textile workers and owned by the mills. Some five hundred persons were crowded into the sixty rooms of each tenement. A single outdoor tap provided the drinking water for all five hundred. As Snow described the scene in his diary:

The rows of houses stand only about five feet apart. Down the center of the lane dividing them runs an open sewer, which carries off the urine, garbage and other filth from the thirty ground floor rooms in each tenement, and the thirty upstairs. Little emaciated children, naked, run up and down the center of this drain. They splash themselves with its filth and carry it on their little feet into their dark, dirty, windowless hovels, where they are forced to retire during the heavy rains of the day, and at night.

Meanwhile, at the luxurious Taj Mahal Hotel, Snow added, "their foreign and Indian mill-owning oppressors" quaffed drinks and reclined comfortably in their white flannels, "while making superficial comments about Bach and Brahms." (In the typical incongruities of these situations, Snow too was staying at the Taj Mahal.)[28]

Snow's growing awareness of Marxist thought while in India came also from a well-publicized trial of Communists then taking place there. The thirty-one Indian and British defendants, many of them intellectuals, had utilized the lengthy proceedings to expound on all aspects of Communist theory and practice—all of which had been duly reported in the Indian press. "When one reads back through the newspaper files since the trial began," Snow noted, "it is an education in the economics of Karl Marx, and their revolutionary application by Lenin, his associates, and their successors." "Some of the most trenchant criticism ever directed at British rule in India has come forth at the Meerut trial," he added.[29]

Snow wrote against the traditional degradation of women in India and gave prominent play to the growing role (the "revolt") of educated and politically conscious women as a potent new feminist force in the Indian nationalist movement. Such women fought, he wrote, both for the emancipation of women in the home and of India as a nation. In Bombay he had been taken in tow by a young Communist activist named Suhasini, from the remarkable and illustrious Chattopadhyaya family. Snow described her as "the most beautiful Indian woman I have ever met," and a "one woman revolutionary movement in herself." Her sister, whom Ed also came to know well, was the celebrated poet and Congress political figure Sarojini Naidu. There were two other sisters, one a leading educator-philosopher and the other a dramatist and noted authority on Indian art. An elder brother, Virendranath (Chatto), was a major Indian revolutionary nationalist, active also in the European Communist movement. He had had a stormy common-law marriage to Agnes Smedley during the 1920s in Berlin. Interestingly, it was Snow, when covering the war in Russia in 1943, who obtained confirmation that Chatto had died at Stalin's orders in Russia in 1941 or 1942.[30]

Suhasini, the first avowed Communist Snow had met, was one of Ed's guides through the Bombay worker tenements. She attempted to proselytize him on communism, but Snow was not about to embrace doctrinal absolutes, especially one with its own godhead in Moscow. Nonetheless, as Snow later put it, Suhasini and others "did make me realize there were two revolutions (i.e., national and social), not one, struggling for birth and power over men in India as in China." Thus, despite his great admiration for Nehru, Snow considered him to be "fundamentally an aristocrat; secretly he is shocked or frightened at the thought of power suddenly being wrenched from the present controlling elements and administered by Indian peasants and laborers." Ed confided similar misgivings to Mildred about the Indian Congress leaders. They were "not opposed to unlimited exploitation by capitalists and they have no program for the agrarians."[31]

There is little doubt that the new intellectual and political horizons opened by his eventful 1930–1931 travel year pointed the way to *Red Star*. "All my experiences [of that year]," Snow recounted a quarter century later, "were going to shape my life and work beyond any capacity of mine as yet to appreciate." Meanwhile, fortified and chastened by his broadened outlook, Snow (with stops in Ceylon, Malaya, and the Dutch East Indies) headed back to Shanghai. There he would begin his personal discovery of the Chinese left, and in time of that deeper stage of Asian revolution he now considered both necessary and inevitable.[32]

CHAPTER 6

Shanghai Again

While still in India, Snow had come down with another of his chronic head colds caught in the bitter chill of Simla, high in the foothills of the Himalayas. He had arrived there from the torrid plains below clad in summer shorts. This had in turn set off one of his low, homesick moods. But, he wrote Mildred from Simla, "my dilemma is that I can't quite decide whether it is nostalgia for China or America. I am strongly inclined to believe it is China." Still, the decision to stay in Shanghai was painful if pragmatic. "Often I get suddenly frantic and long to cry out against the necessity of this long separation," he confided to his father before leaving Bombay for China. But necessary it was. His travel year had been "a losing proposition." In Shanghai he could at least live cheaply while doing all the writing he had in mind. He reluctantly turned down a tempting offer from Charlie Towne to share the comforts of Towne's Manhattan lodgings and summer cottage. He could not allow himself to "abuse" such hospitality, Ed wrote Towne from Shanghai; he would feel obliged almost immediately to look for a job—probably some "silly stunt" like selling advertising. Beyond this, driven by a feeling of unattained goals as time raced by, Ed could not return home while still "far from achieving what I set out to do." Even more, he was acutely conscious of all that had changed for him in America. Were it not for the family and one or two others, he told J. Edgar, "the thought that I might not see America again for two or three years would not agitate me." There was no going back to the old life. "I have outgrown that— or it has outgrown me."[1]

Back in Shanghai (for which he seemed to be developing a love-hate relationship) by mid-summer 1931, Ed was immediately laid low by a malarial attack that added to his rundown condition. Still convalescing, he met Helen Foster on the very day of her arrival in Shanghai from the States. She was twenty-three, unusually attractive, upbeat, and freshly American. Armed also with a portfolio of Snow clippings, she was a bracing tonic for Ed's malaise. Ambitious, keen-minded (and sharp-tongued), she was determined to make her name as a writer. Though born in Utah, she strongly identified with her Welsh-English, Puritan New England roots, summed up in the tenets of Morality, God, enter-prise, and hard work. The contrast in personality and mind-set between the two was great indeed, but Ed was always drawn to strong-willed, brainy, and good-looking women. "There are many kinds of interesting minds;" he had earlier written Howard, "some of them have a soft curve at the hips." Peg (the nickname she used in those years) had a remark-able role in China over the next decade, both in her own right and in Ed's life and work.[2]

By the fall of 1931 Ed resumed his part-time arrangement with Con Press, at eighty dollars a month. Though it left him free to write for other publications, Snow was annoyed both by the minimal compensa-tion and the penny-pinching limitations imposed on him in doing his job. Newspapers at home generally relegated Asia news to the back burner. He argued for a much more substantial commitment to the Shanghai operation, an argument underscored by Japan's Manchuria aggression that September. "All evidence is that very deep social, eco-nomic, and political changes, of vital effect on the world, are soon to take place," he wrote Epes in October. The issue was not simply money. He could make a good deal more doing other things (such as ad agency jobs in Shanghai for which he had no stomach), "but that is not what will keep me here." However, budgetary constraints in the severely strapped newspaper field back home precluded greater outlays, Epes told him. Ironically Snow, who feared facing the bleak depression prospects in America, was feeling its fall-out in China.[3]

Epes did prove slightly more generous with extra compensation and expense monies as the China situation and Ed's duties heated up—par-ticularly in his eyewitness reporting of the Shanghai fighting in early 1932. He had also taken over Powell's relinquished post as correspon-dent for the London *Daily Herald* (as a stringer). Despite the shoestring character of his one-man operation, Snow's reportage of the Shanghai battle garnered rich praise. The managing editor of the *Sun* told Epes he "had never seen a better job done by a correspondent working alone and with so little contact with the home office." The *Daily Herald* foreign editor equally wrote Powell that Ed's cables "during the Shanghai trouble have given great satisfaction here."[4]

In early September 1931 Snow went up the Yangtze River with the press corps to view the vast devastation wrought by massive flooding along a nine-hundred-mile stretch of the lower Yangtze. It was one of the great natural disasters of the century and left some two million people dead and many more millions homeless and destitute. Snow's *Herald-Tribune* article on the catastrophe was reminiscent of his 1929 piece on the great northwestern famine. Yet the two reports also gave a good measure of the distance Snow had come in his thinking and perspectives. In 1929 he had written of the famine victims through the eyes of a compassionate foreign observer. In the flood account, Snow put himself in the place of the individual peasant in all his agony, despair, and inner fury, for whom the flood was "the culmination of a long series of afflictions." Snow described these "afflictions": extortionate tax collectors, looting soldiers and merciless militarists worse even than bandits. Granaries were left bare, Snow went on, and only landlords and usurers retained any silver, which they hid as they trembled in fear of "the long range and thrust of the wild new cry of Communism." In 1929 Snow's criticism of the government had been virtually nil. In 1931 there was a searing indictment of "a militaristic regime which for callous indifference, tyrannous oppression and ruinous incompetence has not been surpassed anywhere in this era." "I have seen so much pain and suffering," Snow ended, "that it has entered my own blood." The Chinese peasants "merit better treatment than they have received from the elements and from man."[5]

Snow had just returned to Shanghai from the flood areas to hear news of the Mukden Incident. A minor explosion on September 18 ripped the tracks of the Japanese government-owned South Manchurian Railway at Shenyang (then, Mukden), capital of Manchuria. This contrived pretext was the signal for the rapid takeover of southern Manchuria by Japan's well-prepared Kwantung Army operating out of the railway zone. Before the end of the year Japanese troops had conquered all of northern Manchuria (where they met more determined Chinese resistance). These events ushered in a period of continuous Japanese pressure against China, leading to the all-out attempt to subjugate that nation in the "China Incident" of 1937. Manchuria shattered the fragile structure of world order built in the 1920s, symbolized by the League of

Nations, the Kellogg-Briand Pact renouncing war, and the Nine-Power Treaty affirming respect for China's independence and territorial integrity.

Snow went up to Manchuria with a press party in early November, by which time the Japanese conquest was a fait accompli. The newspapermen arrived in frozen northern Manchuria (till then considered a Russian sphere of influence) in the immediate aftermath of the fighting there. Chinese bodies lay everywhere, a testament to the courageous resistance by the local Chinese forces led by a plucky general. The manner in which these men had fought in the face of certain defeat, "is the most heroic thing I have seen in China," Ed wrote Howard. In Mukden he interviewed the commander of the Japanese forces, General Honjo, and the Chinese puppet governor. The latter, a classical scholar, had been forcibly installed by the Japanese. He acknowledged to Snow that "we are the last to hear of actions and policies credited to us" by the Japanese. In like manner the Japanese thrust the last boy emperor of the Qing dynasty, Pu-yi, into the role of chief executive of the Japanese-created state of Manchukuo the following March.[6]

Snow, in Shanghai again by early December, was downhearted and contemptuous at the failure of the Young Marshal, Zhang Xueliang (in Peking with most of his Northeast Army), and of Generalissimo Chiang Kai-shek, in Nanking, to resist the Japanese. Ed's mood was worsened by a bout of sinusitis, brought on by a severe head cold contracted in the arctic climate of northern Manchuria; it forced him to cut short his trip. In Shanghai he required hospitalization and then convalescence at home through the Christmas–New Year holiday period. This sinusitis, he told his father, "is the most vitiating thing I know." The only pleasant aspect of his illness, Ed further informed J. Edgar, was the attention he received from his "charming neighbor," Peg Foster. It was his first mention of Peg to the family. She was a "lovely child" (all of two years younger than Ed!), and they had become "warm friends." "It occurred to her that she would like to be Empress of Asia, so she put on her roller skates and came out. She is quite mad, but very cheerful and quite intelligent." Before coming to China, she had read everything he had ever written, and is "really rather splendid because she quotes to me from my own 'works.'"[7]

It irked him, Snow wrote Epes at this same time, to be sidelined by illness "during these exciting days in China." But he was now recovered, and ready to go north again should the situation require. As it turned out, however, Snow would be in the right place at the right time when the Japanese launched their attack on Chinese Shanghai two weeks later.[8]

Snow's frustration over the Manchurian events was directed also at the ineffectual response of the world community. "I suppose," he voiced his feelings to Howard, "there are still people in the West who will believe in the efficacy of prayer, and the Kellogg Pact, the Nine-Power Pact, and the League of Nations to outlaw war. All of them obviously are failures." (He took an equally jaundiced view of Washington's "non-recognition doctrine" in January 1932.) "What a farce" it all was. Neither did Snow show much sympathy for the ousted Manchurian overlords. He had no doubt, he told Howard, that the inhabitants of Manchuria would fare better under Tokyo's rule. But there remained "the ethical problem"—did any nation have "the right to take over the land, property, and government of another merely because that latter is hopelessly incompetent?" And as a confirmed anti-imperialist (reinforced by his travels in colonial Asia), Snow knew that no people were truly "better off" under foreign conquerors—particularly ones as arrogant and ruthless as the Japanese military. The future for the Chinese people seemed dismal indeed, whether under Japanese masters or Chinese oppressors.[9]

In a wide-ranging 1932 New Year letter to his father, Snow touched on topics from Chinese communism to American capitalism and much in between. The key targets of his stark and radical analysis of the state of the world were imperialism (Western and Japanese), militarism (Chinese and Japanese), and fascism (European and Asian)—all of them part of a collapsing capitalist global order. China entered the new year in a more "pathetic condition" than ever before. Chiang's "ruinous dictatorship" was toppling, but new leaders (who temporarily replaced the "resigned" Generalissimo) had nothing better to offer. Either way, the country remained in the hands of "war barons." "What a perennial tragedy poor China is!" There had not yet appeared a single man "with any real genius for leadership and statecraft"—a more restrained version of Ed's earlier call for a "Great Redeemer." Communism in China was now stronger than ever, an "accurate barometer of the people's despair, disgust and dissatisfaction with the record of the past three years," Snow continued. The Communist leaders possessed "a vigor and enthusiasm" that could soon carry them to important victories, barring some "revolution" in the Kuomintang. The world was in for a dark time. Japan's Manchurian conquest "squashes any hope of a pacific world for years to come." Liberalism was on the wane. The Western imperialist powers would be adopting "reactionary" foreign policies, including a tougher line toward their subject peoples. Fascists were on the rise in Italy and Germany. America might have made a difference the past year but has had little better leadership than China's. ("Mediocre," "vacillating," "weak," "cowardly" were only some of the pejoratives Snow directed at the Hoover administration.) "Oh, for a man in the White House with courage and a clear mind and clean heart that would refuse to compromise with the stench of rottenness and corruption that pervades our national as well as local politics." Capitalism itself was in decay in Europe and America. It was "economically unsound, antiquated from our time, and moribund." Its overthrow in Europe was "only a matter of time." Even in America, where capitalism had been the "premise" of the country's unparalleled development, it was also running out of steam. An earlier period of "freedom and comparative equality of opportunity" had vanished. "We are entering a period of consolidation of the forces of capitalism and imperialism against our rapidly increasing masses who are the victims of the system. The crisis in America will come more gradually and the outcome will take different forms than elsewhere, but I believe that fundamental changes in the economic machinery are clearly visible ahead." It was all pretty heady and heavy stuff to go along with Ed's New Year greetings to J. Edgar![10]

Snow's gloomy *Weltanschauung* carried over into his personal mood. He seemed quite at ease unburdening himself to his as yet unmet sister-in-law, Dorothy (Dotty). Perhaps the younger brother was also trying to project a sophisticated image of the world-weary veteran foreign correspondent. He was jaded with the Chinese, he wrote Dorothy in January 1932, and found the Europeans and Americans mostly stuffy or boring. Nor were prospects among the women especially enticing. (Peg, the obvious exception, was unmentioned.) "So you end up at a Chinese dinner listening to high-pitched singing girls and feeling a little sad because it is no longer as thrilling as it once was."[11]

Snow's ennui was soon dispelled by Tokyo's move against Shanghai later that month. The city had become the center of intense anti-Japanese popular feeling over the "national humiliation" in Manchuria. It took the form of an effective boycott, and of labor strikes against Japanese-owned factories. The mayor of Shanghai, prodded by Nanking, capitulated to an ultimatum to suppress the movement. But despite this surrender Japanese naval and marine forces struck on the night of January 28. They sought to terrorize the Chinese and prepare the ground for penetration of the lower Yangtze Valley.

The Shanghai assault proved to be a serious blunder. Spearheaded by the strongly anti-Japanese Nineteenth-Route Army under its dauntless commander, Cai (Ts'ai) Tingkai, the Chinese waged a brave thirty-four-day struggle against powerful enemy naval, air, and army forces. Casualties were heavy on both sides, and there was great loss of property and civilian lives from indiscriminate Japanese bombing—a new factor in modern warfare. The Chinese were finally forced to retreat, but for the Japanese government it had been a stunning embarrassment and for the Chinese people an inspiring act of resistance. After a truce, the Japanese withdrew in May. In effect, their plans for the Yangtze region were put on hold until 1937; meanwhile they concentrated on the takeover of Inner Mongolia and northern China. General Cai became a national (and international) hero, much to the Generalissimo's discomfort. Chiang shunted him off with his denuded army to more remote Fujian province. Cai continued through the years to be a maverick figure in Kuomintang politics and ultimately joined the new Communist regime in 1949.[12]

Snow was in the center of the battle (his first real experience under fire), operating from his base in the adjoining International Settlement. His eyewitness accounts (including a first-day scoop), cabled to his American newspapers and the *Daily Herald,* got front-page play and much praise from his editors. Ed had been the first to alert the manager of the railway's north station in the Zhabei district about the imminent Japanese thrust, near midnight of the twenty-eighth. He thereby had a part in saving some ten million dollars of rolling stock from destruction. As Snow related the incident in *Far Eastern Front,* a Chinese officer soon arrived on the scene and confirmed Ed's news to the skeptical station manager. Years later, in *Journey,* Snow added more drama and suspense to the story. The verifying officer disappears from the new account. The station master is forced to make an immediate and agonizing decision to move the equipment based solely on Ed's unofficial and unverified warning.[13]

Snow's account of the Shanghai battle described its tragic human toll. He also stressed the inspirational impact of the struggle on the Chinese. "The lessons of the Shanghai war," he wrote in *Far Eastern Front,* "stimulated in all classes, particularly in the youth both in and out of the army, a new manhood, a self-reliance and self-respect, with an apparent determination to resist." Chiang Kai-shek, in contrast, moved his government farther inland to Luoyang out of harm's way during the fighting. It was becoming evident to Snow that China could be saved only by a national groundswell of the kind he had just witnessed in Shanghai. Later in Peking, he and Peg would themselves become part of that developing momentum among the educated youth.[14]

For the while, however, Tokyo's inroads in the north and Nanking's acquiescence in them went on unabated. The prospect, Snow wrote Epes as the Shanghai fighting drew to a close, was that "Japanese operations in China will steadily expand in scope," with the aim of subjugating that country. The notion that the economic costs and sacrifices entailed could bring Japan down was simply an illusion, Snow added. "The Japanese people are capable of enormous sacrifices to uphold national honor or prestige." The vast territory of Jehol (later, Rehe; eastern Inner Mongolia) was invaded in February 1933, its conquest completed in but ten days. It was a further humiliation for the Young Marshal. While he stayed in his Peking headquarters, a substantial portion of his remaining Northeast Army was lost in the Jehol debacle. He resigned his northern China command and quietly left for Europe.[15]

The Japanese followed up their victory by moving south into Hebei province, menacing the Peking-Tianjin (Tientsin) corridor. By May 1933 the infamous Tangku Truce had been signed with Nanking, creating a neutralized and demilitarized zone in northeastern Hebei. Chinese defense of the area was in effect abandoned, while Japan proceeded with plans to control all of northern China by orchestrating "autonomous" (puppet) movements there. Earlier, in March 1933, Tokyo had responded to the League of Nations' condemnation of its aggressions by withdrawing from that world body. A year later, Pu-yi was enthroned as emperor of the expanded state of Manchukuo. Chiang Kai-shek, Snow caustically noted, had achieved the "astonishing feat" of remaining supreme commander of China's armies during a de facto war with Japan, without once taking active command in defense of Chinese territory. Ed bitterly noted that some 400,000 of Chiang's best-equipped troops, and his air force, were engaged in fighting the Reds in central China, "when needed to defend the country against the Japanese."[16]

With the end of the Shanghai war Snow was back to his part-time assignment with Con Press (plus his new *Daily Herald* connection). He had received an extra $500 from Epes for his work on the Manchurian and Shanghai stories and was now put on a $145 monthly stipend. Snow accepted appreciatively but remained disappointed at the limitations of the job, which once more restricted him mostly to mail copy features. Restive as always, he was anxious to get away from Shanghai and its Shanghailanders. "There is an unfathomable desire in us," he wrote his sister-in-law, to "travel and explore and exhaust everything in an environment and a person" until it was all utterly predictable and "no more fun." After four years in the East he felt "infinitely older" and "more resigned to the limitations of life," he told Mildred. He was "restless, discontented, dissatisfied." He had few truly close friends in Shanghai—"a suspicious city." This new bout of despondency, he thought, could be due to all the suffering, sorrow, and stupidity he had recently witnessed. His attitude and modes of thought had all been shaken. There seemed no sense or purpose to it all. Faiths, he averred, were "merely treacheries for the ensnarement of the naive"; nevertheless, he envied those "not troubled by questionings." But of course, precisely such questioning and seeking were the making of him.[17]

In May Ed broached the idea to Epes of moving to Peking, where he could be closer to impending major developments in the north. He thought also of a trip to the central Yangtze region, with the aim of personally investigating Red-controlled areas south of the river. Snow's interest in the Communists had been further whetted by contacts he was making in left-wing circles in Shanghai. But the unexpected opportunity to do a fast book on the Manchurian and Shanghai wars caused him to put aside other plans. Howard and Dorothy had come up with a publisher, and a New York agent, interested in a book from Ed to be completed in time for fall publication. The publisher (Century Company) bowed out, but the agent, Henriette Herz, stayed with Snow for much of his writing career. Ed was doubtful of what he could produce in little more than two months to meet an August 1 deadline in New York. He nonetheless got to work, put aside his Yunnan travel book, and in June arranged for a forty-day unpaid leave from Con Press. (Given the extremely tight cash flow situation, Epes told him, "you couldn't have selected a better time to lay off.")[18]

Once begun, the book became "an obsession" for Ed, and "a race against time." The manuscript, fifteen chapters and 76,000 words, was completed on July 19, his twenty-seventh birthday. "Earsplitting" renovation work going on in his apartment building, and an unbearably hot and humid Shanghai heat wave had been added obstacles. The heat left him "limp and with no desire but to lie still, exercising neither mind nor body." He vowed to make this his last Shanghai summer.[19]

Snow, a writer who meticulously checked and painstakingly revised and polished his work, was dissatisfied with a product turned out under such frantic circumstances. He anticipated its rejection, which would not find him "sorry." In fact, it took almost another year of persistent effort by agent Herz to find another publisher. There was then even a greater rush to update, revise, and enlarge the original manuscript for its October 1933 publication. It was like doing a new book, Snow noted.

The final result was undoubtedly much stronger than the original effort, and one that he felt "will not hurt my reputation (if any) as a journalist." Once he shipped it off, he had no opportunity for any further changes, nor was he able to correct final proofs. He was dismayed at the inordinate number of typos and other errors ("some with rather tragic consequences") that marred the book. (It was a criticism made by many reviewers as well.) Ed was especially irritated that the dust jacket incorrectly identified him as correspondent for United Press. The book had no maps or index. The publishers, Harrison Smith and Robert Haas, operated on a shoestring, without publishing or distribution facilities of their own. (Smith later joined Random House, which became Ed's permanent publisher.) Public interest in Far Eastern conflicts was limited in depression-ridden America and there had been a flood of books on the subject. Nor did his publisher do much to promote Snow's book. Rather expensively priced at $3.75, the book sold fewer than 700 copies; Snow earned nothing beyond his $250 advance. Foreign editions later netted him a bit more.[20]

Yet *Far Eastern Front* was an important, even extraordinary, work and had many of the hallmarks of future Snow books. It combined informative background and solid, prophetic analysis with striking depictions of major actors and events, all recounted in a vivid personal style. Snow occupied a conspicuous place in the drama, as an "in the thick-of-battle" eyewitness, and as an unsparingly frank commentator on the overall scene. There was outrage at Japan's aggressions, scathing notes on the puppet charade of Manchukuo, scorn at the nonresistance policies and oppressive venality of China's militarist rulers, admiration for the patriotic heroism of Shanghai's defenders, and empathy for the human cost of it all. Snow's writing and persona were still maturing. His prose could become overheated and melodramatic, and there was a penchant for the fancier word when simpler ones would do. His first-person mode might call for more quietly assured and less breathless handling ("the stirring adventures of Edgar Snow," one reviewer sarcastically remarked). But these were peripheral points to a style that already had Snow's punch, color, personality, and humanity.

American reviewers invariably used such descriptive terms as "riveting," "absorbing," "readable," "dramatic," calling Snow an exceptionally able and intelligent writer. In Shanghai, the *Review's* lengthy assessment saw Snow as a new breed of modern, liberal China expert—in sharp contrast to the treaty port mentality of old China hands. The noted Chinese literary critic and author Lin Yu-tang gave the book particularly high marks, not only for its eminently readable qualities, but its "heartfelt sympathy for the Chinese people." There was "no humbug, no heaviness, no Shanghai mind, no capitalist bias," Lin wrote. A dissenting view came from the *China Forum,* a pro-Communist journal published in the International Settlement in the early 1930s. It was an anomaly Snow would often face from the orthodox left, despite (in this case) his vigorous condemnation of the anti-Communist Kuomintang regime and his essentially sympathetic assessment of the Chinese Communists. Harold Isaacs, the reviewer and the youthful American editor of the *Forum,* had come to China three years earlier after graduating from Columbia College in New York and would shortly break with the Stalinist Communist movement. Isaacs later continued to take a jaundiced view of Snow, but from an opposite standpoint—that of a disenchanted former "insider" who now saw Snow as a naively sympathetic "outsider"—or "fellow traveler."[21]

But Isaacs's chief complaint against Snow in 1933 was of his typically "liberal" failure to deal with events in Marxist class struggle terms. Snow thus offered a purely "ocular narrative"—he "sees all but knows nothing." Isaacs reluctantly granted that Snow had described the Shanghai fighting "with some power." There were also "a few passages of interesting facts," especially on the evils and weaknesses of the Nanking regime. Snow deserved "some credit" for this, since most "bourgeois" journalists ignored such matters. Isaacs reserved his greatest scorn for Snow's proposed "solutions" to the Far Eastern problem. In truth, Ed himself doubted they would be acted upon. Other reviewers had also (though much less disdainfully) dismissed them as little more than a forlorn hope.

In the concluding "Destinies of Asia" chapter of his book, Snow grappled with the dilemmas and contradictions stemming from his analysis of the realities of the Asian and world scene. (He also presumably kept in mind the noninterventionist attitudes of his American audience.) In the main this analysis continued to be key to his thinking, as well as a point of departure for his later perspectives. In this sense, Snow's ultimately more realistic stance incorporated the visionary reflections of 1933. The picture Snow drew was discouraging. Japan, propelled by its militarists' sense of national destiny and prestige, would inexorably continue its offensive against China. Further, Tokyo's expansionist drive would eventually challenge the entire Western position in Asia. "The rise of an Eastern Power great and daring and determined enough to defy the European Powers and America," Snow concluded on a Spenglerian note, "probably marks the twilight of Western mastery."

The "new" imperialism of Japan, Snow argued, was essentially no different from that of the earlier European empire builders. In any impending contest with Japan, the Western powers' primary concern would be self-preservation of imperial interests, not self-determination for Asian peoples. But the West, defensive, passive, and beset by a rising tide of colonial unrest, lacked Japan's push and spirit. The latter had the additional great advantage of the color issue, a potent factor in an Asia dominated by white racial supremacy and prejudice. Snow thus faced the dilemma of his "damned if you do and damned if you don't" view of the Western position in Asia. Failure to stand up to Japan inevitably meant Japanese ascendancy. But if the West ultimately confronted this challenge, it would do so only out of unworthy imperialist motives. As for America, while Snow had earlier derided the efficacy of the Hoover-Stimson (and the League's) nonrecognition stance, he now reasoned that neither the relatively small American economic stake in China nor the defense of the treaty system justified what would be an "absurd war" with Japan. Even should the United States prevail, at great and calamitous cost to both sides, America would end up in the role of Japan—the dominant, and highly unwelcome, imperial presence in China. (Snow here gave a foretaste of America's unhappy role in China following Japan's defeat in 1945.) The problem of Japanese militarism was primarily one for the Japanese people to resolve. A pacific Western posture might help encourage the "moderates" there.

China itself, divided, weak, and engaged in internal strife, was an easy prey for Japan. Preoccupied with its campaigns to suppress communism in the hinterland, and imposing a "White Terror" on radical and liberal elements in the cities, the Nanking regime had neither the will nor capacity to take on Japan. Under these conditions, no effective national resistance movement had emerged. China could even end up as a subservient partner in a new Japanese East Asian order. In brief, in its "present condition," China was both unable to save itself and unworthy of external rescue. America's only option for restraining Japan, Snow concluded, would have to be diplomatic. Here nonrecognition of Manchukuo needed to be supplemented by equal determination to move on with the liquidation of America's own "imperialist adventure" in the Philippines. This in turn should be the lever to pressure the European powers into adopting a twenty- to thirty-year plan leading to full self-government for their Asian colonies. If the Japanese managed to break the militarists' grip, Snow saw a "faint hope" that Japan might respond by similar moves in Manchukuo and possibly Korea. These measures would, for the first time, attack the fundamental causes of all conflict in the Orient. "It would require the Western Powers to yield up themselves that which they deny to Japan." The alternative was continued advance by "a triumphant and belligerent Japan," a race among the powers for markets and military primacy in the Pacific, and the "fatal progression" toward another world war, "this time to be fought on a Far Eastern Front." His proposals would be regarded as "visionary," Snow acknowledged. Yet his glimpse of the end of empire in Asia would become the reality, but it would take "a series of bloody conflicts" also envisioned by Snow. Japanese militarist wreckers, American power, and Asian revolutionaries would all play their parts.[22]

Snow had shown an interest in the Communist movement in China even before embarking on his 1930 Asian travels. He had made an initial foray in print on the subject in a piece for *Current History* that appeared during his journey. It displayed a fair amount of information (secondhand and not always accurate) secured from Shanghai sources. Snow's approach to the Reds was uncertain and ambivalent. He alternated, in somewhat schizoid fashion, between two images of the Communist-led peasant uprising. On the one hand, the Reds "looted and pillaged" captured cities and towns, "ravaged" the countryside, and killed thousands of men and women of the "upper classes." Snow also pointed to "the directing hand of Moscow" and financing through "Russian agents" in the treaty ports. On the other hand, he pictured the movement as an effectively led, powerful revolutionary force with great potential and promise for China's oppressed and impoverished millions. It was the deplorable conditions of Chinese life, and the Kuomintang's failure to better them, that had won the Communists their successes and the support of poor peasants and "half-starved" workers. Snow was thus already moving away from the simplistic "Red bandit" portrait propagated by the Chinese government and most press reports. His article was in fact paired and contrasted with one titled, "Banditry in a New Guise." But Snow's assessment also revealed the built-in contradictions for him as a liberal-humanitarian, sensitive to the conditions that led to inevitably violent and ruthless social revolution.[23]

Snow's further education on the revolutionary movement in China came from a very special source. Some time after the Shanghai war ended in 1932, he sought out Madame Sun Yat-sen (Soong Qingling), to do a profile of her for the *Herald-Tribune*. Madame Sun's credentials were truly formidable. As the widow of the officially revered Dr. Sun, with her younger sister married to the Generalissimo, her older sister to China's top banker and major government figure, and her brother T. V. the financial wizard of the Nanking regime, Qingling was clearly a most inconvenient but personally untouchable odd woman out. She openly and uncompromisingly condemned Chiang and his regime as betrayers of Sun's legacy and retained links to, and support for, the liberal and revolutionary opposition. She was a guiding force in the China League for Civil Rights, which sought human rights in general, and legal protections and fair trials for the thousands of political prisoners, usually accused as Communists.

Soong Qingling was a radiantly lovely and well educated modern woman, with a subtle intelligence, indomitable will, and independent character. She clearly had the qualities Snow found most appealing in women. (He had already written a paean of praise to China's "modern" emancipated new career women.) Ed later characterized Qingling as "the conscience and constant heart of a 'still unfinished revolution.'" Harold Isaacs, equally smitten, remembered her as "advancing her causes not just by the power of her name but by the quality of her person and her presence."[24]

Snow's first meeting with Madame Sun (known to her close foreign friends by her Wesleyan College sobriquet, Suzie) took place at the American hangout in Shanghai, the Chocolate Shop—also the site of Ed's first encounter with Peg. Madame Sun and Snow became good friends. Through her, Snow recalled, "I met the thought and sentiment of China at its best." She introduced him to "young writers, artists, and fighters who were to make history." She told him about the Chinese revolution and its politics in a way he "could never have learned from books." Perhaps most important, she made him "comprehend that the Chinese people were capable of radically changing their country," and raising it once again to its rightful place in the world.

Snow was a frequent guest at Madame Sun's home on the Rue Molière in the French Concession, where she presided over something of a left-wing cultural-political salon and befriended also the American radical journalists Agnes Smedley (who became an important figure for Snow) and Harold Isaacs. Unlike them, Snow was never part of Madame Sun's inner political circle of clandestine revolutionary contacts and undertakings, though he did tap into it for his trek to the northwestern Red base in 1936. As Israel Epstein notes in his recent biography of Madame Sun, though she had visitors from "all sections of society," she generally kept them "strictly separate, even if they knew each other, were trusted by her, and were close in outlook." This was actually the pattern in Shanghai's leftist circles during those years of the White Terror.[25]

Lu Xun (Hsün) was then another major force in Snow's development. He was China's foremost modern literary figure, and the revered exemplar of its revolutionary young writers. Born in 1881 and raised in the scholarly classical tradition, he became a champion of the new vernacular literary style, and a biting critic of all the "man-eating" malignancies of Chinese life. His short stories, essays, and parables dealt with the sham, hypocrisy, self-deceit, inhumanity, and injustices in Chinese society. Snow felt that Lu Xun, whose essays left readers "between bitter laughter and indignation," might best be described as "China's Voltaire." Lu Xun became strongly hostile to the Kuomintang after 1927 and moved toward the Communist opposition. He was an active figure in the Red-inspired League of Left-Wing Writers founded in 1930. But he affirmed always the creative independence of the writer from all political dictation. From "the standpoint of the [Communist] Party apparatus, Lu Hsün was a prickly kind of supporter to have," Isaacs recalled. On Lu Xun's death of tuberculosis in 1936, ten thousand people joined his funeral procession on a route closely guarded by armed police, to his burial place in Chinese Shanghai.[26]

Snow met Lu Xun through Madame Sun; Lu in turn introduced Ed to the new writers and literature of the left. These writers lived, as did the famed Lu, in the shadow of the Kuomintang terror, even in the supposed sanctuary of the foreign enclaves. "During these years," Frederic Wakeman, Jr., writes in his study of the Shanghai police during the 1927–1937 Nanking decade, "the Nationalist government was expending a large proportion of its resources on the extirpation of Communists and other progressives, who were either jailed or killed, or offered the choice of defection or betrayal with its material rewards." Western radicals had extraterritorial protection, but Chinese leftists were at risk. It is true that Chinese dissident organizations, publications, and individuals might find some haven in the foreign settlements, either covertly or on a semi-legal footing. (The Communist party's central leadership functioned underground in Shanghai until probably 1932.) But the International Settlement courts quite routinely turned over accused Communists to the Nationalist authorities, many of them to their deaths. These courts, according to Isaacs, "handed over 326 real or alleged 'Communists' to the Kuomintang" from 1930 to 1932. Patrick Givens, the "charming Irishman" in charge of the Special (political) Branch of the International Settlement police, "personified" this collaborative policy, Wakeman states. (Givens had also been the one who compiled the infamous Shanghai "red" dossier on Snow.) When Givens retired in 1936 as assistant commissioner, he was awarded the Chinese medal of honor, along with a letter from the mayor of (Chinese) Shanghai, noting that "in the course of [Givens's] duties in securing evidence against Communists, he frequently worked in close cooperation with the [Nationalists'] Bureau of Public Safety."

The fascist-like Blue Shirts of the KMT also intimidated the regime's critics in the foreign concessions through kidnappings and assassinations. Ex-Communist informers added to the fear-ridden, conspiratorial atmosphere. Isaacs, who maintained very carefully circumscribed contact with the Communist sponsors of his journal between 1932 and 1934, later recounted, "It did not do for any vulnerable Chinese to be seen in my company." He never knew the real names of the ones who worked for the *Forum,* and "if I ever did meet any important Communist figures in Shanghai in those days, I never knew who they were. What one did not know, one could not tell."[27]

The execution in February 1931 of five young writers was a particularly infamous case. They had been among twenty-four persons arrested in a British police raid on a secret Shanghai meeting of a Communist opposition faction, all of whom were turned over to the Nationalist authorities and executed at the notorious Lunghua killing grounds outside Shanghai. (A story by one of the executed writers was included in Snow's *Living China.*)[28]

Snow, while deeply influenced by his radical contacts, had no inside picture of the revolutionary network. Isaacs, however, was close to the Communist movement and knew at first-hand its rigidly imposed "line," its control mechanisms, its harsh treatment of deviationists, and lethal reprisals against defector informers. Through Madame Sun, and less closely Lu Xun, Snow dealt with compellingly attractive and outspokenly independent leftist figures, who saw his sympathetic but autonomous position as an asset and in his writings found more prominent expression for their radical views. Lu Xun encouraged and assisted Ed in collecting representative short stories of the new literature of protest, which Snow translated (with Chinese assistants) and edited. Stories by Lu were the centerpiece of this *Living China* book, which included also an essay on him by Snow. And with the volume's dedication to Soong Qingling, "whose incorruptible integrity, courage, loyalty, and beauty of spirit are burning symbols of the best in living China," Snow affirmed his admiration for these two influential figures.[29]

Snow always responded more readily to the humanistic approach to the larger China equation, rather than to abstract ideological analyses or detached Western treatises on the subject. He once observed to Howard that the "few translations we have of Chinese fiction and philosophy are more valuable than all the thousands of pages poured through the lens of twisted foreign perspectives." The Chinese were "real people like ourselves," he wrote a publisher, and he saw his *Living China* project as an antidote to "the impossible fiction on China" turned out by Western writers. It was to the human condition ("all kinds of people, and what they thought and said and how they lived"), and to the misery of it all in China, that he reacted most intensely.[30]

The line between liberal democrat and radical revolutionary was a thin one in Nationalist-ruled China. Liberal political options were then (and since) in very short supply. The Nanking authorities applied the "Communist" label broadly and freely to its opponents, though such elements among China's intellectual and cultural circles covered a broad political spectrum. "In the revolutionary literature movement," Snow observed in 1935, "there were, for example, disgruntled *bourgeoisie, salon* socialists, liberals, Communists, Menshevists, Trotskyites, and whatnots." In this context, Snow (perhaps a bit disingenuously) could later lump together as critics of the regime the independent revolutionary writer Lu Xun and the urbane literary satirist Lin Yu-tang. They were both "merely Western-oriented liberal individualists"—a rubric Snow presumably applied to himself as well.[31]

In Snow's continuing China education, the role of Soong Qingling was somewhat akin to J. B. Powell's in 1928. The personal qualities of both individuals immediately captivated Snow, particularly their courageous independence—Powell's pro-China stand in the face of "die-hard" Shanghailander hostility, and Madame Sun's outspoken condemnation of the Chiang regime in the harshly repressive atmosphere of the early 1930s. She gave Ed a view of China's recent political history that reflected her support for the leftist forces crushed in 1927. Madame Sun had been an active figure in the Kuomintang-Communist alliance. She saw its destruction as a counterrevolutionary betrayal of Sun's cause. For her, the banner of the "unfinished revolution" had been taken up by the Communists, and other remaining leftist and liberal dissident forces.

Snow, of course, was no longer the China novitiate of 1928. Soong Qingling reinforced many of the conclusions he had already reached while she explained the leftist view of the revolutionary events of the 1920s. She liked and trusted Ed and utilized him to publicize her opinions in the "bourgeois" American media. At the same time, by copious quotations and attributions to Madame Sun, Snow could project his own "liberal-leftist" views on China in a less politically compromising manner. (His writings would nevertheless raise some hackles back home, as well as in China.)

Thus in a September 1932 dispatch, Snow quoted Madame Sun to the effect that the Kuomintang had become a "moribund institution doomed to extinction." She thinks, Snow went on, "that the Chinese Communist Party is the only real revolutionary force in China today," and that it would soon conquer the entire country. Snow cited her judgments on the rulers in Nanking: "mediocre men," lacking any "progressive social or political concept," with "darkly feudal minds," who have brutally destroyed the spirit and principles of the Kuomintang. In his profile article on Madame Sun the following year, Snow elaborated on these themes, again by numerous citations from her. It was also a thoroughly admiring portrait. "I have never met anyone who inspires such instant trust and affection," Ed declared. In reporting Madame Sun's condemnation of the Chiang regime and all its works, Snow somewhat cautiously added, "These are opinions which not many would dare voice so strongly, but which, although there are mitigating circumstances, it would be impossible to confute completely." Clearly, they were views Ed himself endorsed.[32]

It was in Snow's closer attention to the Chinese Communists that Madame Sun's impact was most evident. In June 1932 Snow expressed to Epes a strong interest in "the Communist situation in central China," noting that a trip to those regions would "offer particular lure since practically no reliable information has yet been secured from actual investigation." Apparently through his new Shanghai contacts, Ed attempted for some months to gain entry to the Red areas, but to no avail. Madame Sun "strongly sympathizes" with the Red armies fighting in central China, Ed wrote in his profile on her. "A woman of unusual grit herself, perhaps she admires their spirit." Snow linked the Communist label often attached to Madame Sun with her opposition to Nanking's anti-Communist suppression campaigns, to her key role in many "liberalizing movements," and to her "ceaseless effort to relieve the oppressed." Again, Snow associated his own views with these positions. "I do not know much about these 'Chinese Red Armies'; accurate information is hard to secure," he wrote. "It is impossible for anyone familiar with the present tragedy of rural life in China to deny a certain admiration for this little band of fighters." Noting that the Reds now "had the audacity to declare war on Japan," Snow expressed "a modicum of contempt" for those Nationalists waging war on the Communists while the Japanese pushed down from the north. And again in line with Madame Sun's convictions, Snow expressed the view that Sun Yat-sen and the Communists he had united with before his death had shared "the same avowed purposes"—"achieving social, economic and political unity and justice," uplifting "the masses of men who toil," and "making them into human beings."[33]

In *Far Eastern Front* Snow reiterated these themes with his usual ample references to Soong Qingling. The Kuomintang's "revolutionary character" had become "a grim joke and earned the tragic laughter of China," while the Communists had carried on the agrarian revolution and implemented basic social, economic, and political reforms that appealed to "the vast landless, propertyless classes." Yet Snow questioned whether this would become anything more than a "destructive" peasant movement that could bring down the corrupt and decaying old order. It "remained to be seen whether the movement would produce something better to replace it." On the indications thus far, he rather curiously (and obscurely) declared, Communist victory "would mean the triumph of ochlocracy" (mob rule). He faulted the movement for its lack of "ideological background and instructed leadership," dubiously citing as key evidence the absence of any translation into Chinese of Marx's *Capital*.[34]

Perhaps Snow was then influenced by his Shanghai radical intellectual contacts who reflected the conventional urban Marxist suspicion of a peasant-centered revolution. In any case, Snow already saw the rural revolution in typically human terms—"peasants who call themselves Communists, but who are in reality men who have been crushed, oppressed, robbed, bullied," and "are at last in a revolt for freedom," he explained to his father in early 1933. Still, Ed's unease with such impoverished, desperate peasants who needed to be uplifted into "human beings," may have been a residue of his American middle-class origins. It may also underlie Snow's intellectual attraction to the "uplifting" social reformism of the British Fabian socialists. And on the American scene, he was still apt to think in terms of his "own kind." Commenting to Mildred in November 1932 on the birth of a son to Howard and Dorothy, he could remark on the responsibility of "the well-bred, the intelligent, the worthwhile element of the population" to "perpetuate itself."[35]

Snow's strongly asserted China views were bound to raise problems for him both in China and back home. He remarked to Howard in September 1933 that his newly published *Far Eastern Front* "will probably result in making enemies for me in certain quarters in China," and he also expected his Madame Sun article to arouse "considerable antagonism among certain officials." And Peg wrote to Ed's father that "we await with some slight anxiety the repercussions from the book next month, especially among the Chinese and Japanese." In July of that year in Peking Snow consulted the American minister to China, Nelson T. Johnson (subsequently ambassador), about his Shanghai British police dossier that had followed him around Asia since his early days in China. This had become of greater concern to him since he had heard, according to Johnson's memorandum of the meeting, that "the story was going about town that he was under suspicion as being a friend of radicals, a subversive character, etc." Johnson noted that "Mr. Snow informed me of his friendship for Mrs. Sun Yat-sen and for one or two others of the younger China group in Shanghai who have been prominently engaged in the propagation of liberal ideas." The minister's basic counsel was for Snow to ignore the matter, "leaving his actions and his writings to prove the falsity or truth" of the allegations.[36]

Snow's subsequent "actions and writings" did not ward off his detractors. He would have numerous run-ins with the Nanking authorities through the years. He discussed some of these in a February 1937 letter to Ambassador Johnson in Nanking. Referring to his *Living China* volume, Snow responded typically. "I learned very much while doing this book—probably too much, along certain lines, for the powers that be to look upon me benignly again," he told Johnson. "You cannot enter a thing like this very deeply without coming to share some of the feeling that produces it—and to begin to have feelings about a country and its people may prove a good road to ruin for a 'foreign correspondent.'" The Japanese, equally unhappy with Snow's reporting, had him on their blacklist from the early 1930s.[37]

There were some repercussions on the home front too. Howard, now working for the ultra-conservative National Association of Manufacturers, wrote Ed in June 1935 that he had "heard indirectly" that Ed was becoming "leftist" or "Communistic." Snow reacted sharply, as he would always do on such charges. (Nor could he resist needling Howard on his new job: "Is it your task to get more manufacturers to associate or to promote company unions among the workers?") As to the "Communistic" rumors, "You must know very well that it would do me no good in my work to have such stuff circulating. There is hardly an editor in America who would print a thing by me if it were thought I was a Communist.

And for your satisfaction, I am not." He belonged to no political organization and adhered to no "ready-made economic or political doctrine whatever, whether Marxist or Leninist or Mussolinian or Rooseveltian."

Ed's reply to Howard gave him an opportunity to sum up his social and political thinking as it had evolved by 1935, just a year before his journey to the Red northwest. There was a clear distinction between his approach to America and China. Toward the former, he affirmed his belief in its democratic principles, while favoring the reform of its "hopelessly archaic economic system" along more planned, socialistic lines. He saw this in essentially Fabian terms: it did not require revolution, only the "intelligent" exercise of the vote by the citizenry. The ideals of the founding fathers could be made consistent with "a decent civilized system of life and economics which will fairly soon put the control of the means of production in the hands of the people, and for the widest social benefit." China, however, was a very different matter. There, the "man with the biggest pile and the biggest army casts all the votes." Now, finally, millions of starving peasants and workers were attempting to organize their own armies and seize the power. "They are in revolution," which was "sometimes the only thing that will save a people," and "is tried only when every other means of resolving intolerable situations has been exhausted." The Chinese Red Army was thus the "technique" used by the long-suffering masses "to cast their vote in the national will." Now "volcanic and catastrophic in its manifestations," it is "the people's thumbs-down on the rulers of the realm." (All in all, we might wonder just how reassuring Ed's letter was to Howard! Actually, up to the 1950s nearly all of Snow's reporting was for generally conservative American newspapers and journals, and the anti-Communist British Labor *Daily Herald,* and he avoided writing for avowedly radical publications.)[38]

This letter in its essentials expressed Snow's standpoint on the Chinese revolution and on social revolution generally. Any remaining ambivalences he had on the Red Chinese cause (such as his image of its unbridled peasant fury) would be largely dispelled in his 1936 journey of investigation. But it is time to backtrack to another much more personal and pleasing challenge to Snow's independence—courtship, marriage, and life in ancient and beautiful Peking. This former capital, a focal point of Japan's expansionist aims in northern China, would soon be the site of a student-led surging anti-Japanese tide. Helen and Ed Snow would be important participants.

PART 2

Peking Interlude, and the Red Star

CHAPTER 7

Peking

Words and Action

Helen Foster had arrived in China determined to become a rich and famous great author. Born in Cedar City, Utah, she was of English heritage, with some Welsh on her mother's side. To Helen, her Foster forebears who had come to Massachusetts in 1635 were builders of a "uniquely Puritan civilization, all English and a yard wide." She herself was "strong for the principle of law in the British tradition" and "strong for Western civilization and Protestantism." The work ethic, individual initiative, personal morality and fidelity, and an activist sense of mission loomed large in her makeup. "I had always thought out everything for myself," she wrote in her later years. "As a result, I had a kind of instinct for being a prime mover and for getting other people to bestir themselves, even the Chinese who are quite immovable usually."[1]

She saw her marriage to Ed as a partnership dedicated to work and achievement, with a responsibility on her part to press Ed on (prod him, he often said) to ever higher levels. "Together we decided to do everything left undone by Americans in the Far East before us." She liked to repeat a remark made to her by their good friend, Marine officer Evans F. Carlson, "Keep criticizing and pushing Ed. It is the making of him." Not that Peg needed much encouragement! James Bertram, a young New Zealander Rhodes scholar and close friend of the Snows in the Peking days, also thought "Peg spurred Ed into doing his best work." A lifelong admirer of Peg (and Ed), Bertram pictured their marriage as "a beautiful give-and-take in the earlier years." Acknowledging that she could be "scolding" at times, he rejected as "very wide of the mark" any notion of Peg as being "continually nagging." The late Harvard sinologist John K. Fairbank who, with his wife, Wilma, socialized with the Snows in Peking, described Peg in less flattering and perhaps male-slanted terms, as "driven by ambition," and in "obvious rivalry with Ed." In *Journey*, Snow wrote of her as "the very unusual woman who was to be my frequently tormenting, often stimulating, and always energetically creative and faithful co-worker, consort and critic" during their married years in China. There was indeed a delicate balance in her relationship with the proudly independent and highly sensitive Ed; its dynamics were evident both in their signal accomplishments together and in their eventual estrangement. And not unlike Ed, Peg equated engagement in the Chinese revolutionary cause with her English-American values, though with more of a compulsively "do-gooder" missionary fervor than Ed's more restrained humanist-journalistic impulses. Her "prime mover" part in the wartime Chinese Industrial Cooperatives, with its self-reliant and democratic producer ethic, embodied many of the principles she held dear.[2]

Helen's father, John Moody Foster, graduated from Stanford University in 1906, the year before her birth. A chemistry and geology major, he taught science at an academy in Idaho, where he met and married a fellow teacher, Hannah Davis. After a teaching stint in Utah, he moved on to law school at the University of Chicago and practiced law out west specializing in mining claims. Interested in physical culture and women's athletics, he encouraged Helen in such training. He expected top academic performance from his children, and Helen obliged as a straight A student. Her parents were civic-minded people (in their Chicago days, her mother participated in the women's suffrage movement), though her father was a remote personality. "He never raised his voice, never showed his feelings, and seldom talked at all." In this he was unlike his daughter—always an animated, rapid-fire talker (and writer) with a mind "that races along at a 90 m.p.h. clip," Carlson wrote of her. Though Ed was engagingly sociable (his "Irish charm" side, Helen described it), his quietly unassuming manner ("well-bred," she said) perhaps reminded her of the father she greatly admired.[3]

After a few years at the University of Utah (like Ed, she did not stay to graduate), Helen worked for the American Mining Congress, an influential silver lobby. Having passed the necessary civil service examinations, she landed an overseas post as private secretary to the American consul general in Shanghai, Edwin S. Cunningham. China was on the silver standard, and she was expected to report back on and promote the cause of silver. "I thought of myself as 'Miss Silver' when I sailed for China in 1931."[4]

Trimly built, with a round, blue-eyed "baby doll" face, in her words, Helen Foster was an outstanding example of "beauty and brains." (She mentioned turning down twenty-one proposals of marriage before accepting Ed.) She had a sharp intelligence ("a rapier style," according to Bertram) that could sting those against whom it might be directed, and an avid intellectual appetite. (In later life her favorite reading was the *Encyclopaedia Britannica*.) She too planned to travel around the world, write travel books and "at least one good novel," and not marry "until I had accomplished something on my own." Before sailing for the Orient, she assiduously collected press clippings on China (part of her silver lobby job), including virtually everything Ed had written. She also made arrangements with a Seattle-based press association to write pieces to help revive the dormant tourist business in the "glamorous" East. Neither silver nor tourism would hold her interest for very long. "Shanghai is a marvelous place for an enterprising young person with ideas," she wrote home in October 1931. "It is a total loss for many things, but I see so many opportunities that I can hardly decide what to do." Peg Foster was an enthralling image of the wholesome America the dispirited Ed still longed for—a distinctive and all-American girl.[5]

The Snow-Foster courtship developed rather fitfully. After their first meeting in Shanghai in August 1931, Ed was soon off to cover the Yangtze flood, then to the Manchuria front; after his bout of illness in December came the Shanghai war the next month. But there had been opportunities in the fall of 1931 and the next spring for jaunts to the nearby "tourist" cities of the Yangtze delta—Hangzhou, Suzhou, and Wuxi. These were mostly in connection with Peg's tourist promotion activities. (In Hangzhou, a passing coolie expressed his appreciation—*ding hao!* [the tops]—of Peg's looks.) Then Ed was holed up for most of the summer and fall of 1932 in the crash writing of *Far Eastern Front*.

Neither of them seemed temperamentally suited for the matrimonial bond—at least not yet. Ed was wary of being "tied down," and Peg was set on her travel and writing. Nor was Peg willing to enter into an affair with the infatuated Ed. Yet their free-spirited ambitions and interests were themselves sources of mutual attraction. "We believe or disbelieve in about the same things, have similar dreams, aspirations, hopes and sinicitis [*sic*]," Ed wrote to Mildred and J. Edgar. "She is free-lance, one of the romantic free company like myself, and our plans seem to coincide." Ed also enthused over Peg's literary talent. As a poet, "some of her things will make Shelley and Blake seem quite as dull as my old razor blades." (Peg would have many of her poems published, and three of

them were later reprinted in a *Saturday Review Treasury* anthology.)
Snow came up with the "Nym Wales" nom de plume Peg wrote under
into the 1950s and was always supportive and proud of her China writing accomplishments.[6]

Peg finally agreed, on a blustery day in December 1932 on the Shanghai Bund, to marry Ed. To mollify her protests that she had not yet written *her* first book nor traveled to all the unexplored places, Ed worked
out an extensive South Seas honeymoon itinerary. After that they would
relocate to Peking where the couple could live inexpensively and settle in
to do their writing. Peg insisted also on a high noon Christmas Day ceremony in "nice and clean" Tokyo. (She was beginning to take charge.)

Snow made the plans for their trip through a Japanese steamship line,
surprising perhaps, considering his hostility to Japan's actions in China.
But Japanese passenger-freighters regularly plied these less traveled
routes and were also the least expensive. Snow in fact enjoyed holiday
visits to Japan and in Shanghai his Japanese acquaintances included journalists (and once, a woman friend). His view of Japan was tinged with
respect for that nation as a dynamic latecomer to the imperialist club in
the East, successfully challenging a declining Western dominance that
Snow had little faith in or liking for. Besides, he wanted a closer look at
this rising force in Asia and arranged with Epes to submit copy on the
trip to help defray expenses. (He parlayed the wedding episode into a
slickly charming "Christmas Escapade" account for *Travel* magazine.)
Epes also agreed to the move to Peking. Ed carefully avoided linking his
travel plans with a honeymoon, but Epes, in cabling approval, added,
"Incidentally, happy honeymoon!"[7]

The Christmas Day ceremony in the American Embassy in Tokyo
was handled by Snow's former Shanghai roommate, John Allison, a foreign service officer in the embassy and a future American ambassador to
Japan. Typically, Ed broke the news to Mildred and J. Edgar in a tardy
letter from Shanghai that reached them only after the event—reminiscent of his 1928 leave-taking from New York. ("Oyez, I am getting married," he announced. "Do not laugh; it does look rather silly, but then it
appears to have happened to both of you.") A Tokyo newspaper friend
cabled the story back home, and the Snow and Foster families' first
knowledge of the marriage came through their local papers on Christmas morning. Ed had been just as circumspect in spreading the news in
Shanghai, Madame Sun being one of the few to know. She had already
met and liked Peg; she arranged a Chinese banquet for the two and gave
them an American-made percolator.[8]

After a train journey through Japan, the couple sailed from Nagasaki as the only Caucasian passengers on their Japanese ship. Peg was something of a clothes horse in those days and took aboard (much to Ed's annoyance) a large wardrobe trunk with attire for every possible occasion. (Before leaving Shanghai, she had insisted on outfitting the reluctant Ed with a full set of English-tailored clothes—which lasted him through his remaining years in China and after.) The cruise was a "shakedown" one for Snow in adapting to the marital state in general and to Peg in particular. His even-tempered affable manner could mask a touchy quality. He brooded a bit in his diary at Peg's uninhibited tendency to voice her irritations and criticisms. He noted a few such mild reactions in his entries during the honeymoon trip, but it all seemed par for the conjugal state. "Hmmm," Ed jotted down at one point with "several minor complaints" by Peg, "trials of married life begin." In a last gasp of the freelance spirit, he facetiously mused that he had thought his father "demented" when going about the house "muttering lines of Shakespeare to himself, . . . but now I realize that it was only that he was married." But more important, marriage and a home in Peking marked the end of what Snow called his "nomad" existence, and the start of the most fruitful and significant stage in his career.[9]

The two-month honeymoon included visits to Formosa, the East Indies, Singapore, Hong Kong and Macao, and the southern China ports up to Shanghai. The newlyweds had taken along volumes by Fabian socialists H. G. Wells and George Bernard Shaw, and read to each other aboard ship. The democratic socialist concept appealed to them; they were less impressed by the Fabian gradualist approach. "We thought it was typically British, slow as cold molasses in December," Peg remembered.[10]

Aside from the Indies, the trip was a reprise of some of Snow's 1930–1931 travels. His impressions of Dutch and British rule in the East Indies did nothing to change his hostile view of European colonialism, but he came away further convinced of Japan's determined and effective pursuit of its imperial ambitions. The disciplined and centralized Japanese state and society could mobilize its resources completely and rapidly, the military was in firm charge, and Snow thought there was little chance of civilians regaining control for at least another ten years. He found the Japanese foreign minister he interviewed in Tokyo to be "cold, haughty, with old samurai pride and insolence." The Formosa sojourn reinforced his earlier opinion that Japanese rule was "certainly an improvement on three centuries of Chinese rule." Although conquest is "never a palatable thing to a proud people, if it must be in the Orient then perhaps the Japanese rule of Orientals is preferable to any Western rule," he recorded. Aside from the army and its methods, ordinary Japanese colonizers were less prone to the "deep disdain of race and color that white men bring." Discussions with the ship's officers were lively: "The real extent of Japanese distrust and dislike of America [was] hitherto not grasped by me."[11]

In Borneo Snow met British colonials who had found the status they lacked at home. Ed pondered the role of an "inferiority complex" applied to nations, as "possibly explaining to a great extent England's conquests, France's, Japan's." In Bali the Snows encountered a New York Jewish schoolteacher couple on a sabbatical trip around the world. Ed's diary entries exhibited both his naturally warm interest and liking for them as individuals and yet a trace of his homegrown sense of their "otherness."[12]

The reputedly more enlightened Dutch rule in the Indies was no more attractive to Snow than the English and French varieties. Bali was the one exception—which he found to be a seductively alluring and still unspoiled oasis in the expanse of European empire. "The body is taken for granted here, as is sex itself. . . . And [that] is good." The gentle Balinese, their art, music, dancing, and social organization he thought altogether admirable. They needed nothing the West could offer, he concluded. In *Journey,* Snow dwelt nostalgically and luminously on his Bali experience. Bali became a metaphor for his vision of a nonpredatory, nonviolent world, though "it was too late to export Bali to the white-skinned people," he sadly acknowledged. At a stopover in Hong Kong on the return trip to Shanghai, Snow met Shaw, then on a world tour. Shaw twisted the British lion's tail with some Shavian anticapitalist "Bolshevik" epigrams in a Hong Kong University lecture. Snow clearly savored the performance.[13]

Snow's impressions of the Japanese and of their colonial enterprise were embodied in an article he wrote up soon after the honeymoon, on the decline of Western prestige, similar in theme to *Far Eastern Front.* Its equanimity at the prospect of a Japanese-dominated new Asian order was the product of Snow's disdain for the European record in Asia, for the Kuomintang's in China, and for the failure of both to face up to the Japanese challenge. Nor should America take on the task of pulling European imperialists' chestnuts out of the fire. "It is perhaps well, after all, that an Eastern country inherit the mandate that the West was given, for nearly a century, but did not know how to use," he remarked to his father at this time. He would soon dramatically alter his thinking on the nature of the Japanese threat and on ways to deal with it.[14]

By early March 1933 (coincident with Tokyo's conquest of Jehol) the Snows had moved to Peking. They spent a couple of weeks in the cavernous Grand Hôtel de Pékin on the broad Avenue of Eternal Peace, directly across from the legation quarter diplomatic enclave. The hotel's roof garden, overlooking the yellow-tiled vista of the Forbidden City, was then a favorite night dancing spot for Peking's social set—which soon included the Snows. The couple rented a new Chinese-style house close to the massive wall surrounding the city proper. It was the first of three residences before they left the old capital in the wake of the Japanese occupation in 1937. These Peking years saw their immersion in a social and cultural way of life that seemed removed from the harsher China realities and perils of the times. Peking, surrounded by its massive city wall, within which the now unoccupied imperial palaces of the Forbidden City stood surrounded by their own wall and moat, presented to foreigners an image of old China at its most authentic: towering gates, broad avenues, and innumerable lanes (*hutong*s) lined with gray walls behind which were one-story residential compounds with their interior courtyards and gardens. Foreigners, in the fashion of a now vanishing Chinese scholar-gentry elite, occupied the grander compounds, complete with a retinue of servants, each with an assigned household status. Of that period, John K. Fairbank wrote in his China memoir, "We savored the amenities of foreign life in China. Only gradually did we become aware of the prospects of Japanese invasion and social revolution that were all too soon to burst over the land."[15]

This gracious if somewhat weary city had a charm and ambience that ensnared virtually all Westerners who came there. Most of the diplomatic corps still preferred their Peking embassies to the new seat of government in considerably less attractive Nanking. Officially, the city's name had changed in 1928 to Peiping (northern peace). But the inhabitants and foreign residents largely ignored this. Peking (derived from the French *Pékin*) was the preferred designation by foreigners and Western-educated Chinese. The Chiang regime never did succeed in winning the hearts and minds of the city's residents. "I think Peiping will still be PEKING despite all that the Nanking crowd can do about it," Ed wrote his father soon after settling down there.[16]

In contrast to foreign-dominated, business-centered Shanghai, which seemed to personify all the evils and vulgarity of its hybrid Sino-Western modern civilization, "gentle Peking," as an American expatriate fondly recalled it from the 1930s, remained a quiet stronghold of the old China favored by its ingrown foreign community enjoying the perquisites of the good life. Even the ricksha men had the courtesies and manners, along with the Peking-accented Mandarin speech that was part of the city's style. Still, as China's foremost academic center, Peking spawned major intellectual currents of change, both liberal and radical, which the May Fourth Movement of 1919 highlighted with its anti-Confucian individualism, anti-imperialist nationalism, and call for science and democracy as the path to a modern China. From the prestigious National Peking University had come the first leaders of the Chinese Communist party and the nation's most influential liberal reformers. The American missionary-founded Yanjing University, Qinghua (then, Tsinghua) University (established with American Boxer Indemnity Fund support), and Rockefeller Foundation–financed Peking Union Medical College were other major institutions in the city and its outskirts. Peg Snow attended classes at Yanjing, and Ed would do some teaching in its Missouri-linked journalism department. The two Snows and the students were to have a special connection in the anti-Japanese movement to come.

The Sino-Western Peking set lived by rules of "proper" etiquette, complete with calling cards. A round of dinner parties, teas, receptions, polo, the racetrack (where a Snow gamble paid off handsomely enough to help keep him from the grind of a regular Associated Press job), art and antique collecting, the Peking Club, and weekend excursions to nearby western hills temples, marked the social routine. It was a cultivated community of educated Chinese, foreign diplomats, missionaries, journalists, and Western expatriates seeking the wisdom and life-style of traditional Chinese high culture, antiquarians and sinologists. Many of the Westerners studied Chinese at the Peking (North China Union) Language School run by the American Board of Foreign Missions. The study of Chinese language and culture was popular among the foreigners (in contrast to the attitude of Westerners in treaty-port Shanghai); Ed undertook his first sustained study of the language, and Peg of Chinese philosophy, art, and economics. There were some notable personages in the Snows' circle. Evans F. Carlson, then adjutant of the U.S. Marine legation guard, and his wife, Etelle, were good friends. Another was Teilhard de Chardin, the brilliant and iconoclastic Jesuit paleontologist-philosopher who challenged church orthodoxy with his social-ethical application of evolutionary theory. Peg had many spirited and intellectually stimulating discussions with him, as they strolled atop the city wall. James

Bertram vividly remembered Teilhard "in full flight in argument with the attractive and irrepressible" Peg. Transient visitors who became their friends included Pearl Buck and her future husband, Richard Walsh, whose John Day publishing house and *Asia* magazine were print outlets for the Snows; J. P. Marquand, John Gunther (doing the Asia volume of his popular *Inside* series), and the Swedish explorer Sven Hedin, who gave Ed and Peg their beautiful white greyhound, Gobi.[17]

Among their friends in the younger sinological community were John and Wilma Fairbank, and Owen and Eleanor Lattimore. Agnes Smedley would visit with the Snows on trips from Shanghai to the city. Ed and Peg were close to a number of the Peking-based correspondents, especially F. MacCracken (Mac) Fisher of the United Press. He too (as well as James D. White of the Associated Press) was a Missouri journalism product and had been a student in the Department of Journalism at Yanjing University from 1931 to 1933. He shared the Snows' intense hostility to mounting Japanese aggression in northern China, knew and sympathized with the student leaders, and would do much in tandem with the Snows to publicize the emerging anti-Japanese student movement in late 1935. (In Chungking after Pearl Harbor, Fisher headed up a newly created American information service in China, which became the Office of War Information there.)[18]

Particularly as Snow took on his *Living China* work, he also maintained links with a very different, leftist group of writers and young Chinese translator-assistants. He also met at intervals with Lu Xun and others in Shanghai in connection with the project. A private language tutor came daily at a total cost of $5 per month for both Snows. While Ed's spoken Chinese reached serviceable levels, for written materials he remained heavily dependent on translations. His reading competence in Chinese by then was "just enough," he later recalled, "to check translations and to do a very slow translation of *bai-hua*," or vernacular, texts. But even for full-time Western students of the language, achieving genuine reading capability was a daunting ordeal. As Fairbank remarked of his Peking Language School days, "Some refuse to believe the writing system can be the way it is and suspect a conspiracy." Even Snow's limited but serviceable competence in the language made him an exception among American reporters in China of his time. Peg, who worked closely with Ed on the *Living China* project, developed her own contacts with writers and artists, did much research on the literary scene, and contributed a substantial essay on the modern Chinese literary movement to Ed's volume.[19]

Low living costs were a key to the foreigners' Peking life-style. It was one in which, as Snow put it, "a newspaper correspondent [and a poorly paid one at that] could become accustomed to living in the style of a bank president." The Snows' comparatively small first house had six rooms and bath, plus servants' quarters and bath. Located along one of the city's residential lanes, it was a typical one-story walled compound with interior courtyard of trees and garden where freshly blooming plants could be constantly replenished at minimal expense. (In recent decades the compound has become a crowded multifamily dwelling.) All this, and a staff of servants, could be had for little more than $1,000 U.S. per year. Rent plus servants' wages (including a fine cook) came to about $25 U.S. per month. Imported luxuries, such as Ed's Camel cigarettes, Maxwell House coffee, and Gillette razor blades, were the much more costly extras. Small coal-burning stoves provided the winter heat, mostly reserved for Ed's office-library, Peg complained. Silk-padded long Chinese gowns were the indoor winter wear of choice for the Snows. Their street lane (Mei Cha Hutong) translated unglamorously as "coal residue" or simply "Clinker Street," Ed informed his father.[20]

The low cost of living was just as well, given the declining fortunes of Con Press, Snow's single steady source of income. Within weeks of the couple's arrival in Peking, Epes informed Ed that his salary would be reverting to $80 per month. The "bottom has almost fallen out" of the newspaper world in America, he lamented. Snow's efforts to obtain work with the *New York Herald-Tribune* in the summer of 1933 were unavailing. Fortuitously he had sent off his "Decline of Western Prestige" piece to the *Post,* a long-shot gamble, he thought. An acceptance check for the incredible sum of $750 U.S. duly arrived in the mail, followed by a congratulatory letter from the editor, George Lorimer. Though Snow had been intent on alerting his readers to the facts of Japanese power and ambition, his opposition to any American military involvement may have had particular appeal to the isolationist-minded *Post.*[21]

The *Post* windfall not only resolved immediate financial pressures, it was enough to cover nearly a year's expenses. It also bolstered Ed's determination to pursue his freelance mode of writing and established a connection with the *Post* that would ultimately blossom into a decade-long regular relationship. The magazine, Snow later estimated, paid him nearly a quarter million dollars, most of it during the 1940s. Even the occasional *Post* check during the Peking years made all the difference. He was able to take some unpaid leave from Con Press for final revision of *Far Eastern Front,* and to undertake the even less commercial *Living*

China work. He could devote himself to Chinese studies, read widely with special attention to fascism and communism, and take on a part-time journalism teaching assignment at Yanjing. None of these activities paid many bills (not even Peking ones); and the infrequent pieces he did for *Asia*, the *Herald-Tribune* magazine, and other journals paid very modestly, as did his stringer arrangement with the *Daily Herald*.[22]

Snow's only "steady" income (reduced in value even further by a sharp drop in the exchange rate in late 1933) vanished entirely with the demise of Con Press at the end of 1933. Despite what had been the meager financial rewards of this affiliation, Snow and Horace Epes had developed a genuine long-distance affection and esteem for each other. Their correspondence has a gentlemanly civility, graciousness, and warmth we rarely associate with "hard-boiled" journalistic images, particularly of the depression-era thirties. Yet these characteristics were always a hallmark of Snow's professional relationships—which tended to become long-lasting personal friendships. This was already the case with J. B. Powell and would be equally so of Snow's dealings with the editors Ben Hibbs and Martin Sommers of the *Post*, with the publisher Bennett Cerf and with Snow's editors at Random House, with his literary agent Henriette Herz, and many more.[23]

The *Sun* did come through in the spring of 1934 with a grand retainer of $25 for a monthly feature article. Notwithstanding this slim sum, Snow was comfortable with this kind of arrangement, which also allowed him to retain his professional identity as Peking correspondent of the *Sun*. He had already turned down an Associated Press offer to be their regular correspondent. "I am doing this," he wrote the *Sun's* editor, "because I think there is a definite need for a writer, on the scene, who can give in magazine articles a wider interpretation of Far Eastern news events than is possible in ordinary newspaper correspondence."[24]

Snow's situation had been buttressed by a move in January 1934 to the village of Haidian on the outskirts of Peking and directly adjacent to Yanjing University. A Chinese banker friend and Yanjing alumnus rented the Snows his newly built modern retirement villa, complete with small swimming pool, for even less money than their Peking house. With an acre of gardens and trees, and a picture window view of the western hills and the Summer Palace, the spacious residence was the perfect setting for the more contemplative study and writing Snow had in mind. It was also ideal for his new teaching chores at the university.

The Snows remained at their Haidian retreat until the summer of 1935. While Ed taught a course on feature writing, Peg enrolled in virtually full-time academic work at Yanjing. The two also bicycled to nearby Qinghua University for a class in the history of Chinese philosophy under the noted scholar Fung Yu-lan. (At a "confessional" session at Peking University in 1970, the then elderly philosopher described himself to Snow as "a reactionary academic authority" now being remolded along the revolutionary path charted by Mao. "'So I must now regard your work [on the history of Chinese philosophy] translated by Derk Bodde as a poisonous weed?'" Snow recounted in his diary. "'Oh yes,' said he, 'a *big* poisonous weed.' [laughter] 'Then I am still under its influence,' said I.") Ed and Peg each had separate studies in opposite wings of their U-shaped compound. At teatime in the afternoon Ed would usually read aloud to Peg his morning's writing, which they discussed in detail. He "edited and cut and re-wrote tirelessly," Peg recalled. He was a "natural" writer and journalist, who "enjoyed his work always." Ed worked on his short story translations, wrote some magazine articles for his major income, kept up his stringer *Daily Herald* connection, and did occasional mailers for the *Sun*. He continued to work sporadically on the Yunnan travel book. "The year has been thoroughly enjoyable," Snow wrote Epes in April 1935, "but financially a bust—particularly with the steep drop in value of the deflated dollar."[25]

Ed had taken on the Yanjing teaching assignment in part to get some lecturing experience. In his perennial hopes for at least a visit to America, he had tentatively agreed to do a lecture series in the States in the fall of 1934. "I do not like to lecture, I'm miserably unconvincing at it," he wrote J. Edgar in the spring of 1934, "but just now it seems to offer the only possibility of financing my much-needed visit to the States." In truth, public speaking never really did suit Snow's more deliberate, soft-spoken style. Nevertheless, his Yanjing course proved popular, and his public talks after his return from the Red area would fascinate his listeners. But like all his previous plans for a return home, the 1934 lecture project was unrealized.[26]

Instead, Snow was offered the opportunity, from his publisher Harrison Smith, to do a book on Chinese communism. He was offered a $750 advance in March 1934, which "in a moment of optimism" he accepted, promising to finish a manuscript by the end of the year. As already noted, he had been interested in such a project as early as 1932, but his efforts had come to naught; "at the last moment the CP's [Communist contacts] through whom I worked became suspicious of me, and disappeared; I never saw them again." Snow had never relinquished his interest in the subject. The task, however, was an intimidating one, given the dearth of reliable information in print, either in Chinese or foreign languages. What was available (chiefly propaganda tracts, official handouts, gossip, and hearsay) could not be depended on for truth or accuracy. "This means," Snow told Henriette Herz, "that if a book on Chinese communism were to be of real value it would imply a large amount of original research." And to be "valid," he added, "it would have to include at least one visit to an important Red area, for first-hand study."[27]

As Snow himself soon realized, 1934 was a particularly unpropitious year for attempted journalistic forays to the central China Red base. The Red armies were then waging a desperate battle against the Nationalists' fifth and final annihilation campaign. Squeezed ever tighter by an encircling blockhouse strategy, the major Communist forces slipped through the blockade in the fall of 1934 and began their epochal 6,000-mile Long March, reaching a Communist base in remote northern Shaanxi in the fall of 1935. But even though "the whole of Soviet China may be obliterated," Snow felt in early 1934, the Communist movement will continue to exist and grow, "*sub rosa,* on a national scale. It will definitely be an important factor in the immediate destiny of China and the Far East, even if it does not become the dominating factor." A properly documented book on the subject, he prophetically noted, "should be one of the most vital and interesting imaginable." Yet Snow continued to harbor the conventional Marxist wisdom that "a successful mass revolution" was unlikely to develop "until the industrialization of Manchuria produces a proletarian leadership for the backward peasant millions of China."[28]

For the time being, as Snow later recounted to Ambassador Johnson, he found it impossible "to write such a book without ever having seen a 'Red' soldier." He did take a stab at a more academic approach to the project by applying to the Guggenheim Foundation for a two-year grant to study the agrarian crisis in China, with particular reference to communism. Despite strong backing from a diverse group of distinguished people, Snow's proposal was turned down in favor of a presumably less controversial proposal by a Columbia University psychologist to study Chinese facial reactions to differing emotional stimuli—on the assumption "that starvation looked 'different' on a Chinese face," Snow bitingly observed. He expected the rejection, noting to Epes in April 1935 that foundations like the Guggenheim "generally choose projects that are pretty safely moss-covered, and unlikely to get anyone agitated . . . save a few intent scholars." Snow's contract with Smith and Haas was taken over by Random House with the merger of the two publishing firms in

1936. Meanwhile events were moving in ways that would bring a convergence of time and circumstances for Snow's opportunity to meet his first Red soldiers. *Red Star* would appear three years after the original contractual deadline, but at a far more propitious time and as an immeasurably more significant book.[29]

The Yanjing-Haidian period brought Snow's first sustained contact with China's tiny and elite student-academic community. Yanjing provided a very pleasant and attractive setting, with its pastoral, wooded campus, lovely "No-Name" lake, and modern Chinese palace style architecture. Bertram remembered the campus of those years as "one of the most attractive college settings I have known." Bertram recalled also the "misleading" impression given by "these elegant women in their colourful slit gowns cycling demurely about the grounds, the men in slacks and pullovers, American campus style." Yanjing was a progressive Sino-American Christian institution with partial extraterritorial immunity. It was under the liberal leadership of J. Leighton Stuart, later to be America's last ambassador to the Nationalist government on the mainland. Less subject to the repression of student activism in the state universities, Yanjing's students (and to a lesser degree Qinghua's) could function much more freely. (Students from the state-run National Peking University, within the city, "who wanted to read the Marxist classics with impunity borrowed them from the Yenching library.") Yanjing students came largely from Westernized, influential, and affluent urban business and professional families, and they were generally imbued with a strong anti-Japanese nationalism. The admission of a number of Manchurian refugee students after 1931 added strongly to such sentiments. An American missionary school such as Yanjing, John Israel writes, "produced free-thinking, socially conscious, politically active undergraduates." Unlike other colleges, it had an active student government organization and a sympathetic college administration. The school would take the lead in the famed anti-Japanese student movement of December 1935, with its journalism majors in the vanguard. Snow's rapport with those students would have its special significance in that historic event. But first we need to look at Snow's political state of mind as he reacted to European and Asian developments before that occurrence.[30]

By the mid-1930s the fascist powers in Europe had joined Japan in mounting an attack on the crumbling Versailles world order. Fascism's ultranationalist expansionism, its smashing of all domestic leftist and liberal opposition, and its proclaimed anti-Bolshevist crusade, gave credence to the Marxist-Leninist view that fascism had discarded the facade of bourgeois democracy in the attempt to save a dying capitalism from the forces of the proletarian socialist left. This view jibed with Snow's opinion of the "moribund" state of world capitalism and of the need to move on to a more "rational" system of planned socialist economics. In China, he saw the Kuomintang regime as a dictatorship of the right, waging a relentless war against the revolutionary left, adopting in the process many of the trappings and methods of fascism. This included creation of the militarized and rabidly antileftist Blue Shirts, and of a youth corps modeled on European fascist counterparts; inculcation of the "leader" principle around the Generalissimo, and the use of German and Italian military advisers.[31]

Snow highlighted this picture of the Kuomintang in a scathing mid-1935 article: "Arrest, torture, imprisonment, possible death are penalties threatening all, from the pale Pink to the deep-dyed Red." But Nanking's efforts to build a fascist-style nationalism, he wrote, did not fit its compliant pro-Japanism. The Chinese, Snow concluded, were "too old a people, too cynical and too fundamentally realistic to be made into flag-waving cousins of the Italians and the Germans. And they are far too hungry." (The Chinese people were always the saving grace for Snow. "What a wonderful if also terrible place China," he wrote at this time to Richard Walsh. "It is good to get back to her after a sojourn among the darkly sane and regimented Japanese.") The real possibility that the Nationalist government might collaborate with Tokyo in the latter's declared aim of "saving" China from communism only sharpened Snow's viewpoint. And reading books about fascism, Snow much later wrote to antifascist author George Seldes, "helped me see what it was necessary to oppose in the world even if I didn't yet see clearly what was worth supporting."[32]

Japan's role now took on a much more ominous character for Snow, in contrast to his earlier somewhat complacent reaction to Tokyo's imperial ambitions. To Charlie Towne he had observed in March 1933 that "conquests merely rejuvenate, do not destroy China." The Chinese people are "satisfied" that in fifty or a hundred years, "the little islanders will be absorbed, and the fruits of their strenuous adventures will be enjoyed by their [Chinese] posterity. A curiously reasonable people, the Chinese." Following an extended trip to Manchuria (now become Manchukuo) in the fall of 1933, Snow described the Japanese military's moves to transform that vast and resource-rich area into a formidable political, economic, and military redoubt and base for future expansion.

But in noting the great migration of Chinese into the region, Snow added, "They go north because years of misrule under Chinese satraps have ruined them economically," and while "Manchukuo is no earthly paradise," it "still offers the Chinese peasant greater safety, security and opportunity than his erstwhile Middle Kingdom." And through their attachment to the soil, "it is these sturdy immigrants who may ultimately reclaim Manchuria for China."[33]

By 1935, however, Snow argued precisely *against* this thesis in an *Asia* article subtitled, "The belief that China always absorbs her invaders is challenged by the record of Japonization in Formosa." Snow now forcefully rejected this oft-expressed Chinese maxim as merely a rationale for Nanking's do-nothing policy toward Japan. Nippon was not only effectively assimilating Formosa but had undertaken a similar process in Manchuria. Under Japanese hegemony, "the Chinese people stand to lose. . . . the liberty to build up a new civilization according to their own will and choice." When that happens, Snow quoted Madame Sun, "a nation ceases to exist." China had at most a decade to save itself, but that would take a "revolutionary program of coordinated social, economic and political change"—an impossibility under the nation's present leadership and policies.[34]

This scornful view of the Chiang-led Kuomintang remained at the heart of Snow's unremittingly bleak view of China's prospects. In a mostly unflattering portrait of the Generalissimo in 1934, Snow had implied that Chiang might have reached some "understanding" with the Japanese whereby his central China base would be safeguarded in return for a free hand to Tokyo in the north. In further pursuit of this theme, Snow wrote a fellow journalist in mid-1935 that Chiang's military buildup was more likely aimed not against Japan, but at creating "a first class police force" to "patrol" the country for the benefit and profit of Tokyo. All in all, "In my time in China, I cannot recall when the situation looked more hopeless."[35]

Convinced as he was of the imperatives for radical change in China, and of the fascistic, appeasement-prone proclivities of Nanking, Snow gave closer attention to the alternatives from the left. He would soon find renewed hope for China in the courageous anti-Japanese demonstrations of the Peking students, and even more among the Red revolutionaries in the northwest. These rising forces seemed to mesh with an emerging international antifascist front in which the Communists, with the Union of Soviet Socialist Republics as their central bastion, appeared to be the principal spearhead. (In the context of such a front,

Snow noted decades later, liberal-minded foreign visitors to the Chinese Red area "needed to believe that there were people in China as good as the Reds seemed to be.")[36]

All this activism whetted Snow's interest in the Soviet Union and in Marxist-Leninist writings on fascism and world politics generally. He had reported to his father in March 1934 on "a most illuminating talk on Russia" given in Peking by a Harvard scholar returning from several years study in Moscow. Snow was impressed by the latter's opinion that Russia now held the "key to the peace" in Europe. The Soviets were now "one of the strongest nations on earth and have joined the 'status quo' powers against the revisionists [aggressors]," he told J. Edgar.[37]

Snow did his more systematic reading of Marxist literature (begun earlier in India) during his Haidian-Yanjing "sabbatical" year away from more active newspaper work. The books came mainly from the Left Book Club of England, organized by the influential left-wing socialists Harold Laski and John Strachey, and the publisher Victor Gollancz—who would later bring out the best-selling English edition of *Red Star*. At the request of the Yanjing president, J. Leighton Stuart, Snow prepared a lecture on fascism to the faculty in December 1934. For it he consulted an array of sources ranging from the Marxist works he had been reading to the writings of Hitler and Mussolini and lesser fascist ideologues. The lecture, self-consciously academic in tone and heavily larded with citations, was a bit out of character for Snow. It lacked the personally experienced, vividly anecdotal, "human" qualities he usually brought to his work. Nonetheless, it was not only a skillful and well researched effort; it also gave insight into Snow's evolving political perspectives.[38]

Snow described the generally accepted elements of European fascism: militarism, ultranationalism and glorification of war, racial-cultural doctrines of supremacy, single-party dictatorship, demagogic leaders, and terrorist tactics against all opposition. But he moved on to a considerably more radical interpretation. Fascism, despite its socialist rhetoric, preserved and defended capitalism. It was a counterrevolutionary response "to the social and economic problems which the decay and ever-nearing collapse of modern capitalism are everywhere posing today," he declared. Fascism appeared precisely to avert socialist revolution. In essence, it was capitalism without democracy. Snow acknowledged that fascism and communism were both dictatorial. Yet the latter, he emphasized, saw "proletarian dictatorship" as a necessary but transitory "evil" on the way to "a classless society." Fascism viewed the "Absolute State" as "the ultimate political form."

Snow put the principal blame for the defeat of the socialist forces in Europe on the social democratic parties and leaders. When in power they had practiced a "self-defeating" reformism, throwing away the chance for genuine socialist change. And in the crunch, as in Germany in 1932–1933, while the capitalists moved to save themselves against a rising Communist revolutionary tide, the social democrats in effect opted for fascist dictatorship rather than for a genuine social revolution under proletarian rule. (Actually, according to William L. Shirer, though the Socialists did not cover themselves with glory in the collapse of the Weimar Republic, the Communists bore a heavy share of responsibility, precisely by attempting to narrow the political choices to the extremes of right or left.)[39]

The lecture—in itself unimportant, its subject one for which Snow lacked firsthand knowledge and relied heavily on pro-Communist sources—nevertheless gives us a glimpse of Snow's political thought on the threshold of a dramatic new stage of his China journalistic career. His disdain for the "reformist" European socialist parties mirrored in part his China experience, where moderate political alternatives seemed hopeless and almost irrelevant. Revolution (as Ed wrote Howard in 1935) was the only "vote" available to the Chinese. This conviction was further buttressed by Snow's larger, Marxist-colored world view: Western capitalism (and colonialism) in terminal crisis, with socialism as the inevitable next stage of social development. The Soviet Union symbolized the socialist future, while fascism represented a regressive capitalism. But while Snow fell back on Marxist theory to justify a dictatorship of the left, there was a critical difference between his view of it as a "temporary evil," and that of contemporary Communist pronouncements that hailed the Soviet "dictatorship of the working class" as "the highest type of democracy, *socialist democracy*." The realities of Stalin's rule would become increasingly evident to Snow (never an ideologue) in the Moscow trials and purges of the middle and later 1930s. He continuously grappled with what he saw as the "good-evil" equation of the Communist system. He tried to balance what he regarded as the greater good of the social and material advancement he felt revolution had brought to formerly feudal societies, against the lesser evil of the absence of (never experienced) political freedoms. It remained an unresolved dilemma for him and would come sharply to the fore on his later visits to Communist-ruled China beginning in 1960.[40]

In the China of 1935, however, such issues seemed marginal at best. "There is one thing about the left movement [in China] that most people can't understand," Peg Snow wrote Richard Walsh at that time—reflecting Ed's views as well. "These Leftists are always the most intelligent, most promising, and most *popular* students and teachers in China. They are not a little fringe of disgruntled intellectual dilettantes as in America, for instance, but the leaders in every sense."[41]

By the summer of 1935 the Snows had moved back into Peking, where Ed again plunged into his journalistic activities. The *Daily Herald* had upgraded his status to special correspondent, and he retained his *Sun* connection. Once more, the couple found an ideal place to live at an inexpensive price. It was a foreign-style rather palatial residence, shared with a Swedish geologist who spent half the year back in Sweden. The large compound, adjacent to the ancient east wall of the city, boasted steam heat, marble baths, a tennis court and stables, and a garden greenhouse Ed used as his summer office. He spent a month in Manchuria that summer, gathering material for articles. The 2,000-mile trip took him as far as the Outer Mongolia frontier. He wrote Howard, in a strangely prophetic comment, that though a Russo-Japanese war could come in a year, "there is not historic necessity for it till, I figure, about 1945." The Japanese had done more to modernize Manchuria, he told his brother, than the Chinese had accomplished in all China since 1911. "They [the Japanese] are cocky, self-assured, conscious of their role as empire builders." "The Chinese," he remarked, in line with his now pessimistic view of the entrenched nature of the Japanese conquest, "fade more and more into the background, becoming mere rural scenic effect."[42]

In the fall, Tokyo began to tighten its hold on northern China by maneuvering to set up an "independent" North China, à la Manchukuo. Orchestrated by the Kwantung Army's master intriguer, General Doihara, the Japanese sought by a combination of bribes and threats to force the regional Chinese commander, General Song Zheyuan (Sung Cheyuan), to declare the "separation" of the northern China provinces that were already partially under Japan's control. The Nanking government, it seemed, would be unable or unwilling to intervene. This was the situation by mid-November when the students in Peking gained an inkling of what was about to transpire.

There is some controversy on the relative roles of various actors in the drama that ensued. Was the December Ninth Movement essentially a spontaneous reaction of youthful patriotic outrage at the sellout of northern China? Did the Chinese Communist party (whose organized presence in Peking was then virtually nonexistent) play a part, leading or otherwise? Did the Snows provide the initial "spark" to the students that set off the demonstration? The truth seems to be all of the above, in the order of importance listed.

The Snows had become close to a number of the Yanjing students, primarily from among those in Ed's journalism classes. They included Manchurian refugee students who tended to be among the most ardent anti-Japanese activists. The students visited the Snows first at Haidian, and then at their new Peking home in the later months of 1935. They discussed the impending crisis, and the Snows shared with them their own intense antifascist views, with special reference to the Kuomintang. Ed and Peg in turn gained an appreciation of the latent power of China's idealistic and patriotic students, who might yet be the nation's salvation. Though a minuscule fraction of the population, the students commanded a respect traditionally accorded the intellectuals as voices of the nation's moral and political conscience. And since they came from the more influential families, the college students were handled a bit more circumspectly (but only a bit) by the suppressive machinery of the Nanking government. Snow was the recipient of the natural esteem Chinese students accorded their teachers; beyond this he exemplified the liberal American values and style they had come to admire as Yanjing students. His friendliness and warm support solidified their feeling of trust.[43]

The Snows provided a safe haven for student leaders to meet in strategy sessions. The couple gave inspiration and encouragement, offered tactical suggestions, and channeled information that Snow came by as a correspondent. (The students referred to the Snow house as "a window to the fresh air.") Ed could offer foreign press coverage, while Peg reported on the student movement for Powell's *China Weekly Review*. Among other things, Snow arranged for the delivery (apparently through Agnes Smedley) of a letter from the students to Madame Sun in Shanghai, and for her reply in which she urged the youths on to action. As one of the Yanjing activists later recalled, Snow used the pronoun "we" rather than "you" when talking with the student leaders.[44]

Those (Chinese and Westerners) who were then involved with the Snows retained sharp impressions of their widely disparate personalities and styles. Peg struck them as highly emotional, impetuous, excitable ("talking like a machine gun"), and free with her energetically expressed opinions and suggestions. (Give the students "the devil for their inactivity and sleepiness," she wrote the Yanjing student leader Zhang Zhaolin in November 1935. "Why be a vegetable?") But they also saw her as a resourceful and original thinker, and a tireless worker for the causes she embraced. Li Min, secretary of the Yanjing Student Association and Peg's special protégé, would often visit the Snows carrying a small suitcase that Peg filled with antifascist materials she had typed up for Li Min to take back to the university. Peg wrote a lengthy and impassioned poem on the expected cave-in of northern China to the Japanese, "Old Peking." Published in *Asia,* it was translated into Chinese by Li Min and had wide impact among the students. It was all emotionally draining for Peg. The "impact of China was tremendous on me," and "I would be half dead from nervous and physical exhaustion," she later recounted. As a Western friend put it, Peg both "rocked the boat and propelled it forward."[45]

Ed, by contrast, came across as quietly thoughtful, gentle, unruffled, and much more reserved in passing judgment or offering advice. At the same time he was one who enjoyed talking with friends, old and new. Peg probably described him best in her account of the student movement: very popular with the students and teachers, he had "a naturally democratic and easy manner," was "casual but friendly, and did not force his opinions on anyone, but confined them to his typewriter which was always busy." She aptly characterized herself as "full of overflowing affection for the human race in general, but spiced with acid comment on people and things of which I did not approve." She could be counted on for some verbal fireworks in her spirited discussion-arguments with Ed; on the whole, however, the two operated as a highly effective and productive team. The students relied on and confided in them both.[46]

During the fall of 1935 the students watched with growing dismay as library and museum collections were packed and moved south in anticipation of the impending separation of northern China. Rumors had it that the universities themselves would be relocated. As student leaders gathered in the Snows' house in early December, Ed kept them abreast of the latest developments. Peg, with Ed's concurrence, urged a mass street demonstration as a replay of May 4, 1919. The students apparently had been working on the same idea. Of course, the street demonstration tactic was a time-honored one in modern China where more "civil" avenues for open discourse and dissent were closed. The Snows alerted members of the Peking press corps of the planned event, and at the demonstrations on December 9 and 16, the presence of the Snows and other Western correspondents (with cameras) inhibited police violence. (On Ed's advice, student organizers held a press conference for foreign journalists on December 12.) The United Press's Mac Fisher, with his own Yanjing ties and his reportorial links to the local English-language press, was a particularly valuable ally. "The students dearly loved Mac," Helen Snow later related, "an affection which grew with every news article [of his] that appeared in the *Peking Chronicle* or the *North China Star*."[47]

At the December 9 demonstration, nearly a thousand Yanjing and Qinghua students marched five miles to the west gate of the city, only to find it barred to them. But some students had slipped into the city the previous evening and were able to join two thousand marchers from Peking-based schools and colleges. The Snows walked alongside, with Peg irrepressibly shouting slogans and exhorting the students. It was a triumphant beginning, despite some beatings and arrests and an icy water hosing of the marchers. Ed cabled the news to his London and New York papers that evening, and dispatches by the other correspondents gave the event world coverage. It was even reported in the censored Chinese press. "Nym and I were ordinarily no parade-watchers," Snow later wrote, "but we took our place beside the leaders of this one proudly."[48]

December 9 was followed by a student general strike, and a much more massive and well-organized demonstration on December 16 in which up to ten thousand students from twenty-eight schools and colleges participated. On this occasion, Snow climbed atop the Qianmen (front gate) tower, where he used his new movie camera to film the event. Lu Cui, the vivacious Qinghua standardbearer, emerged as the hero of that day when she crawled under a bolted city gate in a thwarted attempt to unlock it and allow entry to the city for her five thousand fellow marchers. The police hauled her off into custody. Snow soon appeared at the police station and was able to interview her and express his sympathy and support. During a Kuomintang crackdown the Snows gave her sanctuary for some days and helped spirit her away by train for Shanghai, where she worked on organizing student associations.[49]

The movement mushroomed and spread throughout China in the spring and summer of 1936 among students, workers, and business and professional circles. Despite Kuomintang repression of left-wing activists, a National Student Union was formed, and a Shanghai-based All-China National Salvation Association. In the wake of the December demonstrations, students from Peking and Tianjin went to the surrounding countryside to rouse the peasants. (The Snows came out on a frigid January day to see the Peking students off to the villages. Ed gave them an elaborately packaged box of chocolates he jokingly told them contained "tear gas bombs" for their protection.) As for the northern China autonomy scheme, Japan was forced to retreat from its more ambitious plans. Buttressed by the strong expression of public opinion, General Song demonstrated considerably more backbone in dealing with the Japanese. All these developments encompassed the December Ninth Movement of 1935–1936. It "was the beginning of the end of China's non-resistance policy," Snow would recount.[50]

In the personal style of *Journey*, Snow headed his account of December 9, "We [he and Peg] Spark a Rebellion." And Helen, firmly convinced of her "prime mover" role, declared in her China memoir, "It is a charming irony that Doihara and all his mobilized armies had to retreat when faced with two little anti-Fascist Americans living on U.S. $50. a month—but armed with a piece of the truth." To a considerable degree these extravagant estimates of their part in the movement rested on assumptions about the lack of direct Communist input. Nor were the Snows anxious to find any—an attitude easy to understand at a time when CCP people in the Kuomintang-ruled White areas operated in secrecy and anonymity, even from fellow members. An organized party apparatus in northern China was probably created only at the end of 1935, and left-leaning students would have found it truly difficult to make such contacts. As one of the December Ninth leaders later recalled, "The Party, where are you? At that time we had not yet joined the Party. Under the White Terror and during those dark days, where could we find the Party!" And neither were such students apt to parade Communist sympathies openly. Thus Snow could declare in *Journey* that "there was not a Communist" among the student leaders who came to them for advice and support.[51]

Later Communist claims to an initiating and directing role in the December Ninth Movement were undoubtedly overstated. Nevertheless, leftist and Communist influence among the student leaders was significant and was to some degree channeled through the Snows' "safe house." The recollections of a number of these leaders, though colored by the party's line, attest to this. The testimony of Huang Hua (then known as Wang Rumei), one of the Yanjing students closest to the Snows who would become a top foreign affairs figure in the Communist regime, is pertinent. Acknowledging in an interview for this book that the student movement had "a kind of spontaneity," he insisted that the party underground, though small, had been active also. More important (and perhaps more accurately), he noted that he and other left-minded students had some covert access to Communist pronouncements such as its August 1 Declaration calling for a united anti-Japanese front and an end to civil war. He had already read Marxist tracts and was inspired by accounts of the Long March and the Red Army's arrival in northern Shaanxi that had appeared in the Tianjin press. But direct contact with the Communist party came only through individual student (or ex-student) Communists whom the other students met at the Snows, and probably elsewhere, perhaps on the eve of the first December demonstration. David Yu (Yu Jiwei) in particular, who carried larger party responsibilities in northern China, soon took a guiding hand in the student movement. "I could see they were taking instruction from David," Helen Snow later recalled of the meetings in her home, "but I had no idea he was anyone important." Chen Hanbo, one of the participants in these sessions, remembered David Yu as "a spellbinder" whom the others "adored." "We got to know the Beijing leaders of the underground Party organization in [the Snow's] small sitting room," he added. David Yu would also be an initial intermediary for Ed's 1936 Red journey.[52]

Snow had a Peking reunion in 1960 with some of the student activists he had known in 1935 and 1936. One of them, Yao Yilin, told him that he and David Yu held party meetings at the Snow house. In his notes on the reunion, Snow commented, "I suspected that but didn't care to know too much about it." (David Yu became mayor of Tianjin and was a state minister in the Peking government at the time of his death in 1958 at age forty-six. Yao became a party economic expert and one of the top state leaders.) Snow seemed prepared to believe in 1960, as then claimed by Yao and others, that the demonstrations were planned by the "*tang-jen*" (party people) and that "participation of foreigners (as protective screen of newsmen) was merely fortuitous as was likewise my advice and encouragement that such an action be taken."[53]

Probably reflecting this 1960 experience, Snow afterward downplayed the "spark" version in *Journey*. The "few pages devoted to the student rebellion were not offered as history *entier* but were obviously presented as an aspect of personal adventure," he wrote in 1966. Though the party did not "direct" the December 9 demonstration, he added, "From its inception and throughout its growth into a mass movement, student anti-Japanese action served to provide sanctuaries for radical youth which effectively ended the Communist Party's isolation in urban China." In fact, by spring 1936 the party was already in a key position in the organized student national salvation movement. But perhaps most to the point was Snow's observation in *Journey*, "This experience taught me that, among all the causes of revolution, the total loss of confidence by educated youths in an existing regime is the one indispensable ingredient most often neglected by academic historians of the phenomenon." Ironically, December Ninth leaders such as Yao Yilin would find themselves one day arrayed against another generation of such disenchanted youth.[54]

The surging left-propelled anti-Japanese movement had given Ed a new confidence in the resistance potential of the Chinese people. It thus added urgency to his long-held desire to visit the Reds and also did much to create an opportunity for such a journey. And Snow's role in the December demonstrations had opened the necessary underground contacts for him and solidified his credentials as the ideal non-Communist Western journalist to report the Reds' story to a wide Chinese and Western audience. In so doing, Snow would find himself even more caught up in the events he recorded.

★ CHAPTER 8

Redstar-Struck

In the Land of the "Better" People

Young Marshal Zhang Xueliang, back from Europe invigorated and drug-free, had been transferred to Xi'an in the northwest in 1935 with his Northeast (Dongbei) Army. He had been ordered by the Generalissimo to do battle against the Reds, now ensconced some 150 miles to the north after completing the Long March. Marshal Zhang, designated the deputy commander of Bandit Suppression Headquarters, moved against the Communists in October and November 1935 but suffered resounding defeat. His army, restive, homesick, and intensely anti-Japanese, fought half-heartedly. Prisoners taken by the Communists (including many officers) were released carrying the Reds' message of unity in resistance to the common external enemy. A similar theme began to appear among the ranks of the Northeast Army and in the schools and the press in Xi'an, spread by the hundreds of youths who flocked there in the aftermath of the December student demonstrations. (Journalism students from the Snows' Peking circle were especially influential as editors of a major army paper.) Marshal Zhang, and the commander of the smaller regional Northwest Army, were won over to the Communists' anti–civil war call, and by the spring of 1936 a de facto truce prevailed, with close liaison between the two camps. The Red security chief Deng Fa was secretly staying in the Young Marshal's own residence when Snow arrived in Xi'an in June.[1]

The atmosphere was tense and conspiratorial. Chiang Kai-shek's Blue Shirts hunted down suspected Communists in the city, while Marshal Zhang gave protection and encouragement to leftist-inspired anti-

Japanese activities. These cross-purposes would shortly lead to the historic Xi'an Incident in December. Meanwhile, they were the backdrop for Snow's appearance there, at the optimum moment when Xi'an offered a covert gateway to Red northern Shaanxi for this American journalist with the right (left?) connections.

Snow embarked on his trip in a more buoyant temper than earlier over China's prospects in the deepening Far Eastern crisis. In the post-December patriotic upsurge, backed by the Communist revolutionaries in the northwest, he had discerned genuine prospects for effective popular resistance to Japan, and to the appeasers in Nanking. Perhaps the mood he now detected in China was best exemplified in a volume published in Shanghai that year by leading literary figures headed by the renowned social realist writer and close ally of Lu Xun, Mao Dun (Shen Yanping). The book brought together contributions randomly solicited from people of all strata throughout the nation and designed to reflect "the face of China" on one particular day, May 21, 1936. As the anti-Japanese Mao Dun summed it up, behind the portrayal of "the ugly and the evil, the sacred and the pure, and the light and the darkness, we can see in it optimism, hope, and awakening of the masses of people." For Snow, the new mood promised at long last a practical, progressive, and authentically anti-imperialist means for thwarting Tokyo's empire builders. "China's cause was now my cause," he later wrote of the onset of war in 1937, "and I linked this sentiment with a commitment against fascism, nazism and imperialism everywhere."[2]

As he waited in the early months of 1936 on final arrangements for entering the Red districts, Snow produced a series of articles on the Far Eastern situation and American policy options. The themes were vintage Snow: a plague on *all* Asia imperialisms, and opposition to any American military involvement there. These opinions were updated, however, by his growing apprehension over Japan's European fascist links and ambitions, and by his newfound faith in the ability of a Chinese "people's war" to frustrate those ambitions. It therefore allowed him (for the time being) to hold to his non-interventionist position in a China-Japan conflict he now regarded as inevitable. It is instructive to compare these articles with one written just prior to Snow's student movement experiences. It was based on his previous summer's visit to Manchuria and underscored again the key role that region was scheduled to play in Japan's plans—"Empire in Manchuria foreshadows empire in China." Tokyo's takeover was complete, with the Chinese there reduced to "vegetable subjects." The Japanese were taking no nonsense from the white man either, Snow added, cognizant as always of the color issue in Asia. "All the anguish of wounded pride accumulated over Western acts of discrimination against the yellow man here finds its outlet in Japanese authority, as colonial masters, of yellow over white." Their former inferiority complex had been transmuted into "an equally Freudian superiority complex." And Tokyo's envoys were finally getting "respect" in Western capitals. Only through defeat in "a major foreign war" (involving the United States, Britain, and/or Russia) could one "now envisage any failure of Japanese imperialism," Snow concluded. How long the latter's empire in China could stand "in the fluid world of today" Snow left to the "speculation" of his readers.[3]

A few months later Snow was reaching quite different conclusions, expressed in a two-part series for the *Post* and a follow-up in *Foreign Affairs*. (A serious bout of malarial fever and dysentery had delayed his work.) He was no less pessimistic on prospects for China under a supine and "tottering" Chiang Kai-shek: the country was going bankrupt at a "breakneck" speed accelerated by "every economic and political obeisance" Nanking made to Tokyo. China, self-destructing since 1931, had lost the chance to construct "a modern capitalist nation of will and power and social progress." Again raising the likelihood of a Japanese collision with the Western powers, Snow asked rhetorically, "Is it too late for us to keep out?" Much as he had in *Far Eastern Front,* Snow warned against America being sucked into a conflict to maintain "the international status quo in the Far East." There was no American stake in China even remotely worth the costs and sacrifices involved. Applying his earlier prescription specifically to the United States, he urged Washington speedily to relinquish its special privileges and military presence in China. America had no empire to defend—let others fight their own wars. This was "in no sense a policy of isolation, but an active policy of insulation," he maintained.[4]

Snow acknowledged that Tokyo's "Imperial Idea is not going to die until it is killed" but now added his conviction that the Chinese themselves were "fully capable" of this task. Tokyo's relentless advance "will shortly provoke an effort of resistance that will astound the world," against which Japan "will break its imperial neck." The effort would come from the growing mass of patriotic Chinese "disgusted" with the policy of "the compradore regime which rules them." In the final extremity, Nanking itself would be forced to fight, Snow predicted, to avoid "destruction by universal insurrection of the Chinese people." The ensuing struggle for self-determination would likely lead to the demise of imperialism ("reversals of fortune," Snow called it) not only in China but "elsewhere" in Asia, by setting in motion "revolutionary developments of great consequence." A nonimperial America need not fear these eventualities, Snow argued. Her true interest lay in peaceful commerce, and its great expansion actually required a revolutionized, emancipated China. "Beyond that we need ask for nothing. Beyond that, we can, in justice demand nothing." The thesis that a capitalist (but nonimperialist) America could live peacefully and profitably with social revolutionary Asian nationalism remained a cornerstone of Snow's thinking to the end.[5]

Snow's anti-British empire, no foreign entanglements approach was, as before, congenial to the conservative and nativist-isolationist *Post* editor, George Lorimer. Ed discreetly saved the fuller exposition of his views on China's revolutionary future for the more academic pages of *Foreign Affairs*. Lorimer, after all, found even the New Deal much too "socialistic" for the *Post's* taste. In *Foreign Affairs,* Snow focused on Japanese Prime Minister Hirota's call for a joint anti-Red front with Nanking. This proclaimed duty to save China from bolshevism could be "the vehicle" for Japan "to ride into China," Ed wrote. But even should the Generalissimo seriously consider some such collaboration as a short-term expedient, the Chinese Reds, now "expressing the growing political will of the Chinese masses," had in effect closed that door to him. In the current national crisis, the Communists saw the opportunity to lead the struggle "not only for social and economic but also for *national* liberation." In contrast to the Chinese "warlords," the Reds have nothing to lose by war with Japan, "and there is a socialist world to be won." For Chiang to cast his lot with Tokyo against the Communist forces would fatally compromise him among virtually every segment of Chinese society. China's leader, Snow prophesied, would characteristically stall for time, while making "a supreme effort" finally to annihilate the Reds. But he faced the inexorable choice of war or submission. When "the bombs begin dropping at his feet it is possible to believe that he will fight." The Reds, however, might well take that power of decision away from him. In that case, Chiang will have only two alternatives: "Japan, and the preservation of capitalism but the loss of China's independence; or communism, and the end of capitalism, but China still sovereign."[6]

In early 1936 Snow understood the nationalist-cum-revolutionary message of Chinese communism. Indeed, he saw the CCP as the key to a successful resistance war. In this sense, his journey to northern Shaanxi would be one of confirmation and reinforcement as much as of discovery. The

China scenario he had sketched touched on the central issues then in (largely sub rosa) dispute within the Communist camp. The CCP and its Comintern mentors were in general accord in pushing for an end to civil war in China and for a unified "national defense" government against Japan. The ascendant Mao leadership, however, saw these objectives from the vantage point of Chinese revolutionaries on the spot. For Moscow, Soviet Russian foreign policy and security considerations were primary. Already moving toward rapprochement with Nanking, the Russians pushed vigorously for conciliation between the Communists and the Nationalists. The Soviets looked to a unified and ostensibly democratic China under the Generalissimo, prepared to take on Japan. Mao, on his part, focused on the growing Communist-supported urban national salvation movement, and the CCP's mobilization of the peasantry, as the keys to creating an anti-Japanese national front—preferably without Chiang. Mao envisioned a principal role for the Communists in a resistance war and contemplated active Soviet support for the Reds in such a conflict.[7]

On the Marxist theoretical level, the issue boiled down to an assessment of the class character and goals of an upcoming China-Japan war. To the Comintern forces it was a "bourgeois-nationalist" battle for China's independence led by the Kuomintang, with any subsequent "proletarian-socialist" stage relegated to an indefinite future. For Mao, however, the resistance struggle would itself be an integral part of an ongoing revolutionary process. Ultimate socialist objectives depended on how effectively the Communists did their work during the wartime phase. And—Mao declared to Snow in Bao'an in July 1936—the peasants' demand for land reform must be met, without which "it is impossible to lay the broad mass basis for a successful revolutionary struggle for national liberation." The current "national democratic" stage of the revolution, Mao more bluntly told Snow in Yan'an in 1939, will "*after a certain stage . . . be transformed into social revolution.*" The present "becoming" would "turn into its 'being'—unless our work in the present phase is a failure," Mao added. Snow was already prepared to react sympathetically to Mao's dialectical linkage of resistance and revolution, and to the concomitant challenge to the Kuomintang. It would give *Red Star* its markedly prophetic character. And rather curiously, Snow and his book would serve both as surrogate vehicle and target in the often-obscure CCP-Moscow dialogue on these questions. First must come the story of Snow's sojourn in the land of the Reds.[8]

Snow's growing convictions about the major role the Communists were soon to play rekindled his interest in investigating the Reds for himself. The Communist troops were now potentially within striking distance of Japanese military operations in northern China, underlining their claim to be a patriotic vanguard force. With the auspicious truce on the Shaanxi battlefront, the Red zone became accessible through Xi'an, an 800-mile rail journey from Peking. For the Communists here was a highly opportune moment to publicize their anti-Japanese unity stance and image among the nation's now very receptive urban circles. It was a critical moment for the CCP, its supplies and troops depleted by the massive Long March losses, and awaiting another "final" Kuomintang annihilation campaign. The Mao leadership was intent on putting the greatest possible pressure on Nanking (with whom it had opened inconclusive secret negotiations), while seeking alternative political strategies.[9]

As a trustworthy but non-Communist Western journalist, Snow appeared ideally suited to bring out the Reds' story. He had broad access to the bourgeois media in China and the West as well as extraterritorial protection for what he wrote. Not only would his reports carry more weight than those by an avowed Communist, but the very fact of his independence from Communist ties made him more likely to grasp the broader implications of the message Mao wished to convey. Thus Snow, who had already been an inadvertent channel for Communist contacts with the Peking students, would now become the "medium," in his later words, "through whom [Mao] had his first chance, after years of blockade, to speak to the cities of China, from which the Reds had long been isolated."[10]

Snow apparently first made overtures for the trip through David Yu, whom the Snows had befriended and sheltered after the December student movement. David, an important if youthful functionary in the tiny party underground in the north, left in March 1936 (wearing an old tweed suit of Ed's) for Tianjin, where he contacted the newly arrived northern China party chief, Liu Shaoqi. David soon wrote the Snows that Ed's "problem" would be "settled a few days later. . . . I think they have no reason to refuse your requirement." "When shall Ed start his travelling," he queried them in a follow-up note. Hearing nothing further from this source, Snow went to Shanghai in May to enlist Madame Sun's help in expediting matters. This seemingly worked; he was shortly put in touch with a Northeastern University professor (and secret party operative) in Peking, who passed on to him an invisible ink letter to Mao, and instructions for contacting the Red underground in Xi'an. That letter, Snow was told on his 1960 visit to China by the Shanghai mayor, Ke Qingshi, had been authorized by Liu Shaoqi and written by Ke.[11]

As Helen Snow pungently noted, "Ed packed up his sleeping bag, his Camel cigarettes, his Gillette razor blades, and a can of Maxwell House coffee—his indispensable artifacts of Western civilization." Still feverish from a series of last-minute inoculations, and with his cameras slung around his neck, Snow hastily slipped out of Peking on the midnight train for the two-day ride to Xi'an.[12]

There are a number of variations on this basic (and documented) scenario. In Snow's own accounts he emphasized Madame Sun's role, leaving out David Yu. Rewi Alley, whose Shanghai house held secret radio equipment for communicating with the Reds in the northwest, stated that a "call" had come for an "honest" foreign journalist and a Western-trained doctor. According to Alley, Madame Sun then asked Snow if he would go and he consented. But whatever the sequence of events, Snow was the one who took the initial step. Hamilton, in his Snow biography, recounts the part supposedly played by a Russian émigré professor at Peking University named Sergei Polevoy. As told by the deceased man's son, Polevoy had links to important Chinese Communist and Comintern figures in China in the 1920s, and in 1936 Snow approached him as another potential go-between. Ed may have raised the matter with the Russian, who continued to have left-wing contacts in Peking, and who visited the Snow home on one occasion. For someone whose Chinese Communist ties had been largely through the Comintern, Polevoy appears to be little more than a bit player. Harrison Salisbury in his book on the Long March surmised that a Comintern "recommendation" to the Chinese Reds to "establish international connections" may have "opened the way" for the Snow invitation. But this surmise is hardly plausible. In Comintern jargon, "international" meant connections and loyalty to the Moscow center, particularly so during the years of Stalinist centralization of power over the international Communist movement. The Russians were indeed suspicious of Mao's "nationalist" (China-centered) orientations, and unenthusiastic at his elevation to party leadership during the Long March, without the imprimatur of Stalin—not to mention the continuing disagreement on how best to deal with the Kuomintang. The lone foreign Comintern representative with the Chinese Communists, the German Otto Braun (known to the Chinese as Li De) regarded Snow cautiously in Bao'an, "rebuffed" his inquiries about the Red Army and the CCP, and (perhaps from a later political perspective) saw in Snow's compilation of "invaluable information" on the Reds the possibility of an American "secret agent" connection. At any rate, Snow's reports were bound to highlight dramatically the political (and revolutionary) profile, history, and policies of the Chinese Communists, something the Comintern seemed anxious to avoid in the delicate pre-united front maneuvering in China. There is little reason to believe the Comintern initiated or pushed the idea of a Snow visit.[13]

On more mundane levels, Snow, as a working journalist, was busy making his financial arrangements. He remained under contract for a book, and *Red Star,* in addition to its other attributes, would also be the big "off-the-beaten-track" travel book he had always wanted to write. And he thought in those terms. "I shall call it 'I Went to Red China'," he jotted in his diary during his northwestern stay. With plans for the Shaanxi trip falling into place by the beginning of June, his London and New York editors enthusiastically offered the necessary support in return for a series of exclusive articles. "If I succeed" (in interviewing the Red leaders), "it will be a world scoop," Ed wrote the *Daily Herald.* On his return from Red territory, he impressed on the *Herald* editor the value and uniqueness of the copy he was sending him. "I do not know that anything of the sort has occurred elsewhere in modern journalistic history, for the situation is so unusual that it can scarcely have had a counterpart." The total bill Snow ultimately submitted to the *Herald* and the *Sun,* covering his expenses from June 14 to October 25 (including the cost of substitute coverage during his absence from Peking) came to $1,334.50 Chinese currency—about $450 U.S.! Almost four months of "no frills" living in Red China ran him well under $100 U.S. Compare that with our high-powered, high-living media stars of today. He had made no agreement (with the Reds or anyone else) as to what he would or would not write, he assured Ambassador Johnson, "and wherever my personal sympathies may lie I continue to be from Missouri." For the Communists, of course, this stance was one of Snow's assets.[14]

In Xi'an Snow put up at the new guest house, interviewed the provincial governor (a former Communist himself), and the commander of the Northwest Army, Yang Hucheng (who would be one of the ringleaders in the December coup against the Generalissimo), and awaited his secret contact. It soon emerged in the person of a rotund gentleman in a gray silk gown called Pastor Wang. A theology graduate of St. John's University in Shanghai, Wang had served under the warlord "Christian General," Feng Yuxiang. Now he was one of a clandestine network of Communist liaison agents who shuttled between the Red and White Chinese worlds. He had carried out high-level missions for the CCP, including the initial truce arrangements with the Young Marshal. In true conspiratorial fashion, Snow and Wang produced their halves of a card with English verses and matched them up. For the better part of a week Pastor Wang (whose name was Dong Jianwu and who spoke excellent English) briefed Snow on the Communists, colorfully interlaced with many personal yarns and reminiscences. Wang and Liu Ding, another important operative from the Shanghai underground who was then functioning as secretary to Marshal Zhang, introduced Snow to Deng Fa, the Red security chief staying with the Young Marshal. Deng Fa, nattily dressed in the attire of a Kuomintang official, was bursting with glee and high spirits in disclosing his identity to Snow during a jaunt to the Han tombs west of Xi'an. It was he who briefed Snow on the particulars of travel and other arrangements for the Red area. These three key contacts, Pastor Wang, Liu Ding (a German-educated engineer known to his foreign friends as "Charles"), and Deng Fa, would all come to tragic ends. Deng was killed in a plane crash in 1946, while the other two underwent persecution and imprisonment during the Cultural Revolution years, in good part for the extensive (and dangerous) liaison work and foreign connections they had put to the service of the revolution. When Rewi Alley privately told Snow in 1970 of Liu Ding's mistreatment, Snow "snorted and used a Chinese obscenity." As for Pastor Wang, in December 1970 he was being denied emergency medical attention as a "bad" element but, on word that Snow was coming to Shanghai and wished to see Wang, was hastily hospitalized. He died before Snow's arrival.[15]

Snow additionally met up with George Hatem in Xi'an, a young American doctor also heading for the Red base. He had been part of a close-knit circle of foreign radicals in Shanghai, among whom Rewi Alley and Agnes Smedley were prominent. They often provided safe houses and communication channels for the party and its operatives. These radicals gravitated around a left-wing bookstore and a Marxist study group in which a German Communist intellectual, Heinz (or Heintz) Shippe, held forth as guru. Hatem was a politically less sophisticated member of the group. Raised in Buffalo and North Carolina of poor Lebanese immigrant parentage, he studied medicine on scholarships at the American University in Beirut, and at the University of Geneva. As an adventurous young man, he took off for Shanghai in 1933 and set up a practice that consisted largely of "cleaning up" women from the brothels "until the next dose," he related. Treating venereal diseases was a lucrative business for a Shanghai doctor but not what had brought Hatem (known as "Shag") to China. Appalled at these conditions, he was further radicalized by what he saw while accompanying Alley on the latter's factory inspection tours for the Shanghai municipal council. Hatem was attracted to the bookstore and the study group and was influenced by the intensely committed Smedley. She in turn introduced him to Charles (Liu Ding). Hatem's office was sometimes used for secret cell meetings while the young doctor stood guard. Based on these connections, Hatem agreed to be the medical person the Reds wanted and joined Snow in Xi'an for their shared odyssey. Both would be crossing their "Red Rubicon" (in Snow's phrase), but on divergent lifetime paths.[16]

Hatem, a warmly engaging, amiable, and gentle personality, entered the Red districts hardly knowing a word of Chinese. (Snow's Chinese was adequate for both.) Hatem would devote the next fifty-two years of a remarkable medical career to the Chinese Communist cause. At his death in Beijing in 1988 he was a revered medical figure. He had taken a Chinese name, Ma Haide, and married a beautiful and charming Chinese actress, Zhou Sufei; they had two children and four grandchildren. After the Communist victory in 1949, he led a campaign that eliminated venereal disease and prostitution (a vindication of his early Shanghai career). In his later years he concentrated on leprosy, using his "remaining energies," he told me in 1987, to "help rid the world" of that disease. He and Snow became lifelong friends; Dr. Ma and Alley, and to an extent Madame Sun, would be Snow's major links to China in the cold war decades and serve also as his "progressive prods." Hatem would lead a Chinese medical team sent to Switzerland to minister to Snow in the final weeks of his terminal illness in 1972. Oddly, Hatem never appears in the pages of *Red Star* nor in any of Snow's writings until the 1960s. Hatem had requested this omission, evidently fearing (in the case of *Red Star*) that such publicity might endanger his Shanghai friends and contacts. Actually, Hatem's absence from Snow's account of their expedition probably enhanced the narrative quality of *Red Star,* in which the image of the lone intrepid (and attractive) foreign explorer was especially effective.[17]

Snow and Hatem finally took off one morning in early July in a Dodge truck that belonged to the Northeast Army. Their destination was Yan'an, then still in Kuomintang hands and the last major outpost bordering Red territory. From there they proceeded on foot, with a single muleteer guide and a donkey to carry their gear, including medical supplies Hatem was bringing. Ed's cameras, watch, and good leather shoes offered tempting targets for bandits of whatever variety or political coloration, he nervously thought. In fact a Red detachment sent to escort them had been sidetracked by a clash with anti-Red marauders. The fantastic contours of the treeless orange-yellow loess landscape in this heartland of ancient Chinese civilization lent an eerie tension to their excursion into the unknown and unpredictable. The "infinite variety of queer embattled shapes—hills, like great castles, like rows of mammoth, nicely rounded scones, like ranges torn by some giant hand, leaving behind the imprint of angry fingers," Snow described the scene. The "incredible and sometimes frightening shapes" could also take on a "strange surrealist beauty." The peasants' habitats were carved into the loess, with entire cave villages honeycombed into the hillsides. Snow's description remains the perfect rendering of its impact.[18]

After a two-day trek, Snow and Hatem arrived at a village headquarters to be greeted by a bearded slender soldierly figure who turned out to be Zhou Enlai, the thirty-eight-year-old commander of the East Front Red Army. He welcomed Snow in halting but intelligible English, as a "reliable" journalist, "friendly to the Chinese people." Over the next couple of days he briefed Snow on the extensive itinerary planned for him and responded at length to Ed's queries on Communist policies, strategies, and history, and on his own background. Snow found this attractive, cultivated, and ardent revolutionary of Mandarin antecedents to be "every inch the intellectual"—a "scholar turned insurrectionist." More generally, he noted in his diary at the time, the Reds he encountered "go about remaking the world like college boys to a football match. . . . Every house rings with singing at night, laughter and good humor." The lads ("little Red devils") who did chores for the army had a "personal dignity" Snow had never before seen in Chinese youngsters. They were "cheerful, gay, energetic and loyal—the living spirit of an astonishing crusade of youth." Snow was thus launched on his compelling portrayal of Chinese communism "with a human face"—of many distinct and attractive visages. "It is the human epic in the story of the Red Army that interests me, and the politics only secondarily," Snow perhaps disingenuously assured his *Herald* editor after his return to Peking.[19]

Significantly, Zhou Enlai's comments to Snow on the dynamics of a resistance war hardly squared with the contemporary Comintern line. The revolution, he declared, would "probably come to power on the vehicle of the anti-Japanese movement." And as for Chiang Kai-shek, the "first day of the anti-Japanese War" will "put a stamp of doom on his hegemony." But as events unfolded in China and led to a KMT-CCP rapprochement, Snow would be urgently entreated by Zhou to keep such remarks out of his book. Irritated at this, Snow discarded as well much of Zhou's biography because the personal story had been so interlarded with strongly anti-Chiang material.[20]

After a further two-day journey on nags well past their prime, and accompanied now by a twenty-man Red Army escort, the two travelers arrived at the Red headquarters in Bao'an. (The following month, both men received gifts of two fine horses captured by the Reds from Moslem forces.) On entering the walled town, in a valley among the surrounding hills, they were greeted by welcoming banners, a military band, and (with the exception of Mao) the top echelon of Red leaders in residence. "It was the first time I had been greeted by the entire cabinet of a government, the first time a whole city had been turned out to welcome me," Snow recorded. "The effect produced on me was highly emotional." Bao'an, Snow remembered, "was the ruin of a once sizable frontier city reduced by years of war and famine." Snow and Hatem were put up in what Ed called the *waichiaopu* (foreign office) compound, in a small hut with two mud *kangs* (sleeping platforms) and a simple table and benches. After sleeping outdoors during the journey, it looked like "the genuine Waichiaopu article" to Snow. An unexpectedly lavish banquet followed, at which they were joined by government functionaries including Mao, still looking sleepy, with his "mass of black hair uncombed." All in all, a typically courteous Chinese welcome to special guests.[21]

Mao struck Snow as "a gaunt, rather Lincolnesque figure," and someone who "may possibly become a very great man." However, Snow added, "I never met a Chinese Red who drivelled 'our-great-leader' phrases," an obvious jibe at the Stalin cult. Snow was then not privy to Mao's political downgrading before his comeback at the Zunyi conference during the Long March in January 1935. Nor, for that matter, was he aware of that watershed event itself, nor of the continued challenges to Mao's leadership. Snow's powerfully impressive portrait of Mao and the famous Mao autobiographical centerpiece in *Red Star* significantly enhanced the Red leader's prestige and renown in China and abroad and undoubtedly added to his political "capital" on the road to his own "great leader" status.[22]

In rounding out his portrayal of the chairman, Snow pictured Mao in earthy human terms: searching for lice under his belt or removing his trousers in the heat of the day—both in Snow's presence; and as a "plain-speaking and plain-living" leader who strolled of an evening casually and unobtrusively among the townsfolk of Bao'an. But though he had "the simplicity and naturalness of the Chinese peasant," Mao was also a classical poet and student of philosophy, a person who delighted at the sight of a lovely moth in the candlelight. It was the beginning of a lifelong attraction for Snow; interestingly, he was not only the first foreign journalist to interview Mao but also the last to do so, in December 1970. And with singular impact on both occasions.[23]

There was immediate rapport between the forty-three-year-old Chinese "peasant-born intellectual turned revolutionary" and the thirty-one-year-old middle-class heartland American turned "friend" of China and the revolution. Snow not only responded to Mao personally, but also to the Red leader's peasant populism, his determined commitment to both national and social revolutionary goals, his friendly overtures to America, and his independent-minded though cautiously expressed distancing of himself from Moscow. It was a Maoist package Snow could identify with and enthusiastically communicate. As for Mao, after reading the Chinese translation of *Red Star*, he stated to a Yan'an cadres' conference that the book "truly represented our situation and introduced our party's policies to the world." He conveyed the same opinion to Snow personally in 1939.[24]

Mao generally slept until midmorning, breakfasted almost to noon-time, then worked late into the night. His meetings with Snow took place in the evenings, on an irregular schedule, in the leader's spare, candle-lit cave dwelling. The two men would talk well into the night, often ending with a shared meal at midnight (or later). In this poor and primitive first bastion of the Red forces in the northwest, cave living was the norm. The Red Army "academy" occupied a cave-lined cliffside for its classrooms, and the students sat on stone stools.[25]

Mao devoted an extraordinary amount of time and attention to the Snow interviews, which totaled some twenty thousand words. At Ed's request, the Yanjing student Huang Hua followed Snow to Xi'an and Bao'an to be his interpreter. (He left Peking just days before final exams and graduation.) Huang arrived too late for the Mao interviews but accompanied Snow on his subsequent travels through Red territory. Wu Liangping, Mao's secretary, served as Snow's initial interpreter. Wu, a Long Marcher, had been educated in Shanghai and at Sun Yat-sen University in Moscow and spoke fluent English and Russian. Snow's interview notes, based on Wu's oral translation of Mao's replies, were re-translated into Chinese by Huang Hua, read and corrected by Mao, then translated again into English by Huang. At the same time, Snow practiced much more of his own spoken Chinese during his northwestern sojourn than in his previous two years of "desultory" study of the language in Peking.[26]

At the base of the Mao-Snow relationship were overriding political considerations on Mao's part, and professional journalistic ones on Snow's. Later, as China's leader, Mao could discard or take up the Snow connection as it suited his and China's larger political purposes. Yet between the two men there remained an extraordinary personal thread from beginning to end of their meetings. "I've missed you a great deal since you left," Mao wrote Snow in March 1937, alerting Ed to shifts in CCP policies. "We are all grateful to you," he added. And in their very last conversation in December 1970 Mao could, rather disarmingly but not unmeaningfully, tell Snow, "from our first meeting thirty-five years ago up to the present, . . . we have remained unchanged and treated each other as friends." The "basic relationship between us two has not changed," he reiterated.[27]

Much of what Mao had to say to Snow in 1936 (beyond his autobiographical narrative) was directly cited or attributed to Mao in *Red Star;* other comments, often made more informally, remained in Ed's notes and diaries at the time. But they all clearly provided the background for Snow's own analyses of Chinese Communist policies and prospects. On the strategy of a resistance war, Mao articulated his concepts of a protracted, mobile, guerrilla-style struggle, based on a mobilized and revolutionized peasantry. It assumed an independent and major role for Communist-led forces, within the framework of an overall national front. Mao further declared that the Soviet Union could not remain neutral "in the struggle against Japanese imperialism." Once "the Chinese people have their own government and begin their war of resistance," the Soviets will be "in the vanguard to shake hands with us." It was a point of view that could only cause irritation and discomfiture in Moscow. The U.S.S.R. was then particularly intent on discouraging any unilateral CCP anti-Japanese (and anti-KMT) actions, such as the Reds' recent thrust into adjacent Shanxi province. The strategically located new northwestern Red base was uncomfortably near Russian-dominated Outer Mongolia. The Soviets feared the Chinese Communists might provoke Chiang and the Japanese into joint anti-Soviet moves.[28]

Mao, though evincing his loyalty to the Comintern, and openly praising the leaders of the internationalist (pro-Moscow) faction of the CCP, did not hesitate to criticize earlier Comintern-guided policies and agents in China that had led to disasters for the Chinese Communists in 1927.

He emphasized, in so doing, his own maverick and radical agrarian policies of that period. He castigated Michael Borodin, Stalin's chief political agent in China from 1924 to 1927, for his "rightist" stance of being
"ready to do everything to please the bourgeoisie"; Mao's remarks
seemed to have much relevance to the contemporary controversies over
Communist united front policy. Though Mao spoke of the common
ground and interests a Communist-ruled China would have with its
"brothers" in the U.S.S.R., he stressed that any future socialist "world
union" could succeed only if each member nation retained full sovereignty and could enter or leave at will. "We are certainly not fighting for
an emancipated China in order to turn the country over to Moscow!"
"Who is Moscow's 'Moscow'?" he tellingly asked Snow. The Chinese
revolution, Mao declared, was already the "key factor in world revolution"; when it achieved power, the peoples of many colonial countries
"will follow the example of China and win a similar victory of their
own." (This last was a foretaste of the later CCP call to such countries to
follow "the path of Mao Zedong.") Mao's account of his own intellectual and political development against the backdrop of dramatic revolutionary events in China during his student years in Changsha underscored the indigenous Chinese and diverse foreign influences on his
thinking before he finally embraced Marxism at age twenty-seven in
1920.[29]

The Red leader naturally had a compelling interest in portraying himself and his movement as staunchly patriotic defenders of China's national rights and interests. But at the same time the China to be saved
was a China to be transformed. Mao was determined to pursue a course
designed to ensure, first and foremost, the survival, growth, and eventual triumph of the forces of the revolution. In retrospect, Mao's historic
talks with Snow not only underlined the continuing Communist national contest with the Kuomintang but contained equally the opening
salvos in a still nascent Maoist challenge to the Stalin-controlled international Communist establishment. Snow, as the messenger, would be
branded with a permanent "mark of Mao" in Moscow's eyes.

Peg's first (and only) news of Ed came through a secret Red Army
courier (and former Tianjin student) named Wang Ling, who showed
up at her door one September day with a letter for her from Snow. Ed's
letter, written after his first weeks in northern Shaanxi, was composed in
one of the rather naive but creative "codes" the two Snows henceforth
adopted for such missives. He had begun work on his "botanical collection," he informed Peg. "There is a tremendous number of wholly new

specimens here unknown to the scientific world and the project is a much greater one than I imagined." Life there was "an austere affair"; his chief worry were the bugs, "which I am also collecting for the Smithsonian Institute: fleas, ants, spiders, bedbugs, lice, mosquitos, flies, etc. I'm being devoured by epidermal inches." But the experience was worth all that and more. "It is exhilarating in many ways but most of all because of contact with heroic young scientists working under conditions just as bad (or worse) as for me." He wished Peg were there to share the experience. "What lively conversations and discussions you could have here; the air sparkles with intelligence." But the health-conscious Peg, he felt, would have trouble with "the bugs and the filth you despise." It was probably no accident that Ed used the "scientist" symbol for the Reds.[30]

Peg instantly took Ed up on his "half-invitation" and, with the surprisingly enthusiastic encouragement of Wang Ling, prepared for the journey to Xi'an and entry to the Red district. Actually, Peg's earlier articles on the student movement had made a strongly positive impression in Bao'an. Wang Ling in fact inquired of Snow on the latter's arrival there (as noted in Ed's diary), "Why my wife had not come along. He extracted a promise from me that she would come next time." To Wang's remark to Peg that Ed would be "surprised and glad" to see her, Peg retorted, much to Wang's amusement, "No, he won't be glad, he'll only be surprised."[31]

Peg had taken over Snow's *Daily Herald* and *Sun* correspondence in his absence and used this newspaper work as her chief cover in Xi'an, where she arrived at the guest house in late September. (She asked Mac Fisher to handle Ed's newspaper duties in Peking in her absence.) Charles (Liu Ding) soon visited, sportily dressed in golfing tweeds and cap. He was much less sanguine (or enthusiastic) than Wang Ling had been on the prospects of smuggling Peg into Red territory. The situation in Xi'an had become increasingly tense and risky. Peg, however, felt her youthful appearance and college girl apparel worked in her favor. ("I was certainly harmless looking and a little vague in manner, looking upon everyone as a friend.") Charles apparently thought otherwise. Perhaps in part to mollify her and speed her departure back to Peking before Ed's soon anticipated return to Xi'an, Charles arranged an interview for her with the Young Marshal, after which she would leave for Peking where her story could be cabled to the *Herald*. The interview turned out to be a bombshell. Marshal Zhang responded to Peg's questions with his characteristic candor. Possibly incautiously, the lead sentence in her cabled report was Zhang's declaration that, "If the Chinese Communist armies can sincerely cooperate with us under the leadership of the Nanking Government to resist the common invader, the problem of China's civil war can perhaps be settled peacefully." The dispatch in the *Herald* appeared under the heading "Prefers Red Army to Japanese." As the first public statement of Zhang's stand against Nanking's anti-Red policy, it was bound to ring alarm bells in Nanking and was a prophetic foretaste of the drama to come. Thus, while chagrined at her failure to pierce the blockade, and reluctant to leave the "good story" unfolding in Xi'an, Peg nonetheless returned home with a major journalistic coup of her own. (In *Red Star,* Ed would prominently feature a Xi'an report by "Miss Nym Wales.")[32]

Meanwhile, Ed had embarked on a monthlong inspection of the "real" Red Army on the Gansu front. Traveling horseback and accompanied by a young Red "Foreign Office" functionary, the trip took him through much of Communist-ruled territory, and added further to his collection of Red Chinese portraits. Peasant hosts along the way were invariably "kind and hospitable," sharing their crude huts and meager food with the "foreign guest." Despite minor grumbling, they were unanimous in their support and appreciation for the Reds, in contrast to their experiences under White rule. In the primitive "industrial center" of Wu-ji-chen, an earnest-minded Communist engineer who had come to the northwest from Shanghai "complained" to Ed that the workers spent "entirely too much time *singing!*"—which, to Snow, epitomized "their spirit of socialist industry, even if they lacked its materials!" In his diary, Snow recorded a less welcome reception from a landlord's family. Going up to the house in search of food to buy, he found two women in rags sitting on the kitchen floor. To his food inquiry, "they replied in a surly tone, we are poor people, we have nothing." Snow's Red Army companions "explained" that such landlords buried their wealth and put on their poorest clothes when the Reds arrived. Most of them fled; generally only the smaller landlords remained.[33]

At Commander Peng Dehuai's First Front Army headquarters, the soldiers "believed they were fighting for their homes, land and country." Personal morality among the youthful peasant warriors of this unique army was puritanical. ("I think easily more than half the Red Army must be virgins.") They were fiercely and patriotically anti-Japanese, with an extraordinary spirit and morale founded on a deeply instilled "revolutionary consciousness." Snow viewed a stimulating theatrical performance by the Red Army Players and compared the experience to the

Peking scene: "a contrast of life and death, between a living force and a dead one, a young and growing culture, and an old, disillusioned, spent and diseased one," he recorded.[34]

The harrowing details recounted to Snow of Kuomintang atrocities against the civilian populations in the central-southern areas recovered from the Reds had only steeled the Red Army's resoluteness. It had "marked the matrix of their minds with a class hatred ineradicable for life." Snow was also told of instances of Red terror in central China against landlords and White officers at a time (1930) when the party had been dominated by "the Li Li-san line and the Trotskyists," but he saw no evidence of any such violence during his four-month stay with the Communists. He observed a landlord family under arrest, was aware of "several political prisoners" jailed in Bao'an, and knew ("from unrestricted inquiry") of just two civilian "counter-revolutionaries" executed in that period. "During all my stay in the Soviet districts," a diary entry stated, "I never saw a child struck or mistreated, a woman abused nor an old man offended." He had not even witnessed "a fistfight either between a soldier and soldier or between a soldier and civilian." In a subsequent interview with an official of the Red internal security forces (Political Defense Bureau), recorded in his diary but not in *Red Star,* Snow was informed that only sixty prisoners (mostly spies) were then being held in the entire Soviet district, and that in the year since the Red Army had arrived in northern Shaanxi, "not over twenty political prisoners had been executed." As to the level of political "freedom" allowed, the security chief assured Snow, "Nobody is arrested for only expressing an opinion or saying a sentence or two against the regime, but consistent exposition of anti-Soviet views is not allowed and is punishable."[35]

The story of doughty General Peng Dehuai symbolized the new "people's army": after a bitter, deprived peasant childhood, he ran away from home at sixteen to become a soldier and rose to high officer rank in the Nationalist revolutionary army in the mid-1920s. Peng became a Communist and led his troops in revolt in 1928 and joined Mao and Zhu De on their mountain stronghold. His military exploits and inspired leadership under the incredibly harsh living and fighting conditions he and his men endured were legendary. He was second only to Zhu De in command of the Red Army; the latter, in fact, was then still en route to the northwest with the Fourth-Front Army of Mao's political rival, Zhang Guotao. Snow depicted Peng as "a gay, laughter-loving man," with an "open, forthright, and undeviating" manner and speech—rare qualities among Chinese, Ed thought. Snow's extended interviews with

Peng resulted in one of the more influential sections of *Red Star*—the Red commander's outline of the military and political principles and tactics of Red partisan warfare. These tenets remained at the core of Chinese Communist strategy up to the climactic final battles of the 1946–1949 civil war. As recorded by Snow, they would become something of a text for anti-Nazi partisans in wartime Russia, and for revolutionaries in India and Southeast Asia. As Commander Peng summed it all up, "We are nothing but the fists of the people beating their oppressors." For Snow, Peng's recital of his revolutionary military experiences and successes against overwhelming odds must have seemed the living example and proof of his own growing faith in the efficacy of people's war against both foreign aggressors and domestic oppressors.[36]

On his return to Bao'an in September, Snow had final interviews with Mao and Zhou Enlai in which they transmitted to him a new and more conciliatory united front line. Based on a variety of domestic military and political considerations, it reflected as well intensifying pressures on the CCP from Moscow. By this time the Red Army had ceased offensive actions against Nanking's troops and had now officially embraced the formula of a CCP-KMT united front under a democratized, firmly anti-Japanese Nanking regime—"a national defense democratic government." But with Chiang still evidently determined to launch another major offensive against the Reds, Mao privately criticized the Comintern's "faulty understanding" of Chinese realities. An internal party directive affirmed the CCP's leading role and stressed the party's continuing intent to unite with anti-Chiang, anti-Japanese armies as the key to "pressuring Chiang" to resist Tokyo. Mao still believed that unity could be obtained "only through struggle" and "could not be bought cheaply," the historian Jerome Ch'en notes.[37]

Mao's ambivalent and skeptical approach to the possibilities of rapprochement with the Chiang government, and his views on how and on what basis it might be achieved, were candidly expressed to Snow in their September talk. The "meeting of the minds" of the two on these issues was evident from Snow's diary account. (It was actually Snow who raised doubts regarding Chiang's aims and motives, with Mao concurring.) Mao did talk of "the reunion of the two parties" as essential to effective prosecution of a resistance war and called for "a united people's democratic government" whose writ the Communists would implement in the Soviet district. And given such a truly "national salvation front," the Red Army would place itself under a unified command. But Mao added, "One thing is certain: the Red Army will continue to exist and will have the right to expand, as the army of a revolutionary base whether or not it is known as the Red Army, the Anti-Japanese Salvation Army, or something else."[38]

Pressed by Snow as to whether the CCP was now prepared to postpone "class or agrarian revolution" until national independence had been "firmly established," Mao replied in somewhat circuitous fashion. The "anti-Japanese program cannot be realized without relief to the peasants." Agrarian revolution, he observed, had been carried out in "bourgeois democracies" and was a requisite for the development of capitalism. "And the main point is that just now we are not against capitalism but imperialism." Wouldn't Chiang try first "to eliminate or narrowly limit Communism as a military force," Snow queried, and went on essentially to answer his own question. Only after achieving such an objective would the Generalissimo be willing to make some political concessions, Ed observed. This in turn would enhance, not limit, Chiang's full control of the terms of war and peace with Japan. "As I saw it," Snow's diary version continued, "Communism now offered the sole opposition to Chiang's dictatorship and as such the only force capable of challenging or modifying his power of decision on the Japanese question."

Snow reasoned that the Nanking leader would make one final effort to destroy the Red Army, or at the very least confine it to a small economically backward area that would severely restrict its expansion possibilities during a war. Chiang might then grant the Reds some sort of recognition politically. He would thereby augment his own political prestige and power, seem to "unite" the nation behind him, gain major support from the Soviet Union, and perhaps active assistance from Britain and America too. Mao "in general agreed" with Snow's analysis but added that after "testing" the Red Army in battle again, Chiang would "perhaps conclude" it was best to give up the ten-year anti-Red struggle and join hands against Japan. A new attack on the Reds would only result in strengthening them militarily and politically. In the end, Snow summed up Mao's view, Chiang "would be obliged to submit to the United Front with his own role minimized therein." The CCP, however, was stronger politically than at any time since 1927 "and destined during the national liberation struggle to reach a maximum never before attained." In the current negotiations with Nanking, Mao declared, the CCP was ready to "cooperate" in the unlikely case that Chiang could be "persuaded" to take on Japan. But if the Generalissimo preferred civil war, "the Red Army was also ready to receive him."[39]

In a follow-up talk with Zhou Enlai, the latter told Snow that he saw "little real hope or possibility" of reforging the mid-1920s union with the Kuomintang. Too much had changed. There was now a strong Red Army, a large Soviet area, and a Communist party with ten years of fighting experience and an independent status. The Communists "will no more give up this Army and the Soviet district than will Chiang Kaishek relinquish his hegemony of the Nanking government." Chiang's current negotiations with the Reds, he stated, "are part of his strategy to destroy it, or minimize it as much as possible." Even as a new stage of CCP-KMT unity was finally threshed out the following year, Snow himself never really abandoned the views he had expressed (and heard) in these interviews—nor for that matter did Mao. As delineated in the final pages of *Red Star,* at a time of proclaimed amity between the two parties, it would cause problems in certain Communist circles.[40]

As Snow waited in Bao'an for a suitable moment to slip back into the Nanking-controlled "White world," he worked on his notes, and relaxed among his new Red friends. There were tennis foursomes, and Snow-initiated "high-stakes" (in matchsticks) poker sessions with the Communist elite, occasionally including Mao. But with Nanking troops gradually replacing Marshal Zhang's Dongbei forces along the Red front, it became imperative to leave while a friendly outlet still remained. When Snow finally departed on October 12, the Red hierarchy and cadets turned out to see him off, as they had welcomed him four months earlier. And again, the late-sleeping Mao was the sole exception.

The experience had been an "exhilarating" one. Snow had met the revolution and its revolutionaries in the full bloom and hope of youth. The "little devils" with the Red Army seemed the perfect metaphor: "the incarnation of the spirit of the army—boundless energy, the endless stream of youth, the eternal hope rising anew in China." Snow had felt himself in the company of valiant Davids who, despite their losses and privations, stood confidently ready to take on the Goliath forces arrayed against them. All good things seemed possible and attainable. A genuine bond had been forged with these "undevious and scientific-minded" Chinese with whom he had been as comfortable "as if I were with some of my own countrymen." On leavetaking, "I felt that I was not going home, but leaving it."[41]

There was still one trauma to endure on arrival in Xi'an—the disappearance of his precious bag of notebooks, diaries, films, and documents. Somehow, inadvertently, it had been thrown off his Dongbei truck at an ordinance depot north of Xi'an. At Snow's insistence, the driver immediately turned back while Ed waited in agonized suspense for the bag to be found and brought back to the city. And none too soon. All roads were blocked the very next morning, as the Generalissimo flew into Xi'an on a surprise visit to complete preparations for a "final" assault on the Reds, and to staunch the powerful anti–civil war, anti-Japanese currents in that supposed stronghold of the Bandit Suppression campaign. (Snow suffered a mini-reprise of this experience in 1965, when flying home to Switzerland from a China trip. His briefcase with his China notes and interviews had slid beneath his seat to the rear of the plane. Frantic that he might have left it behind somewhere, Snow joyfully hugged the stewardess who eventually located it.)[42]

While in Xi'an, Snow met up with Smedley, who was staying at the famous Tang-era hot springs resort at Lintong—the scene of the Generalissimo's "arrest" that December. The two had dinner at the home of Dr. Herbert Wunsch, a German dentist and CCP contact. There they had a happy reunion from Shanghai days with the prominent leftist writer Ding Ling. Arrested in 1933 by the Kuomintang, she was now living under cover at Wunsch's home before breaking through to the Red district to the north. (In a strange mischance, on the day of the Xi'an Incident Dr. Wunsch would be shot down by anti-Chiang soldiers of the mutinous Northwest Army as he tried to enter the Xi'an guest house.) A few days later Ed turned up at the door of his Peking home "grinning foolishly behind a grizzled beard and looking like the cat that had swallowed the canary," Helen recalled in her inimitable, slightly disparaging style. He plucked from one of his many bundles "an old grey cap with a red star on its faded front," put it on, and pranced about the room "pleased as Punch" at his coup while demanding of the cook fresh eggs, milk, and coffee.[43]

A quarter century later, on returning home from his initial visit to the People's Republic of China, Snow thought back to his pioneering 1936 journey:

I had gone to the Northwest before any other Westerner and at a dark moment in history for the Chinese Communists as well as for all China. I had found hope for the nation in that small band of survivors of the Long March and formed a favorable impression of them [the "better" people] and their policies of that day against my own background of seven years of life in China. I admired their courage, their selflessness, their single-minded determination to save China (under their leadership) and the outstanding ability, the practical political sense, and personal honesty of their high Commanders.

To a certain extent Snow had become a vicarious extension of their cause, which he saw as China's cause at its best. Though "I was not an active participant in the revolution, I could not deny some responsibility. The words I wrote had helped bring others to action."[44]

Thus as Snow surfaced again in Peking, against a backdrop of fast-moving, climactic events, his words would themselves become factors in a many-sided and not always clearly discernible drama.

PART 3

Red Star over China, and Elsewhere

CHAPTER 9

Writing and Making History

Snow had planned to hole up for a while after his return from the northwest and quietly get out his films and articles (oddly, through Japanese-held Dalian) without censorship problems. But rumors of his "execution" by the Reds, carried widely by the wire services, forced him to surface almost immediately. He divulged the main facts of his trip at a hastily called Peking press conference at the American embassy; his story, published abroad, was reported back to China and throughout the Far East. The next weeks and months were filled with frenetic activity. Ed rushed to develop his films and send them off to his agent in New York. Aside from their monetary and journalistic value, they were incontrovertible proof of his journey, which Nanking publicists were now calling a "hoax." Peg had "never been more thrilled" than to view the prints of the Red leaders. While Ed prepared his formal Mao interviews for speedy publication, she pored over his notebooks and spent days "happily" captioning and annotating the photos.[1]

The Mao interviews appeared in Powell's *Review* in November; with its wide readership among China's business, professional, and intellectual circles, it added to the groundswell for national unity. The *Herald* received the interviews in London just in time to run them together with the sensational news of Chiang's December 12 kidnapping-arrest in Xi'an. *Life* paid a thousand dollars for seventy-five of Snow's photos and featured many of them in two prominent photographic-essay displays early in 1937. A series of some thirty articles, the core of *Red Star,* followed for the *Herald.* The paper promoted him to chief Far Eastern correspondent, and he covered the first three years of the China war for the

Herald. Asia ran six of his *Red Star*–related pieces during 1937, and in an article for the *Post,* Snow made use of the title he had once considered for his book ("I Went to Red China"). His news, he wrote the *Herald* in February 1937, "is causing a mild sensation here in the Orient."[2]

Snow sent Ambassador Johnson a copy of the Mao interviews, which the latter forwarded to Washington. It was an example of the mediating part Snow increasingly tried to play between China's revolutionaries and American policymakers. Johnson's rather snide references to "Mr. Mao Tse-tung" was an early sign of the frustrations the journalist would encounter in such efforts. (Roosevelt, with whom Snow established a personal relationship from 1942 until F. D. R.'s death in 1945, appeared to be the exception.) America's wartime foreign service officers in China fared worse for their efforts when they tried to alert Washington to the decisive role the Chinese Communists would play in China's future. Snow's ability to get through to his readers, especially in *Red Star,* would be quite another matter.[3]

The Xi'an Incident of December 12 put a world spotlight on the very forces and issues that were at the heart of Snow's recent experiences and writing. The forcible detention of the Generalissimo, who had again flown up to Xi'an to put an end to the anomalous situation there, was to be a crucial turning point for China despite its strangely anticlimactic ending. For Snow, this exercise in "military persuasion" by the Northeast and Northwest armies of the Young Marshal and General Yang Hucheng, respectively, substantiated his belief that only maximum pressure could force Chiang to alter course. In an eight-point declaration issued by the Young Marshal the generals called for an end to civil war and for united resistance to Japan under a reorganized, broadly representative Nanking government, guarantees of democratic rights, and release of all political prisoners.[4]

The Communists, after some initial rejoicing at Chiang's seizure, soon took a more conciliatory tone (evidently with some pressure from Moscow) and used the situation to press their united front proposals on him. At the invitation of the Young Marshal, the astute Zhou Enlai led a Communist delegation to Xi'an for direct talks with the captive Chinese leader. (Zhou had worked closely with Chiang in the united front days of the 1920s.) In the end the Generalissimo was released on Christmas Day to nationwide acclaim. The Young Marshal (against Zhou's advice) voluntarily accompanied Chiang back to Nanking in the reverse role of a penitent. Though "pardoned" by Chiang after sentencing by a military court, Marshal Zhang remained in custody of the Generalissimo and his successors, on the mainland and then in Taiwan. It was the Young Marshal's final quixotic act of patriotic, if naive, loyalty. There were no publicly announced or signed agreements at Xi'an, and Chiang in fact soon removed or reorganized the rebellious forces in the northwest and imposed control by Nanking troops along the front with the Reds. The latter, on their part, had utilized the crisis to expand their holdings and in January 1937 had occupied Yan'an, which became their famous wartime capital. Nevertheless, Chiang's anti-Communist crusade was ended, and with much theatrical sound effects and political posturing, the two sides inched gradually toward reconciliation during the spring months of 1937. Statements on renewed CCP-KMT cooperation were issued separately by the Communist party and the Generalissimo in late September, more than two months after Japan's attack in July.[5]

Snow, completely immersed in writing his articles and book, had arranged with the *Herald* for Jim Bertram to cover the Xi'an events in his stead. Under the tightened security and travel restrictions during the crisis, the young New Zealander took a circuitous route from Peking that brought him to Xi'an two days after Chiang's release. Snow had entrusted Bertram with a bulging sealed envelope to pass on to the Communists (presumably for Mao). "Keep it in your inside pocket," Ed advised him. "We don't want any of Chiang's Blue Shirts reading that little lot." Fearing a police search at one point in his travels, Bertram hurriedly burned Snow's letter in a moment of pure panic. Bertram stayed on in Xi'an, where he and Agnes Smedley, who had arrived there before Chiang's arrest, made daily radio broadcasts to the outside world that did much to counter the highly slanted version of the Xi'an affair then being circulated by Nanking. There was still a tension-ridden atmosphere in the city, and the northwestern revolt did not wind down until February. Radical younger coup leaders then escaped to the Red lines; General Yang Hucheng (who had taken an adamant and more threatening line toward Chiang) was eventually arrested by the Nationalists and held prisoner until his murder in Chungking by KMT special agents just before the capture of that city by the Reds in 1949.[6]

Snow's reactions to the Xi'an developments were expressed in an important talk he gave in January 1937, when the situation in the northwest remained fluid and unresolved. Ed, as we know, never enjoyed such speechmaking and lacked a flair for it—compounded in this case by one of his bad head colds. But he was speaking on a topic (the Reds and the northwest) on which he now had unrivaled personal experience, and he could deal with the Xi'an affair with special insight and some authority. He gave his talk at the monthly dinner meeting of the men's forum of the Peking Union Church. The group represented a cross-section of the foreign community, including members of the diplomatic corps; the gatherings, held at the Peking Hotel, were black-tie affairs. It was far indeed from a radical setting. Ed insisted on wearing his favorite Shanghai-tailored Harris tweed outfit, asserting both personal comfort and independence. His lengthy presentation was a great success. Many in the "intensely interested" audience of some two hundred "nearly turned handsprings over him afterwards," Peg exuberantly reported. The chairman of the meeting, "an old diehard" from the British embassy, "announced afterward that so far as he was concerned the Reds could march on Peking any day if they can do all the things Ed related in his talk!" Snow's talk, forwarded to Randall Gould, was published in full in Gould's *Shanghai Evening Post and Mercury* in early February. (Ed worried a bit that his disclaimer to be examining the background to the current situation "from the viewpoint of the Chinese Communists" would be overlooked.)[7]

To Snow, the Xi'an events marked the direct clash of two opposing currents in China. The Nanking regime represented one—"Rightist, fearful of any mass movement whatever, opposed to democracy, opposed to any compromise with the Communists or any opposition which can threaten its dictatorial hegemony of power." On the world scene, the Kuomintang leaned toward the fascist powers, with an extremist minority seeking joint action with Japan first against the Chinese Reds and then against the U.S.S.R. As for the other side, its position was best summed up in the Young Marshal's eight-point declaration. It found its support "among the anti-Japanese armies, the national patriotic associations, the student movement, all opposition progressive political parties, the Red Army, etc." It was aligned with "the worldwide democratic front" of the western democracies and the Soviet Union.[8]

Given these views, Snow was shocked and incensed at Moscow's reaction to Chiang's detention at Xi'an. Apparently anxious to dissociate the Soviets from any hint of involvement in the Xi'an revolt, and to affirm support for Nanking, both *Pravda* and *Izvestia,* the Soviet party and government newspapers respectively, harshly condemned the act. In their eyes, it undermined the growing national unity under Chiang and "objectively" aided and abetted the Japanese aggressors. In a clear statement of the crux of Moscow's China policy, *Izvestia* declared, "In as much as the Nanking government conducts the policy of resistance against Japanese aggressors, the united popular front struggle against Japan should be regarded by all its participants not as a front against Nanking but as a front together with Nanking." Snow, in a memo he penned at the time, referred to this statement as an "observation which is no doubt made possible by the long-range field glasses in *Izvestia's* office but which is imperceptible to the naked eye of the observer on the spot."[9]

The Soviet stance could not be attributed to any "misunderstanding" or ignorance of the facts, Snow felt. He himself had sold to the *Tass* office in Peking copies of the set of articles he was writing for the *Herald* and the *Sun,* and he had confidentially briefed *Tass* on the cooperation between the Reds and the Young Marshal (as he had briefed two military attachés in Peking, the Soviet and the American [Colonel Stilwell]). Peg Snow, in her impassioned and best "prime mover" fashion, had immediately taken off for the *Tass* office (dragging a reluctant David Yu along), in a futile effort to hold up distribution of the Russian press materials. In *Red Star,* Snow would pointedly write that the Japanese "had met their masters in propaganda in Moscow's press." In the latter's denunciations of Marshal Zhang and their "hosannas" to Chiang Kai-shek, he added, the Soviet media had "invented a story . . . so antipodal to the facts that even the most reactionary press in China had not dared to suggest it, out of fear of ridicule." It was but one such "anti-Soviet" remark in the book not calculated to endear Snow to Moscow.[10]

Snow much later wrote that this had been "one of the personal experiences which would convince me that as long as Russia made Comintern policy it would always and everywhere be made first of all in the strategic interest of the U.S.S.R., as the Kremlin saw it—or, more baldly, Soviet Russian communism first, and international communism second." He might have added that the Soviets expected the international movement to adhere to these same Moscow-first principles. Snow also revealed at that time that he had been told by Madame Sun in 1937 that Mao had flown into "a rage" on receipt of a telegraphed Moscow "order," soon after Chiang's capture at Xi'an, to release the Generalissimo. Snow's opinion of the Soviet response to the Xi'an crisis reflected his always ambivalent, if not contradictory, attitude toward the U.S.S.R. For Snow, the Russians were the major antifascist power and a still potentially dynamic revolutionary force in world affairs. But his independent leftism made him bridle at the idea of Stalinist overlordship of the Chinese Communist movement. "I am dubious about [the Reds'] relationship to Moscow (especially since the recent mass executions)," he had written Ambassador Johnson in early 1937.[11]

Ironically enough, the Xi'an Incident provided the lever that opened the way for the united front under Chiang that the Kremlin had so assiduously sought. It also enabled the CCP to reach agreements with the KMT that included the minimal guarantees Mao had stipulated to Snow in Bao'an for such a united front. In the aura of conciliation in the early stage of the China war, and with the Generalissimo at the height of his political prestige and popularity, all sides—Nanking, the Chinese Communists, and Moscow, seemed in relative harmony. Longer-term issues and conflicts were largely in abeyance. Snow's book, in which he looked beyond and beneath surface amity, would be an irritant in this respect— not least in its provocative but prophetic title.

Snow showed his northwest movie film and photos, and bits of his *Red Star* manuscript, to selected groups of Yanjing students, while his Mao interviews in Powell's *Review* were translated and published in the student newspaper. Thus inspired and informed, a student group (with the help of a map drawn up by Ed) made its way to Yan'an in the spring of 1937, posing along the way as a vacationing college youth group. The students talked with Mao and other leaders, rode horseback with Smedley, and practiced shooting. Back in Peking, they in turn passed on their experiences to other students, some of whom undertook a similar trip. Snow thereby had an early impact on what would become a migration of many educated youth from the northern China cities to the Red areas, stirred by the national resistance stance of the Communists.[12]

Snow was also anxious to get his account to a wide Chinese audience as quickly as possible. It was all in keeping with his growing role as engaged participant in as well as reporter of China events. A student from the Northeast named Wang Fushi (known then as Fullsea Wang), who had studied at Yanjing and knew the Snows, supplied the answer to Snow's quest. His father had worked closely with the Young Marshal in Peking and ran a newspaper there financed by Zhang. The Snows rushed material to young Wang, who not only did much of the translating into Chinese but served as editor and publisher. Through his father's newspaper plant, a book of some three hundred pages, complete with maps and photos, was secretly printed in five thousand copies by March 1937. With the innocuous title of "Foreign Journalists' Impressions of the Northwest," it included much of (and in some instances more than) what later appeared in *Red Star* plus Snow's men's forum talk, and related materials from Western and Communist sources. The book, appearing in the post-Xi'an climate of uncertainty and confusion, circulated widely and did much to acquaint urban educated circles with the

Communist message—particularly through the Mao interviews, and Snow's analysis of the Xi'an affair. Snow later noted that this early partial version of his book (which made its underground appearance many months before the publication of *Red Star* in England and America) "provided countless Chinese with the first authentic information about Chinese Communists." Mao himself soon received a copy, presented personally to him by Wang Fushi, who went to Yan'an, as Helen Snow's interpreter, shortly after the book's publication.[13]

A Chinese translation of the regular English edition of *Red Star* was just as rapidly (and covertly) produced in Shanghai by February 1938, and again with Snow's active cooperation. He was then back in Shanghai and had given a copy of the newly arrived London edition to a member of a group of anti-Japanese, Marxist intellectuals who met secretly each week as the "Tuesday forum," in the Shanghai foreign concession area. (Chinese Shanghai had already fallen to the Japanese after a lengthy battle.) The forum group of twelve, apparently with the approval of the Communist party underground, took up the translation project as a collective task. They raised the necessary funds among themselves and by selling tickets to prospective readers to be redeemed when the book appeared. The group created their own publishing house, collectively translated the work, and rushed it into print with the cooperation of patriotic printing workers. Snow provided a special preface, in which he waived his copyright for this edition. The book, under the title *Xixing Man Ji* (Journey to the west), went through four printings by November 1938 and was widely circulated in occupied and free China and in Communist-controlled areas. It remained the standard Chinese version of *Red Star* for the next decade. Strangely enough, Snow's classic was considerably more accessible to Chinese readers before 1949 than for the quarter century following the Communist victory.[14]

The Snows took on yet another project in the months preceding the outbreak of the Sino-Japanese war in July 1937, designed also to advance united front policies along the lines of the Young Marshal's Xi'an declaration. An intensely earnest-minded American, J. Spencer Kennard, visited the Snows one January day in 1937, with an offer of one thousand dollars gold from the Friends Society (Quakers) to found a journal of "applied Christian ethics," with Snow as editor. Though fully involved in writing his book, Snow found this an offer he couldn't refuse, especially with Peg ready as always to take charge of yet another China "missionary" endeavor, and be the "active Snow" in the venture. An editorial board was quickly assembled, including a few liberal Yanjing professors,

Chinese and American, together with the two Snows, and Ida Pruitt, a China-born missionary social worker and writer who would become a major figure in another Snow undertaking—the Indusco movement. The Snows corralled John Leaning, a coolly sophisticated but strongly antifascist young Englishman then passing through Peking, as editor. There was a total clash of personalities between Leaning and Kennard, which added fuel to the usually argumentative free-for-alls of board meetings. Attendance at these meetings, Ed later observed, "was worth the price [$150] of a share" in the joint enterprise. The journal was baptized *democracy* (with a small *d*), and the editors quickly dispensed with Kennard's originally stipulated "Christian ethics" subtitle. Only five issues of the semimonthly appeared—from May 1 to July 8, the last dated the day after the Japanese attack on northern China and Peking, which ended the journal's brief life. Yet in those few months it had provided another valuable channel for spreading excerpts from Snow's *Red Star* (including his portrait chapter on Mao), and for much discussion of the state and fate of democracy in China and the world. J. Leighton Stuart, president of Yanjing University, contributed his thoughts on the outlook for democracy in China (a sharp contrast to one written by Peg), and also an "appreciation" of Chiang Kai-shek. The predominant motifs of the journal were anti-Japanese, antifascist, and pro-united front.

"To our astonishment," Snow wrote in 1940, "the magazine proved very popular, and subscriptions were coming in nicely when we had to fold up." Hubert Liang, the journalism chair at Yanjing and a member of the editorial board, wrote to Peg decades later, with some hyperbole, that the magazine had been "an immediate, sensational success, taking China's intellectual world by storm." Kennard and others made efforts to revive the journal in 1939–1940. He again approached Snow, who took the position that the initiative should now come from liberal elements within the country. With China now at war, there was "nominally a United Front, nominally the right of free speech and organization. If the Chinese liberals will not now demand and fight for their right to democratic processes, no amount of foreign agitation will get very far." While these remarks reflected Snow's jaundiced view of Nationalist-ruled wartime China, they did not really jibe with his continuous firm support for, and personal practice of, progressive foreign intervention in China's affairs. The revival idea remained stillborn.[15]

All these activities further undercut Snow's standing with the Nanking authorities. His post-Bao'an writings had aroused the ire of the Chinese government, Ambassador Johnson informed him. Similar news had come from "other quarters," Ed replied to the American envoy in February 1937. In answer to a somewhat threatening letter from the foreign ministry's director of intelligence and publicity, Snow rejected the charge of "propaganda" leveled at his work. For the real thing, he dryly pointed to the lurid (and manifestly false) tales on the Xi'an affair that had been circulated by the government news agency. His reports on the Reds, Snow told the official, could help provide the facts and understanding so vital to bringing about "a strong, united and effective China." As an American journalist, Snow rather loftily concluded, "I have a right (as a Chinese journalist has in America) to publish the truth as I find it."[16]

The Nationalist regime specifically banned a lengthy list of Snow reports (in Chinese translation) on the Reds. And after Snow returned to the States in 1941, the Generalissimo apparently personally directed the Chinese ministry of information carefully to monitor Snow's published pieces in America, and to funnel refutations of his "false propaganda" to "friendly" American media outlets. In February 1944, American Ambassador Gauss reported from Chungking to the secretary of state, the "opinion" of Chinese observers that "the Generalissimo and many high ranking Kuomintang officials are convinced that the favorable publicity received by the Chinese Communists in the past resulted from (in their view, the distorted) picture drawn of conditions in that area by Edgar Snow." Gauss's observations referred to a projected trip to Yan'an by foreign correspondents, reluctantly agreed to by the Kuomintang. The ambassador shrewdly added that "Kuomintang critics" thought the trip "may result in the Kuomintang having to face 'eleven Edgar Snows' instead of just one." Yet, as we will see, in the early wartime united front years the Nationalist-Snow relationship was, at least overtly, a more compatible one.[17]

Snow faced other, more personal, complications and interruptions as he worked on his book in the winter and spring of 1937. He fainted one March day from a kidney stone attack, and was taken to the Peking Union Medical College hospital where the stone was removed by cystoscope—without anesthesia. Infection set in, entailing a lengthy and painful convalescence. He would be plagued for the remainder of his life by recurring kidney infections and urinary tract problems. Ed had his operation on the same day that proofs for the inaugural issue of *democracy* arrived at the Snow house. Peg was a bit nettled that Ed wasn't around to oversee the unfamiliar task of making up the dummy for the print shop. She and Leaning managed, however; they dropped it off at the printers and only then proceeded on to the hospital to see how Ed was faring.[18]

Peg had worked closely with Ed in transcribing his northwestern notes and was particularly intrigued by the life stories he had brought back, most especially by the Mao autobiography. "As soon as I read Mao's story," she subsequently recounted, "I knew I would have to go to the Red areas to write down some more of them." For her, these personal narratives were "the best sources of history" on the Communists. According to her various accounts, Helen Snow argued vehemently with Ed to keep Mao's autobiography intact for his book. Snow, she asserted, felt the many Chinese names and details might be too much for his readers and was at first inclined to cut and rewrite much of it. Mao's story, of course, did become a classic centerpiece of *Red Star,* and an enduring and indispensable source on Mao's early life, education, and radicalization. The Communist leader was himself a talented communicator and could relate his life in pithy, colorful, and personal terms. His narrative was thus exceptional not only as a paramount primary document but as an engrossing read, and Snow surely appreciated this. He did lighten it a bit by deleting some of the Chinese nomenclature.[19]

But the debate between the two Snows, at least as Helen told it, did illustrate their very different writing philosophies, and perhaps talents as well. Her overriding concern was didactic—delivering the message, "boring though it might be to some potential readers." Her China books and monographs contain rich and valuable source material on the Chinese Communist movement and its protagonists, but they did not yield "the one good book" of wide popular appeal she always aspired to write. Yet when she moved away from doctrinal-political instructive material to a more personal vein, her writing took on considerable verve and color with sharply etched characterizations. Possibly poetry has been her most effective literary mode, including a talent for Ogden Nash–style versifying. (The most absorbing and "literary" of her China books is the intimate and wrenching story she took down in Yan'an in 1937 of a Korean Communist active in the Chinese revolution in the 1920s and 1930s.) "It's a kind of do-gooder public service," she remarked of the hurried writing (for immediate Chinese translation) of her *Inside Red China* in 1938, "just giving out information, not being a writer." Her work, she observed, "was an example of plain facts plainly explained." Her painstakingly recorded and cherished Yan'an notebooks gave her "an exaggerated sense of every small detail and scrap of paper. . . . History was sacred to me." *Red Star,* she readily acknowledged, had "charm, humor, the sense of discovery, and suspense. And it is written to make the story more attractive." She considered her own work to be "medicinal." While Ed could communicate, "I can diagnose and prescribe."[20]

When David Yu (now evidently able to surface more safely in the new political climate) informed Helen that a major party conclave was to meet in Yan'an at the beginning of May, she dropped everything else and prepared for the trip to Xi'an and Yan'an. It would be a rare chance to gather many additional accounts from important Communist figures Snow had not met. She was particularly intent on collecting material about revolutionary activists who were women. Ed, still finishing up *Red Star* and slowly recovering from his painful kidney ordeal, watched her pack for the journey with mixed feelings. It would be an opportunity for her not only to do a book of her own, but to obtain additional photos and updated information for his book. And he always supported her journalistic and literary endeavors. (When Peg's *Inside Red China* was accepted by Doubleday the following year, Ed wrote her from Hankou that he thought the book "will at once establish your name and reputation." He signed off, "With salutations to the Great Nym, from Mr. Wales.") Yet there were the worrisome health risks and other dangers she would face. And he would be left to fend for himself—with a retinue of servants, of course. Offsetting Peg's absence, though, might be the benefit of a less frenetic setting in which to do his work. All in all, it was an example of their supportive-competitive partnership in action. In a note to Ed, written on the way to Xi'an, she gave some long-distance medical advice-commands on diet and rest, "as you look very thin now and bad generally (and act worse!)."[21]

In Xi'an Peg encountered a situation very different from what Ed had found the year before. Nanking troops had taken full control, with the Young Marshal's forces dispersed elsewhere in China. "The whole atmosphere here is very depressing," she wrote Ed. Despite the united front negotiations then underway, the local authorities were intent on preventing journalists, especially another Snow, from entering the Red districts. The police were "gunning for you," she warned Ed, advising him to stay away from the city. Under constant police surveillance, Helen was "nervous, frightened, but resolute." "What an incredibly horrible country," she told Ed. "Thank God for extraterritoriality among these feudal-savages." "Be sure to get your book out immediately and don't waste any more time," she enjoined him, "because I'm leaving China after this experience!" But despite all the hyperbole, she intrepidly managed a celebrated midnight "escape" from the first-floor window of her room at the foreign guest house. With the unlikely connivance of an adventuresome China-born young American Standard Oil man, she slipped out of the city at dawn in a "borrowed" military car and reached the Communist lines at Sanyuan north of Xi'an on April 30. The American, Kempton Fitch, was a member of a pronouncedly pro-Nationalist missionary family. But, "political opinions aside," he wrote Snow after depositing Helen at the Red Army outpost, "a lone American always sticks up for another lone American, and it seems that a young man always assists a lady in distress." As to whether Helen was, in his estimation, one of those women who "make the grade in a bit of adventure," he observed in somewhat inverted gallantry, "your wife is not one of these, if such exist, and should not be allowed to roam around without the gentle hand of restraint ever at her elbow."[22]

Helen was deferentially received, both in her own right and more specially as Ed's wife. Snow was "famous" in the Red areas, George Hatem had earlier informed Ed, while Agnes Smedley wrote Snow from Yan'an shortly before Helen's arrival that "They ['our comrades'] all like you, admire you—both your work and your personality." Mao and Zhu De paid a joint courtesy call on Helen soon after her appearance in the Red capital. (Ed himself had failed to meet Zhu the previous year; the Red commander had arrived at the northwestern base in late 1936, after Ed's return to Peking.) In the press of events, however, Mao showed considerably less urgency in meeting with her than had been the case with Snow the previous year. Helen had planned on a relatively short stay, but it was well over four months before she was able to leave. It was a tense and critical period in united front negotiations, and she had to bide her time into the summer waiting for definitive political pronouncements, and for appointments with Mao and other leaders. The onset of war in July, and torrential rains that made travel impossible, further delayed her departure until mid-September. In due course she had her talks with the Red leaders and their surrogates and assiduously collected dozens of autobiographies. Most of the latter were eventually published by Stanford. She returned with enough material for four books, and for much other writings over succeeding decades. "I've been a prisoner of these notebooks for twenty-three years," she wrote when compiling her Yenan (Yan'an) notebooks in 1961.[23]

The remarkable and rather intimidating Agnes Smedley was also in Yan'an during Helen's stay, and they left together for Xi'an by horseback with a Red Army entourage. Helen had a gingerly relationship with this moody, often charming, and demanding woman. A painful back injury Smedley suffered in August intensified the problems; she had to be carried by stretcher for much of the ten-day journey. Smedley's intense feminism had stirred up a minor storm among the socially conservative Communist wives in Yan'an. The dance lessons she gave and the square dance parties she organized did not help. These functions attracted the male hierarchy and the new wave of young people from the cities, but not the wives. Smedley later told Snow about a particularly bizarre and violent quarrel involving Smedley, Mao's wife, He Zizhen, Mao himself, and a beautiful young actress called Lily Wu (Wu Guangwei). Wu had come to Yan'an early in the year and became a confidante and interpreter for Smedley. She made quite a splash among the men, including Mao, who got into the habit of visiting Smedley and Wu (who had adjoining cave accommodations) for conversation, and exchanges of poetry with the educated and modern-minded Chinese actress. One night He Zizhen showed up and bitterly berated Mao, accusing him of a romantic liaison with Wu in which Smedley had colluded. In the upshot of all this Wu was sent off to the war fronts, He Zizhen ended up in the Soviet Union, later divorced by Mao, who then married another young actress, Jiang Qing. As for Smedley, her departure, whether or not it amounted to banishment, undoubtedly caused much relief in Yan'an.[24]

Smedley took up other, probably equally intractable if less nettlesome, causes in Yan'an and enlisted Snow's help from Peking in dealing with them. Bothered by hordes of possibly plague-carrying rats in the cave at night (as was Helen, who woke everyone in her compound with screams whenever a rat was caught in a trap set under her cot), she undertook a one-woman rat extermination campaign. As Snow told the story, "Soon after her arrival [in Yan'an], she wrote to ask me to ship from Peking, where I was living, *2,000 rat traps!* . . . I sent in a suitcaseful at a time, whenever I heard of a student or journalist going in that direction, until I exhausted Peking's supply of rat traps." But this crusade also came up against some Yan'an social realities. "I distributed [the traps] free," Smedley subsequently ruefully reported, "but soon I found they were being sold in the market!" She followed this up with further urgent requests to Snow for hybrid corn seed, and literature on chemical farming, public hygiene, medicine, birth control, and much else. He was unable to find a phonograph she wanted for her dance sessions, but she procured one from Shanghai together with worn records of American folk songs. Snow related all this after Smedley's death in England in 1950 and the burial of her ashes in Peking. He ended, "I suddenly seemed to see the evil rats scurrying for cover" and "hear, above the sweet fragrance of the noble mimosas [of Peking], the faint music of an old phonograph record grinding out, 'She'll be coming round the mountain when she comes.' "[25]

Compared to this older stalwart revolutionary, Helen Snow must have appeared (misleadingly) as something of an ingenue. "Peg Snow," her admirer Jim Bertram has remarked, "was surely the only foreigner to make a Red Army uniform look chic." Normally very thin, she contracted dysentery, ate only sparingly of a few "safe" foods, and left Yan'an weighing less than a hundred pounds. (When finally back in Peking she needed a spell in the hospital to recover, in a room at the German Hospital that came complete with a picture of Hitler on the wall.) Ed had sent some care parcels of American canned and packaged foods for her, Hatem, and Smedley, but only one parcel arrived, catching up with them on the way back to Xi'an. "I can't imagine where you get the idea that 'everything' can be bought here, or that when I climbed out of a window I was able to take a truckload of food with me," she testily wrote Ed in late June. But since she never paid much attention to what she ate, "except for starving it doesn't bother me in the least."[26]

Many of Peg's letters to Snow from Yan'an (carried out by courier and mailed to a secret mailbox in Peking) apparently did not come through at the time, adding to Ed's worries about her and to his uncertainty and consequent irritation as to when she would be returning. She did send out many of her notebooks and films and a letter brought back from Yan'an by a visiting group of American Asian specialists, including Owen Lattimore. Ed was able to include some of her photos in *Red Star*. When she left the Red capital, traveling on foot or horseback, Helen carried all her remaining notebooks (without covers) in an improvised belt under her coat.

The Communists would have preferred that Snow come to Yan'an for briefings on the party's now much more conciliatory line toward Chiang and the Kuomintang. In lieu of this, they pressed him through Helen to take account of these changes in his virtually completed book. Snow had already been obliged to revise the final chapters to reflect post-Xi'an developments, he informed Helen in early June. He worried that the trend of events was undermining the main thrust and significance of his book. He remained skeptical on prospects for democratic changes under the Kuomintang, was deeply suspicious of Chiang's motives and plans, and felt, as he acidly expressed it to Helen, that the Reds had "[thrown] in the sponge." The "obvious meaning" of the Xi'an Incident was now clear, he confided to her. In effect, the Communists had conceded national leadership to the Kuomintang "for possibly many years to come, that, and nothing more. It weakens the whole structure of my book very much, but that is nothing." Chiang's "decisive" and "perhaps unavoidable" victory was now "abundantly manifest."

In reply, Helen warned, Ed would "make a lot of enemies if you say [in the book] what you did in your letter about the united front position here, and it may be very harmful for them [the Reds] also." Such criticisms were now considered "Trotskyist," she added. "The Communists are giving up everything to organize a legal movement in the white districts," she continued, "and reestablish the CCP in working order for a mass movement there along purely political lines under the democratic slogan, etc., etc." In essence, Helen was delineating the position advanced by the influential internationalist wing of the party led by Wang Ming. (Later in the year, Wang flew into Yan'an from Moscow and was effusively greeted at the airstrip by the entire party high command.) Mao would in due time counter this line, which Maoist historians castigated in terms reminiscent of Snow's 1937 views. Actually, it was Zhou Enlai and not Mao who was pushing Snow to delete anti-Chiang remarks and anecdotes confided to Ed the previous year. Mao apparently shared his friend Snow's apprehensions about Chiang's intentions. In a confidential letter to Ed, shortly before Japan's attack, he expressed "anxiety and dissatisfaction" over negotiations with the Kuomintang.[27]

Tell Zhou "not to worry," Ed wrote Helen on July 26; he had instructed his publisher to delete the entire Zhou chapter from Red Star. "Don't send me any more notes about people reneging on their stories to me, as it's much too late to do anything more about it." Snow did use some Zhou Enlai biographical material (shorn of anti-Chiang barbs) in a Post article he was then doing. In it he highlighted Zhou's role in securing the Generalissimo's release at Xi'an and noted that he was once again working with Chiang as he had done in the mid-1920s. Snow, however, did not refrain from making his usual point that Chiang's obsessive anti-Red campaigns had allowed Japan to take over large chunks of China.[28]

In his late July letter to Helen, Snow also brought up "the purgation in Moscow," suggesting to her that she question the Yan'an people on their "attitude toward this, and what it means, and why it doesn't shake their confidence, and why this couldn't happen in China, etc." Snow's caustic queries reflected not only his current annoyance with the Chinese Reds, but his distaste for the Stalinist dictatorship and his distrust of the CCP's Moscow connections. Yet Snow remained convinced that the U.S.S.R. was Japan's primary target, and that the Soviets would become a key player in deciding the China conflict. No one in either the

Communist party or the Kuomintang "really believes that the war against Japan can be won without Russian help," Snow wrote in his November 1937 *Post* article. "Everything in this struggle depends on whether or not Russia is drawn in." Readers of this book should keep in mind that the optimism Snow had felt in 1936 for a successful Chinese war of resistance had been predicated on his vision of a broadly based revolutionary anti-Japanese coalition spearheaded by the Reds, a "people's war"—the only kind he considered to be both effective and worthwhile. In a diary entry soon after the start of the war he derided the "naive" view of many Peking intellectuals that "the Reds would be the ideal rulers of China if only they'd give up social revolution!"[29]

Thus, while Snow remained uncertain and uneasy over the new direction of Communist policy, he also continued to affirm his belief in the Reds' ultimate revolutionary destiny. Their moderated line, he observed in his *Post* article, seemed "to remove the fight for Socialism in China to a remote future" and would likely then be waged "within the framework of democracy, rather than by armed insurrection." He nevertheless wondered whether the Red leadership in the course of a protracted struggle would "prove ingenious enough to transfer the loyalty and devotion of its following to the banners of pure Chinese nationalism," without destroying the "political morale" originally derived from "the immediate practical gains of class warfare." But taking his cue from his 1936 talks with Mao, Snow declared that the Reds were "serenely convinced" that the war would inevitably lead to "a mighty victory of Socialist democracy" in Eastern Asia. As the party "best able to mobilize, train and lead the peasantry" in a long and costly conflict, and with an army most expert in mobile warfare, "the Communists think they will be able to conclude the war with a firm grasp on national leadership, as well as with the credit for a great triumph over Japan." *Red Star* would strike an even stronger similar note.[30]

For now, however, the realities of China's humiliating defeats in northern China and his deeply pessimistic views on the immediate course of the conflict had put Snow into one of his despondent states. The passive, inept, and disastrous Chinese defense of Peking, witnessed by Snow in the weeks after Japan launched its war in northern China on July 7, further soured him. "Well, it's all over," he recorded, after Chinese forces evacuated the city on July 28. "The idea of organizing the people for a 'Madrid' never entered the old fool's [the commanding general, Song Zheyuan] head." It had been a "debacle and sell-out." No Nanking troops or planes had come up from the south to join the fighting. Chiang would fight only if Japan invaded "his territory" south of the Yellow River. Even then, Snow gloomily (and inaccurately) felt, the Generalissimo could not be depended on to conduct a sustained and serious struggle. As for the Communists, he bitterly noted, they were most likely to follow a "live and let-live" policy toward Chiang, in which case "we can expect little more from Red leadership."[31]

Snow's dark mood was accentuated by his loneliness and worry about Helen, from whom he had heard nothing since the start of the war. The accumulated strain of the intense work and activity of the past year (his book had been finally completed just days before the Japanese attack) had also taken its toll. After covering the fighting around Peking, he was expected by the *Herald* to go down to Shanghai to report on the battle raging there, but his uncertainty about Helen kept him immobilized. His expenses were mounting, and monies due him from the *Sun* and *Herald* were not coming through. The *Post* and other journals wanted war articles from him, which he felt unable to produce. Added to all this, his Peking house had become a refuge for many Chinese on the Japanese blacklist. In mid-August he and Jim Bertram shepherded such a group, including Deng Yingchao, Zhou Enlai's wife, herself an important leader in the party, to Tianjin on a refugee-packed twelve-hour train trip. (Deng had been living secretly in the western hills outside Peking taking a tuberculosis rest cure.) Ed got her through the Japanese security check, in Tianjin, with Deng posing as his amah, and into the safety of the British concession.[32]

These were "mostly days of worry and misery," a diary entry reads from Tianjin at the beginning of September, where he had returned again, unsure whether to go on to Shanghai or to meet up with Helen, perhaps in the seaside resort city of Qingdao on the Shandong coast. After ten "miserable and expensive" days, and some garbled and confused telegraphic messages from Helen, he took a steamer to Qingdao together with Bertram, to await further clarification. "Everything about my personal life is in chaos," he brooded. He had been "a lousy traitor" to the *Herald,* which had ordered him to Shanghai a couple of weeks earlier. Two pieces for the *Post* remained unwritten, and hinging on them, "the possibility of becoming their regular correspondent in this war." Other journals were "clamoring for copy. What a pity that I cannot write a line! . . . I am so afraid something has happened to [Peg] that I cannot sit or stand still a moment; must be always moving and with people to keep from worrying about her. Nor can I write a line, except this sort of thing which gives direct expression to my nervous apprehensions."[33]

Ed and Bertram proceeded to Xi'an where they just missed Peg, who had left hours before by train for Qingdao. She was taken off her train and returned to Xi'an. (The Snows later passed the express on which she had traveled, wrecked by Japanese bombers with many passenger fatalities.) Ed found her to be "rather pale and thin" but "in good spirits." In Xi'an, Snow saw Smedley and visited with old Red friends from Bao'an at their Xi'an liaison office, now functioning openly and legally, though under police scrutiny. Ed and Peg went on to Qingdao while Bertram entered the Communist areas for his own stint with the Reds.[34]

For almost two weeks the Snows enjoyed the lovely, deserted beach at Qingdao, still untouched by the war. "Days of rest with Peg," Ed recorded. "Sleeping, eating, sunbathing, long talks and quarrels and talks. Joy of reunion; tears and roses." Ed took passage for Shanghai on October 9, in time for the final phase of the fierce battle there. "These have been costly and chaotic months in my personal life," he wrote the *Herald* from Shanghai, in appealing to them for some reimbursement of the heavy expenses he had incurred since the start of hostilities. Peg returned to Peking, to close up the house and get medical treatment for her recurring dysentery. She arrived in Shanghai by ship in late November, a few days before the Japanese victory parade there. She brought with her, Snow glumly noted, "14 trunks and 13 pieces of hand luggage, poor kid." Snow preferred to travel light. Helen still carried around her waist the notebook-stuffed "life belt." The two were soon involved in another momentous chapter in their China lives, with Helen as usual setting the pace. They would initiate a movement for the kind of grassroots mobilization of human and material resources Snow always believed crucial to the Chinese war effort.[35]

The first copies of *Red Star* arrived from London just before the end of the year and were soon sold out—a small sample of the strikingly successful reception the book was getting first in England and then America. It came as a surprise to Snow, and a great boost to his morale (and finances). There would be some equally unexpected, but unpleasant, jolts from the left.

CHAPTER 10

The Strange Life of a Classic

Snow's dejection in the early months of the China conflict extended also to his expectations for *Red Star*. Despite "bits" that were "surprisingly good reading," he wrote Helen about the completed draft, "I'm afraid I can't say much for it." Besides, he added in a further letter to her in Yan'an, he believed the American public took "a noticeably waning interest" in the Chinese Reds since they had buckled under to the Nationalists. Yet it was precisely Snow's book that stirred Western interest, sympathy, and admiration for the Chinese Communists and helped inspire an optimism about China's prospects that Snow himself for the while noticeably lacked.[1]

The "truth is," Ed dispiritedly wrote his father from Tianjin in September, "that I am a little tired and tired especially of the Orient." (Though once again he added the refrain: a return home would have to wait, perhaps for the duration of the war.) As for the China hostilities, all wars were much alike "so far as human suffering and brutality and stupidity are concerned"; this one particularly "seems a rather sordid and unglorious business." Whereas he felt China, now in a "fight or perish" situation, should in the end prevail, it would be because of "greater endurance at hardship and misery." Japan would finally break economically, rather than militarily. (It was a point he had once dismissed as wishful thinking.) Great power intervention was also to be expected. He reiterated his oft-expressed conviction that Russian intervention in one form or another "will come and will be decisive." He predicted to J. Edgar that America would be involved no later than 1940. The Japanese military, bogged down on the China mainland, he prophetically continued, would become increasingly reckless, as probable Western sanctions sapped Japan's resources. It was a cheerless kind of "optimism" that had little of his prior expectations for China of an entire people fully mobilized for war under broadly based leftist-patriotic leadership.[2]

Rather incongruously, the eventful and calamitous course of the first six months of hostilities that so depressed Snow appeared to his American publisher to be fortuitous "timing." It was "almost a miraculous break," Bennett Cerf exuberantly declared. *Red Star* reached the bookstores "just in time to have the headlines on the front pages of every newspaper in the country act as an advertisement for our book!" And "throwing caution to the winds," Cerf predicted sales of at least a hundred thousand. *Red Star* appeared first in England, published by Victor Gollancz, one of the founders of the Left Book Club Snow had long subscribed to. Available there in an inexpensive edition as a selection of the club, the book became an immediate success, selling over a hundred thousand copies in its first weeks. In America (a larger but much more insular market), the Random House edition had considerably lower total sales of 23,500. This was nevertheless a new high for a nonfiction work on the Far East. (The attacks on the book in the Communist press and the party's boycott undoubtedly cut into the potentially substantial demand on the left.) Its reissue in Random House's Modern Library series in 1944 sold an additional 27,000 copies. Actually, the 1938 Random House edition may have just missed becoming a Book-of-the-Month Club selection, which would easily have put sales over the hundred thousand mark its publisher had anticipated. Cerf later confided to the Snows that only the negative vote of Heywood Broun, a member of the club's board and a selection judge, had prevented this. (Richard Watts of the *Herald-Tribune* informed Snow in 1939 that Broun had told him he did so "because he thought another book would come out next month disproving *Red Star*.") It was a strange political twist since Broun, a popular newspaper columnist and author, was noted for his leftist views. He later converted to Catholicism and broke with the left (events apparently unconnected with his stance on *Red Star*) shortly before his death in December 1939.[3]

Of course, more than timeliness, the empathic public response to *Red Star* reflected awareness of the tragic realities of the conflict Americans were reading about—especially the great human cost and material devastation of the protracted battle for Shanghai, and the Japanese military's savage terror against the civilian population of Nanking following its occupation in December 1937. In Shanghai, Snow recorded in his diary: "In the midst of this tragedy of a people one can talk—talk is a release—and yet to write of it is difficult. Difficult because one realizes the emptiness and limitation of words and everywhere the necessity for action." But *Red Star* would be a prime example of just how potent words could be.[4]

Snow's book touched a responsive chord, particularly among intellectuals in the West searching for resolute heroic figures on the bleak landscape of unchecked aggression in Europe, Africa, and Asia. The uncertainty surrounding a purge-ridden Soviet Union, and the passivity toward and even abetment of the aggressor states by the Western democracies, added to the somber perspective. Thus Harold Isaacs noted in his later volume on American images of Asians that *Red Star* had made its "deepest impression on increasingly worried and world-conscious liberal intellectuals." It had been "well and widely received," with an impact far beyond its relatively limited sales figures. Among the almost two hundred influential Americans Isaacs interviewed, Snow's volume was cited second only to Pearl Buck's blockbuster popular novel and film, *The Good Earth,* as a key source of their picture of the Chinese. Harry Price, the Snows' good friend in Peking who taught economics at Yanjing before returning to the States, wrote them from New York: "I don't know any book that is being more discussed now," and "time and time again I have heard people say, 'Well, I had no idea that the Communists in China were really like that!'" Snow had "scotched" the Communist "bug-a-boo," particularly among those "most responsible for influencing and determining American foreign policy," Price enthused. Roosevelt told Snow at their first meeting in 1942 that he "knew him" through *Red Star* and enlisted Ed as one of his unofficial wartime overseas sources of information. In a 1938 interview with Admiral Harry Yarnell, then commander of the U.S. Asiatic fleet, Snow described the Reds in much the same terms as he had in his book, to which the admiral responded, "Well, they sound just like oldfashioned patriots to me." Snow's vividly and dramatically written account of the epic Long March made especially inspiring, even thrilling reading. Harold Ickes, Roosevelt's outspoken secretary of the interior, told another former Yanjing colleague of Snow's, after reading *Red Star,* that "any people that can do what the Red Army did during the Long March and after" were "positively invincible."[5]

There was an amusing sidelight to the attractive picture Snow's writings on the Reds were evoking in America. A coffee company wished to use Ed's published photo of Mao and Zhu De seated at a table on which one of the company's coffee cans was prominently displayed. But the photo was hardly evidence of a thirst for American coffee in tea-drinking China; it showed merely that salvaged empty coffee tins made highly useful containers for the supply-starved Communists.[6]

Aside from a few cautious caveats that Snow had perhaps painted too bright a picture of the Reds, mainstream reviews in England and America were lavish in praise. The book was hailed as both a stunning and significant journalistic coup and a writing achievement of the first magnitude—an "epic story, superbly told," his own *Daily Herald* declared. Snow had turned out an engrossing personal adventure travel book, told in his most engaging and colorful style, as well as a fascinating, Marco Polo–like depiction of previously inaccessible "Red China." ("A Chinese State Hitherto Unknown to Us," the *Herald-Tribune* headlined its review.) Pearl Buck, the China novelist and 1938 Nobel laureate, called *Red Star* an "intensely readable" and "extraordinary" book, "packed with incident and information, living with unforgettable character sketches, every page of it is significant."

Red Star was replete with appealing and confidence-building portraits of Red leaders, commanders, and soldiers; their selfless fortitude, indomitable spirit, and historic destiny were epitomized in the Reds' year-long trek to the northwest. The book read very much like a modern morality play of good against evil that transcended its immediate Chinese setting. Snow's good friend Marine Captain (later Colonel) Evans F. Carlson was especially intrigued by this moral dimension. Carlson read Snow's book in manuscript in Shanghai and resolved to see this very special army for himself. With Ed's encouragement and help, he spent months with Zhu De's Eighth-Route Army forces on the northwestern war front. A deeply religious man of strong convictions, Carlson came away convinced that he had witnessed among the Reds a unique example of Christian ethics and brotherhood in practice. (He had told Zhu De, Carlson divulged to Snow on his return, that he "would be glad to serve under him any time.") He transmuted the Communists' egalitarian principles into his own concept of "ethical indoctrination" and applied them to his famous Marine raider battalion during the Pacific War. Carlson adopted the logo of the Snows' Indusco movement, Gung Ho, as his motto and in the process put it into the American vocabulary.[7]

Red Star's delineation of the Communists' highly effective mobile warfare techniques, their solid base among an awakened and responsive peasantry, and their anti-Japanese nationalism and supreme confidence in final victory uplifted Western readers dealing with the mostly disheartening war news from China. It "may portend the long-predicted awakening of the Chinese people and the ultimate frustration of Japanese imperialism," the *New York Times* reviewer thought. Despite Snow's (and Mao's) careful emphasis on the Reds' Marxist-Leninist credentials and goals, it all left a lasting impression that these revolutionaries were only so-called Communists. What Snow had found, literary critic Henry Seidel Canby asserted, "was an agrarian revolution and an organization so Chinese in its character as to suggest that 'Communist' was an inaccurate term of description." If Snow's book "has been correctly interpreted, the significance of Red China is not that it is red but that it is Chinese," the *New York Times* seconded. "The 'Red bandits' bear a close resemblance to people whom we used to call patriots," the *Times* reviewer added. And Pearl Buck compared the book to the classic Chinese "Robin Hood" novel, *Shui Hu Chuan* (Water margin), in which a brotherhood of "good bandits helped the poor and despoiled the rich." It was a reaction that saddled Snow, unfairly, in later less sympathetic times, with responsibility for the "agrarian reformer" view of the Chinese Communists. Still, on a less simplistic level, Snow had accurately pinpointed the indigenous peasant-oriented characteristics that would give Maoist communism its distinctive qualities. The *New York Times* reviewer drew the inference that though the Chinese Communist leaders had read a good deal of Marx, Lenin, and Stalin, "they were largely influenced by the immediacy of events in China itself."[8]

John Gunther described Snow's book as "one of the best books of historical journalism ever written." Gunther and his wife, Frances, spent time with the Snows in Shanghai in the spring of 1938 while gathering material for Gunther's *Inside Asia*. Ed found him a keen-minded, sharp questioner, interested "in every cause with a strong man or interesting character in it." He "has royalties blood in his veins," Snow quipped. Frances Gunther came up with a bon mot on the Generalissimo: "There's Methodism in his madness."[9]

The British journalist Freda Utley, who would in time become a bitter anti-Communist crusader against Snow in America, lauded *Red Star* in 1937 as "a piece of brilliant and unique reporting." (She mildly suggested that a "slightly more critical approach and fewer personal histories of leaders might be preferred by some readers" but immediately added that the book was "of absorbing interest.") She had been a member of the British Communist party but left after six disillusioning years in the Soviet Union and the purge of her Russian husband. She retained liberal persuasions in the later 1930s and was receptive to the view of the Chinese Communists as "a different breed" from their Russian counterparts. Oddly enough it was Utley, following her own journalistic experience in China in 1938, who proclaimed the thesis that the Reds had become merely a party of "social reformers and patriots."[10]

Red Star was not only timely; it took on a more enduring "timelessness" precisely because the Mao-led CCP had no intention of "throwing in the sponge," as Snow had feared. (In Shanghai, early in 1938, he brooded as before over this "surrender" to Chiang, which he attributed to Russian intervention and pressure at the time.) The very title of his book voiced his underlying conviction that the Communists were still ordained, even required, to occupy a central place in the war and after. Soviet and Western Communists tended to see this in reverse. "Little remains" of the period Snow wrote of, stated a reviewer in December 1938 about the revised edition of *Red Star* in *China Today* (a journal subsidized by the American Communist party). "The 'Red Star Over China' is a closed episode" of a civil war period now replaced by the "wholly fulfilled" essential of national unity. When a truncated Russian version of Snow's book appeared in 1938, it carried the blandly apolitical title *Heroic People of China*.[11]

Despite the book's extraordinarily influential role in fostering an admiring Western opinion of the Chinese Reds (though also in part *because* of it), the Comintern had major complaints against *Red Star* and voiced them forcefully through surrogates in the American Communist party. As Harry Price had written to the Snows, "It is curious that the right-wing press and journals have sung your praises most highly, with potshots coming from left-wing groups. Apparently the latter are not satisfied that you think 'to the line.'"[12]

The American Communists were placed in an uncomfortable position in mounting their attack on Snow. Rather than give him high marks for his powerfully admiring portrayal of the Chinese Reds whose exploits against the Japanese invader were now heralded daily in the Communist press, the *Daily Worker* simply ignored Snow's book until he had produced his slightly "laundered" revised edition later in 1938. Yet at the time it was deemed essential to counter his "Trotskyist slanders" against the icons of international communism—Stalin, the U.S.S.R., and the Comintern. Aside from more fundamental political considerations, reviewers needed to alert readers on the left who could easily be "disarmed" by Snow's book. "We have presented this critique of 'Red Star Over China,'" a lengthy analysis in the American party's political organ declared, "with the aim of placing its readers on guard."[13]

Snow had indeed referred to Stalin's "dictatorship" and contrasted his "great leader" image to Mao's unpretentious and "Lincolnesque" persona. (Snow told a "horrified" Madame Sun in mid-1938 that he thought the new Soviet "Stalin Constitution" an "excellent" vehicle for keeping the Communists in power, but a "joke" as a democratic instrument.) More substantively, Snow implicated the Stalin-led Comintern in the disasters that befell the CCP in 1927. He also took a hard look at the alternative policies advanced by the Trotskyist opposition at the time. He judged that Trotsky's more radical proposals would have had even more detrimental results. In any case, Snow concluded, the Trotskyists, in pursuing their own political agenda, had greatly exaggerated Comintern culpability for an outcome largely predetermined by "overwhelmingly adverse" objective conditions. Stalin subsequently tightened his grip on both the Soviet Communist party and the Comintern, Snow noted (with a skeptical aside for the Moscow trials)—the Comintern itself becoming "a kind of bureau of the Soviet Union, gradually turning into a glorified advertising agency for the prosaic labours of the builders of Socialism in one country." Snow added fuel for the Trotskyist fire building under him by asserting that in the event (as was likely) the Soviets were drawn into an expanded Asian conflict, they would be in a position decisively to influence the outcome of the Chinese revolution. The success of that revolution might thus hinge on whether the U.S.S.R. was able to move from "a programme of Socialism in one country to Socialism in all countries, to world revolution," he wrote in his conclusion. This last reflected Snow's continuing conflicts on the Soviet world role. On the one hand, as he also wrote in *Red Star,* he felt that the non-Soviet Communist parties "have had to fall in line with, and usually subordinate themselves to, the broad strategic requirements of Russia" (the Stalinist "Socialism in one country" syndrome); on the other, he believed the U.S.S.R., as a fundamentally "progressive" anti-imperialist socialist power could be expected, when push came to shove in world affairs, to act in tandem with Asian revolutionary nationalism. Snow would eventually find Soviet-sponsored "socialism in all countries" to be primarily an expansionist projection of the interests of "socialism in one country."[14]

The harsh and even vindictive American Communist reaction to *Red Star* was expressed in a review in *China Today,* and more exhaustively and authoritatively in a lengthy commentary in the party's theoretical organ, *The Communist.* The editor of *China Today* was Max Granich, back from Shanghai with his wife, Grace, from their party-assigned task as editors of the now-defunct *Voice of China*. Granich read Snow's book on board ship in galley sheets given him by Ed. The Granichs had become friends of the Snows through Madame Sun. (Granich later remembered a Peking dinner with the Snows. Ed, who always enjoyed his drink, took along an ample supply of brandy, solemnly informing Granich that it was needed to kill off any germs ingested with the food.) On reading Snow's book Granich immediately felt Ed's offending Comintern chapter to be "pure Trotskyism." "I said, 'Oh my God oh my God, what he has done,'" he recalled.[15]

The *China Today* reviewer, Philip Jaffe (writing under a pseudonym), was a Far Eastern specialist and editor of the left-wing monthly, *Amerasia*. He and his wife were in the American foursome that visited Yan'an in June 1937 while Helen Snow was there. He carried "greetings" from the American party chief, Earl Browder, to the Chinese Communist leaders. He met Snow in Peking before going into the Red base, and the two had talked of Ed's nearly completed *Red Star*. "What was it," Jaffe now rhetorically asked in his review, "that impelled a man of Snow's remarkable reportorial ability to write the most glorious pages about the Red Army of China and its leaders, and at the same time pepper them with unsubstantiated attacks against the Soviet Union, Stalin, and the Communist International." While it was certainly "difficult not to believe that Snow is a Trotskyist," Jaffe magnanimously chose to think Snow was not "a conscious counter-revolutionist." It was more a case of theoretical ignorance, a misunderstanding of the Chinese revolution, and just plain "confusion" on Snow's part. Jaffe's review appeared some four months after *Red Star's* publication in the United States. His "kinder" judgment on Snow was presumably based on his awareness of changes Snow was making for a revised edition of the book—changes Jaffe later claimed were made "in part with my assistance." Actually Snow was much irritated that his intended revisions had been leaked to the Communist party. The changes consisted mostly of eliminating a number of obvious "anti-Soviet" buzz words and phrases that Snow needed no help in identifying. While the revised version was still far from being politically correct from Jaffe's point of view, he held out hope that Snow would continue to mend his ways. "And then," he concluded, "we may hope for the final corrections which will make *Red Star Over China* the important book it should have been." (Both Granich and Jaffe, who later broke with the Communists, would come to regard *Red Star* as "a great book.") Meanwhile Harold Isaacs, in his own 1938 classic and genuinely Trotskyist-oriented book on Communist policy in the

Chinese revolution, sharply rebuked Snow for having "lightly parroted calumnies" against the Trotskyists. Adding further to the ideological stew, Snow found his book being used by a reviewer in Powell's Shanghai journal to substantiate a pro-Trotskyist view of the united front and the resistance war as an example of Communist betrayal of revolutionary goals. Snow felt obliged to write a lengthy rebuttal separating himself and *Red Star* from these opinions.[16]

In his diary Snow reflected on these attacks by Jaffe and Isaacs. Both concluded that "I know nothing of the Chinese Revolution," he noted. "It's all very amusing, but really not so amusing as tragic because both these people fancy themselves working for the betterment of man in a quick and big way." The Comintern and its Trotskyist foes both embrace the myth of their own "scientific" godlike infallibility. "If you disagree or see another point of view you are an ignoramus." As a critical-minded friend of the left, Snow would face the problem often in the future.[17]

In Shanghai, he was enduring similar attacks from Western Communist circles there. "How childish these people are," Ed jotted in his diary in December 1937, "always carrying out their Boy Scout duty by finding a Trotskyist daily!" Heinz Shippe, the intellectual leader of the Shanghai Marxist circle, spearheaded the assault. Formerly connected with the German Communist movement, he had writing connections with Comintern and Soviet publications. He also wrote on Chinese affairs for Western journals under the pen name Asiaticus. In *Pacific Affairs* (the journal of the Institute of Pacific Relations), Asiaticus launched into a long-winded, highly theoretical Leninist disquisition on the various stages of the Chinese revolution. Aimed specifically at discrediting Snow's *Red Star* views, it all boiled down to his affirmation of the orthodox Communist position on the current united front phase of anti-Japanese resistance, which he characterized as "bourgeois nationalist" in content and leadership by the Kuomintang. "As such," he declared, "it is distinctly different from the later period of struggle to realize Socialist revolution for China." Any attempt, "open or covert," to intertwine the two stages would only isolate the Communists from "the national and democratic revolutionary front." In his rejoinder, Snow showed himself no slouch at Marxist dialectical discourse. Even though the struggle against Japan "has been initiated by, and is still under the hegemony of the bourgeoisie, with the loyal cooperation of the Communists," he summed up, "it is a grave error in dialectical thinking to imply from this that the Communists would not be prepared, if conditions imposed the task upon them, to accept the full hegemony of the revolutionary war themselves."[18]

Snow was restating his bedrock convictions on the direction, character, and goals of China's resistance war, which he had spelled out in his *Red Star* conclusions and linked to the sentiments he had heard in Bao'an:

They [the Communists] foresaw that in this war it would become necessary to arm, equip, train, and mobilize tens of millions of people in a struggle which could serve the dual surgical function of removing the external tumour of imperialism and the internal cancer of class oppression. Such a war, they conceived, could only be conducted by the broadest mobilization of the masses, by the development of a highly politicized army. And such a war could only be won under the most advanced revolutionary leadership. It could be initiated by the bourgeoisie. It could be completed only by the revolutionary workers and peasants.[19]

Though Snow contemptuously rejected the allegations of Trotskyism leveled at him, he was nevertheless feeling the pressure to make some "corrections" of his more "inflammatory" comments. In the overheated political atmosphere engendered on the left by the Stalinist purges, the Trotskyist label was an especially heinous one—a synonym generally for apostate "spies and traitors" to the cause. Shippe had visited the Snows in their Shanghai apartment and, according to Helen Snow, had threatened politically "to destroy" Snow and his book. Particularly in view of the substantial influence the American party had in intellectual and cultural circles during the 1930s, these charges were creating barriers to the progressive audience Snow wished to reach in support of the Chinese resistance fighters. And the U.S.S.R., after all, was the single main power giving substantial aid (through the Kuomintang) to China. Snow had received a much gentler (and more honest) hint in that direction from Madame Sun (herself an admirer of Stalin) in Shanghai. She told Ed his book was "wonderful" but when pressed further by him responded with a smile, "Well, you are perhaps too frank in some places." Helen, who always gave primacy to getting the word out, was urging Ed to remove any impediments to this goal. In his *Pacific Affairs* polemic with Shippe, Snow had already indicated a willingness to alter possible "errors of judgment and analysis," some of which concerned the Soviet Union. "The views I have expressed are subject to revision."[20]

Later, in July 1938 in Hankou, Communist leader Bo Gu (Qin Bangxian), who was linked with the internationalist wing of the party, told Snow that he had been "a little too strong" in his criticism of the Comintern. As to Snow's final chapters with their perspectives on the Communist role in the resistance war, "you are quite right," Bo Gu remarked, "but we don't want to talk about these matters now." Mao apparently saw these things in a somewhat different light. He had been the one to pass on to Snow much of the criticism of earlier Comintern policy, and he would shortly again begin to assert policies in keeping with the political perspectives so effectively outlined and publicized by Snow.[21]

Thus Snow was much reassured to learn, also in Hankou in July, of Mao's personal reaction to Shippe's critique of *Red Star*. (Shippe had been going around Shanghai "telling everybody," Snow earlier noted in his diary without comment, that Mao and Zhou Enlai agreed with Shippe on *Red Star*.) Through Rewi Alley, he now heard that Shippe had gone up to Yan'an to present his views directly to Mao, only to be harshly rebuffed by the Red leader. It was "a serious offense" to attack *Red Star,* Mao reportedly told Shippe. Snow "is our good friend, and to attack him is a counter-revolutionary act." A devastated Shippe returned to Shanghai, where he told Smedley of his ordeal. As Smedley relayed this to Snow, Shippe kept repeating that "Mao was really too cruel" to him.[22]

The hostile response of the American Communists to *Red Star* seemed to confirm Snow's contentions on Soviet Russian control and use of the world Communist movement to further its overriding strategic and political ends. It was a point Snow was quick to make in a curious letter to the party head, Browder, whom he had never met. Snow wondered, in citing the Communist ban on his book, at "the logic behind the decision." His book was an honest, first-hand account, and its "testimony was on the whole warmly sympathetic to the Chinese and the world revolutionary movements," he argued. It had won "understanding and support for Communists, not only among influential foreigners, but among Chinese themselves." Having said this, Snow then deftly referred to his much criticized point on the Comintern as a bureau of the Soviet Union: "I am somehow unconvinced that a banning of the book at the behest of some arbitrary order, necessarily proves such a remark to be incorrect." On the contrary, he maintained, it tended to support "the critical view I expressed." Snow then carried this point considerably further. Had the decision "rested with those responsible for the boycott," his book would never have been published, the manuscript probably burned, "and it is just possible that its author might have been shot." In another jab Snow added, "I am convinced that I have been of more service [to China and the Chinese Communists] than the people who banned my book in New York." His few ("good humored") critical comments on the Comintern, Snow continued, were "extremely restrained" in utilizing the "abundant information" at his disposal. If motivated by the "malevolence" ascribed to him, he might have employed such material "in a very harmful manner indeed." As his contribution to what he evidently anticipated would be some backtracking on both sides, he concluded by informing Browder that "some weeks ago" he had "voluntarily" asked his publisher "to excise certain sentences from any new edition of my book—sentences which I thought might be offensive to the party." Snow couldn't forego a parting shot: "By the way, the last time I saw your old friend Chou En-lai he asked me to send you his warm regards." It was all a clear example of the duality and conflict between his China-engendered radicalism and his liberal-minded instincts.[23]

The changes Snow did make for a revised edition appearing later in 1938 took out most of the "slanderous" comments that the Communists considered most egregiously "anti-Soviet." Snow partly rewrote a brief chapter that softened and revised his original assessment of Comintern responsibility for the strategic political and military decisions made during the final pre–Long March phases of the Jiangxi Soviet that contributed to its defeat. He did not tamper with his more substantive critique on the Comintern's China policy, on the Stalin-Trotsky controversy, and much else the left had found objectionable. However, the "corrections" were deemed satisfactory enough to enable the party to extricate itself from its increasingly awkward "dog-in-the-manger" rejectionist stance on *Red Star*. Actually, the major change in the new edition was an add-on section on the first year of the China war and its probable future course.[24]

The party's *Daily Worker,* which now belatedly reviewed the book, pronounced it "a serious improvement" over the original. But while welcoming the "modifications" Snow had made in his earlier "malicious" and "slanderous" statements, the reviewers held that the book still contained "serious flaws" on matters of Soviet Russian and Comintern history and policies. The criticism centered now primarily on Snow's allegedly woeful ignorance on issues far beyond his depth. Snow, "lacking in ideological equipment, has proved unjust to himself and to history." Despite such weaknesses, *Red Star* was "a valuable and rich book"; with "the above criticisms and reservations we can strongly recommend this book to all friends of China." Max Granich, in a brief review in *China Today,* added his stamp of approval. While also regretting the continued inclusion of material "which seriously compromises the political content of the book," he wrote that *Red Star* was "nevertheless one of the finest books written in the past decade on China's stirring history." And so Snow and his American Communist detractors made their edgy and prickly truce.[25]

Yet deeper enduring issues remained. Snow had not simply pointed to the Soviet national interest behind the policies pursued through the Comintern. He had counterpoised to this a Chinese communism imbued with its distinctive characteristics and "revolution in one country" preoccupations. In Moscow's eyes Snow, by bad-mouthing Stalin and the U.S.S.R. while glorifying Mao and a national Chinese communism, had raised far-reaching challenges to the Soviet concept of a Communist world order in which Marxist-Leninist "proletarian internationalism," as defined by the Moscow center, was the indispensable cementing ingredient. And most important in this, Snow was clearly venting and transmitting Mao's own counter standpoint. Recall the chairman's pithy query to Snow in 1936, "Who is Moscow's 'Moscow'?" Snow had introduced his famous Mao autobiographical account: "Then Mao Tse-tung began to tell me something about his personal history, and as I wrote it down, night after night, I realized that this was not only his story, but a record also of how Communism grew—a variety of it real and indigenous to China, and no mere orphan adopted from abroad, as some writers naively suppose—and why it won the adherence and support of thousands of young men and women."[26]

At the time *Red Star* appeared, Mao was the recognized and acclaimed leader of the CCP and had no apparent differences with the Comintern on wartime policies and goals. In Communist political culture open criticism of a ranking leader was avoided until and unless he was being cast into oblivion—political or otherwise. (To an extent Mao's candid criticism to Snow of earlier Comintern China policies violated these norms.) Snow divulged unsettling evidence of Mao's independently Chinese cast of mind. And in promoting an influential image of a different and attractive breed of Red revolutionaries in China, Snow was also laying the groundwork for a possible American connection. In all the major issues raised in the *Red Star* controversy, the nationalist-internationalist question loomed large, whether over the Comintern's proclaimed infallibility and its relationship to the Soviet state and party, or over the appropriate united front role and strategic perspectives of the CCP in the anti-Japanese war.

The Chinese Communists were the first, and as yet the only, non-Soviet party with its own army, area, and government, and a decadelong experience of intense armed struggle. The themes sounded in *Red Star* presaged the rise of national communisms challenging the imperial Moscow center. Snow in fact portrayed the U.S.S.R. itself as a prime example of national communism. Writing of the Tito "heresy" in 1948, Snow would see it as "a head-on collision, not between nationalism, on the one hand, and internationalism on the other, but between two sets of nationalisms within the 'socialist system of states.'" In the following year, with Communist victory in China, Snow wrote, "in the long run the Chinese Communist Party probably cannot and will not subordinate the national interests of China to the interests of the Kremlin." Not surprisingly, it was in 1960, when Snow's prediction had become the reality, that he was welcomed back to China by its Red leader. And in one of the supreme ironies of history, Russian and other Soviet nationalisms have resulted in the disintegration of the Soviet Union itself.[27]

For the while in 1938 the onus remained entirely on Snow, with the transparent claim that he had spoken only for himself, and in direct conflict with the "Marxist-Leninist" position of the CCP leadership. As the polemic in the American party's theoretical journal amply demonstrated, the attack on Red Star served to restate and reaffirm the Stalinist line for China from the 1920s to the current resistance war. It was in effect an early warning signal aimed especially at any Chinese Communist "nationalist" deviations. (Later and more directly in Soviet sources, during open Sino-Soviet conflict Snow would again be targeted as a front man for both American imperialism and Maoist communism.) After the standard praise for his "warm presentation of life under the Chinese Soviets," the American party journal launched into a point by point refutation of Snow's "Trotskyite interpretation of the Chinese revolution." It accused him of drawing "a false and unfriendly picture" of the U.S.S.R., making it "the villain of the piece." "Can one be a friend of the Chinese people and not a friend of the Soviet Union?," it posited. (While Snow rejected out of hand such true-believer definitions of friendship, the question was nonetheless a vexing one for him, as his Red Star revisions illustrated.)

The Communist authors focused on Moscow's protégé, Wang Ming, and extolled his role in "bolshevizing" the CCP in the early 1930s. They pointed to the Comintern-inspired August First (1935) Declaration, drawn up by Wang Ming in Moscow, as setting the guiding principles that led to the KMT-CCP unity arrangements of 1937. (These were of course all matters on which Mao had had his serious reservations and differences.) The writers took Snow to task for his skeptical view that there was no likelihood of "the Kuomintang quietly signing its own death warrant by genuinely realizing bourgeois democracy." In the purest statement of the "Wang Ming line," later denounced by the Maoists, the article claimed that the Kuomintang was "reviving its earlier [1925–1927] revolutionary tradition." There was, therefore, a "long-range perspective" to KMT-CCP collaboration, "not only in driving the Japanese imperialists out of China, but in building a united, democratic republic." Almost as if in direct rejection of these 1938 attacks on Snow, a Mao message to him in Hong Kong in August of that year urged him to come to Yan'an for "a long talk" on the new stage of the war. Snow, however, was unable to accept the invitation until September of the following year.[28]

Meanwhile Moscow was producing a translated version of *Red Star* from which officials could delete anything and everything they found objectionable—something the American left was of course unable to do. It was both a much more subtle and effective way of dealing with the political pluses and minuses of the book. The brief Soviet volume consisted of excerpts from selected chapters, mostly on the Red Army, the Long March, and Peng Dehuai's recital of Red military tactics, rearranged and packaged to suit the editors. It came complete with a new title and an introduction setting forth, with copious quotations from "the great Stalin," the correct line for its readers. It emphasized above all the paramount importance of the united front as "the sole key" to victory over Japan. Mao's autobiography was relegated, in much attenuated form, to a final section on "Sons of the Chinese People," which included also sketches of the major Red Army commanders. The Mao segment devoted less than a page to his entire post-1921 activities, in other words to his entire career as a Communist! It thus neatly avoided virtually all Mao's version of Chinese revolutionary history. Nor did Snow's admiring profile of Mao find a place in the book. Nevertheless *Red Star,* properly sanitized, was evidently politically too useful and perhaps impolitic to ignore. Even more than in the West, Snow's account had great inspirational as well as informational value for a Soviet audience.[29]

Rather intriguingly, a much more complete Russian edition of *Red Star* may have been contemplated in some quarters. The Soviet publication *Book News* in early 1938 reported on Snow's book (citing its original title), which it said "will be coming out." The fairly detailed description of the contents clearly fitted the original text much more closely than the bowdlerized product actually published. A subsequent issue of *Book News* simply carried a review of the latter volume. There is no record of any other version published in the U.S.S.R. More than this, nothing further of Snow's writings appeared in Russian translation for almost half a century, despite his highly favorable wartime reporting from the Soviet Union for the *Post*.[30]

Snow appeared to be unaware of the treatment his book was receiving in Russia. In an early 1938 diary entry he reported hearing that *Red Star* "had been translated and was being widely read in Moscow." After his return to America in 1941, Soviet Ambassador Oumansky told him in Washington (just a few days after the Nazi invasion of the U.S.S.R.), that he "believed" *Red Star* had been translated in Russia, "I hope with omissions." He added that he "understood" such omissions had Snow's "permission." "I said not that I know of," Snow recorded in his diary. "He (Oumansky) said he thought 'verbal permission.' Seemed quite well informed on this point!!!" We may infer from this cryptic exchange that neither the ambassador nor Snow was "well informed" on the Russian *Red Star*.

In a somewhat odd twist, in 1942 Snow contributed to the Red Pioneers the royalties (in rubles) he discovered were due him on the book. Adding to the confusion was another strange tale Snow heard about his book in Moscow. The secretary of the Foreign Writers' Union, whose task it was to select foreign books for translation, had read and liked *Red Star*. Lydia told Ed she had made a "rough translation" of a few chapters and sent it to the Soviet Writers' Union. "Then I went to the hospital," she continued her story. "When I came out the book was already published! I was terribly ashamed, my translation was rough and not meant for publication at all. But the Youth Congress was meeting and wanted some new inspirational book at once. They printed 25,000 copies and sold them in three days." Snow apparently bought this account, which seemed accurate only in the fact that 25,000 copies of the Soviet edition were printed. The Russian translation was actually a professional job and was quite obviously edited and produced under authoritative political supervision. Snow encountered others in Russia who told him they had read his book, including a young partisan fighter on the Smolensk front who just happened to cite his book as the source of her knowledge of guerrilla tactics. Surprisingly, during those years Snow apparently never checked further or saw a copy of the Soviet edition. In contrast to these encomiums, Snow had had great difficulty securing a visa for entry to the Soviet Union as wartime correspondent for the *Post*. And after the war his chronic "Titoist" or "Maoist" sympathies for national Communist challenges to the Kremlin would bar him from that country permanently.[31]

During the brief post-1949 span of Chinese solidarity with a Soviet-led socialist camp confronting a hostile America, Snow was clearly out of the loop in both the new People's China and the United States, not to mention the Soviet Union. At the very time Snow was enduring the antagonistic McCarthyist climate in America, he was getting some of the fallout from the supercharged, Korean War–fueled "anti-American imperialism" campaign in China. The prevailing Chinese line on him appeared in a 1952 piece in the *China Monthly* [formerly *Weekly*] *Review,* which had resumed publication in Shanghai after the war (with a very different political stance) under J. B.'s son, Bill Powell, and which continued to appear under the Communists until 1953. It criticized Snow for discoursing "learnedly on whether Titoist subversion is or is not suitable as a pattern for restoring China to the imperialist sphere," and in terms reminiscent of the 1938 Communist attacks on *Red Star,* it accused Snow of "writing slanders on the Soviet Union which are only faintly distinguishable from those of the most shameless reactionaries."[32]

Although unofficial Chinese editions of *Red Star* appeared in Shanghai and Peking in the looser setting of the initial Red takeover in 1949, by the 1950s outside of a few libraries a copy of the book was almost impossible to find. Though circulated and read by people all over the world, wrote a Chinese scholar about the book in 1980, "the people that had given birth to the book had been having a difficult time reading it openly." Snow disappeared from view as far as the new China was concerned. When Snow finally returned to China in 1960 and met his old friend Chairman Mao, the latter evidently knew little of Snow's personal life in the intervening decades. He thought Ed was still married to Peg and that his nine-year-old daughter, Sian, had been born in her namesake city many years earlier. As for Snow, he was equally uninformed of the nonstatus of his book in China. In the late 1950s he imagined he could pay his expenses in China, should the opportunity to visit arise, with the royalties *Red Star* and other writings might have earned there.[33]

Coincident with Snow's 1960 visit to China, a somewhat expurgated and limited Chinese edition of *Red Star* was prepared for internal (*neibu*) party distribution. Snow's trip came at a time of openly escalating Sino-Soviet tensions, and of consequent renewed Chinese Communist interest in pursuing an American opening. "Too proud to say so directly," Snow reported of his 1960 talks with Chinese leaders, "they were obviously hopeful that my visit might help to rebuild a bridge or two." In his massive book on the 1960 journey, Snow pointedly quoted at length from his earlier Titoist-style projections on the long-term Sino-

Soviet relationship. But it would take another decade to translate these and subsequent developments into the Sino-American rapprochement of the 1970s.[34]

Notwithstanding all these developments, it was not until 1979, seven years after Snow's death, that a full Chinese edition of *Red Star* finally became publicly available in People's China. The volatile politics of the Cultural Revolution, and the purges of Red leaders featured in Snow's book, had delayed such publication, bizarrely enough, until after the death of Mao and the end of the Maoist era Snow had been identified with. This edition, which sold well over a million copies, mostly through party committee channels at all levels, was a newly translated one based on Snow's final revised and heavily annotated 1968 edition. Snow's estate apparently received no royalties as China then was not a member of the International Copyright Union.[35]

Red Star also surfaced again in Soviet sources during the 1970s, in reaction to Snow's supposed role in laying the groundwork for the new U.S.-China relationship. Moscow now openly (and exaggeratedly) targeted Snow's classic account as providing the first and most influential signal of Mao's "nationalist and anti-Soviet" heresies and of his overtures to America. While Snow was being hailed by the Chinese as the prime "bridge builder" (also overstated) of Sino-American amity, the Soviets naturally saw this matter quite differently. *Red Star,* they asserted, was the originating source and principal propagator of the Maoist line in American historical and political writing and thought. Snow himself had been the conscious intermediary in the ultimately achieved "collusion" of Maoist communism and American imperialism. ("Moscow has paid me the honor of attacking me several times," Snow wrote to a friend in September 1971, just months before his death. They should have "better misinformation on me," he added, "plus lots they must have exchanged with CIA.") By 1981 a Soviet historian, focusing on the final decade of Snow's writings on China, concluded in escalated rhetoric that they showed "beyond any doubt that his earlier declarations of sympathy for the national liberation movement in China were merely a disguise for his real identity of an imperialist, anti-communist politician and writer."[36]

In 1938 Snow had been castigated by the Communists for maliciously and ignorantly misrepresenting the views of the CCP leadership; now he was accused of having been an all too understanding and sympathetic accomplice in then transmitting the Maoist message at a time when the Chinese leader was not yet in a position directly and openly to proclaim such opinions as official CCP policy. *Red Star*'s "interpretations of the Chinese problem previewed—sometimes many years ahead—the true, long-range Maoist plans," a Czech Communist anti-Mao polemic declared. "Snow's comments," the writer continued, "turned out to be the comments of a perfectly instructed emissary enjoying the status of an 'independent journalist.'"[37]

In the context of the intense Sino-Soviet enmity of the 1970s, Russian historians went back to the 1936 Mao-Snow connection and assigned a seminal role to *Red Star* in the emergence of a "pro-Maoist conception" of Chinese communism in Western historiography. Though now viewed through an inflamed anti-Maoist political prism, these commentaries harked back to many of the themes in the Communist critiques of Snow's book in 1938. The American party's attack on and boycott of the book at that time was approvingly noted—substantiating Snow's contention to Browder on the real source of the banning edict. These Soviet analyses, however, now fingered Mao as the chief villain in the *Red Star* political saga, with Snow in a major supporting role. Though aimed at showing a direct "American imperialist" link between Snow in Bao'an in 1936 and Nixon in Peking in 1972 (conveniently leapfrogging over two decades of intense American hostility to Mao's China), these commentaries were most revealing on just why *Red Star* had originally rankled the Soviets so deeply.[38]

As the argument went in these sources, by the mid-1930s American business interests in China had lost confidence in the Kuomintang's ability to bring unity and stability to China, and to defend the country against growing Japanese aggression that threatened the long-term American position in the Far East. This concern kindled their desire to obtain accurate intelligence on the Chinese Communists, particularly in view of the latter's call for a national front against Japan. Snow, representing these elements, made the initial serious effort to gather such firsthand data. Mao, on his part, sought U.S. support not only against the Japanese, but also for his upcoming contest with the Kuomintang. Mao, then emerging as the CCP's leader, and personally resentful of the Comintern and the U.S.S.R., was bent on convincing the American journalist that he (Mao) was "first of all" a Chinese nationalist, independent of and "unfriendly" to the Soviet Union. Snow believed in and transmitted Mao's "Trotskyist lies." The Red leader entrusted Snow, in their confidential talks, to carry the message to American "ruling circles" that they had nothing to fear from Mao-led Chinese communism. Thus, these Soviet writers explained, despite the fact that *Red Star* was a "panegyric" to the Chinese Reds, the bourgeois press "opened its pages" to Snow and widely acclaimed his book, which had a "noisy" success in the West. Snow had clothed his glowing portrayal of the Communists in Maoist garb, and his account became a "landmark" in forming this image. Mao therefore gained considerable personal "political capital" through *Red Star.* Snow was the first to popularize and glorify the then still relatively unknown Red leader. Mao's life story, recounted by Snow in the party head's own words, especially served to promote Mao's stature and publicize his version of Chinese revolutionary history. *Red Star* in Chinese translation had wide currency within the CCP and helped advance Maoist domination of the party. Mao was naturally pleased with Snow's exalted treatment, and while other Communist parties were rightly faulting the book's Trotskyist line, the Chinese leader praised it as "telling the truth about us." ("Your *Red Star Over China* is famous," Mao would pointedly remark to Snow in their final talk.)

By presenting Mao as a "democratic" revolutionary leader standing apart from the international Communist movement, these Soviet critiques maintained, *Red Star* strongly appealed to liberal American readers. (Here we note a Russian version of the "agrarian reformer" thesis.) Other "Edgar Snows" followed in journeys to the Red regions over the next decade and modeled their reports on *Red Star.* Snow was particularly useful to Mao in expressing views that the Communist leader could not as yet openly articulate. (By the same token of course, Moscow was able indirectly to attack this "Maoist line" in 1938 by aiming at Snow.)[39]

Did Mao "set up" Snow, as John Fairbank somewhat flippantly suggested? The evidence tends to show Mao and his Boswell to have been in essential agreement on the overall Chinese political scene, and on the strategic and revolutionary perspectives for the upcoming struggle with Japan. Snow's independent-minded commitment to China's national salvation and his deep distrust of the Kuomintang as leader of that cause jibed with Mao's own independently nationalist outlook and equal suspicion of the Moscow-promoted pro-Kuomintang united front line for the CCP. Mao clearly encouraged (or did not discourage) these inclinations in Snow. The Red leader did gain much "political capital" (and Snow much "journalistic capital") from *Red Star,* as did the Chinese Communist movement as a whole and the larger resistance battle. Curiously, in seeing Snow and his "followers" as having aided and abetted Maoist communism in its drive for power in disregard of its internationalist obligations and loyalties, the Russians produced their own "loss of China" scenario. It was the reverse image of McCarthyist allegations that America's China hands in government and journalism had been responsible for the loss of "our" China to the Russians. In Moscow's eyes, essentially the same nefarious group were culpable in the loss of "their" China to the Americans. Both sides had basically the same complaint against these China experts: with Snow leading the way, they had foisted a pro-Maoist line on American thinking and policy. As a final ironic touch, at the time when Snow's "collusive" American imperialist activities were allegedly finally bearing fruit, he himself in those Vietnam war years was at his bitterest toward the American "ruling circles" he supposedly represented.[40]

In sum, *Red Star* holds a unique place as a journalistic tour de force, as an integral factor in the history it recorded and as a remarkably potent political instrument and symbol that brought the Chinese revolution and its revolutionaries to life in the minds of readers around the world. It prophetically charted the dynamic course of that revolution and possibly even more significantly proved to be a harbinger of what would be the disparate power centers and conflicting nationalisms behind the monolithic "proletarian internationalist" facade erected by the architects of the socialist camp. In its implications for China in particular, Snow had already observed in his book that although the CCP was still "an adolescent of sixteen years," it was "the strongest Communist Party in the world, outside of Russia, and the only one, with the same exception, that can boast a mighty army of its own." Finally, Snow effectively communicated his discovery of a new China under the Red star, with its promise of a liberated and transformed nation and people. "The secret of *Red Star Over China*," Helen Snow perhaps nostalgically writes, "is that it is a positive, happy book, telling of a wonderful new and happy experience." *Red Star* remains a legacy of that revolutionary promise: the redeemed, the unredeemed, and the betrayed.[41]

Let us now return to the embattled China of 1938, where the Snows involved themselves in another historic enterprise that would have a liberating potential of its own.

PART 4

The Battle for Asia
to the Battle for the World

CHAPTER 11

Gung Ho for a Wartime China

On a bleak January day in 1938 Snow walked with Rewi
Alley beyond the perimeter of the International Settlement into war-
ravaged Japanese-occupied Chinese Shanghai. He felt both depressed
and angry as the two surveyed the human and material wreckage left by
the protracted battle for the city. (Chiang had committed his crack divi-
sions to the hard-fought battle for the city, which had lasted from August to November 1937, with a loss of two hundred fifty thousand Chinese troops.) "Miles of debris: bricks, stones and broken timbers.
Hardly a house standing intact," a diary entry noted. Unburied and de-
composing bodies of Chinese soldiers and of civilians caught in the intensive Japanese bombing and shelling lay everywhere. "Walking along
one saw here and there a clenched fist sticking up from the soil or an arm
or a leg." Half-starved people scrounged among the corpses for any
money or valuables to buy food. In sharp contrast, at the Metropole
Hotel in the settlement "silk-gowned, pomaded Chinese blades" were
absorbed with the dancing girls in shimmering white silk that clung to
them "like gauze." How "degenerate" the bourgeois Chinese residents
of Shanghai, and how fine and courageous the peasant soldiers of China!
China's hope, Snow wrote, lay not in corrupt, gangster-ridden Shanghai, but in the vastness of the land and people beyond it.[1]

Snow was equally outraged that no provisions had been made to
evacuate any of China's small modern industrial plants, mostly concentrated in or near Shanghai. There had been no advance moves to organize and prepare the workers to salvage their machines and move with
them to the unindustrialized interior. "But any such advance arrange-

ments," Snow later dourly wrote, "were rendered impossible under a Government which feared Shanghai labor as much as, if not more than, the Japanese." The poignant sense of loss and of lost opportunity was accentuated for Snow by his New Zealander companion on these Shanghai rounds. Alley, then chief factory inspector under the International Settlement's municipal council, could reconstruct for Ed the histories of hundreds of such destroyed workshops and of their harshly exploited workers. Hundreds of thousands of industrial workers had been idled, and the foreign settlements were jammed with some two million refugees, most of them destitute.[2]

This was the context and mind-set in which the Chinese Industrial Cooperatives (CIC) took form in the early months of 1938. In his characteristically understated and self-effacing manner, Alley eloquently summed this up the following year: "We have brought together engineers and cooperators, and have started a chain of small industry throughout the country. We have made a few engines work that would otherwise have rusted. Put a few people to work who would otherwise have sat in refugee camps. Produced some of the necessities that a people must have whether they are at war or not." And as Ed wrote to a colleague of his own deep commitment to the project, "I could not any longer consider myself a bystander; there was too much work to be done; and without waiting for anybody's invitation, I threw myself in (as [the ample] Anna Louise Strong would say) where my weight counted most."[3]

The cooperative movement was primarily the "invention" (Snow wrote in *Journey*) of Rewi Alley and the two Snows. The original idea and much initial "energizing" of the other two came from Peg. As Ed told the story in a graceful preface to Peg's 1941 book on the CIC, industrial cooperatives were "first of all the brain child of Nym Wales." The subject of cooperatives had come up at a Shanghai dinner party attended by the Snows. Their host, John Alexander of the British consular service, had enthusiastically pushed the cooperative cause as the solution to the world's ills. Peg vigorously rejected the idea: "As usual, she overwhelmed her opponent," Ed wrote. Yet within a day or so she came strongly around to the concept, but for producer rather than consumer units, with particular applicability to China's grim wartime situation. Such industrial cooperatives could give productive work to refugees, mobilize idled skilled labor, and create a decentralized chain of small workshops utilizing the resources of China's vast interior, away from concentrated urban areas vulnerable to Japanese occupation or bombing.[4]

According to Helen Snow, the very next morning after her encounter with Alexander, "the solution to China's chief problem came to me in a flash. Why not organize the Chinese workers into cooperatives owned and managed by themselves, financed by labor hours instead of cash capital?" Under her "usual intellectual prodding," Snow related in his *Battle for Asia,* Alley and he soon saw the light on the great potentialities of industrial cooperation. Peg "stood over" him, Alley later recounted, and said, " 'Now look here, Rewi, what China wants today is industry everywhere. . . . I tell you Rewi, you say you like China, you ought to drop this job of making Shanghai a better place for the Japanese to exploit, and do something that will be useful at this time. The Chinese are made for cooperation.' This she said and much more," he dryly added.[5]

Alley, already working on ideas for building up industry in the interior, went home and typed up a plan based on the concept of a chain of small-scale producer cooperatives throughout unoccupied China. Ed then turned this into a finished version, which was printed in pamphlet form by J. B. Powell's *Review.* Snow came up with the term "industrial cooperatives" (which became known as Indusco abroad from its cable address), and Rewi with the *gung ho* logo, the Chinese equivalent of Indusco that could be literally rendered in English as "work together."

As I noted, Evans Carlson took on the Gung Ho slogan for his famed wartime Marine raiders. To him it represented the spirit of common resolve and equally shared burdens and rewards he had perceived in both the Communist Eighth-Route Army and the CIC movement. Through this avenue Gung Ho entered the American vocabulary to convey an attitude of rather naive "can do" enthusiasm. Truly, there was much of this latter spirit in the expansive claims and aspirations for CIC made by its founding trio. It was proclaimed to be the economic basis for unifying and strengthening resistance forces (including support for Communist-held guerrilla areas), for advancing political democracy, and promoting social and economic change. It was "a people's movement giving encouragement to progressive tendencies," Helen Snow declared, and a "healthy 'middle way' common economic program to prevent a civil war between the Right and the Left in China." Industrial cooperation, Ed wrote, "offered the possibility of creating a new kind of society in the process of the war."[6]

The Snows and Alley gathered with eight others in a Shanghai restaurant in April 1938 and formally constituted the group as a preparatory committee to promote the cooperative project. A prominent Shanghai banker and patriot, Xu Xinliu (Hsu Sing-loh), chaired the committee.

His financial contacts and enthusiastic support were invaluable in these early months; his death that August when his plane was downed by the Japanese on a flight from Hong Kong into China was a serious blow. Snow had talked with Xu in Hong Kong on CIC business just a few hours before his departure. Xu's death "shocked me beyond expression," Snow wrote J. B. Powell. He was "a rare personality of his class indeed, a generous and sincere and honest man, and one of the few first class financial brains in China."[7]

Just as Xu had been an exception to Snow's image of the "degenerate" Shanghai bourgeoisie, he soon met a further exception of a different sort in the British ambassador to China, Sir Archibald Clark-Kerr (later Lord Inverchapel), who subsequently served as ambassador in wartime Moscow and then Washington. As another early convert and ally in the cooperative cause, he clearly did not fit Snow's unsympathetic view of such representatives of the British Raj, or for that matter any other stereotype of the stuffy diplomat. "Archie" and Snow would become trusting and lasting friends. Clark-Kerr had read *Red Star* before coming to China and looked Snow up on arrival in Shanghai in early 1938. Though then representing the highly conservative Chamberlain government, he was himself vigorously "anti-Axis, anti-Franco and anti-Japanese," in Snow's words. He confided to Ed in Hankou (also called Wuhan, for the tri-city complex of Hankou, Wuchang, and Hanyang) well before that city's fall to the Japanese in December 1938 that its Nationalist defenders needed some of Madrid's *no pasarán* spirit. (Snow was clearly of like mind.) A craggy featured, ruddy faced Scotsman ("all he needed was a feather in his head to be an Indian chief"), he impressed Snow with his infectious wit, kindliness, initiative, and self-confidence. "He stands for the highest type of British official—a rare diplomat," Snow entered in his diary.[8]

Snow succeeded in convincing the ambassador of the merits and practicality of the Indusco plan, and of Alley as the ideal leader to make it work. Clark-Kerr then "sold" the package to the Nationalist government in Hankou—primarily through Madame Chiang and the Generalissimo's Australian adviser, W. H. Donald. They were probably the two people with the greatest influence over the Generalissimo and represented as well the staunchest anti-Japanese elements in the regime. Madame Chiang pressured her brother-in-law, Finance Minister H. H. Kung, to back the project with money. He in fact became president of the board of directors of the CIC Association under the executive branch of the government, of which he was then also president (premier). In this capacity, Kung "assumed active direction over all CIC policies, finances, and appointments."[9]

In Hong Kong Snow gained the support of T. V. Soong, who agreed privately to back CIC with a substantial loan. T. V., the "liberal" member of the Soong family and a financial expert and banker, was then outside the government and on less than cordial terms with Kung. With Madame Sun's enthusiastic support also secured, the Snow-Alley trio of cooperators had managed to corral the full spectrum of the Soong clan, from the Chiang-Kung ruling branch on the right, to T. V. in the center, and Soong Qingling on the left.

Already in Shanghai the British ambassador had arranged for Alley's immediate separation from his post under the Shanghai municipal council administration. With his unconditional release and pension monies in hand, Alley gambled all on the CIC project. He was soon in Hankou where, with Madame Chiang's firm support, he was appointed chief technical adviser under Dr. Kung, of the now formally established organization in August 1938. (Alley would also wear a dual hat as field secretary under the CIC's international committee set up in Hong Kong in January 1939.) After many "wearying hours in Hankow talking about our cooperative scheme," Snow wrote Powell from Hong Kong later that month, "(I) had the satisfaction of seeing it launched." The movement was going ahead, he added, "despite all sorts of political intrigue and obstruction centered around it." In describing these developments more confidentially to Bertram (then in England) later that year, Snow wrote that "we had manipulated the fuehrers into compliance with a program which normally they would have regarded with shocked horrification as distinctly rouged."[10]

The fact that the cooperative scheme could get off the ground with the backing of the Nationalist government attested also to the heady atmosphere then prevailing in Hankou. For a moment in time, that temporary capital became a somewhat romantic symbol of a seemingly politically united, all-inclusive, and optimistic spirit of determined resistance to the Japanese enemy. It had taken on (rather unrealistically) a kind of Chinese Madrid symbolism ("a genuine popular front capital," Bertram recollected)—an international focal point, especially for the left, in the worldwide antifascist struggle.[11]

The auto tycoon Henry Ford and the Irish-American Presbyterian missionary Joseph Bailie were unorthodox links in the Indusco chain. The latter had first come to China in 1890 and had early on seen his mission in terms of "helping the poor as opposed to saving souls." In his view, "hungry Christians cannot be good Christians." He had been a principal founder of and professor at the College of Agriculture and Forestry of the University of Nanking and took the lead in promoting rural reconstruction programs. He saw rural educational, medical, and economic development as the foundation for a productively self-supporting, independent Chinese nation and people. He stressed the dignity of labor and deplored those who treated the Chinese worker merely as a coolie. "My theory of life," he declared, in reference to the medical condition of the Chinese countryside, "is that we can never have real culture so long as the so-called cultured can look upon such degradation as we have here without doing all in its power to remove it." In all this Bailie was truly, as Alley said, "the ancestor of Indusco."[12]

This was true in a broader sense as well. Among his many ideas and projects for human betterment in China, Bailie urged Henry Ford in 1920 to consider establishing one or more auto plants and support facilities in China, and in conjunction with this to take in groups of one hundred Chinese students for on-the-job practical engineering experience in a training program at his Detroit works. "I want you to go to China and open up," he told the Ford people, "and it will save you an immense amount of trouble to have a lot of tried men at hand." Ford duly provided such training to youths selected by Bailie, most of them graduates of American engineering colleges. These were to be a new breed of educated Chinese who combined theoretical learning with hands-on work experience at the factory level, not the usual returned student aspiring to and prepared only for a bureaucratic career back home. Bailie thus constantly agitated against what he considered "white-collar engineers." He tended to idealize Ford as a model entrepreneur and benefactor of the American worker, who would come to China to do equally well by the Chinese. "Is there no way," he somewhat naively wrote Ford's secretary in 1921, "whereby when whatever company is organized, the shareholder would receive no more than a definite interest on their money invested, while the balance of the profits after treating the workers as Mr. Ford knows how, would be used for giving elementary education to those villages where very often not a single literate person can be found?"[13]

Though Ford eventually lost interest in a China auto venture, many Ford factory school alumni, most of them Christian and with engineering degrees, would become the core technical-engineering staff of Indusco. With the help of some Ford returnees, Bailie also conducted technical programs for poor factory apprentices and young workers in schools attached to major industrial plants in Shanghai. All these student protégés came to be known as "Bailie Boys."

Alley first met this unusual missionary in 1928. Bailie soon became a mentor and inspiration to the young New Zealander. (It was Bailie who had persuaded Alley to spend his summer vacation in 1929 in the northwestern famine area where he first met Snow.) Bailie "was a great American," Alley wrote in 1940, "standing out as a giant in this twilight where we grope so feebly and do so few of the things we are capable of doing." Discouraged, and ill with cancer, Bailie returned to America in 1935 to be with his family in Berkeley, California. After undergoing surgery, he knew he had at most a few bedridden months to live. "So he faced the issue as he had always faced issues," Alley recounted, "waited till people were away from home and quietly shot himself." The Bailie Boys' role in CIC, and Alley's work in connection with the cooperatives, including establishing a number of Bailie Schools for poor village youths modeled on the missionary's work-study Shanghai project, made a fitting memorial to the old man.[14]

During the 1930s Alley befriended a number of Bailie's engineers in Shanghai, a few of whom worked at high-level jobs for the American-owned Shanghai Power Company. He recruited these skilled and experienced men—still imbued with the Bailie spirit—for CIC, at great personal cost to them of income and security. The secretary-general of CIC and the four administrative heads under Alley were all Bailie Boys, as were others who held key posts in the various regional field headquarters. Their extraordinary importance was underlined by the fact that CIC in those years had a total of only twenty "first-class engineers." The secretary-general, K. P. Liu, had been a model county magistrate in Anhui province where he had organized, as he proudly wrote Bailie shortly before the latter's death, cooperative societies for afforestation, fishing, and credit; built roads and a hospital; and ousted the racketeering local tax collectors.[15]

The CIC planners had set an overly ambitious goal of thirty thousand field units by the end of 1940. (Carrying this further, Helen Snow declared in 1940 that CIC "could probably build 480,000 cooperative factories" for the cost of a one-hundred-million-dollar American battleship.) While such numbers were never even remotely achieved, at its peak in 1940 the movement did have 1,867 functioning societies with just under thirty thousand members, with perhaps a quarter million people in all dependent on Indusco for a livelihood. The "Indusco line," Helen Snow grandly wrote, "stretches in a vast crescent from the deserts of Central Asia to the southern sea." With five main headquarters and depots throughout the country these "vestpocket" industries (Snow's term) operated on three "lines": a first or front line of mobile "guerrilla industries" in the battle zones and behind Japanese lines; a second or middle line of semi-mobile units in the fluid areas between the war fronts and the rear; and a third or rear line in unoccupied "Free China" of more permanently established basic industrial enterprises and the technical and other support services for all three zones.

CIC ran training and vocational centers, clinics, printing and publishing houses, and literacy classes for cooperative members and their families. It operated small mines, machine shops and refineries, chemical, glass, and electrical works and produced a broad variety of goods for both civilian and military needs. Using the wool-raising resources of northwestern China, Indusco units were able to produce some three million winter blankets for the Chinese army through 1942, though not without stretching the cooperative principle to include large numbers of hired contract workers.[16]

CIC's organizational principles and procedures were incorporated in a model constitution drawn up in Chungking during 1939 by cooperative experts and CIC people. It was a lengthy legalistic document and, in Douglas Reynolds' words, "suffered from bureaucratic and intellectual excess." Essentially, as Snow described it, a cooperative unit was financed through low-interest loans and credits. Each worker became a shareholder entitled to a vote. Through deductions from wage earnings the workers bought over their shares, thus paying off the loans and establishing a genuine cooperative. Profits were to be allocated, in prescribed percentages, to reserve, welfare, and industrial development funds or, as bonuses to staff and workers, paid in shares and cash. Each factory unit was envisaged, as Alley expressed it to Helen Snow, "as one link in a co-ordinated chain of production," organized into local federations under each of the five regional headquarters. In the final analysis, as Reynolds states, it was not "CIC's fine procedures and regulations" but only proper leadership in the field that could protect and serve members' interests.[17]

Despite the enormous obstacles it faced, and the inevitable deviations in practice from its ideals and principles, CIC had merits and workability and seemed to many a promising democratic prototype for the future—"tomorrow's hope," Snow called it in his glowingly *Red Star*–like portrayal of Indusco in *Battle for Asia*. CIC also attracted the attention of Nehru in India, who closely followed its progress. He avidly read both Ed's *Battle for Asia* (in its British edition, *Scorched Earth*), and Helen's *China Builds for Democracy* (the latter a gift to him from Madame Sun). On Ed's volume, he wrote that "no part of it held me so much as the chapters dealing with the Chinese Industrial Cooperatives." Nehru emphasized the applicability of the village industry concept to India as well as China. "Possibly the future will lead us and others to a cooperative commonwealth," he concluded in a foreword to the Indian edition of Helen's book in 1942. "Possibly the whole world, if it is to rise above its present brute level of periodic wars and human slaughter, will have to organize itself in some such way." With such shining vistas, so assiduously fostered by the Snows in their publicity work, CIC also became a banner for rallying foreign support for China's overall war effort. And garnering such support, particularly in the West, may have had a certain effect in bolstering the more steadfastly anti-Japanese and forward-looking elements in the Chinese government.[18]

From the start CIC faced the financial and political problems that stemmed from its governmental connection. Kung released funds earmarked for CIC only in dribs and drabs; there were constant cash flow crises alleviated by bank loans and monies collected through committees organized in Hong Kong and the West, and among overseas Chinese in the Philippines and Southeast Asia. Alley and other key staff members lived on a pittance, often dipping into their savings for personal and CIC expenses. As of January 1939, for example, Alley had received only one month's salary since joining CIC the previous July. Snow devoted much of his time and energies to the project during his final three years in Asia, at considerable cost to his own work and to his financial and physical well-being. "End of my second month here, working on Indusco! What an ass!" he dejectedly recorded in Hong Kong in June 1939.[19]

Kung, known irreverently to CIC insiders as "the Sage," for his reputed descent from Confucius (Kong [Kung] Fuzi) was both a plus and (increasingly) a minus for Indusco. On the down side were his penny-pinching, foot-dragging mode of support, his profit-oriented mentality, and his innate suspicion of the "popular front" character of the movement. Additionally, in partnership with his wife, the eldest Soong sister, he engaged in speculative and other nonproductive activities. Snow alleged in a July 1939 diary entry that Madame Kung was "fishing around" to get Indusco to help her establish "model factories," possibly in Shanghai, which would earn a "modest 10%" on her investment. Snow also reported that the Kungs still owned "immense properties" in Shanghai, though he added that most of their money was held abroad. These activities at the top reflected the pattern of self-enrichment prevalent throughout the bureaucracy, and which the cooperatives found it more and more difficult to stave off.[20]

Yet in the early years Kung was also CIC's protector in high places. He was after all considered second only to the Generalissimo in the government hierarchy. "Dr. Kung is certainly to be congratulated," Helen Snow remarked in her book on the cooperatives, "upon the fact that he has not permitted the CIC to fall into the grasping hands of Chungking politicians." The "fulsome praise" accorded Kung and Madame Chiang in CIC publicity material, Snow unenthusiastically noted to Jim Bertram in March 1939, was "the necessary line." Kung, educated in American-sponsored missionary schools, and with degrees from Oberlin College and Yale University, savored such image-making publicity the Indusco promoters gave him in the West. To offset his work to guard the cooperatives from rival factional efforts to absorb or destroy them were Kung's own administrative shortcomings and obstructionism, and the "grasping" qualities of many in his entourage. As a Christian convert and a former YMCA secretary, "Daddy" Kung had a "soft-hearted" (and Snow would add "soft-headed") side to him, which could also be a bit of a trial. He tended to view CIC in paternalistically philanthropic terms that misinterpreted its mission and trivialized its significance. He approved of such Gandhi-like "spinning societies," he told Snow, for they could keep virtuous village girls working at home, away from the evil influences of big city factory life.[21]

At the same time, Indusco's founders had a left-leaning agenda of their own that was bound to collide with the entrenched political and economic interests and constituencies of the Nationalist regime. ("What is the color of your [CIC] organization?," W. H. Donald queried Ida Pruitt, who became executive secretary of Indusco's international operations.) The Snows and Alley aimed to use the cooperatives to advance the kind of popularly based and politically inclusive war effort they found lacking in Kuomintang policies. Donald had also already reacted negatively and sharply to Alley's suggestion of two Hankou-based Communist leaders (one of them Zhou Enlai) for membership on CIC's board of directors. Alley was merely (if naively) expressing his and the Snows' view of the cooperative movement as a united front operation encompassing and aiding both the Communist and Nationalist resistance effort.[22]

Actually, as Alley much later revealed, he was in touch with Zhou Enlai and other Communist liaison people in Hankou in the organizing stages of Indusco. They advised a more politically circumspect CIC approach. It should seek out prominent anti-Japanese "patriotic democrats" for leading roles in the organization, work with and through the

Edgar Snow at age twenty-two, as he embarked from New York in 1928 for the Orient.

Edgar Snow's mother, Anna Edelmann Snow. Date unknown. Courtesy Mildred and Claude Mackey Papers, University of Missouri–Kansas City Archives.

Edgar Snow and father, J. Edgar, in 1941. J. Edgar and Snow's sister, Mildred, and her husband, Claude Mackey, were then visiting Ed in New York and Howard in Boston. Ed had not seen his father and sister since leaving Kansas City in 1926. Courtesy Mildred and Claude Mackey Papers, University of Missouri–Kansas City Archives.

Edgar Snow and sister, Mildred Mackey, 1941. Courtesy Mildred and
Claude Mackey Papers, University of Missouri–Kansas City Archives.

Mildred Mackey and Howard Snow, 1941. Courtesy Mildred and Claude
Mackey Papers, University of Missouri–Kansas City Archives.

Chiang Kai-shek, J. B. Powell (*China Weekly Review* editor), and Edgar Snow, probably 1929 or 1930, in Nanking. Powell, then correspondent for the *Chicago Tribune,* had interviewed Chiang. Courtesy of J. B. Powell Papers, Western Historical Manuscript Collection, University of Missouri.

Peking student marchers, December 9, 1935 (December Ninth Movement). Photo taken by Snow.

Helen (Peg) Foster Snow, in Peking in the mid-1930s. Showing her with her dog Gobi, and her riding attire, the photo exemplified one aspect of the life-style of the Peking "foreign set" in those prewar years.

Helen Snow in the Philippines, 1939, where the Snows resided
from late 1938 through 1940. She was deeply involved in Indusco
promotional work there. Courtesy of the late Polly Babcock Feustel.

Agnes Smedley, 1940s. Courtesy of Mary C. Dimond Papers, University of Missouri–Kansas City Archives.

Edgar Snow on arrival in the Red district in the northwest, 1936.

Mao's preserved cave dwelling in Bao'an, where Snow spent long nights interviewing the Communist leader in 1936. Photo by Evelyn Thomas.

Mao and wife, He Zizhen, Bao'an, 1936. Mao later divorced her to marry the actress Jiang Qing.

Hillside cave dwellings of Mao and other Red leaders outside Yan'an, where Snow interviewed the chairman in 1939. Considerably more "upscale" than Bao'an, it remained Mao's headquarters until 1947. Photo by Evelyn Thomas.

George Hatem (Dr. Ma Haide) and wife, Sufei. Inscribed on back, "To dearest Rewi from George and Sufei in Yenan [Yan'an], 1945." Courtesy of Mary C. Dimond Papers, University of Missouri–Kansas City Archives.

Edgar Snow and Evans Carlson, in the Philippines, 1940.

James Bertram during visit with the
Snows in the Philippines, 1940.

Edgar Snow and Soong Qingling (Madame Sun Yat-sen), in later 1930s. Courtesy of University of Missouri–Kansas City Archives; gift of Soong Qingling Foundation, China.

Edgar Snow as a war correspondent at Stalingrad, February 1943, after the Russian victory there. Courtesy of Smedley-Strong-Snow Society, China.

Edgar and Lois Snow with children, Christopher and Sian, 1954.
Courtesy of Lois Wheeler Snow.

Edgar and Lois Snow with China group in Geneva, 1961. *From left to right,* Chinese consul general Wu, Lois Snow, Madame Wu, Chen Xiuxia, Gong Peng, Edgar Snow, Qiao Guanhua (Ch'iao Kuan-hua), and Israel Epstein. Aside from the consul general and his wife and the Snows, the others were in Geneva for the 1961–1962 international conference on Laos. Foreign ministry officials Qiao and his wife, Gong Peng, were old China friends of Snow's. Courtesy of Lois Wheeler Snow.

Rewi Alley outside his Peking home, 1960s. In much the same garb he trekked through China's hinterland in his wartime Indusco work. Courtesy of Mary C. Dimond Papers, University of Missouri–Kansas City Archives.

Edgar Snow, Zhou Enlai, and Mao in Peking during Snow's 1964–1965 China trip.

Edgar Snow and Puyi, the last Qing emperor, in Peking during Snow's 1964–1965 visit.

Edgar Snow with friend and literary agent Yoko Matsuoka in Japan, at a journalists' seminar she arranged for him in Tokyo, 1968. Courtesy of Seiko Matsuoka.

Edgar Snow and Huang Hua, in front of Mao's Bao'an cave, during Snow's final 1970–1971 China visit. Note the diplomat Huang's "politically correct" cultural revolutionary attire.

Lois and Edgar Snow at a Peking dinner party, 1970.

Edgar Snow at home in Eysins, Switzerland, September 1971, just months before his death.

The Snows' home in Eysins. Courtesy of Lois Wheeler Snow.

Kuomintang, and develop as much international support as possible. CIC should not go into Red-controlled areas "except in the course of popular front work that covered all unoccupied regions," Alley related. This counsel seemed in keeping with the orthodox Communist interpretation of the united front line at the time—to avoid any moves that might undermine the joint Kuomintang-led struggle. It was a line with which Snow would have his differences.[23]

In any case, the dynamics of the war, with its great expansion of Communist power vis-à-vis the increasingly conservative and debilitated Nationalists, could only heighten the inherent tensions between the two camps. The tiny CIC united front forces, relying heavily on foreign support and funding, could in no way set the course in China's increasingly polarized wartime politics. The reverse, as Douglas Reynolds's study of the CIC has demonstrated, was the case. CIC thus faced such formidable obstacles as continuous financial cutbacks and crises, anti-Communist vendettas against many of its staff, and persistent efforts at takeover ("reorganization") by rightist elements and time-serving and often corrupt bureaucratic hangers-on. As a crowning irony, what remained of the original CIC would find short shrift and internment under the Communists after 1949.[24]

But in the relatively unified political climate of the early war years, and with an eye on CIC's interests, Snow conspicuously tried to emphasize the positive when writing on the Chiang-Kung patrons of Indusco. A 1940 item he did on the three Soong sisters, who were displaying their joint backing of CIC, was a case in point. In their support of the cooperatives, Snow rather transparently concluded, "One perhaps sees in best focus the generous instincts which all three sisters possess." Ed could hardly have put his heart into even so mildly likening his idol, Madame Sun, to Madame Kung. (Madame Sun, in passing on scandalous tidbits to Snow on the profiteering activities of H. H. and Madame Kung, herself cautioned Ed, for Indusco's sake, not to put any of it in print.)[25]

In a *Foreign Affairs* article on the Generalissimo published in the summer of 1938, just as CIC was moving into place under Nationalist auspices, Snow showed a willingness, despite the past, to give the Chinese leader the benefit of his (Snow's) doubts, and to accord Chiang high marks for his stubbornly courageous, if autocratic, war leadership. "His outstanding virtues," Snow wrote, "are courage, decision, determination, ambition and sense of responsibility." (Snow had a personal interview with Chiang in Hankou that July, a meeting that could take place, he surmised, because the Generalissimo "did not know who I was.")

Snow took even what he considered Chiang's most pernicious past policies (appeasing Japan while waging ruthless war against the Reds) and managed to give them a considerably more affirmative twist. He thus declared, "we may be absolutely certain that Chiang exhausted every practical possibility of reconciliation with Japan before the current bloodbath began." And as for the Generalissimo's "implacable war against the Reds," it could be taken as evidence of Chiang's tenacious character, now put to better use against the Japanese. "This stubbornness," Snow argued, "is in fact one of Chiang's qualities that make the Chinese Communists respect and support him today," expecting that he "can be made to fight" with equal determination against the Japanese. (In a *Post* article at this time, Snow stressed that Chiang had "faithfully adhere[d] to his united front pact" with the Reds.) With adroitness Snow concluded that the "objective conditions which are the instrument of Chiang's fate today are relatively dynamic and progressive, and it is because he continues to reflect their nature that his leadership remains secure."

In another piece on Chiang, over two years later, Snow pursued much the same line of reasoning, but by now raising warning signals for the future. He pointedly declared that the Nationalist leader "must soon either undergo a further transformation with the period or dwindle to a figure of relative insignificance." Chiang could retain his role as "the Leader by common consent only as long as he continues to symbolize the united national struggle against imperialism," and he would "lose his prestige overnight if he were to betray that trust," he asserted. Snow, however, was still ready to applaud the Generalissimo's "steadfastness" under that test, which "has helped to stamp China's fight for independence with the dignity of one of the heroic causes of our time." On the proposition that a man can be judged only against "the milieu and limitations" of his own time and place, Snow finally pronounced, "it seems likely that, despite his prejudices and contradictions and counter-revolutionary past Chiang Kai-shek will be remembered as a great leader." But, Snow emphasized, citing views he attributed to the Communists, the broader "the revolutionary mobilization of the masses," the "deeper would become the revolutionary mission of the war—and the more revolutionary a leader Chiang would be forced to become, if he wished to hold his place at 'the center of resistance.' "

It was equally evident that, for Snow, CIC itself was a crucial element in the military and political dynamics of the China equation. In a *Post* piece in the spring of 1940, in which he appraised China's protracted resistance effort both positively and optimistically, the Indusco story was in the forefront of this relatively sanguine picture. "I believe," he ended, that "a better nation" will emerge from "the valley of slaughter" than the one that entered it. This article even elicited a warmly commendatory letter from Chungking's vice-minister of information (and Missouri journalism alumnus), Hollington ("Holly") K. Tong. "I do not hesitate to say," Tong wrote Ed of his "fine article," that "it is one of the best analysis [sic] I have seen of the present situation between China and Japan."[26]

Snow's public flirtation with the notion that the Generalissimo and his government could or would rise to the occasion of a popular revolutionary-style war effort had run its course by the end of 1940. With the unraveling of the united front and growing possibilities of renewed civil war, coupled with the correspondingly deteriorating situation of CIC, Snow's misgivings would be more openly expressed in his published views. In his personal opinions, as previously noted, Snow from 1937 on continuously took a much more pessimistic and skeptical view of Chiang's wartime stewardship. In this vein, in a letter to Jim Bertram in November 1938, shortly after the loss of Hankou to the Japanese, Snow acidly remarked that Chiang "will simply retire as far back as he is pushed, and it may be best for China that he is pushed to Tali or Bhamo [on the Burma frontier]. Certainly nothing can be done to organize the people, or to mobilize the resources of the hinterland, in areas he controls." Ed (and Helen) therefore saw CIC's primary mission to be one of sustaining the guerrilla-style war waged in the regions of Red military operations. Getting CIC support for "guerrilla industry" became a chief preoccupation of Snow's Indusco work. Though the Kuomintang areas might be the "physical base" of CIC, he told Alley in 1939, the "spiritual base and organizational base must be in guerrilla areas." As always, Snow was deeply influenced in these views by his intense compassion for and emotional attachment to the ordinary people of China and their lives. It is "the youth, the very young, and the farmers, the poor of China, the soldiers, the workers, the men and women, millions of them, who ask so little and give so much in return for it, that make China break your heart!" Snow entered in his diary at the time. The "picture of Chungking and the interior sounds so terribly hopeless from all angles," he added. "Why should it seem such a personal and psychological problem with me?" Perhaps, he pondered, the reason for his strong reaction to all this might be "a conflict between my desire to write the truth as I see it and the loyalties which prevent me from writing that truth?"[27]

Beyond this, of course, was Snow's continuously reiterated thesis on popular mobilization as the key to Chinese victory. According to his reasoning, as the Nationalist armies retreated further into the western China hinterland, their withdrawal gave Japan the opportunity to consolidate control over and exploit the resources of its occupied territories. Only Communist-organized peasant resistance could thwart this outcome, thereby making Japan's China conquests "a costly and entirely profitless venture which may ultimately bring ruin and defeat," Snow wrote Harry Price in November 1938. It would be "a race against time," he told Bertram, "to see whether the Xi'ans [Reds] can mobilize and train and arm the people, in the areas penetrated by the Nips, faster than the enemy can." And CIC was precisely the instrument to provide the essential mobile industrial backup for that effort. As Snow summed it up to Richard Walsh over a year later, "if nothing is done to strengthen the economic basis of guerrilla resistance, China will probably be lost until such time as the fortunes of the Japanese Empire suffer a reversal through major war elsewhere."[28]

In 1938 from Hankou Snow had sent Mao a letter describing the newly launched cooperative movement. The following year he made his second visit to the Red northwest to brief Mao on CIC and secure his personal endorsement. The Red leader told Snow he had fully supported the movement since receiving Ed's earlier letter. Mao especially emphasized to him that CIC "should devote first attention to the guerrilla areas." In a follow-up letter to Mao, Snow noted that "my own deepest dissatisfaction with C.I.C. is that it has failed, thus far, to give important help to guerrilla industry, although that is where the sympathies of nearly all its leaders lie." On his return from the northwest, Snow recommended to CIC's international committee in Hong Kong that it "devote all possible available funds" to develop cooperatives in the guerrilla districts of the north. "Whereas industrial cooperatives are compelled to make all sorts of retreats and compromises to survive elsewhere, in the guerrilla areas alone they can enjoy the fullest co-operation of the government, the army, and the population."[29]

Ironically, as in the case of *Red Star,* Snow was taking a more leftist position, again evidently in accord with Mao's, than the prevailing Communist orthodoxy on just where the political and military center of gravity in the China conflict lay. This was illustrated in an exchange of letters in early 1939 between the Snows and Israel Epstein on the question of CIC priorities and the principal purposes of its international promotional and fund-raising work. Epstein, who had been brought up in Tianjin and had known the Snows in Peking, was an able young journalist in charge of publicity for the CIC's Hong Kong promotion committee, organized by Ida Pruitt in February 1939. Epstein argued for the conventional left line on the Kuomintang-led united front. He had strong reservations about Peg's outspoken views in her correspondence, on CIC's primary mission to help Communist forces in the field. ("Our underlying aim [in starting Indusco]," Helen responded to Epstein, "has been and is now more than ever to make Indusco a medium of helping the people's movement in China, and of securing foreign funds for this in as great a percentage as possible.") As Epstein put it in a rejoinder to the Snows, "if we are not to come to grief, there must be thorough discussion of how Indusco can serve its ends with maximum effect and yet with maximum adherence to UF [united front]. . . . The UF, not some ideal UF but the pulsating and writhing thing that exists at the moment and must be the inevitable environment of our work." Ed, with some asperity, wrote back: if "your committee does not intend to devote its main energies" to raising money for the guerrilla areas "you are evidently under a misapprehension concerning the purposes of the founders of the movement." Snow listed as a fundamental objective of CIC, "to provide indispensable economic bases for the military and political forces of the democratic people's united front"—a distinctly different concept from Epstein's "UF." "Our allies are CDL [Madame Sun's Hong Kong-based China Defence League] and Era and Newfa [the Communist Eighth-Route and New Fourth Armies]," Snow continued, "and not ML and HH [Madame Chiang and H. H. Kung]—whom we must encourage and help, of course, without however dissipating our own slender energies."[30]

Snow's formula for CIC—of working both with and around the Nationalist government—and essentially at political cross-purposes with it—surely had its own contradictory if not mutually exclusive character. (Ed himself seemed to acknowledge this in talking of "guerrindusco" as a discrete entity and undertaking.) For this formula to work at all called for financing and control largely independent of the Chinese government. This goal in turn required vigorous promotional and fund-raising efforts abroad, and the creation of influential externally based committees to funnel the monies raised, through Alley, straight to CIC in the field. As Snow bluntly framed this to Epstein, "I think there is no question that Alley can guarantee the use of all funds secured by us for use in guerrindusco if that is the will of the [Hong Kong promotion] Committee as it most certainly should be, in my opinion." At the inception of CIC in the summer of 1938, Snow had already indicated the semi-adversarial relationship with the Nationalist government he and his fellow Indusco sponsors anticipated. "We may suffer rebuffs, we may be disowned," he had written Helen, "we may irritate and provoke the Gov., but there is no other way to make them act except to keep the movement going outside and push them along."[31]

Snow worked hard in the next months to help organize an international committee for CIC. Its first meeting was in July 1939, with the respected and social-minded Anglican bishop of Hong Kong, Ronald O. Hall, as its chair. Chen Hansheng (Han-seng), a noted agrarian specialist and acute observer of the China political scene whose links to the Communist movement became known later, was secretary of the committee until the Japanese occupation of Hong Kong in December 1941. (Thereafter the committee was based in Chengdu in western China.) Snow was a member of its board of trustees and Alley held the post of field secretary under the committee, which had auxiliary status in Kung's central headquarters in Chungking. The committee had a continually uneasy, competitive relationship with Kung, who sought control over it and of the funds channeled through its hands. "It is fair to say," Alley wrote Ida Pruitt in August 1940, "that without foreign interest and help, the CIC would have been wrecked long ago."[32]

Ida Pruitt had gone on to the United States to organize promotional-funding work there. With branch committees operating in various cities, Indusco, Inc., American Committee in Aid of Chinese Industrial Cooperatives, was established in New York in September 1940. Eleanor Roosevelt headed its advisory board, Admiral Yarnell (now retired) chaired the board of directors, with many luminaries (including Pearl Buck and her publisher husband, Richard Walsh) on the board. CIC "was fast becoming a major (and easily romanticized) factor in American thinking on China." In a March 1939 letter to Madame Sun urging her to join the board of the impending Hong Kong international committee, Snow emphasized that through fund-raising efforts around the world, "It seems likely that ten million dollars could be got under the control of this Trustees Board in a year or two. If [the board] is correctly constituted, in its membership, two million at least—let's be very conservative—can go to the guerrilla industry in which we're most interested." Actually, through 1945, the international committee had disbursed an estimated total of five million dollars (U.S.) to CIC, raised through promotion committees abroad. The American committee for Indusco itself provided some $3.5 million for CIC up to the Communist takeover in 1949–1950.[33]

As to the extent of guerrindusco support, a CIC center was set up in Yan'an (initially sanctioned by Kung), following a visit there by Alley in early 1939. Through 1941 (after which all such contributions apparently ceased), a total of some $1,500,000 in inflated Chinese currency—worth only a fraction of that in U.S. dollars—came to this office through CIC sources. Much of it came from fund-raising efforts by the Snows among the generally prosperous overseas Chinese business community in the Philippines. The latter were also the major source of funds to finance many highly useful CIC projects in areas of New Fourth Army operations. "In those days [in the Philippines] I thought nothing of asking Chinese millionaires for fifty thousand dollars or so for the Communist regions for Indusco work," Helen Snow later recalled.[34]

However, by far the major share of financing for the Yan'an-based CIC operation (especially after 1940) came from the border region government there, and the great majority of the Indusco cooperatives had been organized by the government before their incorporation under CIC. This reorganization had apparently been carried out as a result of Snow's visit to Yan'an in September 1939. "I told them," Snow wrote Ida Pruitt, "if they would reorganize and adopt the CIC constitution I'd try to get some help for new capital from IC [international committee]." Evidently in anticipation of such funding, Alley designated the Yan'an CIC an "International Center." While the Indusco example and experience may have influenced the pattern of the major production movement launched under Mao in the border region in the early 1940s, it much more directly reflected Mao's own "new democratic" concepts of a less "statist," more decentralized, village-based, mixed economy of household, cooperative, and small-scale private entrepreneurial production units. In a long letter to Alley, written just days before Pearl Harbor from his new home in Madison, Connecticut, Snow summed up the results of all their work on behalf of guerrindusco: "I often grow discouraged about the results of our own efforts through these years. Except for the little money we raised in the PI [Philippines] we haven't done anything for the guerrindusco people and I am ashamed." In America, Snow added, "never a cent has been earmarked" for guerrilla industry, and the international committee "never remits a cent itself from our funds." Perhaps reflecting these disappointing results, as well as the general decline of CIC after 1941 as it slipped away from its founding ideals, purposes, and leadership, Chinese Communist leaders themselves came to have little regard for or confidence in CIC.[35]

In September 1938 the Snows left by ship from Hong Kong to Manila (with Helen's usual thirty-eight pieces of luggage), and from there by car to the "air conditioned" mountain resort of Baguio in northern

Luzon. They looked forward, in this mini-American setting, to an extended and much needed respite from their exhausting immersion in the China drama. The last three years, from the December 1935 student movement on, had been a period of particularly high intensity, physically and emotionally draining. "I feel so completely lousy," Ed had written Helen from Hong Kong, just weeks before the two left for the Philippines. He had no appetite, had lost weight, and couldn't sleep in the summer heat, he told her. Helen herself was still recovering from her Yan'an-contracted dysentery. Baguio, at five thousand feet elevation, was an unexpected treat with its "pine clad hills and clear fresh crisp air," Snow recorded. "I had grown used to the China air so that I thought the smell was a chemical part of all air and a universal." The couple rented a four-room cottage at the country club, where Snow played a round of golf the next day. It all seemed a perfect recipe for recuperation. The food at the club was "marvelous: huckleberry pie, hot rolls, baked beans, milk-fed chicken, American lettuce. . . . Everything is on the American scale." But they had not escaped world realities. A few days later came news of the Munich pact. "To me it appears to be the most cynical deal in human life and property ever made by a responsible self-respecting people to save its own neck," Ed bitterly noted of the roles of Britain and France. It was a reaction that would strongly color his thinking on the 1939 Soviet-German agreement and on the early stages of the European war.[36]

Snow had arranged for a leave of absence from the *Herald* and planned to concentrate on his new book about the China conflict. He also looked into the current situation in the Philippines, produced a few articles on the U.S.-Philippines relationship in the context of a threatening Japan, and thought he might quickly turn out a short book on the subject to help defray living expenses. As it turned out, there was no market in the United States for such a work, and as he (and Helen) became ever more deeply caught up in CIC affairs, his big book on the war had to be put aside until 1940. "We came here for a vacation but haven't stopped working for a single day," Helen complained to Hubert Liang after a few months in the islands.[37]

But most of this work brought them no income. They were soon thoroughly involved in committee-organizing and money-raising for CIC, principally among the Manila Chinese, but with much encouragement from the American political establishment there and valuable help from good friends they made in the American business community. It became one of the most successful of such overseas efforts on behalf of CIC, especially in support of the Snows' pet project, guerrindusco.

From the Philippines in 1940 they also drew up and orchestrated a petition to Roosevelt for a $50 million American loan for CIC. Sponsored by Indusco committees in the Philippines and the United States, the document was signed by an illustrious list of Americans. Snow pushed the idea in his first meeting with the apparently sympathetic president early in 1942. Roosevelt sidestepped these efforts on grounds of noninterference in Chinese domestic affairs. He did promise Snow he would personally put in a plug for CIC with the Generalissimo. "I suppose I should have told him that Chiang wasn't the man to take a hint; he had to be pushed," Snow ruefully related in *Journey*. Helen followed up Ed's visit with Roosevelt by sending the president a copy of her book on CIC. In writing the book, Helen wrote F. D. R. in her unsubtle "up front" style, "I had you back in my mind all the time as the great hope for trying to get some American support for the movement." Actually, the Snows' notion that the Chinese government could be effectively "pushed" on CIC through external pressure would turn out to be another less than successful example of foreign efforts to "change China."[38]

Ed and Helen operated as a behind-the-scenes guiding and coordinating center for promotional activities in Hong Kong and Southeast Asia, in England and North America, and for CIC work in China. They clearly regarded the cooperatives as their offspring and were intent on keeping it on the path they had charted, and on guarding it against a hostile takeover from central headquarters in Chungking. They engaged in lengthy, and often frustrating correspondence exhorting, advising, and occasionally badgering those in charge of CIC work, principally Ida Pruitt in America and Alley in China. The Snows viewed both, in their separate spheres, as indispensable to the success or even survival of a relatively autonomous and "progressive" cooperative movement. If "you lose the independence of your Committee," Snow warned Pruitt confidentially, "your work loses its value to RA [Alley] and all the CIC people who are fighting to keep the organization out of the hands of the machine politicians." Alley, Snow continued, "can only be helped through the International Committee, which exists primarily for the purpose of backing up his leadership." There was always another crisis to manage, as well as personality problems to iron out and ruffled feathers to soothe. "No more now, I've spent a whole day on this bloody business," Snow irritably concluded another letter to Pruitt, after a particularly heavy and exasperating day of correspondence on such CIC problems.[39]

Helen Snow carried on an even more massive CIC correspondence, which often tended to take on a "command" quality with long lists of peremptory instructions. A few weeks after getting settled in Baguio, she sent Alley one of her missives. She launched into many pages of directions, under the heading, "Here is what must be done." For poor Alley, more than fully occupied in building the cooperatives from scratch, Helen ticked off a lengthy catalogue of promotional chores—letters, reports, and possible articles to write. Between Alley, the seat-of-the-pants, China-rooted builder, and the more politically focused Snows, differences in perspective were inevitable. "YOU HAVE GOT TO DO SOME PROMOTION WORK. Don't you know that 90% of getting started in China is political? PLEASE STOP WANDERING AROUND YOURSELF for a few days," she ordered, and write up "a full report" on the cooperatives. His "main job" was now organizational, she added. "Don't get lost in the mechanical details." (For Alley, of course, God *was* in the details.) Helen summed up her own standpoint: "The whole world needs fixing so badly that one hardly knows where to start or to stop."[40]

Snow made extended trips back to Hong Kong and China from the Baguio base, on CIC business and for his regular China work—both now closely related. He spent most of 1939 in Hong Kong and Chungking, and in journeying along the "Indusco line" to the pioneering and thriving northwestern CIC center of Baoji, from there on to Xi'an and Yan'an, and back to Chungking. The account of these Indusco travels, and of CIC generally, became a central feature of his *Battle for Asia*. Virtually all his China writing in that period either directly or indirectly aimed to publicize and win friends abroad for the cooperatives. In so doing he sought to preserve a "non-official" status in the movement, in part because he felt his *Red Star*–tainted reputation would not play well in Nationalist circles (though it was an asset to CIC elsewhere). But probably more important, Snow was concerned to maintain his non-affiliated professional journalist role. He was "very annoyed," he wrote Pruitt in June 1940, that some Chinese Information Service material from Washington referred to him as "a leader" of CIC. "I am only a committee member, no official connection, won't be able to do anything for CIC if this goes on," he added.[41]

But in truth, Snow *was* a leader at every stage of the CIC saga through 1941. Rewi Alley's later apt description of Ed as "standard bearer of Gung Ho" was closer to the reality than Snow's own disclaimers. What Snow's (and Helen's) nonofficial capacity did mean was that the enormous amount of effort, time, and expense put into their CIC work was uncompensated, with the exception of a few CIC-related articles Ed did for the *Post* and other journals. "I have spent months of my time, and about all my surplus cash, working on this project," Snow wrote Ma Haide after his September 1939 Yan'an visit, which led to the creation of the international CIC center there. "We have spent all our money again, as usual," Helen told J. Edgar and Mildred, and by the time Ed got down to sustained work on his book in the spring of 1940 (again on leave from the *Herald* "sans pay"), he had "already spent most of the advance royalties, alas!" he wrote his father. In taking hours and days he could not afford to lose away from his book to do necessary CIC writing that summer, Snow reiterated his characteristic journalist philosophy. "I think it is our obligation to put in an oar on the side of decency when we can, if journalism is to retain any dignity or social usefulness," he wrote an editor. His involvement continued even after his return to the States. "I cannot run away from (CIC), as I long to," he wrote Richard Walsh in mid-1941. "I am too deeply committed to some fine people who have given up far more than my little time, and whose very lives are at stake."[42]

Rewi Alley, as a partner in starting CIC and as Ed's personal choice to run the movement, was essential to the Snows' internationally based strategy for keeping the cooperatives on course and out of the wrong hands. ("If RA [Alley] goes, the whole show goes," Snow told Ida Pruitt.) Alley thus became the "star" in Snow's writings on Indusco. The idea was not simply to give this extraordinary man his due. To portray him as the inspirational embodiment of all that CIC stood for was an effective way to rally international support and, it was thought, give Alley the clout he needed for the inevitable infighting over CIC control in China. It would thus be difficult for Chungking to discard him entirely without stirring up an adverse reaction among friends of China abroad—a result that would dry up aid funds not only for CIC but for other China causes as well. "The only thing that is now preserving CIC's leadership from wholesale liquidation [by Chungking] . . . is fear of American and to a lesser extent of [other] foreign opinion," Snow explained to Walsh, then chair of the American Indusco board. By personalizing the CIC story through Alley, Snow contributed significantly to shaping that opinion.[43]

"There is one hero in particular, Rewi Alley," Snow wrote Random House of work in progress on his *Battle for Asia*. Alley's effort to build guerrilla industry in China, Ed went on in an overblown comparison, was "as much of an epic as Lawrence's organization of guerrilla war in Arabia," and it provided "a kind of ribbon of hope" for the latter part of his book. But probably Snow's single most influential writing on Alley and CIC was his *Post* article in early 1941 (a version of material included in his book) called "China's Blitzbuilder, Rewi Alley." It was a deserved paean of praise and admiration for Alley but also an extravagant picture of CIC's achievements and potentialities at a time when the prospects in China, both for Alley and Indusco, were already quite bleak. Who can say, Snow concluded, that in the end Alley's achievement may not "prove of more lasting benefit to mankind than the current battles for empire," and be "the most constructive result of the battle for Asia itself?" But such publicity did have its effect. Since mid-1941, Alley later recounted, "foreign contributions [to CIC] had taken a quantum leap," in part because of the "publicity about me and Gung Ho, especially in a *Saturday Evening Post* article by Edgar Snow." But Kung's central headquarters also redoubled its efforts to gain control over these new funds.[44]

In writing for the mass American readership of the *Post,* Snow dwelt much on Alley's unique foreigner role in China, a point Rewi himself liked to downplay. "Never before, I believe, had a foreigner been given such wide responsibility," Ed declared, "for the actual organization of a socio-economic movement in China." Alley's decidedly non-Chinese appearance was made to order for Snow. With his "fiery hair and hawk-like English nose," Alley was the perfect image of "the kind of foreign devil to frighten the wits out of Chinese children."[45]

Alley was truly excellent material for Snow's promotional endeavors. A twice-wounded decorated hero of the western front in World War I, he had struggled for a bare livelihood in sheep farming in New Zealand before coming to Shanghai in 1927. He already had, in Douglas Reynolds' words, "an instinctive antipathy for the idle rich, and a natural sympathy for the struggling and disdained poor." His China revolutionary sympathies were galvanized by the miserable working and living conditions he tried to correct, as factory inspector in Shanghai. Alley's radical politics came directly out of his compassionate but hardheaded humanity expressed in unfailing respect for those who were poorest and most disadvantaged, especially the young. The China scholar Olga Lang, who accompanied Alley on an inspection tour of Shanghai factories and workshops in 1936, recalled that the young boys and girls who worked in them "greeted Rewi as they would a friend and protector," as "an uncle and father." She was particularly impressed that Alley checked the children for signs of vitamin-deficiency beriberi disease by pressing their skin "without any trace of fastidiousness. . . . These were his own boys, not the objects of charity, not 'the poor heathens' whom one has to help out of some abstract moral [or, we might add, political] considerations."[46]

For Indusco, Alley exhibited a similar mode of on-the-spot personal contact with individual cooperatives and their members throughout the country. By 1941 he had logged tens of thousands of miles, "investigating Indusco in the field, creating it, and mothering and fathering it," in Snow's words. The American writer Graham Peck, who worked with CIC for a time and accompanied Alley to the CIC center at Baoji, related that "as soon as word spread that [Alley] had arrived, Co-op workmen, organizers, and administrators [each with a "special grievance or problem"] poured in to see him from dawn to bedtime." Alley was constantly on the go in his familiar khaki shorts, traveling by wheezing charcoal-fueled truck or bus jammed with every variety of passenger and baggage, by boat, bicycle, or more often than not trudging on his powerful trunk-like legs over the usually roadless interior. Cheerfully he shared and even savored the privations of everyday Chinese life and travel, stoically endured danger and disease, and seemed indomitable and indestructible. "This is my 20th day sick," he wrote Pruitt from a southeastern hinterland CIC base in June 1939, of a severe typhoid attack. "Do hope that other truck comes up so that I can bag it" for the northwest. On virtually all such trips Alley was but one of many hitchhiking ("yellow fish") passengers. "It was a crowded vehicle indeed that Evans Carlson [who was with him on a 1940 CIC trip] and I crawled into in Kanchow the other day," Alley reported. "I went in through the window, as that seemed the quickest and most popular way. Evans being tall, hit his head frequently as he wormed himself over the piles of luggage in the centre of the bus floor." Carlson (who had these same qualities himself) wrote the Snows, "There is a spiritual quality about Rewi which triumphs over disease, fatigue, or any other element which might be expected to leave a mark on him. He is truly one of the anointed."[47]

Whereas Snow was intent on building Alley's international reputation, Rewi himself preferred a less conspicuous role. He was inclined to understatement as opposed to the grand claims made for CIC and himself by its proponents abroad, including Snow. He adapted himself naturally to his Chinese surroundings, spoke fluent and pithily colloquial Chinese, and could regale his peasant-worker Indusco audiences with amusing and self-deprecating anecdotes on such outlandish foreign things as his extremely prominent nose. As he told Graham Peck, "the easiest way to get along with people who are suspicious of foreigners was to make the state of being a foreigner seem ridiculous." While the

Snows and others bemoaned the fact that Alley failed to exploit his international prestige ("face" in Chinese terms) in the political and bureaucratic infighting in Chungking, Alley instinctively understood the pitfalls this involved for him, not only as a foreigner, but as a suspected CCP sympathizer. He concentrated instead on trying to make things work—both people and machines, at the grass roots.[48]

This focus became a source of some contention between Alley and Snow. Ed placed much more weight on the political and foreign publicity aspects of the CIC operation. Rewi put his faith primarily in a "demonstration in the field that will 'save' CIC in spite of opposition," Snow commented in his diary of an inconclusive discussion with Alley in Hong Kong in mid-1939. Alley "thinks he can get to 10,000 [co-ops] on present basis. I tell him we are building the movement in areas of political insecurity." Alley thought Ed greatly overestimated his ability directly to influence matters in central headquarters. "No use to say that I should have stayed in Chungking," he wrote from Jiangxi in June 1939. "Our own H.Q. very certainly did not want me there. And nothing would have happened in these regional H.Q. unless we had got out on the job." Snow had earlier written Pruitt that Alley's position in Chungking was "fundamentally very strong if he uses it but trouble is he's no good at [the] political wire-pulling and intrigue" essential to holding his own in "the rotten system" he was obliged to work with. All the more reason, Ed added in the Snows' familiar and continuous theme, "to strengthen Rewi's prestige abroad, and thereby in the Government." Alley must not "get lost in field work," Helen wrote Ed that May. He was expending all his energy, she complained, "walking around the country and setting up factories with his bare hands." Chen Hansheng put the issue succinctly, in the wake of a major "reorganization" of CIC by Chungking in 1940. "Rewi thinks that if we could build up a strong field force with good coops we will be all right," he told Helen. "I hold a different opinion because I think good coops are eggs of the hen, which, however, now approaches non-fertility."[49]

There was in fact much merit in both positions. Without the organizing, publicity, and fund raising pushed by the Snows, CIC would very likely have withered on the vine early on, and without Alley's total hands-on commitment to the building process, the remarkable achievements of the early CIC years would equally have been impossible. Each side recognized and appreciated the other's contribution. But both had their illusions: Alley that he could safeguard the movement's vigor, purposes, and integrity in the field, and Snow that Alley's continued ability to do so would depend to a good degree on international publicity-derived political capital Rewi could draw on in Chungking.

Ed's position reflected the pronounced foreign vantage point of Indusco, sometimes narrowed to the personal responsibility of the two Snows. "If it becomes impossible to cooperate with Chungking," Ed declared to Pruitt in early 1939, "we will continue it as a purely Era and Newfa responsibility, and for it can tap the same sources of [outside] help." Helen carried this idea a step further in her own letter to Pruitt. If Alley was "kicked out" by Chungking, CIC should not only operate "independently" of the government, but start a campaign to replace Kung by the more CIC-friendly T. V. Soong. "Rewi thinks the way to work with the Chinese," she followed this up to Pruitt, "is to give them the open control and do all the hard work himself." But the Chinese would probably interpret this "as being weak-kneed, especially from a foreigner." The key to influencing Chungking was "foreign approbation," she told Ed. Snow, reacting to CIC's recurrent reorganizational crises, urged Alley in August 1940 to take the lead in developing Western-style democratic mechanisms for shifting power from bureaucrats at the top to the co-op members themselves. He outlined an ascending system of elective bodies from village-level co-op units to a central council at the apex. This council, he declared, should eventually acquire "by whatever methods necessary, the right to approve and finally actually to appoint its own central administration." The people now in charge in Chungking, he pressed on, "must be made to represent the common will of the C.I.C. masses. If you do not recognize that," he admonished Alley, "you will simply be deceiving yourself and evading the responsibility—which is now historic—that a combination of circumstances has put upon you." Just how Alley was to accomplish this takeover from below, in the context of a repressively authoritarian and hostile regime at the head and a traditionalist society at the base, remained unclear.

In any event Alley's way was typically Chinese. In his view, the further away from central headquarters and the less direct contact between it and units in the field, the better. Out in the hinterland, "due to bad communications, one could get progressive administrators appointed more easily," he later explained. But rather contradictorily, he acknowledged that "Gung Ho also suffered many raids and arrests in various hinterland centers throughout 1941–44." Perhaps Alley came closer to the realities in cryptically pinpointing CIC's key problem to Graham Peck in 1941: "We're trying to do it at the wrong time. We are a thousand years too early for the officials and a thousand years too late for the people." The notion of externally "moving" China forward was bluntly put by Helen Snow in her CIC book. "All that [China] needs is a good push from behind." She always identified CIC with her own Anglo-American Protestant ethos, and (with an intent also on garnering American support) underscored the Christian faith and American nurturing of Alley's Bailie Boy lieutenants. "They are the most Americanized Chinese one could imagine," she asserted in her book. "They like American slang and American food and American clothes and American methods."[50]

This Western coloration and reformist-interventionist attitude predictably annoyed conservative Chinese nationalist sensibilities. It gave a semblance of plausibility to the "imperialist" allegations raised in hostile Chinese quarters that added to the threateningly radical image they held of the cooperatives. Alley could thus be painted both Red and imperialist, and Snow found himself labeled a British agent (presumably for his ties to Clark-Kerr) in the gossip of Chungking. (Snow later used the term "missionary"—which had its own Western intrusionist connotations—as best describing his own and Alley's CIC roles.) CIC was similarly accused of facilitating inroads by foreign capital into China. Nor did Alley's Snow-promoted international standing protect him from eventual dismissal as technical adviser by the executive Yuan in September 1942. On the contrary, as Rewi later wrote a CIC colleague, "the starring of my poor efforts have done me a good deal of harm with political people in CK [Chungking]."[51]

Though Alley remained field secretary under the international committee, his title came to have little meaning in terms of overall responsibilities or control of monies. The committee itself, and Indusco's parent funding organization in the United States (United China Relief), increasingly gravitated into the orbit of Chungking. By 1945 Alley was hunkered down in the remote community of Shandan in the far northwestern province of Gansu on the edge of the Turkestan desert. There, he and a resolutely idealistic young Englishman, George Hogg, had built up a Bailie-type work-study center, enrolling peasant youths from this impoverished area. Hogg tragically died in 1945 of tetanus from an infected stubbed toe, and no vaccine available to save him. The Shandan enterprise, under Alley's direct management after Hogg's death, was a perfect example of the style Rewi always found most comfortable and satisfying: personally involved, youth-centered, away from the political spotlight. He had now, as he later recounted, "shifted my attention to training technicians at the Bailie schools to help build a New China which I felt was surely to come." The Shandan school, with help from "progressive forces" abroad, reached a maximum of some four hundred students, with a thriving complex of technical workshops, educational, medical and agricultural facilities. It seemed to embody and demonstrate in microcosm the faith affirmed by Bailie, Alley, and Snow in the mostly untapped potentialities of China's poorest peasant millions.[52]

CIC itself, facing a mounting combination of political-administrative, economic, and financial problems, declined steadily after 1940. Its downward spiral leveled off by 1945 at a total of somewhat over three hundred co-ops, where it more or less remained until Communist victory in 1949. Meanwhile Alley and his school, harassed by government agents, local militarists, and gangsters, ardently and expectantly awaited the arrival of the forces of revolutionary liberation. Ironically, however, the "struggle" tactics of Communist cadres proved no less meddlesome than the takeover methods of Kuomintang bosses. One such "political work" cadre assigned to Shandan by the new regime "set about very steadily to destroy the foundation of the school," Alley much later disclosed. "It was utterly crazy to try to undermine the good boys and say they were all gangsters and to promote the useless ones and send them off to relatively cozy jobs." The school was taken over by the Beijing government's ministry of fuel, Alley's training program for small village industry was "shelved," and Shandan's activities were shifted to the Gansu provincial capital of Lanzhou by 1952. There it concentrated on training technicians for the modern state-run oil industry. All of this was the antithesis of the autonomous, decentralized, small unit, rural-based cooperative network CIC's founders had envisioned. Symbolically, virtually all the buildings of the original Shandan school were destroyed in an earthquake at about that time. CIC was formally terminated by Beijing in 1951, not least for the international ("imperialist") links that Snow had so painstakingly worked to create specifically to ensure CIC aid to Red-controlled areas. CIC was simply "knocked out," Alley told me. The Communists said "it was just an imperialist dodge to get into China."[53]

Thus in the end Indusco became yet another frustrated Western "reformist" attempt to remake China. In many respects CIC was a wartime follow-up of earlier efforts at rural uplift during the prewar decade, in which American Protestant missionaries and their Chinese associates played a large part. The activities of Joseph Bailie prior to that, his later influence on Alley, and the role of his Bailie Boys in Indusco, further underlined these continuities. (In 1933 Snow himself wrote very favorably of the achievements of the widely acclaimed and influential model county project of Tinghsien [Dingxian], in northern China, initiated by James Y. C. Yen, the renowned American-educated former YMCA secretary and initiator of the rural-oriented mass education movement.) As recounted in a study by James C. Thomson, these prewar reformers also faced the daunting challenges posed by their "overly close association" with a government that "stood firmly in defense of the old social order." In terms equally applicable to the Indusco experience, Thomson notes "the grandiose aims and the inadequate instruments possessed by the Americans who attempted to influence the development of modern China in the Nanking [1928–1937] years." Even by those days, "gradualism had been outstripped by the Chinese revolution." Thomson cites one of the Chinese Christian reformers of that era, Y. T. Wu, who stayed on under the Communist regime after 1949. In a mea culpa on his American-linked reformist past, Wu declared in 1951, "All of us have been the tools of American cultural aggression [imperialism] perhaps without being wholly conscious of it." It was, evidently, the CCP's final verdict as well on the Indusco enterprise.[54]

Alley, operating out of Beijing after 1952, became an active figure in China-sponsored international peace and friendship activities. He also traveled widely in and wrote extensively on the new China. He took on the kind of political-publicist role he had previously shied away from. He would no longer find a place in the rural industrial training and development work that had been his life in a decade and more of anti-Japanese and civil war. In response to a 1955 query from Ed on the state of the old cooperatives in China, Alley acknowledged, "In regard to the industrial cooperative movement, naturally it has to wait a bit until heavy industry and the vast agricultural program are attended to." During the Cultural Revolution in 1968, Alley wrote Snow that as "one who had so much to do with Gung Ho beginnings, you may be interested in knowing that amongst those without background of the old society, it is sometimes the fashion to call Gung Ho just a tool of imperialism." As for his original Shandan experiment of self-sufficient small-industry training, he now more frankly told Ed, "I could not get this point understood." But in the China political fashion of 1968, he was careful to place the blame primarily on a "lugubrious Russian" who back in 1951 or thereabouts, had "looked over everything and turned it down."[55]

In the post-Mao climate of economic reform and opening to the West, in 1983 Alley would become chair of a reactivated small-scale Gung Ho (with Helen Snow still doing the "energizing"). But he remained scornful of all bureaucrats and wondered how the new Gung Ho would fare. Shandan had been both a last-ditch stand for Alley in Kuomintang-ruled China and an experimental model and holding operation for the socialist China of the future. Yet after almost four decades of life in that new China, Alley characteristically looked back on his years "with the youth in Shandan" as the high point of his experiences—"the richest and happiest in my life"—he wrote shortly before his death in 1987.[56]

Snow, back in America and viewing the grim perspectives for CIC in December 1941, reiterated both his political approach to and democratic vision for CIC. "I always told you that Indusco could have no future in China independent of the total political picture," he wrote Alley, referring to their earlier divergences on the matter. Ed returned to his thesis that CIC could yet be an instrument for effecting change in that picture and, in a valedictory on the movement, put it in more general terms. Somber prospects notwithstanding, the cooperatives had "an educational value in inculcating democratic ideas among thousands," he concluded. But in truth, the ideals of Gung Ho, with its concepts of genuine empowerment—individual and collective, political and economic—were uncongenial to authoritarianism in China—of the right and the left. Snow summed up what Indusco had meant for him most aptly in human terms. "Your gang are the best people I know," he told Alley, "and have taught me a great deal and cannot be replaced in heart or mind."[57]

CHAPTER 12

Final China Years

Aside from Indusco work during his sojourn in the Philippines, Snow delved into the local political scene. Searching out material for articles, and perhaps a short book, he soon discovered the extent of Japanese economic and political penetration in the islands, circumstances that disturbed him and further jarred his views on the desirability of American disengagement there. Filipino authorities tried to block a public meeting in Manila featuring a China talk by Snow. Only direct intervention with President Quezon by the U.S. high commissioner, Paul V. McNutt, succeeded in restoring the necessary police permit.[1]

Snow's interview with McNutt a few days later was most enlightening on the above incident and much else. The American official confirmed that the Japanese consul in Manila had been behind the effort to stop the meeting. To Snow's rejoinder that it looked as if the Japanese already regarded the Philippines as their colony, McNutt answered that if "the U.S. flag went out the Japanese flag would soon replace it." Snow wondered whether events in China were causing second thoughts among Filipinos on independence. McNutt told Snow he personally favored continued commonwealth status for the islands, in contrast to full independence scheduled for 1946 under the Tydings-McDuffie Act—a measure spurred largely by special American economic interests fearful of competition from duty-free Philippine exports. McNutt tended to agree with Snow's impression that many Filipinos seemed to take a Japanese takeover for granted "and think that's okay." The Japanese, he said, might assume control "without ever firing a shot." With Japan ensconced in the islands, the probable conflict with Tokyo would be a much longer and costlier affair, he added. He concurred with Snow's suspicion that Japan already had "some good friends" among Philippine politicians.[2]

In Snow's follow-up interview with General Douglas MacArthur, commander of the Philippine defense forces, the latter agreed that with complete Philippine independence, the Japanese would inevitably become the dominant economic and political influence in the islands; Japan would have no need to occupy the country militarily, he asserted. In any case, his forces were designed to make such a venture extremely costly. And in the much longer term, the general declared, a greatly expanded Philippine force could handle any Japanese invasion force. To Snow, these optimistic predictions seemed "nonsense." Ed also talked with Emilio Aguinaldo, the legendary leader of Filipino resistance to the Spaniards and then to the Americans at the turn of the century. Aguinaldo was sixty-nine; "the one remaining passion of his life," Snow noted, was to see independence for his country before he died. The old warrior praised America for keeping its promises on independence and complacently assured Snow that a free Philippines could coexist on peaceful and friendly terms with Japan. Citing the China experience, Snow asked whether the Philippines could "stop the Japanese navy with friendliness"—a query Aguinaldo airily dismissed.[3]

Along with the pervasive Japanese influence, and the intense nationalist pressures for independence reflected in Aguinaldo's views, Snow felt that Japan's China aggression had given Filipinos and their leaders—notwithstanding their public stance on the issue—some disquieting second thoughts on independence—as it had done for Snow's views as well. Somewhat at variance with the impressions reflected in his diary entries, he wrote Clark-Kerr from Baguio in January 1939, "Events in China have killed enthusiasm for both Japan and independence." Filipino politicians were now quietly lobbying Washington to retain links to the Philippines. Developments over the next two or three years, he prophesied, will "make it impossible for the Nips to walk in here without fighting America."[4]

In a number of articles during 1939, Snow took up the Philippine question in the context of America's broader responsibilities and interests in the Far East. In the pages of the isolationist *Post,* Snow returned to the pros and cons for American involvement in Asia. He noted, as before, that no current or future American economic interest in Asia could justify the cost of a war there, and that the United States would be fighting for a "phantom—for 'possessions' she no longer possesses or wants to possess." Americans had neither a moral nor material stake in defending the Filipinos who had chosen "separation with insecurity, fully aware of the consequences." Having traversed this familiar ground, Snow then carefully backed away and listed the now compelling factors for a firm and long-standing American commitment to Philippine security. He cited arguments that sound eerily like those Americans would hear from their leaders in later decades for military intervention in Vietnam. The appeals to "political idealism," sympathy for the underdog, and national pride, and a "lingering paternalism" for the Filipinos could be "overwhelming." And beyond these were substantive reasons of "preventive strategy"—to deny the immense resources of the islands to a predatory Japan that would use them to construct "a mighty base of power" to dominate the South and West Pacific. Snow linked this looming threat to the "continued Anglo-American non-interference with the China campaign," thereby conceding "hegemony" in East Asia to the Japanese. The result, Snow direly wrote, would lead not only to the loss of America's Pacific outposts but "force the fight to the mainland for independence itself." Events themselves, Snow concluded on a noncommittal note, could shift American public opinion in the interventionist direction "evidently desired by the [Roosevelt] Administration." The Congress may then eventually "sanctify by law an American 'defense alliance' in the Pacific, the basis of which is really being laid out at this moment."[5]

In further pieces in *Asia* later in the year Snow argued more directly and forcefully for American ties to the Philippines lasting beyond the 1946 independence date. He portrayed the U.S. record in the islands in highly laudatory terms. America, he declared, ruled the Philippines "better than she rules herself." Washington had the "warm thanks" of millions of loyal Filipinos, "not as conqueror but as friend and liberator. And yet more, as protector also." Though Philippine politicians could not openly say so, they now hoped the Americans would stay on, if not by a continuation of commonwealth status, then at least by strong military and economic ties to ward off Tokyo. Snow detailed the latter's "'peaceful' invasion" of the islands, including the buying off of corrupt politicians. If the Japanese were still stymied in China by 1946, they might take up their long-planned southward advance, which would likely include the Philippines. A continued American "union" with the islands, "military, economic, and political" was necessary to frustrate this. But all this was subordinate to Snow's larger and constantly reiterated point. The best way to defend the Philippines and the United States, and avoid war with Tokyo, was to help China successfully resist Japan—by aiding the Chinese economically (especially CIC) and cutting off the trade with Japan that sustained the latter's aggression. (In the early years of the China war, Japan imported from the United States 80 percent of its oil products, 90 percent of its gasoline, 74 percent of its scrap iron, and 60 percent of its machine tools.) As the China war bogged down and the Nazis blitzkrieged western Europe, Snow's projections of Japanese expansionist plans would move into fast-forward.[6]

Snow left the Baguio retreat in April 1939 for Hong Kong and the China mainland. After an extended stay in the British colony, mostly on CIC business, he went on by air to Chungking. In Hong Kong he had caught up with the China news and gossip, which only reinforced his private pessimism on the Nationalists' long-term war commitment. "The war would have ended long ago had it not been for the CPs [Reds]," he confided to his diary. With the Communists in the field, the appeasement elements in the government were "frightened" that their "power would collapse if a peace or compromise disadvantageous to China were made."[7]

Snow arrived in Chungking in the steamy July heat, at a time when the wartime capital was under constant and intensive Japanese bombing. As described in those years by Hugh Deane, then China correspondent for the *Christian Science Monitor*, "When you walk through Chongqing [Chungking] you see shattered buildings, heaps of broken brick and tile, charred timbers, streets meandering meaninglessly through acres of devastation." Snow stayed at first with Peggy and Tillman Durdin in their small house. With the inevitable appearance of Japanese bombers, the three were forced to spend part of the night in the neighborhood air-raid shelter, a dugout cut deep into the rocky hills on which the city was built. When the alarm sounded again a day or two later, Snow resisted getting out of bed and taking cover—arguing, according to Peggy Durdin, that the "law of averages" made any direct hit highly unlikely. But she insisted. When they emerged after the all-clear, their house had been almost entirely demolished by a five-hundred-pound bomb that landed just outside the kitchen. The only personal possession he lost, Ed wrote his father, was a piece of underwear. He was "quite indignant" about this, he went on, since he was traveling with only two pairs, and replacements were hard to come by in the China interior.[8]

While searching with Alley for Indusco units in a village on the outskirts of the city, Snow found "indescribable filth and squalor," with the "stone steps everywhere lined with beggars, destitute, starving, opium addicts, and syphilitics." Yet he was "impressed" with the concentration of new government-built industry outside the city—though he felt as always that dispersed small plants à la CIC was still the better way to go.[9]

Snow left Chungking in late August for his investigative tour of the Indusco line all the way up to the northwestern CIC center at Baoji, which he reached almost a month later. He traveled with fourteen other passengers in the rear of a Dodge truck, "hanging on for life at a corner and sometimes hanging on nothing more substantial than a fellow-traveler's rifle." They stopped for the night (and for many more thereafter) at a "pigsty-like inn" in a "filthy town," where Snow spent a sleepless night battling lice. The next morning he observed the swarms of boys, begging, apparently orphaned or deserted, who lined the village street. It was just such "lost children," he commented in his diary, that the Reds had made into "soldiers and men." Snow had little use for the Chinese conservatives' "glorification of Chinese civilization." For the masses in these parts of China, the realities were quite different: "dirt, lice, fleas, flies, bugs, poverty, famine, filth, . . . eating garbage for food, being kicked and battered here and there. There is nothing, absolutely nothing, worth preserving in this civilization." While Rewi Alley felt equal outrage at such conditions, there was always a sharp contrast in the way the two men reacted and adjusted to the privations and scenes of life on the road in the backwaters of China.[10]

From Baoji Snow went on to Xi'an, and then to Yan'an for his second visit with the Communists. The 150-mile trip from Xi'an took ten days— rain and "loafing" drivers the chief culprits. The old walled town had been leveled by constant Japanese bombing. A new cave city had sprung up in the surrounding hills outside the walls, where the entire population of some forty thousand now lived. Snow was put up in a comfortable enough cave of the foreign guest house and soon met his old companions of the 1936 Bao'an trip, Ma Haide and Huang Hua. It was late September when Snow arrived, barely a month after the signing of the Nazi-Soviet Non-Aggression Pact, followed by Hitler's invasion of Poland and Anglo-French war against Germany. Ma and Huang briefed Snow on the current Communist interpretation of these events, which Mao elaborated on when Snow met with him a day or two later. Mao now lived in what Snow described as a "modern" three-room cave complex carved into the loess hills outside Yan'an. Floors were bricked, and Mao had acquired a spring bed with mattress, more to his southern taste than the typical northern China *kang* he had used in Bao'an. The "apartment" had wicker furniture, there were flowers in the courtyard, and tea, cakes, and Chinese liquor were served. Snow was struck again by the "unusual repose" of the Red leader. "He seems gradually acquiring a kind of benignity that goes with power gracefully held," Ed observed in his diary, also noting that Mao now had two secretaries who "take down all his words of wisdom as from the oracle." Later the two men played bridge until three in the morning.[11]

Mao spoke more explicitly about the ultimate social revolutionary direction and goal of the resistance war than in his 1936 talks with Snow. (After "a certain stage" the national and democratic revolution "will transform into a social revolution.") The chairman, now more confident of his control over internationalist rivals in the party, was poised for the final round in consolidating his "Sinified" leadership and policies. (This would occur in the "rectification movement" [and harsh purges] of the early 1940s.) On issues of the united front, Mao emphasized that the CCP "has never given up its independence for one day, one hour, or a minute. It has never submitted to any party or any group or any person."[12]

As for the drastically altered international scene, Snow found that Mao had taken a sharp leftist turn in keeping with the new European alignments. He strongly defended and endorsed the Soviet-German agreement, condemned the conflict in Europe as "a pure imperialist war," and saved most of his disdain for the Western democratic powers he had previously courted. Such support of Soviet policy and of the world Communist line, however, did not in the least impede Mao's independent pursuit of Chinese Communist interests and goals on the domestic front. And at least in talking with Snow, even the Red leader's defense of the U.S.S.R. could take on a quizzical tone. To the journalist's close and skeptical queries regarding Soviet sales of wheat, oil, and other strategic materials to an imperialist Germany with whom Russia might yet find herself at war, Mao replied not to worry. "Hitler is in Stalin's pocket," he whimsically remarked. When Snow asked if he really meant that, the chairman said "fifty percent." (Snow privately wondered, what if it turns out "there is a hole in Stalin's pocket?") To Snow's questioning of Soviet leases of Sakhalin oil fields and fishing rights to Japan, Mao laughed and said Stalin had learned that from Roosevelt. Snow observed that Mao consistently referred to "Stalin" when talking of the Soviet Union.[13]

Snow came away from his brief visit to the border region (he was back in Xi'an by the end of September) predictably reinforced in his abiding belief that the Communists under Mao's guidance remained the key to victory and China's hope for a brighter future. "Everything I saw and heard [in Yan'an]," Snow wrote from Xi'an in one of his typical "fan letters" to the chairman, "increased my hope and confidence in the future. It is the only place in China where one can derive the feeling of the fundamental soundness and inevitable victory of the Chinese people." And buoyed by his apparent success in enlisting Mao in the CIC cause, he wrote Helen from the northwest, "Do not waste any more breath raising money for CIC in general." If the Philippine Chinese insisted on "sending their money to the New Life Movement and Mme. Chiang, or to non-guerrilla industry, wash your hands of the matter."[14]

In *Battle for Asia* Snow detailed his visit to and impressions of the border region under the new conditions of united war against Japan. His enthusiastic account, a kind of compressed *Red Star* II, had an unavoidable déjà vu quality. It nonetheless gave a uniquely firsthand view of developments there since the start of war. (He would be the last outside journalist able to visit the Red district until 1944.) He emphasized the Communists' expanded military and territorial situation, progress in the economic, educational, and medical spheres, and the broadly representative structure of local government. (Within the next two years, however, the Red areas in northern and northwestern China would face their greatest economic and military crisis from a Japanese annihilation campaign and a tightened blockade and cutoff of financial subsidies to the Red forces by Chungking.) Snow underlined again that as a consequence of the CCP's history of self-reliant armed struggle (away from "the super-minds" of the Comintern), control of its own territory, and immense political experience, it "stands quite apart from all other offspring of the Comintern." But Snow was equally aware of the more orthodox internationalist side of Chinese communism. He pointed to the CCP's "loyal adherence" to the Comintern, and also rejected the notion that just because the Reds now fought for "democracy and national independence they cannot be bolsheviks but are 'only a peasant reform party.'" Those "liberals" who chose to believe that the Chinese Communists were "different" in these respects, he asserted, "were doomed to ultimate disappointment." The CCP would inevitably move from its current "minimum program" of democratic united front nationalism (which Snow described in shining terms) to its "maximum program" of "international socialism."[15]

But Snow was no less at pains to separate the CCP from its counterparts in Moscow and the West. Mao, he declared, was beholden not to

Moscow but to his Chinese comrades and the army. And it seemed to him that the CCP took "the claims and counter-claims" of the Moscow trials and purges "with a grain of salt." He contrasted the revolutionary brotherhood of the Chinese Reds with the petty dogmatic infighting of the "armchair theorists" of the Communist parties in the West. Still evidently unaware of the simmering inner-party power and policy struggles in Yan'an soon to reach resolution, Snow stressed the "solidarity" of the CCP and "the comparative absence of cliques" within it. He attributed this in good part to the "fellowship" of the battlefield. The Chinese Reds, he rather dubiously reasoned, had been "too busy avoiding extermination by their enemies to work out on each other."[16]

Earlier, Snow had mused in his diary on this theme of Chinese Communist "brotherhood" but had approached it from a different and considerably more questioning angle. The comradeship of the revolutionary army on the barricades, he speculated, could well disappear in another setting. Such Red leaders as Zhou Enlai and Bo Gu had acquired "all the mannerisms of bureaucrats" while stationed in the Nationalist capitals of Hankou and Chungking. And the key to the Reds' success in winning the support and trust of the masses in their areas, he added, was "to establish for them the paternalistic infallibility of a parent." A "personality helps to symbolize this," he noted.[17]

Snow's admiring impressions of the border region would be amply seconded five years later by the first Western correspondents able to visit Yan'an since Ed's own 1939 trip. It was by then the command center of a vastly expanded network of "liberated areas" behind Japanese lines. A group of Chungking-based foreign correspondents were finally permitted by the Generalissimo to enter the Nationalist-blockaded Red base in the summer of 1944—an extended trip that resulted in a series of books and articles highly laudatory of the Communists. A. T. Steele, though not a member of this press party, talked with the returning journalists and read all they wrote. He later noted, "A trip from Chungking to Yenan was like going in one sense of the term, from hell to heaven because everything in Yenan looked so orderly and the people were practicing democracy, or so they said, and to a large degree they were. And the Communists seemed to have found a formula that might open the way to a new day in China." Whereas Snow had always stressed the authentically Marxist-Leninist character and goals of the CCP, these latter-day "Edgar Snows" (as the American ambassador dubbed them) tended to downplay this issue. Again as Steele related his conversations with these journalists, "some of them were saying, 'Well, these people are not Communists.

They're promoting a new democracy there,' which they were." (Harrison Forman, in his book on his stay in the border region, wrote that "today the Chinese Communists are no more Communistic than we Americans are.") "We were reluctant to paint them as real Communists," Steele added, "because we knew that that would go against the American grain." To write favorably of Communists, he went on, would raise questions "in the eyes of the publisher," that the correspondent "was maybe pro-Communist." Ironically, this "agrarian democrat" image would itself later fuel the "pro-Communist" attacks on such reporting.[18]

But the more important (and largely unheeded) message for American policymakers emanating from these encounters with the Chinese revolutionaries was articulated by John S. Service. As the foreign service's leading Chinese Communist-watcher, he came to Yan'an with the United States Army Observer Group (generally known as the Dixie mission) which had been reluctantly agreed to by Chiang under pressure from Washington. The small mission under Colonel David D. Barrett began arriving in Yan'an almost simultaneously with the journalists. In an October 1944 dispatch by Service to Washington, in which he cited the CCP's impressive wartime accomplishments, he wrote, "From the basic fact that the Communists have built up popular support of a magnitude and depth which makes their elimination impossible, *we must draw the conclusion that the Communists will have a certain and important share in China's future.*" It was substantively the crux of what Snow had first discerned nearly a decade before.[19]

Sparked by a discussion with a disillusioned American Communist acquaintance in Manila, Snow pondered further on the issue of the bureaucracy as a new exploiting class under a Communist "proletarian dictatorship." If the revolution comes into power with only minority support, he meditated in his diary, it must use "terror" as an instrument of control and must "inevitably resolve into dictatorship of a small group controlling [the] party. It's neither democracy nor 'dictatorship of the proletariat.'" The regime had to rule through a bureaucracy whose loyalty it ensured by granting it special status and rewards. Thus, Snow went on, a "new privileged class" replaced the "exploiting class" of the old society. With its entrenched interest in the system, this new class "will not voluntarily, any more than any ruling class in history, carry out measures for its own destruction or liquidation." This ruling group inevitably itself became an "enemy of the people" whom it would come to view as a threat to its power and privileges. "Is all this what's happened in USSR?"[20]

Seeking an alternative to the bleak scenario he outlined, Snow posed the notion that a revolutionary (proletarian) dictatorship could avoid taking such a path only if it quickly won the support of a majority of the people, who equally rapidly won control of "the political apparatus." He clearly had in mind his Chinese Communist friends whom he saw as good candidates for gaining the majority support that could translate into a "different" kind of dictatorship—a kind of Communist "exceptionalism." Snow's idea that popular control could somehow be shoehorned into a dictatorial political system had curious resemblances (at least rhetorically) to Mao's 1949 oxymoronic description of his new government as a "people's democratic dictatorship," assertedly representing the interests of the vast majority of the people. Snow's 1939 reflections that only a broad popular base could keep a "proletarian" dictatorship from "going reactionary" resonated in a way with Mao's later theories on Soviet and Chinese "capitalist restoration." (Mao's goal, Snow wrote after his last 1970–1971 visit to China, was to overthrow the new "Mandarinate of cadres divorced from the people," and "to restore the purity of the revolution and involve the masses in its direction as never before.") These matters will be taken up further in the final chapters.[21]

Though Snow gravitated toward the left in his overall world outlook, his unvarnished view of the Soviets in the late 1930s tended to give him a more unalloyed insight into the dynamics of Russian policymaking than was true of ideologues of the left or right, and of pro-Soviet liberals in the West. "Quite clearly," he wrote Helen after the 1939 Russian about-face on Germany, "the USSR is acting on the basis of its strategic national interests alone, like every other power." Any other way of judging the international Communist line would "involve idealism and muddled thinking." As early as November 1938, Snow had written Bertram that a "Soviet Russian agreement with Germany in Europe as a self-defense measure is possible, even probable; you must not rule out the possibility of a Russo-Japanese agreement out here." (Both of course would come to pass in 1939 and 1941 respectively.) In a private conversation with his friend Archibald Clark-Kerr the following May in Hong Kong, the British ambassador insisted that Chamberlain would "be forced" into an agreement with the Russians, and that the idea of a Hitler-Stalin get-together, which Snow had raised, was "impossible—Hitler would have to eat every hat on his head." "No more than Stalin," Snow rejoined. In a subsequent meeting of the two in Chungking in October (following Snow's return from Yan'an), the ambassador rejected the Communist allegation that Chamberlain had plotted to turn Hitler east against the

Soviets. The British prime minister "was simply a tired old man hoping by any conceivable means to keep out of the war," he told Snow. Snow reminded Clark-Kerr of their May conversation, and that he (Ed) had "proved a remarkably good prophet." Always sensitive to attacks from the left, Snow noted he would have been accused of "Trotskyism" if he had predicted this openly at that time. "If in the USSR," he added to Clark-Kerr, "I probably would have lost my head!"[22]

On the China front, Snow was now taking a much kinder view of Stalinist policy than he had during the Xi'an Incident and its aftermath. Stressing as always the strategic security factor as uppermost in Soviet calculations, he now applauded the latter's sustained assistance to China's resistance cause, in contrast to Anglo-American policies favoring Japan. But still, he groused a bit that such aid went solely to the Nationalists. From Stalin, Snow wryly remarked in a 1940 *Post* article, the Chinese Reds get "only speeches." Obviously reflecting his own assessment as well, he added that "Chiang Kai-shek believes that Stalin is still more concerned with military security than with political evangelism."[23]

On Europe, Snow essentially took the conventional leftist view of Anglo-French duplicity in dealing with the Soviets for an alliance against Germany. Stalin, in Snow's hard-nosed interpretation, had merely turned the tables on the Western powers in what was a "logical" expression of Soviet interests. Though dubious as to the longer-term consequences of Stalin's trafficking with the Nazis (expressed in Snow's 1939 talks with Mao), Snow was considerably more distrustful of the British and French. His animus against Chamberlain's earlier appeasement policies, and his long-standing conviction that Britain and France would be fighting solely to protect their imperial interests, left him with a thoroughly dyspeptic reaction to the onset of war in Europe. He leaned toward the Communist definition of the conflict as imperialist and wanted America to stay out. In the Xi'an guest house, while on his way to Yan'an, he had run into Jim Bertram who had also been heading for Yan'an. (Jim had shepherded up to Xi'an an overland truck convoy of medical supplies destined for the Red areas, from Madame Sun's China Defence League.) On news of the war, however, Bertram was rallying round the Crown in true New Zealander fashion and planning to return home to join up. Ed looked quizzically, Bertram recalled, and remarked, "Well, it's your war. Or Chamberlain's, don't forget. I wouldn't trust that old bastard an inch." Yet characteristically and contrarily, Ed added, "I suppose I might feel the same way if we were in it"—as of course would be the case. As it turned out, after a return to

New Zealand where his services for the forces were evidently then not in urgent demand, Bertram was persuaded by Madame Sun to come to Hong Kong to work again with her China Defence League. He would be there (interrupted by a stint with the British embassy in Chungking) when the Japanese attacked after Pearl Harbor. He finally had his chance as a volunteer fighter in the British defense of the Crown Colony and would spend the Pacific war years as a prisoner (and laborer) of the Japanese.[24]

On the purely personal level for Snow, the European events that deflected Westerners' attention from the Far East further reduced chances of any major commercial success for the book he was writing. "Ed's new book will probably be a loss" due to the European situation, Helen wrote Mildred and J. Edgar while Snow was in the northwest. This "writing game is really gratuitous work in the interest of public service I guess." (She also told the two Snows in no uncertain terms that she had little time for such "social correspondence." As a final touch for the bitterly anti-Roosevelt elder Snow, she declared it would be "a major tragedy" if F. D. R.'s program were not continued in the coming election of 1940.)[25]

In November 1939, after his return to Baguio from China, Snow provided the fullest exposition of his views on the European situation in a letter of over five thousand words to his good friend in Manila, Will Babcock. The latter, a liberal-minded businessman, had together with his wife, Polly, become staunch and active backers of the Snows' Indusco work in the Philippines. Babcock, a firm antifascist, had argued spiritedly with Ed in favor of early American entry into the war to forestall a Nazi victory and subsequent direct threat to the United States itself. (Coincidentally, the Babcocks would be with the Snows in Madison, Connecticut, on the Sunday of the Pearl Harbor attack.) By defending his own adamantly noninterventionist stand, Ed had an opportunity to sort out his thoughts on the current and future course of world events. There was an illuminating contrast between his detached, loftily Olympian approach to the European war, and his intense feelings on the conflict in Asia. Europe remained a distant, somewhat theoretical arena for him; Asia was personal. And he tended to see the Western powers from this Asian vantage point—primarily as colonial overlords. Asia was where he had lived and worked for over a decade, committed on both the human and political level. He had reacted to Japanese aggression with a sense of outrage and urgency now completely missing from his European outlook. Thus Snow declared that he did not see the European conflict as either "a moral issue" or "a war of ideas," but as a clash of "fundamental socio-economic forces which cause the ideas." Therefore, "I try not to view the war emotionally, or through subjective prejudice," but "to understand it realistically and dialectically." Snow's words did not quite fit this ideal: his judgments were colored by his hostility toward the British empire and distrust of its "ruling class." The current "phony war" stage of military inaction on the Western front only added to his suspicions. (The conflict at present, Snow wrote Helen, "is as uninteresting as a six day bicycle race.")[26]

In brief, Snow asserted that a Nazi conquest of France and much the rest of Europe—let alone of Britain and the British empire—would be so immensely difficult and costly as to be a virtual impossibility. Just the defeat of France, he thought, would cost Germany more than the five million casualties it had suffered in the last war. As for the remainder of Europe (excluding the Soviet Union), "Is it imagined that Germany, at the end of a titanic struggle against France, would still be powerful enough to bully all those people into submission without struggle?" Snow added, equally wide of the mark, "nor has Hitler today got any Chamberlain to compel them to do so." And what prompts the belief, he asked, that "if Hitler took Paris, Moscow would be prepared to leave him there?" The Russians would "gang up" with the other European nations and even England to bring down "a ruined Germany."[27]

In a flight of hypotheses Snow suggested that even should the Nazis surmount all these obstacles and become the new masters of the British empire, America need not necessarily worry. As a "have" power, Germany would mellow—"in John Bull's shoes [it] would become very much like John Bull himself," he imagined. "Is there any reason," he queried, "why we could not live and let live in a world of Pax Germania as easily as in a world of Pax Britannia?" (It sounded disquietingly like the sentiments Americans would shortly be hearing from the America-firster Charles Lindbergh.) In contrast to this, Ed had written Helen, "in the end," America "cannot watch Germany become triumphant in Europe." And "in the end," Snow would have very different answers to a "Pax Germania" as a war correspondent in Russia and as one of the first journalists to come across the horrors of the Nazi death camps in eastern Europe.[28]

Arguing from his Asia-based anticolonial (and Marxist-influenced) perspective, Snow asserted to Babcock, "the war is simply the climax of the struggle between politico-social economic systems, and their rivalry for the earth's resources, raw materials, labor power, markets and the apparatus of control over them"—in sum, an imperialist conflict. Returning to the thesis of his fascism lecture at Yanjing University in 1934, Snow proclaimed that "Hitlerism and British imperialism seem to me equally and both to be the rotting putrefact of an age and a system which is in its last poisonous hours of power." (He dismissed the Nazi führer as "the miserable house painter with an inferiority complex"—one of Ed's favorite psychological gambits.) To avert their mutual destruction, he conjectured, the two protagonists might yet join hands against a "greater antagonism"—the forces of "a new society awaiting—though but dimly perceived—to replace them." Stalin on his part, Snow declared, had already shown "sense enough" to avoid a war moving in his direction. Unable to get his strategic requirements from England (whose "treacheries" Snow detailed), "he took them from Hitler."

But Snow's attempt to portray Stalin as a sure-handed player in the dangerous European power game would soon be confounded by the Soviet invasion of Finland in December 1939. "Stalin was obviously badly advised and miscalculated the internal situation in Finland, as well as the international effect," he wrote Bertram shortly after the Russian action. "The whole move was stupid, clumsy and brutal." He thought it might change "the whole alignment in Europe." Bertram could end up "finding a Red on the receiving end of your machine gun," he needled.[29]

Snow pursued this more disenchanted look at Stalin's European moves in *Foreign Affairs* in the spring of 1940. He wrote of the "Moscow-Berlin Axis," and Soviet anti-imperialist, revolutionary rhetoric as "simply a special terminology of power politics to any one but a devout Stalinist." No matter what the tactics of the moment, Snow insisted, Moscow's long-term interests and goals remained constant and always took precedence over those of Communist movements elsewhere. "No," Snow the "realist" declared, "it is not the Red Dictator but the disillusioned liberals who are inconsistent." Stalin, Snow continued, "taking advantage of a favorable world situation, is grabbing territories wherever possible without (he imagines) risking a 'serious' war." As a consequence of these Russian actions, the "little people" everywhere had lost sympathy for the U.S.S.R. Finland had provided "the anti-Communist standard bearers with a necessary moral slogan." It was now "at least thinkable" that the Anglo-French powers would "eventually find a *modus vivendi* with Germany and mobilize Europe against the Soviets." Snow was in essence exhibiting some of his own disillusioned, "more in sorrow than anger," reaction to the Stalinist realpolitik he claimed to find so logical and understandable.[30]

In contrast to his dismal view of the European scene, Snow took a considerably more upbeat approach to Asia. He discounted the idea, in the same *Foreign Affairs* article, that Stalin might "sell out" China as part of a possible future deal with Japan. Moscow's stake in continued and effective united Chinese resistance to Japan—evidenced in the Soviet track record of aid to China—ruled this out, Snow reasoned. In this strategic picture, the Chinese Reds were "a valuable armed ally" of the Russians, Snow wrote, though he reiterated at some length his "Maoist" independent-nationalist interpretation of Chinese communism that so irritated Moscow. But this very independence of the Reds, Snow further argued, would be an added deterrent to any drastic change in Soviet China policy. Stalin, Ed remarked, was very likely aware that he could not bank on the CCP's "approval" of any reversal of Russian policy "inimical to the interests of China" and of the Chinese Reds themselves.

But for the time being at least, Snow preferred to see no conflict of interest between Moscow and Yan'an, despite the Soviet's exclusive assistance to the Nationalists. Chiang, Snow declared, in the mode of his public assessment of the Generalissimo's role in those years, remained the "pivot" of the united front "which is still the [Chinese] Communists' basic condition for resistance to Japan." The war in Europe made Chungking even more dependent on Russian support. To "conciliate his Communist supporters—Russian and otherwise," Chiang had done "a surprising *volte face*." He had backtracked from steps toward renewed civil conflict and had declared his intent to advance toward representative government. (The Chinese Communists, Snow had written J. B. Powell, were probably "the only Reds in the world" who could be said to have "benefited" from Stalinist moves in Europe.)[31]

Snow's emphasis on the brightened prospects in China dovetailed with the more positively pro-China, anti-Japanese role he wished America to play—including, as we know, government financial support for the CIC. In January 1940 the United States had finally begun to restrict the export of some critical war supplies to Japan. "We are no longer passive objectors to Japanese aggression," Snow declared, "we are taking active steps to check it." He pushed for a Russo-American "pact of amity, restricted to the Pacific," which could have a salutary effect in ending Japanese "bellicosity." To this end, he urged Americans to overcome their "sentimentality and indignation" over Moscow's "stupid and clumsy" Finnish invasion. (In fact it was rather the U.S.S.R. and Japan that would sign a neutrality pact a year later, as the Russians girded for a German attack in the West, while Tokyo prepared for its "southern strategy" against the Western powers.)[32]

Snow's call for a more positive American policy in the Pacific was designed to avert a Japanese-American conflict, in line with his concern to keep the United States out of war, in the Pacific as well as Europe. (American capitalism was faced with a choice between "survival by socialist measures," or the much more tolerable option, "a war to justify vast rearmament," he typically wrote his British agent in February 1940.) But this clashed with his own prognostication in his *Foreign Affairs* piece: "The world is moving with streamlined speed toward a cataclysm of which the current wars in Europe and Asia are but the preliminaries." And he was "inclined to think the casus belli" for American entry, he had also told his agent, "will be out here [in the Pacific], in the beginning."[33]

The rapid Nazi conquest of France and the Low Countries in May and June 1940 presented Snow with dilemmas similar to those of so many of his compatriots equally opposed to being dragged once again into Europe's conflicts. An embattled Britain stood alone against a seemingly invincible and far from "ruined" Germany, now master of most of Europe. Japan had joined Germany and Italy in a Tripartite Pact and was poised, as Snow was well aware, for a move against the West.

He pondered these developments in a major piece published in *Asia* just as he was finally on his way home in January 1941. He acknowledged that European and Asian problems were "indissolubly connected," with the two war fronts seemingly about to converge. He modified his formerly adamant stand on the "imperialist war" and now affirmed his "complete" support for the British "in their struggle for freedom." He declared it important for America to "do everything we can to defend and regenerate democracy in England." However, he added, Britain and the dominions "are not the same thing as Britain the colonial power." Just as he had consistently seen China's resistance war as necessarily taking on a social revolutionary character, in like manner the looming worldwide conflict could be successfully (and justifiably) waged only as a war for colonial emancipation. "We will not have any peace and order on the earth until the subject peoples become free," Snow wrote—a rather millennial vision of a decolonized world.[34]

Snow agreed that America had now adopted the only feasible option left to it in the Pacific—aid to China and active resistance against further Japanese expansion. By thus calling Japan's hand, "War may prove *objectively* unavoidable," he acknowledged. In offering his political prescriptions with that eventuality in mind, Snow was in the process of transforming his anticolonialism from a barrier to American involvement to a banner under which America could legitimately fight.

The United States, Snow thus urged, should sign a "Pact of Democracy" (with military clauses that could automatically kick in) with Britain and the dominions, China, perhaps the Philippines, and it could even be offered to the Soviets. If the British empire can be accepted as democratic, Snow wryly noted, then Washington can "stretch a point in the case of Soviet democracy." On China, he cautioned, Anglo-American aid must not go to "prop up the most backward elements" seeking to suppress "the democratic forces" (the classic dilemma of "good" versus "bad" interventionism). Snow's projected alliance would in fact begin to take shape in the events that brought both the Russians and Americans into the war by the end of 1941. But as a "pact of democracy" it would have rough sledding, as Snow himself hinted of its imperial British, Soviet Russian, and Nationalist Chinese partners.[35]

The Nationalist attack on the Reds' New Fourth Army in January 1941 was the final breaking point for Snow on the Chungking regime. Symbolically, it coincided with his own departure for home and served, as he later put it in *Journey*, "to cure me of my intensely personal sense of obligation to China." He would, however, still be for "the cause of China," for "any measure which might help the Chinese people to help themselves," but "I would be opposed to all uncontrolled charity to the rich-men's government," he added. Just a couple of months earlier he could still write of the Chinese army that, despite everything, "It may yet become a true people's army capable of emancipating eastern Asia." But just before the January attack on the Red forces, he evinced his increasingly pessimistic feelings while drinking in the New Year with Jim Bertram in Hong Kong. In the two friends' forecasts for 1941, Bertram remembered, " 'Civil war in China' was on both our lists." A few days earlier Ed had sent off from Hong Kong a gloomy and revealing dispatch on "the gravest crisis since the beginning of China's resistance to Japan." It was "widely feared that civil war may be renewed on a large scale early in 1941," he reported.[36]

Snow had worked intensively in Baguio on *Battle for Asia* from early spring into the fall of 1940, finally completing it before he and Helen left the Philippines in November after a two-year stay. Helen was on her way back to America, with Ed's immediate plans still uncertain. Both of them felt it would be advantageous for Ed to return to the States via Europe. With that in mind, he was considering a *Herald-Tribune* offer of a "roving assignment" through Siam, Burma, and India, after which he would continue on home through Europe—a kind of replay of his 1930 travel plans.[37]

In Hong Kong, en route from Manila, there were farewell meetings and dinners for the Snows with Madame Sun, Jim Bertram, and other friends in China Defence League and CIC circles. Ed visited with the mercurial Agnes Smedley, who had spent time with the New Fourth Army south of the Yellow River. She was nervous and a bit paranoid, Snow thought. She labeled the New Fourth commander Xiang Ying (Han Ying) a "merciless and ruthless" dictator. As to Indusco units, there was "not a single one" there when she left a year before, she told Ed. Her glum outlook included Russia as well. She thought Moscow had in effect already joined the Axis. "Nothing more—but *that* from Smedley," Snow noted, perhaps ignoring that he himself had earlier written of the "Moscow-Berlin Axis." The Snows went on to Shanghai (the still unoccupied foreign settlement), where Ed saw Helen off on the *President Taft*. A sign of the tense situation for anti-Japanese Americans there: J. B. Powell met the Snows with a bodyguard, and the editor Randall Gould was at customs with Peg, "with hand on automatic in inside pocket," Ed recorded. Coming upriver into Shanghai was even more depressing than usual for Ed: "The unregenerate mud, the gray smoky skies, dirty unpainted buildings, Japs creeping about on shore, lines of coolies marching desolately about in the distance, and sampans swarming with young and old ready to leap into the filthy waters for one American coin."[38]

While in Shanghai, Snow gleaned much additional "dirt" on the Kungs' financial dealings and profiteering. And American Marine brass he talked with bad-mouthed his good friend Evans Carlson, who (for the while) had resigned from the corps. Ed returned to Hong Kong in early December "to pick up threads" on the Chinese political situation and, inevitably, to be told of the latest CIC crisis. It was here that he would be the first foreign correspondent to learn, from his Communist contacts, of the New Fourth Army Incident of January 5, and to send the story abroad just before leaving the British colony on January 8. Snow's account of the incident differed sharply from the version soon put out by Chungking that attempted to lay full blame on the Reds. Whatever the complex background, circumstances, confusions, and motivations surrounding the Nationalist-ordered withdrawal of the New Fourth Army to north of the Yangtze River by the end of 1940, a heavy blow had been dealt to the Red forces and a devastating one to what remained of KMT-CCP unity. In its greatly outnumbered battle with Nationalist troops occupying the surrounding heights, the rear headquarters unit of the New Fourth, still south of the river, suffered losses of at least five thousand combatants and noncombatants killed or captured, with the army's commander taken prisoner and its vice-commander killed. Snow labeled it a "massacre" in *Journey*. The adverse reaction in Western media and government circles to the Nationalist action probably helped dissuade the Kuomintang from further escalation of the internal conflict with the Reds. Snow's report had played its part in this, and it now placed him firmly in the enemy camp in Chungking's eyes. (Lauchlin Currie, who had been Roosevelt's lend-lease emissary to China in February and March 1941, told Ed later in the year in Washington that the Nationalist government considered him "an agent of the Third International.")[39]

But as he continued to go about his business, Snow was gradually sinking into a crisis of his own. The seemingly final unraveling of the united front was but one of many factors that led to a growing personal malaise in the last weeks and days of his long stay in Asia. He had often been subject to low moods, but the accumulated physical and emotional toll and burnout of the China years, the frustrations and financial costs of his Indusco labors, and surfacing problems in his marriage, all contributed to a deeply despondent, distraught state bordering on breakdown. He was malnourished and severely underweight, had little money in the bank (under $2,000) to show for all the years of his China work and accomplishments, and he could see no real prospect of redeeming his fortunes through his new book. His hypercritical tendency to underplay his achievements now showed itself in a pervasive and debilitating sense of failure. Helen's caustic fault-finding propensities had not helped matters.

His diary entries from early December until his arrival in California the next month reveal him brooding and ruminating despairingly over his presumed shortcomings and troubled relationship with Peg. He recalled random derogatory remarks by her (Ed had "ruined her life"), as he agonized over "the possibility of a genuine reconciliation." His distressed state was also manifested in drawn-out, depleting indecision on whether to return directly to the States or go ahead with the southern Asia-Europe plans. He descended into an extreme guilt-ridden stage, intensified by loneliness and sheer exhaustion. On Christmas Day, he recorded, "it has taken spending it away from Peg to make me realize what a complete skunk I have been about a dozen things important to her." Her criticisms of his personal habits (such as drinking and smoking) he now saw as "genuine solicitude for my welfare"; he promised himself he would "carry out a personal revolution: that really is what is needed, no less." Peg's departure for America had actually been understood by both of them, Ed recorded, as a kind of temporary, informal attempt to live apart. He had given Peg an "invitation" to "separate if she liked and find another person who could come nearer meeting her perfectionist demands."[40]

In a slightly more positive (though equally contrite) New Year's Day mood, Snow predicted that he and Peg "shall learn better how to live together." But he continued to castigate himself, cataloging examples of his "selfishness, vanity and egotism" as reasons for Peg "despising" him. "Instead of listening to her I have resented her criticism. I should have thanked her for it with every gesture of gratitude one knows." But beyond the obvious symptoms of stress, Snow's darkly tinted view of his marital relationship mirrored larger, more lasting problems of these disparate personalities who were also highly achieving, talented, and ambitious individuals, working as partners strongly committed to the same causes. It brought its strains, including an inevitable competitive edge. One of the reasons "for our recent difficulties is that we have been living in each other's laps all day long for a year. And at the same time writing," Ed added in his Christmas entry. And among instances of his "selfishness," Snow listed his failure to give Peg "full credit for first thinking of CIC" and "belittling" her contributions "on this and other important work on China."[41]

Snow's inner turmoil was apparently not always discernible at the time even to close friends. Jim Bertram saw no special signs of tension during their New Year's get-together in Hong Kong. But just days later, in a Manila stopover out of Hong Kong, Snow's distraught state ("nervous, hands shaking, somewhat incoherent") was evident to the Babcocks, whom he saw there. (He also made frantic phone calls to Peg from Manila, berating himself as a "failure.") Polly Babcock afterward wrote soothingly to Peg that Ed "seemed a bit tired, but we know that a vacation with you in California will fix him up like new."[42]

On the clipper flight across the Pacific to Honolulu, Snow stayed wrapped in misery and remorse. "Surely this whole period must remain the darkest in my life," he agonized during a Midway Island layover. "Never have I been through the depth of despondency and despair in which my own role has appeared so altogether despicable and contemptible." (Ed later tore this diary page out and handed it to Peg in California—"To show how he repented," she told this writer.) Decades later, Snow would recall his near-suicidal condition on this flight. "I seriously considered jumping out of the plane," he wrote a young friend who was going through a critical period of his own. In those "leisurely days," Ed explained, the clippers had wide picture windows that could be raised or lowered, "think of that!" The captain sensed Snow's mood and, at an overnight stop in Wake Island, confided to Ed how he himself survived, and bounced back from, a suicide attempt induced by a love affair. Snow claimed this helped him "snap out of it." "I had been enormously exaggerating my own share of the guilt," he added in looking back on this dark interval in his life.[43]

In Honolulu he seemed recovered enough for a busy round of activities—meeting with local Chinese community leaders on Indusco and visiting the Pearl Harbor base. There, he was briefed on the large-scale air and naval buildup then underway. "Some" of the naval people he talked with "have the impression U.S. could clean up the Jap Navy in six weeks," he noted. He found Honolulu, with its neon lights, hot dog stands, and Coney Island atmosphere on Waikiki, "hardly recognizable" from the place where he had begun his Oriental odyssey thirteen years earlier. But neither was Snow recognizable as the carefree, romantic, world-is-my-oyster youth who had frolicked there in 1928. In a few days, Ed boarded the *President Pierce* ("in a pickled state") for San Francisco. He read and slept en route but could not concentrate well on either. It was a drearily cold and rainy January day when they docked—"nothing Golden about the Gate" aside from amber lights on the bridge, he morosely felt.[44]

Ed was soon reunited with Helen in the Los Angeles–Hollywood area, where she was already thoroughly immersed in Indusco organizing activities. With wholesome food (he gained thirty pounds in a month), the admiring reception from Hollywood celebrities, and a relaxing vacation at an Arizona dude ranch, Snow soon recovered. "One morning I woke up a whole man again," he later recounted. By mid-March the two were ensconced at the Chelsea Hotel in New York, where J. Edgar and Mildred and Claude Mackey came in by car from Kansas City for their first reunion with Ed since 1926. Mildred and Dad "scrutinized me most carefully and intently," Ed cryptically noted.[45]

The couple's relationship, though stabilized for the time being, remained a problematic one. Helen's no-nonsense, single-minded, work-centered "energizing" style left little room for Ed's more self-indulgent traits—his unhurried and careless unpunctuality and his incorrigible "time-wasting" gregariousness, among others. (Snow's sociable "drinking companion" style and his forgetfulness were exemplified in a later incident recounted to me by Ed's nephew, John Snow. Ed was visiting with John and his wife, Freda, in San Francisco in the late 1960s, during one of Snow's lecture tours. The two men sat drinking and reminiscing, with Ed in an increasingly relaxed and expansive mood. Suddenly, late in the evening, Snow recalled that he had been due hours before at a reception in his honor at a private residence in the city and insisted that John drive him there so that he could make his apologies in person. Unfortunately, the host loudly berated Ed and slammed the door on him.) In Helen's perception of their relationship, the Snows were "not trying to be happy, but to do and think worthwhile things." (During Snow's prolonged stay in Hong Kong in the summer of 1939, enmeshed in the tangle of CIC politics and personalities, she scolded him from Baguio: "EXACTLY WHAT IN HELL ARE YOU DOING THERE for three months? I cannot understand how you can waste so much time and never do a thing to show for it.") Among his New Year's resolutions for 1941 recorded in Honolulu during his emotional downturn, Snow had written, "Do not waste time on useless people when Peg is not willing or prepared—only at definite hours. Do not answer telephone before 5 P.M."[46]

Snow's wartime and postwar assignments abroad put their marriage and its strains on hold from 1942 on, though the two did draw up a separation agreement in 1945. Perhaps exaggerating, Ed wrote Helen in 1946 that he had felt their relationship to be "hopeless" from the time he had left New York's La Guardia Airport for overseas in 1942—"in fact ever since Chelsea Hotel days." Snow halfheartedly offered to make a final try for a reconciliation, on the basis of what he defined as a "give and take" approach on both sides. But neither of them would or could change to satisfy the other. "If you still think you are perfect however," Ed ended this "conciliatory" letter, "there is nothing to do but get a divorce and the sooner the better." Sadly enough, it took years more of increasingly bitter personal and legal wrangling before the final divorce settlement in 1949.[47]

Meanwhile Snow spent the 1941 year rediscovering America and waiting for the larger war he knew was coming. He had witnessed the beginnings of the great global conflict to come in Manchuria in 1931 and would soon be covering its climactic final years for the *Post*. As he waited, he thought much on the meaning of the upheaval, on America's role, and on a world beyond war. In so doing, he continued to grapple with his remaining doubts and inconsistencies on the looming war crisis.

CHAPTER 13

After China

Snow's Vision of a New World

Shortly after arriving in California, Snow met Theodore Dreiser, the crusty, temperamental old literary lion, whose vehemently anti-British, anticapitalist, antiwar opinions put Snow's in the shade. All the arguments Ed had used early in the European war Dreiser now threw back at him: the prewar anti-Soviet machinations and profascist appeasement policies of the British, the subjection of their colonial peoples, and so on. While Snow found much of this "true enough," it was "now 1941," he told the agitated writer. In relating this encounter in *Journey,* Ed stepped gingerly over some of the minefields in his own earlier thinking. "I was against nazism before the [Russo-German] pact," he told Dreiser. "If the Communists want to call it an 'imperialist war' that doesn't change nazism for me." But Snow understatedly acknowledged, "My position had its own contradictions, of course. I wanted us to help China *and* Britain yet I didn't want America to go to war." In what was a final "contradiction," Snow added that he knew "Japan was going to drag us into the war whether we helped anybody or not."[1]

Actually Ed felt that American interventionists focused too narrowly on Europe and ignored or minimized the more immediate threat from the Pacific. At a *Battle for Asia* book-signing session in Philadelphia in early June, Snow told a reporter (who described Ed as "a curly-haired young man you might take to be British") he "would bet" the United States would be at war with Japan within four months, and "practically certain" war would come within a year. Much as he hated the idea of a "nearly self-sufficient" America having to go to war, "our future would not be safe with Hitler in control of Europe, and Japan the master of Asia—and that is the fact we must face," he said. The statement was a good composite of Snow's own isolationist-interventionist mix—and of America's too. Of course, though Snow was surely telling it as it was and was going to be, by drawing attention to the East he also had an eye on the new book he was plugging. (Within days of the Pearl Harbor attack, Ed suggested a new ad campaign to Random House to "revive the sales of *Battle for Asia* by using present interest to call attention to the book"—and proceeded to sketch out a proposed ad with a good deal of hype.)[2]

Battle for Asia appeared almost simultaneously with Snow's arrival in California. But otherwise the timing worked against the book, unlike that for *Red Star* three years earlier. Americans' attention was fixed on Britain's lone epic stand against a Nazi-dominated continent, and on their own country's gradual but steady immersion in the European war. Sales of the book in America over the first year were modest, totaling about 10,000 copies. As in the case of *Red Star,* the book did not become a Book-of-the-Month Club selection, losing out to the revelations of an anti-Soviet defector.[3]

Snow's book kept to his lively and popular personal reportorial style. He took the reader with him through the early pivotal battles of the China war, the birth of Indusco, his travels along the Indusco line, and his 1939 visit to the Red northwest and reunion with Mao. There were vivid descriptions of key personalities ranging from the Generalissimo to Rewi Alley. There were outraged accounts of Japanese depredations and atrocities. (Nowhere "in the present world has the deliberate degradation of man been quite so thoroughly systematized as by the Japanese army.") The volume was interlarded with heavier analytical and background material, and a final section of prescriptions for winning the war and the peace in Asia and Europe. Though Snow had envisioned the work as a wartime sequel to *Red Star,* it inevitably lacked the special chemistry and circumstances, the drama and freshness of Snow's euphoric discovery of a society and people. The book "has the same vivid qualities, but cannot in the nature of things prove as exciting as its predecessor," a British reviewer remarked.[4]

Battle for Asia incorporated the themes and judgments Snow had been putting out in his writings over the previous three years, and many of the chapters were only slightly reworked versions of articles he had produced during that period. The tone was sharply critical of the Nationalist war record to date, but still guardedly hopeful that events could impel the Kuomintang under the Generalissimo to adopt the measures of democratic reform and mobilization needed to save itself and China. (Even so staunch a champion of the Nationalists as the *Time-Life* magnate Henry Luce could write Snow "how deeply indebted" he was to him for his "masterly" book, and hoped it would be read by "many tens of thousands of Americans.") As always, Snow gave full credit to the fortitude of China's ordinary people and soldiery; it was the bureaucrats and generals, and the privileged strata they represented, who fell far short of the mark. To be victorious, Snow declared, China's cause "must carry in it not only the distant promise of improvement in men's lives, but an immediate fulfillment by the realization of a better, democratic, society." Snow added his usual caveats on the potentially disastrous consequences for China of the anti-Communist machinations of right-wing appeasement elements in the government who feared the Reds more than the Japanese. The New Fourth Army episode at that time gave immediate weight to Snow's warnings, as many reviewers noted.[5]

Indusco loomed very large in Snow's account, a story he told in his most persuasively promotional terms. His description of this movement, one reviewer extravagantly declared, "is nearly as thrilling as his account of the famous Long March in his earlier book." Policy toward the cooperatives was a key litmus test of Nationalist intentions, Snow emphasized. If properly supported, Indusco could point the way to success in war and to a progressive future without violent revolution. Snow also championed the Communist war effort (in which Indusco-style cooperatives were doing their bit) as the model of the popularly based policies needed on a national scale. The Red forces, he asserted, were far superior in combat effectiveness to all other Chinese armies. Should the Kuomintang's war resolve falter, national leadership would pass to the Communists. "Though the Nationalist Government is not democratic," Snow wrote, "this had nevertheless been a people's war imposed on the rulers at the beginning against their will." As such it has also "denied to the anti-democratic and defeatist forces the power to enforce a surrender."[6]

Snow gave a chilling recital of Japanese savageries in China, including the infamous "Rape of Nanking" after its fall in December 1937. The occupying troops engaged in a frenzy of looting, rape, and slaughter that left hundreds of thousands of Chinese dead in the city and the surrounding countryside. Snow indicted Japan's feudal-dominated culture and society, and its military's "education for homicide," as the breeding grounds for such brutalities. He also expounded his pet "inferiority complex" thesis as a more "recondite" reason for such Japanese behavior. Here his indignation spilled over into the racist-tinged assertion that "subconsciously" the "individual Japanese is aware of his unfortunate intellectual and physical inferiority to individual Koreans and Chinese, the two peoples subject to his god-Emperor." Yet Snow maintained that ultimately the Japanese people would rise in revolutionary overthrow of militarist imperialism. He cited Japanese leftist antiwar dissidents working with the Chinese as "reminders" that Japan "was full of decent people" who, if their minds could be divested of "Sun Goddess myths and other imperialist filth," and given access to "forbidden dangerous thoughts," could "easily live in a civilized, co-operative world—if any of us could provide one."[7]

In his book Snow turned again to the empire versus democracy issue in Britain's fight for survival. He still saw the world conflict as essentially one of "'ruler' peoples fighting each other for control of subject peoples." Condemning the British record in India, he took a characteristic swipe at Gandhian nonviolence. India's nationalist movement had become so powerful, he maintained, that the British "have mainly to thank Mahatma Gandhi for not having on their hands an armed revolution."[8]

Snow pinned his hopes on America. It was under "no serious danger from any one else" and, he insisted, was "under no obligation to fight any battles abroad on anything but our own terms." And such "terms" called for America to lead the way beyond the age of empire to an era of "truer" social and political democracy on a global scale. He contrasted favorably the progressive record of American rule in the Philippines with that of the British in India. The movement toward "social revolution," he proclaimed, was the order of the day everywhere. All this had the ring of an updated, more revolutionary version of the Wilsonian call to save the world for democracy. Indeed, Snow told the presidential assistant Wayne Coy in Washington that August, "I was for a new 14 points." At a dinner with Washington friends that summer, Snow recorded, "all seemed agreed the old order was rapidly passing." America was the "decisive force" that will either "prop up the corpse of capitalism abroad or bring it down more quickly."[9]

Snow claimed that his strategy of "dynamic democracy" would not only "immobilize" the fascists, but very likely win over Russia. Surrounded by a "cooperative world, the Soviets could feel secure in fulfilling the promise of democracy inherent in their own system," he maintained. This would be particularly so if the Russians were offered "a friendly hand instead of an endless stream" of "holier-than-thou" crusading sermons "against the infidels." This notion of the transitional nature of Communist dictatorship echoes again ideas Snow first voiced in his Yanjing University fascism lecture.

Snow pressed his scheme of a federated union of "democratic states of the world." He called on the British to take the lead in a program of colonial democratization and emancipation as the basis of such a world federation. With the aid of suitably invested Western, primarily American, capital, the developing economies and societies of the liberated colonies would bring benefits and opportunities to the West far transcending those of the imperial connection. Their freedom was "positively essential to the regeneration of external markets," he declared.[10]

The interdependent global economy of today, and the vigorous role in that economy of the Asian nations of the Pacific Rim, attest to Snow's foresight. Yet his sketch of an integrated Western-initiated and constructed cooperative new internationalist order seemed to glide over the forces of nationalism that he himself always emphasized, whether as the mainspring for the subject peoples of the East, or as a pivotal factor in the Communist world. For him, evidently, the end of capitalist business as usual in the world arena would ensure a secure foundation for this new order. But as Michael Hunt observes of the United States, the multiplicity of forces, including noneconomic ones, driving American foreign policy, suggested that a "socialist America" might pursue a foreign policy no more benign than that of the "old capitalist America."[11]

That "democracies based on capitalism" would see the light in time to recover the political initiative seemed improbable, he conceded. But the many-sided world conflict would itself doom both European and Japanese imperialism and seal the fate of capitalism "as we knew it." Snow pictured a future of "cooperative democracy" (or "democratic collectivism") for the West, which could be realized peacefully through the electoral process. (The alternative for America was "some variety" of expansionist fascism.) The liberated and revolutionized societies of the East could then find a place in "a new scheme of intelligent world planning" without challenge from a now more secure Soviet state. Thus global cooperation may become "a reasonably early possibility." With the West showing the way, a "broader and more responsible democracy" could "open up for mankind the limitless possibilities of a civilization based on science and truth."[12]

All the diverse elements in Snow's makeup were present: the liberal democrat, the supporter of revolutionary social change, the colonial liberationist, the firm believer in rational-scientific planned progress. He would try to cast America itself in those roles, with Franklin Roosevelt as its wartime personification (quite a transformation from his earlier skeptical image of the president as a not very successful tinkerer with a failed American capitalism and then as something of a warmonger). He would come to see the president as symbolizing America at its democratic, nonimperialist, world-liberating, and reforming best. Snow came away from his first meeting with the president, shortly after Pearl Harbor, convinced, he later wrote, that given the co-operation of Congress and the people, he would "lead us to victory and a wise peace." (On the day in April 1945 when Roosevelt died Ed was in New York with his publisher, Bennett Cerf, who remembered how shattered the two were at the passing of a man both admired very deeply. The driver of a cab they were riding in made a disparaging remark about the dead president, and Snow insisted they stop the cab and get out.)[13]

Snow's commentaries on America had a peculiarly abstract quality that reflected his long absence from a country he had left as a very young man. In his views was the strong residue of his middle-American upbringing, the conviction, in Henry Kissinger's description, "that America should focus on affairs at home, and that she should promote democracy when she ventures abroad." As Snow himself put it soon after returning home, "For us, as democratic Americans," the policies the nation should pursue abroad could "only be an extension of the political doctrines for which we stand at home." Overlaying this conviction were the radicalized views Snow had developed abroad of America's moribund, depression-ridden, "barbaric" capitalist system. He sought to combine these positions by projecting a fundamental restructuring of American democracy as concomitant with and key to its external reforming mission. It resembles what James Thomson and his fellow authors call the American "sentimental imperialist" syndrome: a "national itch to reshape the world, especially Asia, in their own image." In Snow's case, however, the image was of an America transformed.[14]

The British commentator Dorothy Woodman, in reviewing *Battle for Asia,* acutely pinpointed some of the difficulties in Snow's global "reflections":

Like many others who have championed the "popular front" and found themselves in the dilemma of all good democrats who cannot go all the way with the Communists and who yet see that Socialism is the answer to Fascism, [Snow] begins to build in his mind the structure of the world which might be if the democratic Powers in victory would leap beyond imperialism into internationalism. Whether or not his political speculations are *Realpolitik* or wishful thinking is a question that applies to a broader area than Asia.[15]

Freda Utley, Snow's future nemesis, who by now had turned against Chinese as well as Russian Communists, dealt much more harshly with the issues raised by Woodman. Nevertheless, her review of *Battle for Asia* was still far from entirely hostile. (For 1941 Snow had privately predicted that Utley "will write a review attacking my book.") Snow was a "not yet disillusioned" Communist sympathizer who was "essentially a liberal and a humanitarian," Utley declared. But she found his book to be "the most exhaustive account" to date of the China war, praised its "intimate and realistic quality," its "power of dramatic description," and "generous human sympathies." Her criticisms of his "political chapters," Utley concluded, did not detract from the "essential value" of his China account, nor of the truth of his arguments for colonial emancipation.[16]

Snow, Utley observed, could "still write of revolutionary movements with zest and youthful hopefulness," devoid of any "misgivings" over the Moscow connection. She acknowledged that he had made an "unanswerable case" for the measures needed for victory in China, exemplified by the policies of the "as-yet-uncorrupted" Reds. But Snow had failed to recognize that the revolutionary dynamic thus generated "may serve the interests of German and Russian National Socialism instead of the cause of liberalism and reform." How could Chiang trust a Chinese Communist ally whose moves were dictated by Russian interest? The Reds could reverse their stand overnight, aligning themselves "with instead of against the Japanese enemy" in proclaimed opposition to "the 'Anglo-American imperialist front' supporting Chungking."[17]

Snow of course had opposite (and justifiable) fears that Western assistance to the Kuomintang would shore up the more reactionary pro–civil war faction in Chungking and saw the Communists as the best guarantee of a continued and effective resistance. In the months following the New Fourth Army Incident, Snow's public position on the aid question hardened. With American help finally beginning to flow to China under the new Lend-Lease Act and other credit arrangements, Snow was warning against a no-strings-attached aid policy that would only encourage Chungking in its anti-Communist moves and weaken its stance against Japan. The united front had been little more than a charade, Snow wrote in April 1941, and the Kuomintang now apparently aimed for a war of "quiet attrition" against the Reds. Such outcomes were made even more likely by the prospect that Anglo-American forces might soon carry the brunt of war in the Pacific.[18]

In retrospect, Snow clearly had the better part of the argument with Utley. Stalin, in fact, would promote Soviet interests in the Far East by a pact with the Nationalists in 1945 that to some extent undercut the Chinese Communist position. And Snow's more complex view of the ambiguities in the Moscow-CCP relationship, with its dialectical mix of internationalist loyalties and indigenously based independently determined nationalist priorities, was much closer to the realities than Utley's simplistic notion of total Soviet domination.

Utley's review contained a most telling statement. "It was the tragedy of the progressive movement in China," she remarked, that its close links to Moscow and its earlier "class war" policies "should have driven many of those who might otherwise favor reform into the camp of the reactionaries." This remark pointed along the path she too would traverse and could also be taken as a kind of text on the response by postwar America to social revolutionary nationalist upheavals around the world, seen as instigated and controlled by a Soviet-centered Communist empire.

But these were matters for the future. Snow soon found himself once again entangled with the political left in America, this time on a more personal level. *Battle for Asia* included his usual long-distance barbs at the American Communists for their servile responses to the political twists and turns by Moscow. Their ability "to put themselves out on limbs to be sawed off by Soviet foreign policy seems to be inexhaustible," he commented. He criticized the left for its clumsy attacks on Roosevelt and rearmament at a time when the vast majority of Americans favored a military buildup in the name of security. The Communists, Snow pronounced, "should go far enough with that opinion to mobilize it against the capitalist misuse of armament in organizing fascism at home for imperialist war abroad"—a fuzzy formula that said more about Snow's unresolved conflicts than about the policies of the American left.

As a further example of Communist political ineptness, Snow egregiously ridiculed the party's persistence in nominating a Negro (in the parlance of the time) for vice president, when neither the Negroes nor the working class were "yet prepared for such an advanced (and ultimately necessary) aspiration, any more than the Russians are yet prepared to impose one of their Eskimos as head of the Supreme Soviet." Snow undoubtedly believed he was sensitive and enlightened on the "color" issue—certainly as it applied to the colonial people of Asia he had come to know well. But his life and experiences in America and overseas included no such personal contacts with African Americans; he could hardly be called "ahead of his times" on racial issues at home.[19]

Snow would soon regret these paragraphs. In California, he met American progressives in the flesh. He was lionized by the cultural elite active in leftist circles in the Los Angeles–Hollywood region who showed keen interest in and sympathy for China—most especially for the Snows' favorite cause, Indusco. Helen had already organized a Hollywood Indusco committee headed by the noted left-wing actor John Garfield, one of the Hollywood celebrities the Snows socialized with. Helen and Ed also persuaded Theodore Dreiser to sign the Indusco loan petition to Roosevelt, though we might wonder at the benefit, given Dreiser's public tirades against F. D. R.

Snow was thus attracted and impressed by the many notable and welcoming literary and film people he met, with whom he shared a good deal of common ground. He became more aware of the attacks on the Communists, including the imprisonment of Earl Browder. Now as in later cold war days, Snow was uncomfortable at seeming to aid and abet "reactionaries" in their assaults on the left. In an odd minor replay of the *Red Star* scenario, Snow attempted a last-minute retreat from remarks in his new book that might offend left-wing readers. In a phone call and letter from Hollywood, he appealed to his agent to have the paragraphs on the American Communists deleted. This "now seems to me, after my arrival here, of exceeding importance," he wrote her. In "this hour of difficulty for the LW [left-wing] people I do not wish to add anything more to the calumnies against them." He did not realize, he added, "how tense the situation here in America is, . . . or I would never have ventured such a remark at their expense." But it was in fact too late, and the offending paragraphs remained.[20]

Snow's problematic relationship with the American Communists took a more direct turn later in that first year back home. On arriving in New York in April he was invited to be a main speaker at an American Writers Congress to be held in New York in early June. It was designed by the Communist-dominated League of American Writers as a protest against what it termed the Roosevelt administration's drive toward "war abroad and fascism at home." After glancing through the congress's manifesto, or call, Snow agreed to talk on a China-related topic. He declined, however, to sign the call (something the sponsors usually demanded of participating speakers), though he apparently expressed no open disagreement with its contents at the time. Perhaps the impressive array of progressive cultural celebrities sponsoring the congress influenced Snow's commitment. Among many others, they included Theodore Dreiser, Dashiell Hammett, Lillian Hellman, Rockwell Kent, Langston Hughes, Clifford Odets, Orson Welles, and Richard Wright. To Ed, still fresh to the American political scene, it may have seemed more akin to the relatively broad political spectrum of cultural-intellectual sympathizers of the left he had known in China. Snow naively—especially in view of his earlier *Red Star* experience—thought he could "get along" without fully going along with the congress's line. As Snow later explained the point in *Journey:* though "troubled" by the congress manifesto's branding of Roosevelt as a "fascist," and its total defense of "every act of Stalinist opportunism," he was nevertheless "glad to take any opportunity to arouse people to the danger from the East." He rather lamely added that he had not "quite believed that the Communists were in charge" since he "knew" that many of the writers involved were not Reds.[21]

Actually Snow had been moving steadily away from the adamantly antiwar position of the pro-Soviet American left. The opinions he voiced at his Philadelphia press interview just a few days before the writers' meeting were patently at odds with the avowed purposes of the New York conclave. And he planned in his prepared address to deliver a similar message—squeezed somehow into the antiwar motif of the congress. Nevertheless, he could still write to the executive secretary of the congress, after returning from Philadelphia, that he was "surprised and disappointed" to learn that his prepared speech had been rejected on the grounds that it "fundamentally contradicts the convictions" of the congress. Despite his differences with the call, he added, "That in no way affected my support of the main issues the Call raised nor my readiness to speak at the Congress." It was one of the stranger episodes in Snow's various encounters with the non-Chinese part of the Communist movement.[22]

The text of Snow's undelivered congress address refuted the case he had made to Will Babcock a year and a half earlier. What he had then considered, with some equanimity, as the far-fetched possibility of Nazi conquest of Europe had come to pass, and with it the emergence of the full-fledged Berlin-Tokyo alliance that he had also discounted. He reminded his projected audience of its earlier antiappeasement, antifascist stance and affirmed his support for American aid to the Chinese and British peoples. An independent Britain, he declared, was "a more progressive political concept than a Britain dominated by German Nazism." Even without a decisive victory over England, Snow pointed out, the Germans could move against the Soviets "at any moment. Is it not possible that if Soviet Russia got no help from Britain or America she could be defeated by the armed might of the fascist world?" (When the Nazi attack came just two weeks later, the American Communists clamored for just such aid in what was now proclaimed to be "the life and death struggle between fascism and democracy.") German-Japanese hegemony over most of the globe, Snow warned, would constitute a direct threat to the United States. America would be forced to retreat behind "a wall of arms" and await attack or accept a fascist way of life. But Snow tried to give his argument a "peace" twist. "I do not believe that we run as great a risk of war by giving all-out aid to the Chinese and British peoples as we would run by denying aid and hastening their defeat," he reasoned. Without these conquests, he added, "the Axis Powers have no real bases from which to attack us." Meanwhile, he went on in some tortuous antiwar logic, it was "our duty as writers to see that 'aid for resistance' is not perverted to serve the wishes of the war-makers who want us to enter the war directly ourselves." (As if in rejoinder to his own remarks, he had told his Philadelphia interviewer that America would be actively in the war while "some people are still arguing about whether the United States is going to war or not.")[23]

In turning to China in his writers' congress text, Snow emphasized that "Americans who hope their country will never enter a war incompatible with democratic goals will naturally wish to see certain conditions laid down by Washington in further support of China." It was the CIC syndrome writ large: to reform China through benevolent foreign intervention. Snow ticked off the conditions America should set ("phrased, of course, in the language of diplomacy") in return for aid: no American money or munitions to be used to block internal political progress or to shore up "the present minority one-party dictatorship"; cooperation among the anti-Japanese parties rather than "the recent attempt by Kuomintang generals to destroy the heroic New Fourth Army"; American military supplies to go also to the guerrilla areas, with the Nationalist blockade against the Reds lifted; the Generalissimo to implement "in deeds his 14 annual promises of constitutional democracy"; American aid to be used to help enforce agrarian reform; and finally, that American currency, commodity and industrial credits and technical help "be canalized through CIC, to ensure the democratic industrialization of China." It is interesting to contrast the relatively revolutionary (if "utopian") China role Snow advocated for America, with the China policy of Moscow. Soviet military assistance had been flowing to the Kuomintang since 1937, apparently with few if any of the stipulations Snow was asking of Washington. Snow would later look back ruefully on the China task he had assigned to America: "How earnestly this Candide-turned-reformer pleaded for comprehension in an America which was, he supposed, about to 'take charge'! . . . I was simply dreaming, as many people in China were dreaming, of a 'savior from abroad'—in my case, America."[24]

Snow's remaining doubts on the war issue were being eroded by his steady, if reluctant, recognition that American entry into a war of global dimensions was virtually inevitable. He understood the threat posed by Japan, endorsed the firmest American measures to counter it—economic quarantine, joint defense alliances, and military buildup. He acknowledged that these policies were likely to trigger an attack by a desperate Japan faced with "catastrophe." Yet he portrayed these strategies as still having the possibility of giving the Japanese military pause. The people of Japan must be under no "delusion" that they would only be getting into a "Singapore incident," he wrote, in pressing his ideas for a "political battle of Asia." Stern Western resolve should be linked with an offer aimed directly at those people of "cooperation in the construction of a really progressive New Order." He prophesied that if Tokyo decided against taking on the Anglo-American powers and remained mired in China, "the situation would become so serious as to result in a social revolution in Japan within not more than two years." He conceded, however, that given these grim prospects, and the realization that Japan would only grow weaker relative to Britain and America as time went on, "the outcome might be somewhat different. The army and navy might prefer hara-kiri to surrender." In a mid-1941 *Post* article on the coming "Showdown in the Pacific," Snow emphasized that war was the more likely option for Japan, especially if the China front was neutralized by renewed civil war, and if the U.S. Pacific fleet was weakened by diversion of a portion to Atlantic duty. Japan could likely strike even without these two eventualities. "But we can be sure that if and when those two conditions are realized there will be a blitzkrieg in the Pacific." The Japanese, we know, had their own ideas for weakening the Pacific fleet.[25]

But ambiguities remained. Shortly after the *Post* article appeared, his diary noted his response to the freezing of Axis assets in the United States, and to a recent sinking of an American merchant ship in the Atlantic: "Looks as though R's [Roosevelt's] policy is working out. We are entering war by degrees." In Washington a few weeks later, he described government officials he dined with as "rabid interventionists." There were other inconsistencies. Snow urged the government, as part of a new "propaganda" offensive, to take steps to stop Japanese and Nazi propaganda activities in the United States and its territories, and to "disband" Japanese and Axis-controlled "political clubs and subversive organizations inside American territory." (Snow was concerned primarily with a Philippine "fifth column," but the scope of his proposal was considerably broader.) At almost the same time, he quoted in his diary, evidently approvingly, a letter from Evans Carlson, on the great expansion of FBI power following the fall of France. The bureau had "used the hysteria which followed to gain a cinch hold throughout the country." Strangely, as war with Japan came closer, Snow veered more to the belief that Japan would not "dare" attack. He apparently made such a prediction for 1942 for a *Look* article (which the magazine was able to change in time). As to why he had "abandoned" his earlier analysis, "I'm inclined to believe it was because of the overwhelming front mobilized vs Japan," he recorded on Pearl Harbor day. "I could not believe — though economic interpretation had convinced me earlier of it — that Japan would dare defy such a combination." Just days before, in a letter to Alley, he remained troubled at the extent of the American defense buildup underway, and its global military implications. The country was "militarizing on a scale greater than anything ever dreamed of in history," and American troops will "certainly" be sent to Asia and Europe, and Americans would eventually control the skies in Latin America and Africa. "I don't like the picture and I don't know anyone who does." This sounded more like a presentiment of America's future as world superpower.[26]

During his summer visit to Washington Snow had been offered a commission in Army Air Corps Intelligence. He was evidently expected to help determine bombing objectives in Japan, potential airfield sites in China, and other such matters. (The officer who contacted him on this believed "we would be able to make quick work of Japan," Ed noted.) Snow kept this option in abeyance over the next months, then gave it serious thought when the proposal was reactivated after the outbreak of war. He eventually decided, apparently with a prod of "orders" in that direction from his "Commander-in-Chief," the president, to take on instead a permanent *Post* overseas war assignment. "Oh they'll [the Air Force] manage without you somehow," Roosevelt assured Ed at their first talk early in 1942.[27]

In July the Snows moved into their newly purchased home on some six acres in the Connecticut coastal town of Madison. Helen loved the small colonial-era house, built in 1752, and has lived there continuously for over half a century. (Ed would disparagingly refer to the house as a "shanty.") There was an occasional flare-up between the two in the next months, which Snow brooded on in his diary. In one incident, during a visit by the Babcocks, Helen "screamed" at Ed for a deprecating remark he made on Indusco. "Sweet life," he jotted, "I withdrew." There was also, as previously noted, a warmly pleasant reunion with Ed's old mentor and champion, Charles Hanson Towne, who came up from New York where he was appearing on stage in *Life with Father*.[28]

Snow was anxious, as earlier, to break out of his Asia niche into a wider field of European coverage. "People have put me in a hole marked Far East and they won't let me get out of it," he complained to Alley. He had long desired a Russian post and pursued it again after the Nazi invasion in June. He found no immediate takers, a situation compounded by his continuing Moscow visa problem. He tried also for a London assignment, with no better results. He met with the Chicago department store magnate Marshall Field, to seek a London berth with Field's new Chicago paper. "Have you ever done any writing," Field queried. "Such is fame," Snow noted of the interview. The *Post* put him off as well on the London idea but asked him to do some reporting on how the new draft army was faring—"morale and such. (How absurd—me writing about *morale*)," he told Alley. Nevertheless, he felt it was a good opportunity "to dig into my own country's affairs more deeply to discover what makes the wheels go round." He also hoped that "doing this domestic scene stuff" would help him escape his China pigeonhole.[29]

Snow spent much of the summer and fall looking into army camps around the country, gathering information not only on soldier morale, but on the thinking of the generals, and on the state of American war preparedness. As to why "They Don't Want to Play Soldier," Snow made a point of the nation's anomalous "undeclared war" status. It led to uncertainties and confusions among these draftees as to when, where, and above all why they might be called on to fight. "Some columnists and the Fight For Freedom Committee declared war long ago, but the simple draftee still has peace in his heart." The "most important thing," he recorded, "is the creation of a reason for fighting." For "good or evil," he concluded, "the Army is going to be with us for a long, long time now, and in a more and more dominant role in everybody's life."[30]

Snow cited "nearly all the Negro regiments" among those army units who did have "excellent" morale. "The average Negro soldier is living better than ever before in his life and is learning something, and there is the challenge of proving himself as good as the white boys." Somewhat at variance with this estimate, Snow also forthrightly wrote, "I should think the Army could get along without any officer who habitually refers to black troops in a camp as 'niggers.'" He saw this, however, merely as manifestations of poor "psychology" and "terminology." In detailing the recreational-entertainment efforts of the Army's morale branch, Snow could not resist references to his Chinese Red heroes. "We may think there is nothing to learn from a backward country like China, but its famed Eighth Route Army really has a few lessons for us." He discreetly focused these "lessons" on the less politically charged uses of drama and song by that army. "One thing that explains the magnificent courage and endurance of this remarkable army is the fact that it never gets bored with itself or forgets the importance of humor," he explained.[31]

Back home in Madison in the final months of 1941, Snow waited on events. "As for my personal plans (confidential!)," he informed Alley in early December, "I have none. I am living like the rest of the world, from day to day." Tokyo soon resolved these incertitudes and set the wartime agenda for him as it did for the nation at large. Snow's connection with the *Post* had solidified during that year, in which he produced four substantial pieces for the journal. With the outbreak of war, and a new internationalist-minded editor, Ben Hibbs, at the helm, Snow at long last was given the broader overseas assignment (as *Post* "world correspondent") he so coveted. Still lacking a Soviet visa, he left by clipper in early April 1942, across Africa and the Middle East to India. During the flight he would hear of the fall of Bataan and Corregidor, America's last footholds in the Philippines. Peg had seen him off, but by that time, he later wrote of his marriage, "it was clear to both of us" that its "creative possibilities" were exhausted. Over the next three years and more of the war, Snow would report from virtually every theater of the conflict including, most significantly, the Russian front, and produce two wartime books.[32]

In a bizarre bit of symbolism, one of Snow's fellow passengers on the clipper flight was a navy lieutenant commander (later admiral), Milton ("Mary") Miles, on his way to China on a special navy mission that represented a diametrically opposite perception of America's wartime role in China (and by inference elsewhere) than the vision Snow was taking with him overseas. Miles was heading for a meeting with the notorious Dai Li, head of Chiang's feared secret police and of the fascistic Blue Shirts. By 1943 their collaboration resulted in the organization of the Sino-American Cooperative Organization (SACO) under the joint direction of the two men. It was a collaboration in an active anti-Communist program for the Nationalists that involved arming and training Chinese police, guerrilla, and commando forces for operations against the

Reds. SACO was also associated with the Happy Valley complex out-side Chungking, where Dai Li's political prisoners were incarcerated, many of whom were apparently tortured and killed by his operatives. An increasingly obsessed and unstable Miles would finally be recalled home after the Japanese surrender, later to serve in naval capacities elsewhere in the world. Dai Li would perish in a plane crash in March 1946. SACO was an especially dark foretaste of the cold war–fueled counterinsurgency American interventionism to come. ("Much of what Miles did was opposed by his superiors," Michael Schaller writes, "only because it had been done both crudely and prematurely.")[33]

For the time being, these eventualities were far from Snow's thoughts. On the Far East, Snow had written Edward Carter of the Institute of Pacific Relations before leaving for overseas, "The empires are collapsing and in the last hour the sahibs are discovering they need the people. Great progress may be expected and the old stagnating forms are broken and being plowed under to lay the ground for a broader future." It was a peroration to all he had been writing and thinking about Asia for a decade. As Snow began his new reporting activities, he saw them as an entirely new ("third life") stage in his career. His personal star, however, would always remain linked to the Red star of China.

Epilogue

I covered a few more wars, and near wars (in Russia during Stalingrad was a big point), went home for ten years and cut the lawn and had a family (two) and wrote a few books, until I heard the call of the East again.

Edgar Snow to "Ross," May 8, 1971

CHAPTER 14

Global War,
and Cold War Blues

Snow arrived in India in the spring of 1942, at a moment when that subcontinent was threatened with invasion by Japanese forces that had already conquered neighboring Burma. (The flight across Africa had almost ended in disaster when the plane's radio beam was lost for a considerable time. "You were flying practically by the stars and there were very few," Snow reminisced to the pilot ["Ross"] in 1971, re- calling the latter's "cool in bringing us in.") Ed was predictably caustic on the British Raj, both for the rapid defeat in Burma and the inade- quate marshaling of India's defenses. The British, Snow recorded in Cal- cutta, were relying on America "to win back the empire for them." In a subsequent interview with the viceroy, Lord Linlithgow, Snow pushed his pet Indusco concepts for India's war effort but found the Briton un- receptive.[1]

Ed's arrival coincided with the collapse of the Cripps mission to India. Sir Stafford Cripps (a Labour member of Churchill's cabinet) had come bearing London's proposals for postwar constitutional steps to self-rule, aimed at enlisting the Indian National Congress behind the war. The Gandhi-led Congress rejected the offer, demanded immediate independence, and called for nonviolent struggle against British rule. To Snow, despite his pro-Indian nationalist sympathies and harsh criticisms and suspicions of the British, this amounted to "a declaration of war against Britain instead of Japan."[2]

Snow briefly revisited China from India in late May, flying over the Hump to Chungking. To him, the China situation seemed even further deteriorated since his departure in January 1941. Inflation was rampant, the living standards of workers and white-collar groups were in sharp decline. With America now in the war, the Chinese considered Japan doomed to defeat. As a result, "the important question [in China] now was, who was going to rule the country after the war," Snow noted. It had sharpened the conflict between the Nationalists and Communists — "whereas on my last visit," Ed added, "the Reds were still nominally under the Generalissimo's absolute command, today they do not pretend to obey his orders unless they consider them useful. This reflects a big increase in their real power." Hoarding for future eventualities was now the order of the day in China — "of commodities, of guns, of ammunition, of jeeps."[3]

Ed returned to India and left Delhi in mid-September by air for Teheran. There, in that major lend-lease supply gateway to the Russian front, he waited for the Soviet visa he had applied for many months before; it finally came through in early October. His attitude on entering the Soviet Union for the first time was then at its admiring and sympathetic peak. It was primarily a response to the colossal struggle of the Red Army against the hitherto invincible Wehrmacht, a battle Snow viewed as decisive in determining the outcome of the global conflict. While in India, Snow had pressed Nehru on the Indian National Congress's stance on the war: the "fate of the whole world is being decided in the German-Soviet struggle," he argued to the Indian leader. If Russia is defeated, he continued, "then India, under Britain or under the Axis, cannot survive." And in one of his barbs at the British, he observed that "Indians" (though really he was speaking for himself) know "that Britain was saved, by one thing and one thing only," and that was "the fact that three million Russians died to break the offensive power of a German army that otherwise would most certainly have put an end to the British empire."[4]

Snow was especially impressed by the Soviet Union's ability to marshal its human and material resources for the war — in sharp contrast to what he had witnessed in Nationalist China and just seen in India. About "99 percent of the energies of sixteen united republics seemed to have been mobilized to realize a struggle plan embracing more people and more territory than ever before used to battle an invader," Snow wrote from Russia for the *Post* in January 1943. It strengthened his longstanding conviction on the superiority of a centrally planned (socialist) economy. ("Only the blind can now deny," he wrote in 1944, "that the triumph of the Red Army is the triumph of Soviet socialism, and above all, Soviet planning.")[5]

Snow's writings on wartime Russia reflected the above themes, combined with his "people on our side" approach in depicting the sacrifices, spirit, valor, and humanity of Soviet soldiers and civilians alike. His *Post* articles on Russia from 1943 to 1945 dealt with the superhuman war-production efforts and high morale of factory workers, mostly women; with the exploits of young women partisan fighters he met on the Smolensk front west of Moscow; and with the devastation of Soviet regions recaptured from the Germans. There were also such pieces for his *Post* readers as "What Kind of a Man Is a Russian General?"; "Is Red Marriage Turning Blue?"; and "Meet Mr. and Mrs. Russia at Home." And though Snow underscored the all-embracing "cult of adoration" built up around "that Man in the Kremlin," he could also give the Soviet dictator an earthy "man of the people" touch: in pausing for drinks of water during a wartime radio address to the nation, Stalin "had apologized for this, saying he had eaten too many herring that morning, and Russia roared with laughter," Snow wrote. In reporting the Russian story, Snow saw as always a larger responsibility: in this instance, to promote Allied unity and understanding in war, and to underline the overriding importance of continued Soviet-American cooperation in the peace to follow. It all made for a relatively benign image of the beleaguered wartime Soviet state and its (personally distasteful to Ed) cult of "Stalin the Great." It seemed equally to lead him to a "positive-realistic" appraisal of Moscow's postwar security requirements and of the future in store for a Soviet-dominated, "reformed" and "fraternal" Eastern Europe.[6]

In 1944 *People on Our Side* would sum up Snow's argument for Western accommodation to Russian needs. "The only alternative to mutual recognition of regional security arrangements by West and East," he affirmed, "is the pursuit of a policy of imposing our will by force; it is the policy of preparing for the Third World War, the war of the continents." It was a motif he clung to doggedly, despite souring disillusionments as war ended.[7]

He had come to Moscow at a particularly grim moment when the ferocious, drawn-out, and critical battle of Stalingrad was mounting in intensity. The encircling Russian counteroffensive in November, and final German surrender there by the end of January 1943, marked a decisive turn in the war against Hitler. Snow visited the Stalingrad battlefront with other correspondents in the aftermath of the German defeat. The devastated city, Ed would write, "was demolished Chapei, in Shanghai, magnified twenty times and the bombed districts of London could have been lost in a corner of it."[8]

Snow left Russia in April 1943, after a mostly cheerless winter there. He was annoyed at the obtuse censorship and obstructionism of the press department that faced all the foreign correspondents in Moscow. The "cold impersonal climate in which one works day after day," he recorded, "is what gets one down." The "unbending inflexible character of the whole machine," he added, "kills the average correspondent's objectivity in a very short time." And though he was an ardent advocate of an early Allied landing in western Europe to relieve pressure on the Red Army, he could acidly note, "Wonder why the British never refer to the 2nd front as 'Reopening the First Front' rather than give the R's psychological advantage."[9]

He flew back to India, where the Congress leaders Gandhi and Nehru had been incarcerated by the British. There was a letter from Peg "with orders to form an Indusco committee here." Not quite "as easy as that," Ed reacted. From Assam in the north, he crossed into Yunnan province over the Hump, now a busy Allied air supply route to China. Dotted with newly built American airfields, this formerly remote region of China had been the setting of Ed's memorable caravan journey into Burma a dozen years before.[10]

Ed spent some two weeks visiting American military installations around Kunming in Yunnan, and Guilin in neighboring Guangxi. He received his bleakest picture yet of the China situation from U.S. military and foreign service officers. Skyrocketing prices, endemic corruption, smuggling, blackmarket resale of supplies flown in, foreign currency manipulation and speculation, and much more. The American army was paying for everything at an artificially pegged exchange rate that greatly overvalued the inflated Chinese currency. The "result is general extortion and we are looked upon as Santa Claus," Snow noted. Chinese soldiers were undernourished, weary, and generally unfit for combat, and the Generalissimo, Snow was told, was surrounded by "thugs, gangsters, and racketeers." The Chinese say, an American colonel confided, "we [China] carried the ball for six years, now it's your turn." The major 1944 Japanese offensive sweep through east and central China against crumbling Nationalist forces that engulfed many of the new American air bases evidently confirmed these assessments.[11]

In his 1944 book, Snow would scathingly write, "When I came back to China again from Russia in the middle of 1943, I found that the country's economy had become chaotic, its political life more reactionary than at any time since 1936, and its military efficiency was at its lowest level since the war began."[12]

From India in July 1943, Snow left for the Middle East and then to England for a first visit. He made the rounds of leading British politicians and other luminaries of varying political persuasions. Ed also collected data, for a *Post* article, on the results achieved by the Anglo-American strategic bombing campaign against Germany. For it he interviewed American and British air command figures, including Air Marshal Sir Arthur Harris. He then returned to the States where he remained until June 1944. In May of that year he had his second personal meeting with Roosevelt. In a conversation that ranged over the globe, Snow pushed his Soviet-American postwar cooperation theme, to which Roosevelt readily concurred. The president accepted Ed's renewed offer to write him from Moscow. "Write me a letter and tell me your impressions of Russia since the Teheran Conference." Snow came away with the belief that the president "will accommodate Russia's demands for her eastern frontier," and with an optimistic feeling that civil war in China might be averted. As in the other two Snow exchanges with the president, it all appeared to typify the engagingly informal and persuasive Roosevelt style. But Snow also felt the president had aged considerably since Ed had last seen him, the first weeks of the war. "His hands shook violently when he reached for a glass of water, as he did several times during the talk. It seemed to me his mind tended to wander. . . . He did not smoke. He looked tired."[13]

Snow flew out of Miami on June 5 and learned of D-Day en route to Moscow on June 6. The Soviet capital in summer of 1944, with the Red Army now advancing through eastern Europe, was a bright contrast in weather, mood, and appearance to that of the critical winter months of 1942–1943. Snow was further buoyed by the "astounding" news (received on his thirty-eighth birthday) that his *People on Our Side* had been chosen as a book dividend by the Book-of-the-Month Club. Probably most cheering of all was his reacquaintance with a young Russian woman he had met briefly on his earlier stay. "Ilena" was in her early twenties, and a student at Moscow University. She was "passing fair," with "azure eyes of a singular shape," as Ed romantically described her in *Journey*. They went together for some months until the inevitable pain of parting in another Moscow winter. That capital, Snow wrote, "again became a city of wintry pinched faces and grey frosty souls and streets dark with ice."[14]

While in Russia, Snow made trips to newly liberated sections of Poland and Rumania, getting a sense of the Soviet-orchestrated new political order there. Would the "turn to the left" sociopolitical order in

Eastern Europe lead toward "outright Communism or Socialism," or would it prove to be "the birth pangs of an emancipated society . . . nearer to democracy and the Four Freedoms than this part of Europe has known before?" Snow asked in a November 1944 *Post* piece. It was a question, he wryly concluded, that he "gladly" left to his readers "to think over amid the abundance of America, which everybody in the world hopes to go on sharing with us on the Lend-Lease principle until something better turns up." Snow also saw the Nazi death camp at Maidanek, near Lublin in Poland, and wrote movingly of the searing evidence of its methodically organized mass extermination of victims. He would visit another such camp at Mauthausen, in Austria, the following May.[15]

Snow was home once more in the last months of 1944 and into the spring of 1945. He made a rare visit to see his father in Kansas City and in March had his final talk with Roosevelt—soon after the president's return from Yalta and just weeks before his sudden death in April. Snow had also seen his old friend Evans Carlson, recuperating from his war wounds in California. The president spoke warmly of Carlson to Ed and agreed with the latter's characterization of the marine as "just a good old-fashioned New England Christian reformer." "That's right, Absolutely," Roosevelt rejoined, "but the Marine Corps still insists he's a Red!" (Retired Marine Major-General William A. Worton, who knew Carlson in Peking in the 1930s, in later reminiscences judged Carlson to have been a "Red." He related that after Carlson, who died of a heart attack in 1947, had been given an official Arlington burial ["the works"] by the corps, commanding General Vandergrift had remarked, "Thank God, he's gone." Still, Worton added, "withal, he was a very, very brave and capable man.")[16]

On the political stalemate in China, Roosevelt expressed great disappointment to Snow at the failure of efforts by his special envoy Patrick Hurley to get the KMT and CCP to cooperate. But he evinced full confidence in Hurley and directed his ire at the Generalissimo. "I don't know why Chiang can't get along with these people [the Communists]," he impatiently remarked. "I've been working with two governments in China," Roosevelt "emphatically" told Ed, "and I intend to go on doing so until we can get them together."[17]

Citing in his 1945 book some of these remarks of the now-deceased president, Snow continued to put his hopes for a political solution in China on the great powers. Only "combined Anglo-American-Soviet pressure on both parties in China," he declared, "could impose a formula even temporarily uniting the anti-Japanese forces in our common war." He fleshed out this thesis in a rather complex May 1945 article in the *Post*. His analysis drew on his hopes and assumptions that an era of Soviet-American cooperation was unfolding in postwar Europe, with similar prospects envisaged for Asia. In Snow's view, Washington and Moscow were on a converging course in toughened stances against what Ed described as Chiang's plans: to retain intact the power of his regime of "aging reactionaries"; to reoccupy, with American help, all lost Chinese territory (including "recovery" of areas held by the Communists); and to resume the (futile, in Snow's opinion) task of annihilating the Communist "bandits." In a genuine peaceful settlement brokered by the great powers the CCP might be expected ultimately to prevail, but this outcome need not alarm Washington. A united, "progressive," independent, and still far from fully communized China, and in need of much U.S. economic assistance and investment, Ed argued, would be more in accord with American interests than a "reactionary" and potentially fascistic China under the Kuomintang. And for the Soviets, Snow reasoned, support for "the transition from reaction to progress" in China dovetailed with overall Russian security concerns. Still, Snow added some important caveats to his argument. While "it seems certain that the late President discussed China with Stalin" at Yalta, "what was said is so far a military secret." And "if we are going to fight Russia someday, as pessimists believe," then his analysis "should be 'included out.'" Snow would shortly be getting a rude jolt on the first point and, on the second, later cold war disenchantment.[18]

Moreover, events of the six months preceding Snow's meeting with Roosevelt already cast considerable doubt on the concept of "imposing" an agreement on the contending Chinese parties and their armies. Nor did those events instill great confidence in Roosevelt's resolve or in his full grasp of the realities of the complex China equation. In October 1944 the president had acquiesced to Chiang's demand for the recall of General Joseph Stilwell. The latter had been commander of the China-Burma-India theater and concurrently chief of staff under the Generalissimo for China. He was replaced by General Albert C. Wedemeyer, more acceptable to Chiang, and less abrasive, than "Vinegar Joe." The pompous and increasingly pro-Chiang Patrick Hurley was named ambassador to Chungking, taking over from the resigned ambassador, Clarence Gauss. "The fundamental difference between the Generalissimo and General Stilwell," the correspondent Brooks Atkinson of the *New York Times* wrote after returning from China at that time, "has been that the latter has been eager to fight the Japanese in China without delay, and the Generalissimo had hoped he would not have to." In the Stilwell affair, Michael Schaller notes in his book on America's wartime "crusade" in China, "Chiang had accomplished one of the most crucial victories in his remarkable career."[19]

Neither the Americans nor the Russians could guide or control China's political destiny. With the failure of Washington's final mediation effort, the (General George C.) Marshall Mission President Truman dispatched in December 1945, China erupted in full-scale civil war by the last months of 1946. A contest of arms, by the Chinese themselves, would decide the nation's future. As Michael Schaller concludes, "For a decade, despite a nearly total misunderstanding of China's crisis and an equally murky concept of what it wished to achieve, the United States struggled to become the arbiter of change in China and Asia. Only the fury of the Chinese revolution and the passage of time could begin to erode this arrogance." Snow on his part would soon be revising his stance on such big power interventionism.[20]

Ed was in western Europe in April 1945 for the ending of the war. After the German surrender in early May, he drove with a fellow correspondent to Soviet-occupied Vienna (the first American journalists to enter the Austrian capital) and then back into Germany. (In both countries he heard many anti-Soviet horror stories of looting and raping in Red Army–occupied zones.) Then on to Paris (its "lovely vistas everywhere") and through much of France. He left by military air transport in late July for Stockholm and Helsinki and then reentered Russia at Leningrad for what would be his last visit to the Soviet Union. Leningrad was stark, scarred by the terrible ordeal of the 900-day Nazi siege of that city, which cost the lives of one million of its inhabitants. While it was "certainly a great city by contrast with Moscow," Snow noted, "it seems drab and tawdry now in contrast with the grace and supernal beauty of Paris. The people are shabby—shabbier than I have seen in any country of Europe: far more so than any part of occupied Austria or Germany." Whatever "loot" the Russians had taken from Europe "does not seem to have made any impression on Leningradites." There "is little external gaiety in the place. There is no song, no outward sign of joy of living. The people look old, tired, overworked, hungry."[21]

These impressions mirrored Snow's darkening postwar mood. In Moscow ("lively and animated" compared to Leningrad), he was given a more revealing (and chilling) picture of the Soviet system. Russian acquaintances told of relatives and friends liquidated in the great purges or shipped off to Siberian camps, and other grim tales of Russian life. "How would Chung-kuo jen [the Chinese—presumably the Chinese Communists] regard this kuo [country] if they knew the true ch'ing-hsing [situation]? Have I been deceiving people? Have I told the whole chen-ti [truth]?" Snow privately anguished.[22]

In Moscow, Ed learned the details of the new Sino-Soviet "Treaty of Friendship and Alliance," signed in that city on August 14, the day of the Japanese surrender, and a week after the Soviets entered the Pacific conflict. The treaty (and Russia's war entry) carried out secret accords reached by Roosevelt and Stalin at Yalta in February. Among other provisions, the new treaty restored, in modified form, Russia's pre-1905 railway and warm water port and naval base "rights" in Manchuria; in return, Moscow pledged its "moral, material and military support" solely to the National government led by Chiang. "This is the last and final proof that Moscow's policies are determined solely and only by nationalistic considerations," Snow recorded.[23]

He left Russia in mid-September, accompanying a U.S. congressional party to Saudi Arabia. In Riyadh, he later wrote Saxe Cummins of Random House, he "ate mutton on the palace roof under the moonlight with the King's [Ibn Saud] 39 sons and 60 grandsons, or anyway a good chunk of them." From there he continued on to India, "sat in Delhi for three weeks," and then to Calcutta. He stopped briefly in Bangkok and flew on to Saigon for a week. He found the Indochina scene "very edifying," he told Cummins. After Tokyo's surrender, "the anti-Jap Annamites" had "come out of their holes" and set up an independent government. Then came British troops to "disarm" the Japanese. The British in turn brought in French troops—"Vichyite" troops who had collaborated with the Japanese. "So today it is like this," Snow continued. "Our ex-enemies the Japs, whom the British were to disarm, are advancing as a screen into the interior to push back the poorly armed Annamites. Behind them come Indian troops; behind them come the British. When 'law and order' are restored, the French move in." It was a bitter commentary on the Indochina situation that would remain the baseline of his thinking through the postwar decades of French and American involvement there.[24]

In November, Snow went on from Saigon to the Philippines. There, in the war-devastated capital of Manila ("much more of a wreck than I had imagined"), Snow meditated on his crumbling marriage, thought back on the women he had known in the course of his wartime global travels, and contemplated the personal life he aspired to in the future. "I want to get married again as soon as the r. [right] female turns up—have children, a house with children and a farm, garden, all the rest of it. I want to settle at last." But, Snow continued, "I don't see the female, only females." The "r. female," in the person of Lois Wheeler, would soon turn up, and in time the scenario he had sketched would be fulfilled. However, in the Snow-unfriendly political climate of the 1950s, there would be more settling than he could have anticipated.[25]

From the Philippines, Snow moved on to Japan and Korea at the end of 1945, covering postwar developments there. But not China. He was now denied entry by the Nationalist government as "unacceptable to China," despite a vigorous protest to sympathetic President Truman by the chief *Post* editor, Ben Hibbs. Thus Snow, who had been so notably identified with the rise of Maoist communism, did not witness and report the Red drive to victory in the 1946–1949 civil war.[26]

At a lunch interview with General Douglas MacArthur in Tokyo, the supreme commander for the Allied powers informed Snow he (MacArthur) was saving Japan from the Russians. "I'm trying to give them [the Japanese] a taste of freedom," the general declared, "because I believe when they've had it they won't like regimentation." In Korea, Snow watched with foreboding the emerging pattern of two politically polarized occupation zones, Soviet and American, confronting each other on the thirty-eighth parallel divide. While in Tokyo, Snow saw Jim Bertram, back as an adviser to the New Zealand delegation to the Far Eastern Commission, just months after leaving the same city as a liberated prisoner of war. The two had not seen each other since Ed's departure for home from Hong Kong in January 1941. Snow was now "a little heavier, with his dark wavy hair shot with grey," Bertram remembered.[27]

Ed was back in the States by the spring of 1946—a year that ushered in a key turning point in his personal life. In New York, at an after-theater party given by actors, artists, and writers for Russian war relief, he met Lois Wheeler. It seemed a classic "across a crowded room" attraction between the young actress and the older returned war correspondent and prominent *Red Star* author. Lois, a Californian from Stockton, had come to New York with a scholarship to the prestigious school of acting, the Neighborhood Playhouse, where she also studied dance under Martha Graham. At the time Ed came into her life, Lois recalls, she was playing a leading role in the Moss Hart comedy hit *Dear Ruth*. She and Ed were fully occupied with their different careers but saw each other frequently throughout the following months. When Ed returned to Europe early the next year on a *Post* assignment, Lois was in the Broadway production of Arthur Miller's *All My Sons,* the award-winning play that put Miller on the road to worldwide acclaim. At the end of her contract she joined Ed in Paris; they spent the summer driving through much of the war-torn Europe of 1947. Later, back in New York, she became a founding member of the Actors Studio and worked there with such distinguished directors as Lee Strasberg and Elia Kazan. She continued work in theater, films, and television into the 1950s, until McCarthyism slowly stifled her career.

Lois Wheeler's father had been the mayor of Stockton for a couple of terms and, according to Lois, "a strict Catholic, a Republican, and a bon vivant until he lost all of his money in the crash." He was "a stern and loving father of his four children, and especially about me, endangered by the villains I would meet in New York's theater world." Her mother was ill through much of this time, adding strains on the family. Lois, her brother, and two sisters were educated in Catholic schools, the girls in a convent. ("It's taking the rest of my life to get over that!" Lois recently wrote me.) She worked her way through the College of the Pacific (in Stockton), "jerking sodas and modeling in a local store." The college had an excellent drama department, which "turned me on for life."[28]

In Europe, Ed was plagued by a flare-up of his old kidney infection and spent weeks in the summer and fall of 1947 in two extended hospital stays in Berne, Switzerland. Doses of the newly developed antibiotic, streptomycin, probably saved him from loss of a kidney, but the infection would never be eradicated—"a stubborn and resourceful little beast," he wrote of the offending microbe to the *Post* foreign editor, Martin Sommers.[29]

Once more in Paris at the end of that year, Snow unhappily surveyed the shambles of his visionary hopes for the postwar world. (The kidney problem did nothing to lift his spirits.) His earlier concept of an America of "truer democracy" setting the pace for a collaborative new order to include the liberated colonial peoples and a more secure and thus more agreeable Soviet Union had gone the way of an escalating global cold war. Most of the world, and "you and I," he wrote his friends from Baguio days, the Crouters, are "caught between the U.S. and Soviet rivalry for power. I see no happy outcome to it." Whether America now took an interventionist or isolationist path, he foresaw "years of rearmament and war economy for everybody." Meditating pessimistically on these prospects, he grappled again with the relationship between political rights and economic justice, between his Western-rooted democratic-individualist ethos, and his sympathies for the social liberationist goals of an authoritarian revolutionary left.[30]

Americans can "talk and organize and act on the basis of rights which didn't exist for the common folk even as recently as two hundred years ago," he told the Crouters. And rights once taken away were never voluntarily restored. "So one has to inspect very carefully" the benefits offered in exchange for surrender of these rights to a minority, whatever its claims. But, Snow added, for more "backward countries" with no history or experience of such freedoms, "it's obviously a gain if they win a certain amount of economic democracy by means of exchanging one political dictatorship for another." However, Snow then struck a theme that ran through his prewar diary notes, "There is not now and never has been, any instance of the minority in power ruling in such a way as to help the g.n. [greatest number] at the expense of its own interests," nor to fail to "preserve its own monopoly of power, in terms which seek to convince the world that it is all being done for the good of the g.n." In effect, Snow recognized, there could hardly be true "economic democracy" without its basic political component. (In fact, of course, democracy had been a continuing, if unrealized and variously interpreted, rallying cry of the modern Chinese revolutionary movement since Sun Yat-sen.) Nevertheless, Snow persisted, had he been a Russian in 1917 or a Chinese now, for example, "I would probably be a communist" (i.e., a revolutionary), since in each case "the political experience of the nation was one of violence, despotism, and dictatorship." But for the real (American) Snow, the idea of a "minority dictatorship" of whatever stripe was "anachronistic and retrogressive." Americans, while holding fast to their political freedom, should make their "imperfect" economic democracy the "target of progress," he believed. (Imperfections in political democracy would soon concern Snow more closely, as America entered a decade of antisubversive loyalty probes, purges, and blacklists.) All in all, it seemed, the path to the betterment of humanity remained an extremely tortuous and rocky one.[31]

Earlier, after the Nazi surrender in May 1945, Snow was still looking toward the future in Europe with hope. "In contrast to practically everybody else," he wrote the Random House editor Saxe Cummins from Paris, "I am an optimist about the next twenty years in Europe. . . . We will get along with the Russians, despite all the wails you hear at home and over here, because there is really no very fundamental basis for serious conflict." Russia's "internal needs," he went on, would be "her prime interest and concern" for a long time to come. But by 1947, in the spirit of his remarks to the Crouters, Snow was dismally recording, "I am almost resigned to the inevitability of a Soviet-American war," a prospect for which he began to put at least as much blame on Moscow's intransigence, "blunders," and "methods of forced unanimity and dictatorship," as on American anti-Soviet moves.[32]

Nonetheless, Snow felt impelled to stand against the rising anti-Soviet tide in America, with its high risk of catastrophic superpower war, and its antirevolutionary connotations for Asia and elsewhere in the world. Before leaving Russia in late 1944, he had had a long confidential talk with Maxim Litvinov, former Soviet foreign minister and ambassador to Washington, and now a vice-commissar for foreign affairs, and a sophisticated diplomat with much more experience in dealing with the West than the hard-liners in control in the Kremlin. Snow asked the pessimistic Litvinov if there was any way to "open doors" and dispel "suspicion and distrust" between Russia and the West. "What can a writer do," he queried, "to try to make the thing work and to try to avoid things getting worse and leading to more war?" It was a credo Snow tried to follow despite all the disillusioning developments and intensifying political pressures of the postwar years. The power holders everywhere were beyond the reach of a writer and seemed disappointingly impervious to his prescriptions and aspirations for a peaceful and constructive world order.[33]

He wrote a series of articles for the *Post* in 1947 (incorporated into a book by Random House) to convey, in his characteristic intermediary pattern, understanding of how "Ivan" looked at the world and to advance the thesis (expressed in his 1945 letter to Saxe Cummins) that "Stalin Must Have Peace." (Snow had worked on the articles in the final weeks of 1946 at the well-known Yaddo retreat for writers, artists, and composers near Saratoga Springs, New York. His stay, as one of the working guests at this endowed center, had been arranged through Smedley, a frequent guest there.) In presenting his version of the Russian point of view, Snow included his own critique of postwar American policies (such as Washington's at least indirect support of Western European efforts at colonial reconquest in Asia, and American backing of Chiang in the unfolding China civil war) that ran counter to his concept of a world in revolutionary change. To underscore his theme on the Russians' desperate need for peace, Snow recounted the appalling experiences and horrendous human and material losses to which he had been witness during the Soviet struggle against Hitler. (In one of history's odd twists, the enormous casualties sustained to save the Soviet Union would not be fully recognized in the West until after the collapse of that state nearly half a century later.) Snow replayed his 1941 projections for the postwar world order, with America again in the vanguard. We "need an active policy to promote a co-operative world," he affirmed. The United States, now by far the world's mightiest military and economic power, should take the initiative, seek common ground with the Russians, work for mutually beneficial and attainable agreements (using Big Two summitry), offer major credits for the reconstruction of the U.S.S.R. (and other Allied nations), and promote bilateral cultural, educational, and scientific exchanges. International (collective) security arrangements should prevail over a new arms race. Needed social change "can be reconciled in a no-war world." His aim had been, Snow wrote in a 1949 letter, to suggest a program by which "we [America and Russia] could work together to stabilize peace in a progressive world." But Snow was clearly pressing against powerful currents at home and developments abroad that were moving in quite opposite directions. "To be a best seller [the book] should have been called SMHW [Stalin must have war] in these days," he sardonically told the Crouters.[34]

Snow's Stalin articles provoked a political firestorm back home. As the *Post* editor (and lifelong Republican), Ben Hibbs, later recounted, "I knew when we scheduled the Snow articles that we would be subjected to the most savage criticism, and we were. Despite our almost weekly denunciations of Communism and all its works, we were labeled a Communist publication." The "uproar went on for months." Even so, Hibbs stated, "given the same set of circumstances, I'd do the same thing again. We failed, but we did make our try." Snow's plea for a more conciliatory approach to the Soviets was in many ways a last-ditch attempt to revive his notion of a benignly activist America using its mighty power to "wage peace" in the world. His efforts were evidently no better received in Moscow. Snow's renewed tries that year for a Russian visa were turned down. ("Well, well, the old fight," Ed noted.)[35]

Snow had been equally unsuccessful that year in his one meeting with Truman. Ed had sought to restore with Truman the intermediary-confidante role he felt he had previously established with Roosevelt. "I would like to volunteer my services to the President while I am abroad for the next year, if I can be of any slightest help to him" he had written the White House in requesting the appointment with Truman. In their talk, Snow hoped to impress on the president that for the peoples in countries emerging from feudalism, the struggle was primarily one for human equality and not necessarily for political freedom as Americans

knew it. Snow argued that the Soviet system, though certainly a dictatorship, had brought "some benefits" to the Russian people. But for his
feisty Missouri compatriot, a dictatorship was a dictatorship. "It doesn't
make any difference to the man whose head is under your heel," Truman
pithily told Ed, "whether you think it's done for his own good." (Roosevelt had "picked the right time to die," Truman confided to Snow. "All
the headaches and difficulties I face now would have existed just the
same if Roosevelt had lived.")[36]

Moscow's rejection of any Soviet bloc role in the Marshall Plan, the
creation of the Cominform successor to the Comintern, the Communist
coup in Czechoslovakia in early 1948, and Stalin's excommunication of
Tito that year would be further blows to Snow's argument. He had left
Paris for India in December 1947 (and would be in New Delhi when
Gandhi was assassinated). His diary entries while in India and then
Burma reveal a growing, even extreme pessimism on the state of the
world. In a conversation with a leftist acquaintance in Rangoon, Snow
rejected her attempt to pin him down on where he stood in a "two-
camp" world. Snow testily replied that "Russia had divided the world
into two camps but unfortunately there were many camps." He "didn't
like camps in general," he added, always on guard against efforts to pigeonhole him politically. More broadly, Snow was now perceiving the
Soviet role in Europe as a "New Imperialism." "There was just a chance
we might have influenced Soviet policy at one time," he recorded, "but
it exists no more and only by war." In a "neo-isolationist" reversion to
some of his pre–Pearl Harbor views, he opined, "America's policy
should be one of 'Democracy in One Country,'" a play on Stalin's earlier
"Socialism in One Country" thesis.[37]

On the personal side, Snow's divorce proceedings took on greater urgency as his relationship with Lois developed but remained unresolved
and seemingly stalemated. (He had had a "fruitless" four-hour session
with Helen's lawyers in New York in December 1946, before he left for
Europe.) Well over another year would pass before the divorce was
finally granted on May 17, 1949, in New Haven; Lois and he were married on May 26. Still, despite its lengthy and acrimonious character, the
divorce suited both Helen and Ed at that juncture of their lives. For
Helen it was the opportunity to be free, as she saw it, of "baby-sitting"
Ed—"to be alone and write all my books," clearly her first priority. For
Ed, in his midforties, it was the chance for the warmly secure domestic
life he now found in marriage to Lois Wheeler and the birth of their two
children, Christopher and Sian. (To Helen's way of thinking, Ed "wanted

to marry someone who would think he was wonderful.") Lois was no less strong-minded and determined than Peg but was clearly of a vastly different temperament and style. Though his life was now much "tamer" than the tumultuous China years, Snow would write Bertram in 1952, "it is a life of fulfillment in a personal relationship between a man and a maid."[38]

Away from these personal matters, Snow took up the Tito-Stalin break in an important *Post* article at the end of 1948. He emphasized that the "Tito heresy" had undermined Soviet assertions of a two-camp world, with the Yugoslavs a portent of a "third camp" of rival "communist-socialist" states outside Moscow's orbit. Snow noted that he had discerned this possibility a decade earlier in China, where the Communists had their own army, territory, and administrative responsibilities. (He would pursue this premature Titoist-Maoist-style view of the new China in another *Post* article the following year.) Snow's Tito article was the most forceful exposition of his national-Communist thesis, his long-held aversion to Moscow's domination of the world Communist movement, and his disdain for the unquestioning subservience of the Communist parties in the West to the Kremlin. "What is beginning at Belgrade," he declared, "is not the dis-integration of socialism and communism as a world force, but the repudiation of Russian dictatorship over it." In the end, "repudiation" and "disintegration" would be much more closely and devastatingly linked than Snow envisioned.[39]

Though Snow condemned Stalinist tyranny at home and within the Eastern European satellite states, he stuck by his earlier thesis—now divested of his visions of global partnership in pursuit of international amity, security, and progress. "Now, even more than a year ago," Snow contended, "Stalin must have peace, must view the outcome of a major war as filled with the most profound uncertainties and seek to avoid or delay it." The Soviets, much too weak militarily and economically to challenge the West, were thus ready to settle for the empire they already had in Europe—which was proving troublesome and unreliable enough. "Unless we attempt to drive Russia from eastern Europe by force," he argued, "there will be no general war between us in the foreseeable future." But it was now a bleakly negative picture of that future. The Russians were "very good chess players" and would bide their time. "Just now the stronger pieces are not on its side of the board." They must play for a "peace by stalemate"—a "cold armistice" he termed it.[40]

In a letter written from New York nearly a year later, Snow still defended his 1947 proposals, rather dubiously contending that the United

States might have "weakened" the influence of the hard-liners in the Kremlin—a return to the theme of his 1944 talk with Litvinov. However, the dual triumph of "reaction in our own country," and of the equally reactionary "great-Russian" chauvinistic wing of the Politburo had closed that narrow window of opportunity. Snow held on to at least a residue of his long-held belief that the "better" America would yet prevail at home and abroad. "The defects in our society at home are reflected in the lack of a more enlightened leadership than we can offer to the world." But America's unparalleled power had thus far been used with much greater restraint than would have been the case with others—whether "Hitler, Mussolini, the Japanese militarists, Soviet Russia, Great Britain or France." Seen in this perspective, Americans should not "despair of doing something better for the world" than they "have accomplished to date."[41]

Snow's concept of a "cold armistice" (coexistence?) East-West standoff for a divided Europe, and his belief in a "socialist-communist," non-Stalinist "third camp" outside the Soviet orbit, became the dual linchpins of his world view as the cold war intensified in the 1950s. The latter part contained the crux of his thinking: leftist revolution remained the order of the day in the colonialist or semicolonialist (or third) world, and America need not fear or oppose it. Given their nationalist character and interests, such revolutions, particularly the Chinese, would not necessarily extend Soviet power but could in fact (particularly with wise American policy) act as barriers to such expansionism.

In April 1949, on the eve of Red victory in China, Snow spelled out these points in a *Post* article—to which its editors felt it necessary prominently to attach their disclaimer. "After a dozen years of firsthand study of China," Snow wrote, "I concluded that Soviet Russia would not hold effective domination over the extremely nation-conscious Chinese Communists." China was the first colonial or semicolonial country in which Communists had won power, he noted. And though China's Marxist leaders had always "in theory" been internationalists, "In practice they have been nationalists continuing an independent movement." (Snow here seemed to veer away from his earlier more complex view of the dialectical interaction of internationalist and nationalist elements in Chinese communism.) Mao, Snow declared, "is the only communist leader—Tito excluded—who has publicly criticized Moscow's agents." Snow listed all the factors of the CCP's essentially self-reliant, China-focused revolutionary experience and policies under Mao, and of Stalin's evident wartime and postwar preference for dealing with and supporting the

Kuomintang rather than the Communists. Now Moscow "must deal with a major foreign power run by communists possessing all the means of maintaining real equality and independence." Still, Snow warily added, it would be "illusory" to expect the Russians to repeat the mistakes that had cost them Yugoslavia. "They will proceed with extreme caution, hopefully waiting for the Americans to make the blunders on which their own success could be improvised." In the long run, however, the CCP "cannot and will not subordinate the national interest of China to the interests of the Kremlin." If American policy "is washed clean of interventionism, history may evolve along lines for which all the necessary preconditions now exist. China will become the first communist-run major power independent of Moscow's dictation."

Snow posited twin probable consequences of such an eventuality—both of which would indeed come to pass. Peking might become "a kind of Asiatic Moscow, an Eastern Rome preaching Asiatic Marxism out of Moscow's control." But it might also "set up a frontier against the expansion of Communism *as an extension of Russian nationalism in the East*—a barrier as effective as that erected at Belgrade in the West." The era of colonialism was over in Asia, Snow concluded, it was much too late to restore empire there. "Too late for Russia as well as any other power." (Using Russian and Chinese archival sources, a 1993 study of the Mao-Stalin relationship after the new Sino-Soviet alliance of February 1950 concludes, much as in Snow's 1949 analysis: "Mao did not intend to allow China to become Moscow's satellite. . . . From Mao's point of view, his alliance with the Soviet Union would only be a first step toward reestablishing China's rightful place in the world.")[42]

But, as Snow saw it, there would be "blunders" and "miscalculations" enough to go around—American, Russian, and Chinese. It would take decades more, and much calamitous conflict in Asia, before Snow's projections would work themselves out in Sino-American understanding, in which, appropriately enough, he would be a highly visible participant.

Meanwhile, Mao's China moved swiftly to join the Soviet camp, as an era of unrelieved hostility between the United States and the new China ensued. The outbreak of the Korean War in June 1950 (which Snow had not "the slightest doubt" was begun by Soviet-supported North Korea) locked in the antagonism. Washington intervened directly in the Taiwan Straits, collided with Chinese forces in Korea, and gave full military and political support to the Chiang regime on Taiwan as the legal government of all China. Snow's views on longer-term benefits to the United States of a revolutionary but nationalistic China were definitely out of favor. Instead the "loss" of China consumed American politics, with its consequent McCarthy-style attacks on the China hands, including Snow. And Ed's Titoist-type speculations were no more welcome in Peking (nor of course in Moscow), at a time when Mao was principally concerned to dispel such Stalinist suspicions of him. Snow was beginning to feel himself "persona non grata in all camps."[43]

In a gloomy 1951 assessment for the liberal *Nation* (to which he now began to contribute with some frequency), Snow presented an apocalyptic vision of "undeclared war" on a global scale. Spurred by its massive Korean War–triggered military buildup, America's anti-Communist objective would move from containment to "liberation"—of China, Eastern Europe, and Russia itself. He pictured a counterstrategy of Soviet-Chinese backed revolutionary civil wars everywhere challenging and embroiling America in ineffective and costly interventionism in defense of the status quo. He now saw the Chinese Communists as willing and loyal partners in a "Eurasian Communist axis." Whereas he once stressed the potentialities of a Red-ruled China as a barrier to Russian expansionism in Asia, he now tellingly described China's southern border with Indochina as "the periphery of the Soviet empire," with China the Asian player in the revolutionary strategy of the Communist bloc. Though the Chinese were not "slaves of Russia," Snow commented further in a 1953 *Nation* book review, "Titoist possibilities are at present negligible."[44]

In line with these somber estimates, and in a mood of pessimism edging toward futility, he had written *Post* editor Hibbs in December 1950 (at the height of Sino-American crisis in Korea), "I am sickened by the prospect of terrifying waste and negation into which blind power, rage and stupidity are leading all of us, and the tragic destiny that lies ahead for mankind, and I can't take any interest in promoting this Greek tragedy to the bitter end. All I want to do is holler 'Stop!'" he added.[45]

Snow's connection with the *Post* (his source of livelihood) as associate editor and regular contributor was also entering on troublesome times, as the above letter to Hibbs indicated. Though he continued to enjoy the warm personal regard and support of Hibbs and of the foreign editor, Martin Sommers, the widening gap between his outlook and the unequivocally anti-Communist stance of the *Post* was bound to raise difficulties on both sides—aggravated by the "Communist" label being hurled at Snow from the extreme right. (Ed's name and his now "notorious" *Red Star* came up frequently in the inquisitorial congressional hearings of the day, but he was never hauled before any of these committees.) The furor over his 1947 Stalin "peace" articles for the *Post* had already been a warning sign. A peculiar episode early in 1948 was a further one.

In India, Snow had written for the *Post* one of his most memorable pieces (referred to in chapter 5) on the legacy of the assassinated Gandhi. Rather oddly, the *Post* editors had inserted after Snow's remarks on Gandhi's acceptance of the role of the state "as a necessary instrument in achieving social democracy," the addendum, "though democracy as he understood it was certainly not to be confused with the kind of police state ruled by the Kremlin." Snow reacted angrily to Hibbs at such editorial tampering with his copy without his approval. He was particularly incensed at what he regarded as the gratuitous and jarring intrusion of such "worn and banal" cold war buzz words in an article designed as a paean to Gandhian nonviolence in a "message" to a war-bent planet. More specifically, Snow bridled at being associated with the cold warriors now dominating the media. In a less heated follow-up letter to Hibbs and Sommers from Rome, Snow somewhat tortuously explained his strong reaction to the "police state" insert. To present his readers with this phrase, "as a final verdict against a country I have tried to be sympathetic with and tried to explain in friendly terms in your columns in the past, makes me appear to be a rank hypocrite." There was always an unreal quality in Snow's perception of his "friendly" stance on the Soviet Union, perhaps most especially in those early postwar years. To the Kremlin, it was not standard "imperialist" anti-Soviet rhetoric (or the absence thereof) in Snow's writings that was of any great consequence. Ever since *Red Star* days, Moscow had regarded Snow as a dangerously subversive prime propagator of what would come to be called America's "China card" strategy. Snow himself told Sommers in March 1950 that, despite the repercussions in Russia and China, he was "very glad" he had written his Tito and China satellite articles: "they are among the best I have done."[46]

Hibbs quickly acquainted Snow with the realities on the American scene while Ed had been abroad. To put it "bluntly," Hibbs wrote him, "you have been under vicious and constant attack by a lot of misguided but determined people." He insisted that he and Sommers "have stood up and done battle for you," and continue to do so. Even in Snow's initial outraged reaction, in which he proffered his resignation from the *Post,* Ed added that it "does not at all affect my personal regard for you and Marty, and all that the association has meant to me." The matter simmered down. Hibbs considered a final letter from Ed "reasonable and understanding," making him "feel a lot happier." As for Snow's "resignation," Hibbs ended the discussion, "We want you to continue with us because you are a damned good correspondent. . . . We just aren't interested in any Snow resignations these days."[47]

The key issue for Snow, then and in future, was his sense of his responsibilities as a journalist—in this case, not to contribute further "ammunition" to what he saw as the forces of anti-Communist reaction and war sentiment in America. It was a moral issue that continued to plague him in his work for the *Post*—the more so since his responses to domestic and foreign developments were increasingly at odds. On the one hand, unfolding Soviet policies and actions only deepened his pessimistic views in that area; on the other, the emergence of Senator McCarthy by 1950 greatly heightened his apprehensions at a repressive American political witchhunt that both exploited and intensified Americans' fears of a Red threat at home and abroad.

The issue came to a head during 1950. Sommers had suggested to Ed that he do a profile for the *Post* on Soviet Foreign Minister Andrey Vyshinsky, who had been the notorious state prosecutor of the Moscow trials of the mid-1930s in which a great many of Stalin's erstwhile leading comrades in the party, and a number of his top generals, met their doom. As Snow wrote up his material, it was a scathing indictment of those show trials and the massive purges surrounding them, and of Vyshinsky's cynical role in consolidating Stalin's absolute dictatorship over party and state. Snow dealt as well with Vyshinsky's postwar role in establishing Russian control over the satellite states of Eastern Europe. Still, there was Snow's typically interesting and much more than one-dimensional portrait of the Russian official.[48]

But by the time Snow completed his original manuscript in March, just as the McCarthy phenomenon burst forth, he wrote Sommers that he had decided to withdraw the piece. "What kind of escapist am I, messing about in the Russian privy and ignoring conditions in my own?" As the matter went back and forth between Snow and Sommers, Ed wished at least to preface the article by parallels and warnings for an America embarking on its own (less lethal) political purges. Sommers would have none of this; he saw it as an unwarranted "apology," and there the matter rested for some months. By the late summer Snow, seemingly persuaded that McCarthy was on the run, already discredited by the Tydings Senate committee, wrote Sommers that his article (even without its preface) "may now have some educational value instead of being merely read as support for McCarthy's opportunism." (The fact that Snow was then being paid on a per article basis, with six pieces due each year, doubtless also played its part in the final outcome.) As a concluding twist, Sommers told Snow he had heard that "practically everybody around Lake Success [the United Nations headquarters] read the piece and that almost all the comment was highly favorable."[49]

Even before the Vyshinsky episode, Hibbs had told Snow he thought Ed "should not write any more political articles for the *Post*." Actually, while the Vyshinsky matter simmered, Snow was shunted off to do travel-style pieces for the *Post*'s cities series—colorful places such as Flagstaff, Arizona, and Acapulco. Ironically, these were just the opportunities the youthful Snow had aspired to when leaving New York in 1928. By 1951, Ed finally *really* resigned as an associate editor of the *Post* (accepted this time). "My conscience would not let me remain on the masthead," he wrote Bertram in October 1952, "sharing responsibility for publication of material—particularly about the Far East—which I felt to be malicious, dishonest, and misleading to the American people." Once again, however, he seemed torn between his "conscience" and his ever more cynically disillusioned reaction to the trend of the world. Now, Snow added, he was "not sure I was right in taking such a sanctimonious position."[50]

Snow continued to write occasionally for the *Post* up to 1956, including an article on Zhou Enlai—a straightforward, factual, and fair account of Zhou's revolutionary career, his political style and personal qualities. To Snow's irritation, the *Post* titled it, "Red China's Gentleman Hatchet Man." (Snow's own title had been "Mandarin in a Red Hat," he told Mildred. But to the "editorial overmind" now at the *Post*, "Evil has to be identified in every headline—even though it may be wholly irrelevant to the story following.") Through that decade Snow did shorter pieces and reviews for the *Nation*, some articles on his wartime Roosevelt conversations, a Harvard monograph on his unpublished notes on the Chinese Reds, and some lecturing. It was "a varied and somewhat desultory kind of work," he told his father in 1956. He tried his hand at short story fiction, with but limited (financial) success.[51]

Another project Snow undertook in the early 1950s concerned Agnes Smedley's final book, a biography of Zhu De (*The Great Road*), which she left in draft manuscript form at her death in 1950. Snow had become much closer to, and supportive of Smedley in the last years of her life.

(His wedding to Lois Wheeler had taken place in a Sneden's Landing house where Smedley was then staying as a guest.) She named Ed her literary executor, and he worked with others on her Zhu De manuscript, editing and preparing it for publication. It finally appeared in the mid-1950s, published by the independent socialist *Monthly Review* Press. Before her hospitalization and death in England, Smedley had been staying with Hilda Selwyn-Clarke, her friend from China days. Snow wrote appreciatively to Selwyn-Clarke in London that Smedley was "now in the Valhalla where she said she longed to be, and able to listen to the stories of warriors who died for the revolution." "Personally," he added, "I think she would get bored with that pretty quickly and would turn to setting things right up there where the old guard and its ruling saints have been in power entirely too long." In New York, Snow movingly eulogized Smedley at a memorial meeting he organized.[52]

For the most part, though, Snow's time was spent working intermittently on *Journey,* and "puttering" around their pleasant, rather stately-looking home near the Hudson in semirural Rockleigh, New Jersey, a short commuting distance from Manhattan. The Snows purchased the house in 1952, after renting a house for two years in Sneden's Landing, in Palisades, New York, a favored haven of the Manhattan cultural-intellectual set. Their Rockleigh home was just across the New Jersey state line from Sneden's Landing, and about a mile down the road. "We have [the] usual plagues of springtime and summer chores—vegetable garden, repairs, lawns to mow, etc.," he wrote Mildred in 1953. He remodeled their old barn into "a spacious, sunny, cypress-panelled studio . . . where I now have my office," he proudly informed his sister. (The studio, complete with bath, was later rented out for extra income.) "We are living as we like to live and we count ourselves very lucky," Ed wrote J. Edgar in October 1953. The children, Chris and Sian, were "healthy brown savages," he told his father, and he was "very glad" they had the chance to live where "the air is clean and the open meadow and nearby woods enchant them all day long with their wonder and mysteries." While none of his writing projects brought in much money, the Snow family of four managed to live comfortably enough, though always on the financial edge with continuous cash flow problems. ("Dear Collaborator in Impoverishment," Ed began a financial account to Lois in 1959.) Court-mandated monthly alimony payments to Helen of $187.50, which Ed vigorously objected to in principle (and principal) very often went unpaid. Lois carried most of the financial burden and was an active and accomplished homemaker as well. In the early 1950s she had a good role in the long-running Broadway hit, *The Fifth Season,* and then did TV work in soap operas and "thrillers." She played "a thoroughly detestable nurse" in "The Guiding Light," Ed wrote a friend in 1954. But acting opportunities eventually mostly dried up as she faced blacklisting herself. It was a "tame" existence, he told Bertram in 1952, "compared with our years of wrath, righteous battle and certainty in China and my exaggerated notions of personal usefulness during the war and immediately after."[53]

During this domesticated and bucolic time in Rockleigh, New Jersey, the Red-hunting Hoover FBI (which accumulated a voluminous file on Ed) evidently kept him under security surveillance out of its Newark office. (During those same years Ed became quite friendly with the New Jersey governor, Robert Meyner [a Democrat], the two men occasionally playing tennis together on weekends.) On the pretext of questioning Ed about a journalist acquaintance, bureau agents arranged an interview with Snow at his home in 1953. "Mr. Snow stated substantially," they reported, "that he has never been a Communist, is not a Communist, and will never be a Communist." Snow, they concluded, "was cordial, cooperative, and apparently frank throughout the entire interview."[54]

Essentially sidelined in his journalistic career and livelihood, and estranged from and somewhat disappointed in his erstwhile Chinese friends, Snow had much time to dwell and philosophize on the state of the world and the meaning of it all. Apropos of his continuing work on *Journey,* he wrote Natalie Crouter in July 1954, he was now "equipped with fewer illusions and delusions." He acknowledged that the book would not have the "youth, enthusiasm, and dynamism" of his earlier work. "Then I had just discovered that Evil exists in the world, and then I believed that people were capable of destroying it, fairly swiftly. Now I know that the quick remedies often perpetuate or worsen Evil or only give it a new form. . . . Then I expected too much of man. Perhaps now I expect too little of him." It was "logical and necessary to realize that good actions of today become mingled with the bad or Evil of tomorrow." This was in many ways the leitmotiv of Snow's conflicting outlook: an optimistic belief in revolutionary change and radical reform, and grave misgivings as to the inherent perfectibility of man and society.

In another 1954 letter to his journalist friend Darryl Berrigan, he cited remarks from Pearl Buck's autobiography he was then reading that had much relevance to Maoist socialist salvation crusades. " 'It is dangerous to try to save people—very dangerous indeed! I have never heard of a human being who was strong enough for it. Heaven is an inspiring goal, but what if on the way the soul is lost in hell?' This from the daughter of a missionary, is what I, the son of a Missouri printer, also learned from my brief years of evangelism in China." Nevertheless, Snow's "evangelism" would soon be getting a new jump start.[55]

Yoko Matsuoka, a Swarthmore College graduate from Japan before the war who had become a very close friend of Snow's in Tokyo after the Japanese surrender, evidently discerned Ed's mood of detached pessimism, on a visit to his home in the early 1950s. Matsuoka, a journalist-author after the war, had worked with the foreign correspondents in Tokyo where she met Snow in 1946. She became a politically active leftist and feminist; another of those strong-minded women Snow always gravitated toward, she also became his literary agent in Japan. When she visited Ed she vigorously reproached him for his recent writings for the *Post*. As she narrated this encounter in a postscript to her Japanese translation of *Journey*, Ed "seemed extremely depressed [and] in agony," despite his happy new marriage and the birth of his first child. She felt (from her radical perspective, of course) that "some part of my belief in this man had collapsed." She trenchantly described the scene as she "blurted out" her feelings to Ed: "I was sitting in the living room of his house near New York. Snow, cradling a glass of whiskey in his hand, was silent for some time. I still recall the look of anguish in his face."[56]

Snow finally completed, and Random House published, *Journey* in 1958, but despite "on the whole, excellent reviews," Ed wrote Bertram in April 1959, the book had to date sold fewer than 12,000 copies. Continuing McCarthyist influences, and China lobby and other "reactionary" attacks on the book had hurt, he added. "There is no open-mindedness here," he rather contradictorily complained, "about anyone who has a good word to say for our China friends, however true or historically well-founded it may be." He was perhaps even more disappointed to find that, at least for the moment, there appeared to be no more "open-mindedness" for the book on the Chinese side. He had sent copies to his old friends in Peking—Alley, Epstein, Madame Sun, but the silence from there was deafening. "I've had no reaction from you, IE [Epstein] or Suzie [Madame Sun] to my book," Ed wrote Alley in January 1959. "Too bad people can't get together on the broad areas in which they agree rather than quarrel mole-like in the narrow corners where their recent experience differs."[57]

Apparently Snow's attacks on Soviet imperialism in Eastern Europe and his renewed emphasis on Titoist potentialities in Sino-Soviet relations were not as yet politically correct views in China. Nor did his somewhat indiscreet, and now politically embarrassing, recollections of his 1930s conversations with Madame Sun help. (She never trusted any Chinese politician except Dr. Sun, Snow had written of their talks. She then added, according to Snow, "I distrust Mao Tse-tung less than the others.") Snow's avoidance of any detailed discussion of the new China (of which he thus far had no personal experience), and the inclusion of his romantic interludes in various parts of the globe, probably irritated his politically oriented China friends as well. (Snow, in fact, ended his account in the early postwar years, omitting also his new marriage and life thereafter.) Alley did cryptically write Ed that he had "looked through" the book and "wished that you had been able to spend a little more time in this environment," to which Snow rejoined, "it wasn't my fault that I didn't go back years ago when I asked."[58]

Still, *Journey* would be an important milestone both in reviving his China visibility at home and in preparing the ground for his return to China. He had been "deluged—well, kept busy, at least," he wrote Bertram, "with invitations to speak on radio, TV, before college and civic groups, reflecting among thoughtful people a real hunger for knowledge about a land that by now is as remote from most of us as Cathay of olden times." And in making the case again that the Sino-Soviet relationship did not preclude but instead presented opportunities for a more positive American China policy, Snow was actually setting the stage for his invitation to Peking in 1960. Perhaps not unlike *Red Star* Snow was putting forth a thesis the Mao leadership was itself not yet ready to enunciate or endorse. China "was not ours to have and hold in the 1940s any more than it is Russia's today," he wrote. He then devoted four full pages to a recycling of the key portion of his 1949 *Post* "China Satellite" article. Now, he asserted, "few students would deny the validity" of that analysis. (There were, of course, no further references in *Journey* to Snow's own Korean War–era description of China as part of the Soviet empire.) "China manifestly has become not only Russia's political peer but is in her own right, and for the first time in modern history, one of the four major powers of the earth." However, Snow argued, America's continued activist pro-Chiang interventionist policies against China had overlaid the latent "contradictions" between China and Russia and "constantly improved [America's] position as 'Foreign Enemy No. 1' of the new republic." A necessary and realistic change in such policies, Snow insisted, would instead bring to the fore, in his 1949 words, the "Contradictions between the aspirations of the Chinese Communists and Russian nationalist expansion." It was a point (devoid of its Titoist connotations) the Chinese Red leaders themselves would shortly be transmitting through Snow.[59]

On the larger world canvas, Snow pursued the Taoist theme of the intertwined dichotomy of good and evil he had earlier raised with Natalie Crouter. He saw both Soviet domination of Eastern Europe and American interventionism in Asia in this light—characterizing both as examples of what he called "the new 'imperialisms.'" The Soviets thus played "dual roles as liberator and jailer, as revolutionary and exploiter, as generous comrade and Ivan the Terrible, the vengeful father-punisher." He again went back to his prognostications of 1949 on the Titoist heresy as "the dawn of a new heterodoxy in the world Communist movement"—a process "delayed by savage Stalinist repressions in Eastern Europe, but still going on today."[60]

In Asia, America "verbalized for national freedom everywhere but followed practices which were now pro-independence and now pro-overlord, now liberator and now ally of dictators," Snow wrote. In few cases did the United States openly assist in, or show "notable comprehension" of, the postwar anticolonial revolutions that swept through Asia. Citing here America's role in support of France's failed attempt to reconquer Indochina, Snow concluded his chapter: "In the end it was the French who left, the natives who stayed, and the Americans who paid—and are not through paying yet."[61]

In the face of unwinnable thermonuclear war, Snow saw the cold war moving into a less dangerous stage of "competitive co-existence," which he defined as a global competition between the social systems of East and West. He harked back to the notion of his 1948 aphorism on "Democracy in one country" for America. "No foreign policy is greater than the success of the domestic system which inspires it," he concluded, "and during America's pursuit of cold war aims abroad grave questions have piled up in alarming proportions at home"—education, racism, alienated youth, public health, and more. "For all of us today it is a time for every nation to cast out the beam in its own eyes before seeking out the mote in a neighbor's eye," he ended, eschewing foreign interventionism, American or otherwise. Snow was turning his reforming zeal inward, in a reverse image of his earlier thinking on an America that could raise itself to a "higher democracy" in the process of fulfilling a liberating mission abroad.[62]

In the final year of what had been for him the professionally and politically bleak 1950s decade, Snow was back in the Far East (though not China) as the social science teacher for the 1959–1960 round-the-world

schoolyear junket of the International School of America. Still financially "broke," Snow had accepted the offer expecting that it would also
give him the opportunity to renew contacts in Asia and do some articles
along the way, and possibly a book on his return. In part to cut living expenses, Lois and the children relocated to a friend's house in Switzerland
they rented for that year and sublet their home in New Jersey. With
more and more of Snow's writing assignments now coming from European newspapers and magazines, this would become a permanent Snow
"exile" from America, though with frequent trips to and continued work
connections in the States. The Snows later purchased and renovated an
old farmhouse in the scenic village of Eysins near Geneva. It would be
the site of Snow's final illness and death.[63]

There was a poignancy on this eve of a new decade, just before the
spin of the wheel of world politics reconnected him with China. In
Hong Kong, while on his International School trip, he stayed with
Peggy and Till Durdin but otherwise felt alone, adrift, and without
friends there. He brooded on his next birthday, "(good God!) 55," and
wondered whether he would ever get to China again. "Tonight I felt
suddenly tired, desolate, old, remote, without a person to whom I could
communicate," he jotted in his diary. "Could I work again in this
world?"[64]

CHAPTER 15

Return to China

Snow made his first attempt to revisit China shortly after the Communist victory in 1949. He sent his request to Beijing (addressed to Mao) through his peppery old colleague of Indusco days, Chen Hansheng. The latter, then living in New York, was to return to China in 1950 to live and work under the new regime. As Snow later told it to Alley, he had sent word by "safe hand of Hs [Hansheng]," but "I never heard a beep out of old curmudgeon Hs for years after he returned—to this day [1959] in fact." This silence was hardly surprising in view of Snow's unwelcome writings at a time of the firmly anti-imperialist Sino-Soviet alliance, and of the intense anti-American upsurge in China that accompanied the outbreak of the Korean War in 1950.[1]

In 1955 Snow tried again with another letter to Mao. It was seemingly a more auspicious moment. The Geneva conference on Indochina that year, with Premier Zhou Enlai attending and Secretary of State Dulles as an observer, had worked out an interim settlement of the conflict there—despite Dulles's notorious refusal of a proffered Zhou handshake. Then came ambassadorial-level talks between the American and Chinese sides in Geneva (and later in Warsaw). Snow was then advancing his thesis that the specter of the H-bomb was inevitably mutating the cold war into "competitive co-existence." Though the Geneva talks were going slowly, "talk is better by far than killing and the more things are settled by the former the less likelihood there is of the latter," he wrote Alley in September of that year. "Judging rumors hereabouts," he added, "it may soon be possible for American correspondents to visit China again."[2]

In the letter to Mao a couple of weeks earlier, Snow "wondered why I never received from you any reply to my letter several years ago," though he had been "assured at the time" that the chairman had received it. He now thought, he told Mao, that he could do some "useful reporting based on personal investigation and inquiry undertaken with the freedom accorded me when I wrote Red Star Over China." (Snow was obviously reminding Mao of the benefits of that book to the Chinese Reds, while holding out the prospect of a new *Red Star*.) Should Mao "care" to accredit him to gather material for articles and a book, Ed continued, "I have hope that the State Department might soon waive its ban and validate a passport for me for the purpose." But it would take another five years, and some involuted special arrangements by both Beijing and Washington, to make his trip possible.[3]

Snow did receive an invitation (of sorts) from China in 1957. Early in that year, in what would be an odd episode, he was invited by the vice-chairs of the Chinese Writers Union and of the Chinese People's Association for Cultural Relations with Foreign Countries to come with his family for a stay of indefinite duration. The letter was sent along to Snow by Alley, who cryptically noted, "Enclosed please find an invitation to come here with your family when you are able." Snow replied that the timing was inconvenient. "Right now all I can say is that as soon as I have completed work here [principally on *Journey*] . . . I shall proceed to the Far East as soon as possible." He would "be happy" to see them in Beijing, he added, and would write again in a few weeks, as soon as he worked out arrangements in America to cover expenses.[4]

Snow heard nothing further in response to his letter or to one he sent a couple of months later. We can only speculate that the invitation had been a spin-off from the dramatically liberalized climate of the early months of 1957, particularly in cultural-intellectual circles, under the Mao-initiated policy of "letting a hundred flowers blossom and a hundred schools of thought contend." It would come to an abrupt end with the repressive anti-Rightist crackdown that followed. Yet during that year the Chinese also began to take a more overtly independent, and critical, stance toward Moscow—perhaps the more operative factor in the gesture to Snow.

In December 1957, in reply to various queries from Snow, Alley seemed to encourage Ed by suggesting vaguely that he contact one of Beijing's embassies abroad "and everything will be done to make the trip a comfortable and easy one." The next month (almost a year after receipt of the original letter) Snow wrote his two thus far unresponsive Chinese "hosts" that he was "now anxious to accept your invitation" and proposed a mid-March arrival for a three-month stay.[5]

Snow then wrote Alley, outlining a plan for his trip which, "I wish you to take up, if possible, with Suzie [Madame Sun] or someone on a level where it can be dealt with positively." Central to his proposal was "a long frank interview with chu-hsi [Chairman Mao] himself," which could "possibly prove as important in breaking new land in international relations as the one I did 22 years ago." But Alley now obviously fended Snow off. "Sorry I'm such a weak reed in the matter of helping you out," he finally told Ed in June. "Everyone is so busy, and I see very few anyway." At long last, Ed was beginning to get the message. The "winds seemed to have veered again," he told Alley in January 1959, "as I've had no response from you or others I've queried" on his hopes for a "look see" at China. This was "too bad," since there was now "a wide audience ready to listen" to a Snow report. (He was being "deluged with invites to talk about Chungkuo [China]," he impressed on Rewi.)[6]

Journey may have played some part in delaying Snow's return to China (as he tended to think), though in the longer term it probably helped to bring him there. The time was simply not quite ripe for a visit, with the upheavals of the Great Leap in 1958, and Sino-American brinkmanship in the Taiwan Straits that year. And in truth, Snow faced equally serious barriers in America. "As far as China goes," he informed Alley in mid-1958, "the passport obstacle remains and in turn creates a financial stalemate also." Nonetheless, Snow's points on the benefits his trip might bring China were evidently getting through in Beijing. Alley would shortly be the designated front man for China in a genuine invitation to Snow.[7]

For the while, Snow continued to see himself as out of favor on both sides of the Pacific. "Well, so much the worse for them," he confidentially groused to Bertram in the spring of 1959, "on balance I suppose it would not be far wrong to say that (quite apart from where my long-range sympathies clearly lie) my feelings through this whole wasted decade has been a plague on both their houses." He added, though, that his major disappointment by far was with "my own countrymen's inability to rise above the terms of the conflict offered by the other side." Beyond this, he also told Bertram, it was "amazing that I should still find China so much in mind even after purging myself" through *Journey*.[8]

Strangely enough, news that Snow was now "persona grata" in China would come to Ed through Bertram. It would mark another turning point for him from the "wasted decade" of the 1950s, revive his role as a significant player in the international arena, reactivate his "long-range sympathies" for revolutionary new China, and give him his always coveted opportunity to help his compatriots "rise above" the rigid Sino-American hostility and conflict of the previous decade.

As Snow's International School assignment began to wind down in Europe in the spring of 1960, and while still in the doldrums on his future China prospects, he received unexpected news from New Zealand. Alley was on a trip there and had asked Bertram to pass along to Ed his (Alley's) "personal" invitation to Snow to come to China as soon as possible as his "private guest" for a three-month stay. Snow cabled back his reply: "Please tell Rewi I am anxious to accept."[9]

Snow could come as a "writer," Bertram told him in further exchanges of letters, and it would of course be up to Ed to secure state department clearance. It was evident that, even using the "private" Alley-Bertram channels, his request received approval, as Snow later wrote, "only after reaching the highest level of authority." As he further noted, the Yugoslav and other Eastern European Communists in Beijing "were keenly interested in my admission to China in 1960. They attached significance to it as a straw in the wind of increasingly unfavorable weather in Sino-Soviet relations." Only the state department seemed unaware of such nuances and "did everything to compel me to go to China illegally, if at all." Still, after much back and forth with the Washington bureaucrats, Snow's passport was grudgingly validated for China. In an arrangement worked out between Bennett Cerf of Random House and Gardner Cowles, publisher of *Look,* Snow was accredited as a correspondent for that magazine, reluctantly accepted by the state department after determined persistence and pressure by Cowles. Since *Look* "was one of the organizations authorized to send a correspondent to Communist China," Assistant Secretary of State Andrew Berding wrote Cowles Publications in June 1960, "the Department has no alternative other than to eliminate from his passport the restriction relating to Communist China." (The department was "completely unhappy with the thought that we must validate Snow's passport for travel to Communist China," an internal memo to Berding had stated.) The Random House–*Look* connection also provided Ed with the necessary financial support for his trip. Thus, Snow summed it all up, "Officially, I entered China as a-writer-not-a-correspondent, while in Washington I entered as a-correspondent-not-a-writer."[10]

Once again Snow found himself on the world stage in his habitual role as a journalist-writer with special responsibilities—this time, in an

attempt to alter the frozen hostility between the United States and Red
China, for what he saw as no less than the peace of the world. "To break
our isolation from China was now a task in many ways as challenging as
my assignment in 1936, and far more important," he wrote of his 1960
trip. "I could not refuse a chance to do a great story of some possible
usefulness to history not to mention the survival of our two nations." In
this same spirit, "I felt I had a responsibility to both China and America
and a certain function to perform perhaps vital at the moment," he subsequently wrote Mao Zedong of the visit. "I believe," Ed also told Mao,
"peaceful but competitive co-existence can eventually prevail in relations
between the [two] countries."

Heightening Snow's sense of mission, his old Chinese friends ex-
horted him to bring "the truth" about China to the American people, as
he had done for the revolution in *Red Star*. "I can imagine that every one
you have met [in China] does expect much of you," Madame Sun wrote
him as he was departing China. She urged him to have "the courage to
stand for the truth," despite all the pressures he faced in the West. "Let it
be said that Ed Snow helped people find the path." There was also some
"cautionary-encouragement" from his old friend Anna Louise Strong.
The rather awesome veteran leftist journalist was now working from her
China base as an active writer-promoter of the Chinese position to the
outside world. "We all hope," she wrote Ed soon after his departure
from China, "that your past knowledge of China, plus your recent contacts—in which you were given more access to top people than any
other foreigner has had since Liberation, will result in the kind of book
that illumines a land and an epoch. You have shown the capacity to do
that kind of book but even those who have the capacity do not do it
often." Snow was equally intent on asserting his independent status. "I
came here entirely at my own expense, as a writer," he wrote Bennett
Cerf shortly after arriving in Beijing, "and shall remain as such. I am not
a guest of the government," he insisted, drawing a very fine line, "but
naturally entered by courtesy of the government."[11]

It would indeed be a delicate balancing act for Snow in his role of
"honest broker." "More than anyone I think you appreciate the problems
which faced me in writing this book [on his 1960 trip]," he later wrote
Strong. His book had been directed at "middle class Americans with little background these many years, often using euphemistic terminology to
bypass conditioned reactions, and seeking objectivity invulnerable to academic attack." And there was subtle pressure from Random House as
well. "I am sure that you are trying to give an honest and objective ap-

praisal in your book," his editor, Donald Klopfer, wrote Ed, "and whereas I know it will be favorable to the regime because of its accomplishments, I hope you will be able to point out some of their failures too. God knows, I am not trying to influence what you write, but this book will be read by an American public, conditioned to look upon the Red Chinese as the enemy; consequently, it shouldn't be all white."[12]

Such "objective appraisal" brought a daunting challenge. The politically charged "American imperialist" and "Red China" images were menacing ones and during the 1960s would only become more so. Snow's own ambivalences also complicated his journalistic task. He was drawn to Nikita Khrushchev's peaceful coexistence overtures to the West, while his sympathies were with the more militant stance of a China seen as directly in the line of fire of American interventionism in Asia. As in the past he empathized with the Maoist-style social revolutionary-liberationist path for the "have-not" peasant masses of the third world. Though he was gratified to see confirmed his 1948–1949 projections of an independent Communist-ruled China slipping out of the Russian orbit, he was now more inclined to view this opportunity for a Sino-American accommodation as part of a larger and necessary move toward a post–cold war global East-West détente. And while he considered his primary mission to be that of prodding American opinion and policy in these directions, his thinking on his country's political attitude was far from optimistic. The United States, he believed, was now dominated by its massive "military-industrial complex" and driven by anti-Communist, antirevolutionary zeal. Given the pervasive vested interests sustained by the war economy, America's leaders were not yet capable of dramatic initiatives for peace.

"I do know," he wrote toward the close of *The Other Side of the River: Red China Today* (hereafter *Red China Today*), "that some Chinese leaders have long been prepared to respond to a 'let us begin anew' approach by the United States. Too proud to say so directly, they were obviously hopeful that my visit might help rebuild a bridge or two: that is what they told me in various ways—always with the knowing added note that my imperialist government was not interested in bridge-building." On his return from China, Snow had just a few minutes' conversation with Dean Rusk, the secretary of state in the incoming Kennedy administration. After this cursory meeting with the busy secretary-designate, or "brief colloquy," Snow caustically commented in his book, "I was left with the impression that the Chinese had been right." Nonetheless, he foresaw an inevitable break in the Sino-American logjam. "That it will change," he added, "that it is gradually changing on both sides, is becoming evident."[13]

Snow's "journey of rediscovery" in 1960 was hardly comparable to his 1936 sojourn with the Red revolutionaries in Bao'an—nor for that matter, was this tired and "graying," middle-aged man of fifty-five (as he described himself to Anna Louise Strong) the adventurous young journalist of that earlier time. The 1936 talks in Mao's Bao'an headquarters epitomized the struggle of revolutionary guerrillas against the forces of Chinese state power and Japanese aggression. In the traditional imperial setting of Beijing Snow would now be meeting with Mao (and Zhou) as rulers of an all-embracing, all-powerful "people's democratic dictatorship." His five-month itinerary, from arrival (by Aeroflot from Moscow) in Beijing in late June, took him to Inner Mongolia and Manchuria, Xi'an and Yan'an in the northwest, Shanghai and up the Yangtze to the western interior heartland of Sichuan, and finally to Yunnan in the southwest, from where he left in late November for reunion with his family in Switzerland. His itinerary had been approved by Premier Zhou; there were official tour guides throughout, and interview briefings with local functionaries (cadres) everywhere. There was a private trip and conversation with the premier on his special train. Snow was also welcomed as a "friend" by "dozens" of people he had met in the Red district in 1936. Then "in their youth, ragged, hungry, so-called bandits, now the equivalents of account executives, managers, chairmen of boards, big shots." (Later, in the Cultural Revolution, Snow would label such people in Maoist terms as "Red Mandarins.") The vantage point of a regime in power—one that he viewed sympathetically—would inevitably color Snow's report. It was a perspective considerably reinforced by all his personal long-term friends in China: principally Alley, Hatem (Dr. Ma), Strong, and Epstein among the Westerners; Huang Hua and other officials who had been student friends of his in the old Peking days, Madame Sun, and that leading "big shot" among his former "Red bandit" acquaintances, the "Very High Official" at the top.[14]

Still, here was a unique opportunity for this very special American to see and investigate the new Red China, then no more accessible to his compatriots than the remote northwestern Red base had been in 1936. Notwithstanding the obvious limitations surrounding his formal and informal contacts with a broad spectrum of Chinese in all walks of life, "I think I know more about all these people," Snow maintained, "than I could possibly have understood had I never returned to China."[15]

Snow's "background" conversations with Mao, and his more formal interviews with Zhou were unquestionably the focal points of his stay, and its chief raison d'être. Snow received the summons to his first Mao reunion in over twenty years on a late October afternoon. He found the chairman waiting to greet him at the gate to his home in the Zhongnan-hai residential compound for China's leaders directly adjacent to the palaces of the Forbidden City. (Snow compared Mao's house to that of a successful Long Island insurance salesman.) As earlier noted, Mao seemed unaware of the elementary details of Snow's post-China life, evidently including his divorce and remarriage. Mao made clear that Snow's visit, arranged (by himself and Zhou) as Alley's "guest," did not affect the continued stalemate between Washington and Beijing on the exchange of correspondents. As they thus talked before dinner, Mao suddenly thought that Alley, as Snow's "host," and George Hatem, as Snow's 1936 companion and friend, should be present. In an expression of imperial prerogatives, he immediately had them summoned.[16]

As Snow described the scene in his notes, Alley appeared in about twenty minutes. Hatem, who had been on a bus returning home after a long day's work, was whisked off by car on arrival home. He came into the room looking "rather startled, but very pleased." Perhaps equally revealing, Mao appeared quite vague about these two highly notable and resident "foreign friends" of the revolution. He had not seen either for many years, thought that Alley was Australian and that Hatem (of Maronite Christian background) was Mohammedan. More surprisingly, the Red leader asked Hatem, probably the leading medical figure in the highly effective campaign against venereal disease in Red China, what he had been doing. When informed by Hatem that the disease had been "completely" erased from China (except for cases in Tibet), the chairman was surprised—he had not known that, he observed.

During and after dinner (a simple Hunan-style meal), Mao gave his characteristically unruffled, unhurried forecasts on the Taiwan question, on China's seat in the United Nations (still occupied by Taiwan), and on United States–China relations. A satisfactory (to China) resolution of these matters might take a decade or two, or even longer, but would eventually come to pass. In a typically "Middle Kingdom" view, Mao noted that China in no way felt isolated—it was after all a "United Nations" in itself of myriad nationalities and a huge population. A single Chinese province was in many cases much more populous than most member states of the United Nations.

Mao struck a number of other themes that would show up in Snow's book. He claimed great success for the Great Leap Forward of 1958–1959, particularly in steel production. Yet he cautioned Snow on the latter's too euphoric impressions of China's advances. China remained a poor and "backward" country and would continue to be for a very long time to come. But to Mao's way of thinking, such poverty had its positive aspects. Austerity "steeled" people's (revolutionary) character—"people should know some hardship, some deprivation, some struggle," he declared. It was a premonition of Mao's subsequent cultural revolutionary attack on materialist values and priorities. To Snow's point on the middle-class character of American society, Mao rejoined in standard ideological terms that it was not the middle class but "the monopoly-capital class" that decided things in America.

To accomplish its monumental and long-term task of modernization, Mao impressed on his American friend, China needed peace and would not "run wild" in the international arena, whether in or out of the United Nations. The United States, he added, had an equal responsibility to maintain world peace. "Taiwan," he emphasized, "is China's domestic affair. We will insist on this."

Interestingly, to Snow's query whether Leighton Stuart, the last U.S. ambassador to Nanking, had offered American recognition and aid to the victorious Reds in 1949, if they renounced their ties to Moscow "in the Yugoslav manner," Mao noncommittally "affirmed that it might be so." When Snow asked for Mao's "personal reaction" to Khrushchev's denunciation of Stalin's personality cult, the chairman curtly put him off, referring Snow to CCP pronouncements evaluating Stalin. (Snow would question Mao more specifically in later visits on the sensitive subject of the Chinese leader's own personality cult.) According to Snow's notes, Mao avoided any direct comment on the Soviet Union or on Sino-Soviet relations.

Snow asked the chairman (at a second briefer meeting) about the Hundred Flowers policy of 1957 and the subsequent anti-Rightist response by the regime. Mao replied that "all kinds of people came out in the press with attacks and criticisms of the party," many of them seeking to "overthrow" the government. They had been given "plenty of time" to "expose themselves," he continued. It had revealed the "minority" of "bad people" among the intellectuals, afterwards given "Rightist hats." Mao further emphasized that good people at one stage could become bad at another. Such political labeling, coming down from Mao's perch on high, cast a broad and arbitrarily defined net as it filtered down to the "struggle" levels of local party cadres fulfilling their quotas in exposing "bad" people. In 1970 Mao would rather incongruously complain to Snow about the violence that had accompanied the Cultural Revolution he had himself unleashed.

In a frank peroration on China's Communist ruling elite, Mao told Snow there had been fifty thousand Communists during the revolutionary movement of the 1920s, and only ten thousand after the counterrevolutionary killings of 1927. "Today there are about 800 survivors of all those years. By and large the country is still being run and for some time will depend upon these 800." When saying his final farewell to the Chinese leader, Snow mentioned his interest in doing a full biography of Mao and asked for his cooperation. Mao told Snow to settle for his *Red Star* biography. "Better not write my story any more," he prophetically remarked. "Developments in the future will be a hard thing to write about."

On a lighter bantering note that illustrated the many levels making up the Mao-Snow relationship, Mao handed Ed a toothpick at the end of their dinner. Snow said he thought he would keep it as a memento— "Mao Tse-tung gave me this toothpick." "Have two more," Mao laughed, handing them to Ed for his children.

The full exposition of China's negotiating stance on Sino-American issues was left to Zhou Enlai. Snow's first interview with him took place on the premier's train as they traveled on an August day to the newly completed Miyun dam north of Beijing; a second came a few days before Snow's dinner date with Mao. Taiwan continued to be the key impediment to improving United States–China relations, Zhou emphasized, in a standard statement of the Chinese position. Washington would have to cease "aggression" against China by ending its military intervention in Taiwan and the Taiwan Straits, and also abandon all efforts and policies aimed at creating "two Chinas" in whatever guise. This was an "international question" to be settled between Washington and Beijing. It was separate and distinct from the "internal" Taiwan problem to be dealt with between the sovereign China government in Beijing and the Kuomintang authorities on that island province. These were matters on which agreement should first be reached "in principle," the Chinese premier told Snow; concrete implementation would be a subject for further discussion. There was "no conflict of basic interests between the people of China and the United States," Zhou declared, "and friendship will eventually prevail." Over a decade later, in the Shanghai communiqué marking the close of Nixon's 1972 breakthrough journey to China, the two countries would essentially concur on the basic principles outlined to Snow in 1960. Full diplomatic relations would take longer, and issues relating to Washington's "unofficial" links to Taiwan (as well as other matters) continue to ruffle and at times seriously disturb Sino-

American relations. But what Warren Cohen calls the "Great Aberration" in America's China policy would finally end.[17]

Zhou acknowledged the existence of Sino-Soviet "differences," though insisting they were natural enough between nations. The two Communist powers remained firmly united and committed to each other's defense. On Snow's query regarding Khrushchev's abrupt withdrawal of Soviet experts from China that year, the premier blandly and disingenuously explained that this was merely normal rotation as tours of duty ended. Zhou was putting an understandable diplomatic spin on the rapidly rising but still publicly downplayed tensions between Moscow and Beijing and was perhaps also not yet relinquishing a "Russia card" in any negotiations with Washington. On China's disastrous post–Great Leap Forward economic crisis, Zhou conceded difficulties arising from shortfalls in agricultural output caused, he told Snow, by unprecedented natural calamities. He was otherwise silent on the severe food crisis, let alone on famine conditions, in the country.[18]

In reconnecting with the Chinese revolution and its leaders, and in taking on what he perceived to be a mission of understanding, reconciliation and peace of global dimensions, Snow brushed aside his dyspeptic 1950s "plague on both their houses" attitude. The mission rekindled his fundamental belief in the necessity for, and liberating character of, that revolution in both national and human terms. He had come to the "new China" with a mind-set based in good part on the old China he had known, with its stark images of human misery and degradation, of bad government, and of a weak and divided nation victimized by imperialism in general and Japanese aggression in particular. In contrast, there was now an assertively independent and unified nation, with an effective government proclaiming the interests of the "have-not" majority and embarked on an ambitious, long-term program of economic and social modernization. For Snow, this was the major story he needed to tell—and one his China friends were pressing him to tell. "Going back to China was obviously not the same thing for me that it would be for any other reporter, or even for other former China correspondents," he wrote in the "testamentary" document he sent on to Anna Louise Strong at his return from the China trip. "My position was unique." No Chinese, he further stated, "would for a moment suppose me to be a Communist nor expect me to write as a Communist. Yet they do know," he continued, "that I never joined those who slandered the new regime nor cashed in with exbelievers and professional cold-war propagandists, to help deceive or bewilder the American people about the Chinese revolution and its leaders." It was in this spirit and within these parameters that Snow wrote his massive account of his return to China.[19]

Red China Today, a volume of over eight hundred pages, published in 1962, had the old Snow imprints and more: a colorful personal travelogue style, vividly and warmly depicted personalities from leaders to people in all walks of life, much material on wide-ranging aspects of Chinese life and society, solid discussions of political and economic matters, a positive focus on the regime's social and economic accomplishments and some attention to its more recent setbacks and problems. ("The material was so massive, and the subject so vast," Snow wrote Donald Klopfer of his completed manuscript, that to "make any of it comprehensible to the average reader, far more exposition and background seemed necessary than I had anticipated.") On foreign policy issues, he gave full play to his interviews with Zhou and included a long chapter on Vietnam. A concluding peroration touched all of Snow's visionary themes (his "devotions," he called them)—turning swords into plowshares, with America urged to shift from "war against peasants" to initiative in "a world war against poverty, disease, and ignorance," and for a truly internationalist world in which the "have-not" nations and peoples could find their places in the sun. With Vietnam particularly in mind, he declared that the "eyes of Washington are on the wrong places and on struggles already lost."[20]

For its time, Snow's book was a valuable compendium of information and firsthand impressions by a non-Communist journalist with unique China credentials. It was also a sympathetic, but not uncritical, examination of how China and its people had fared under a decade of Red rule and of how its leaders looked at the world outside. Snow, with his transcendent sense of "responsibility" to help "build a few bridges" (including some of his own), was intent on "balancing" the mostly hostile, and often paranoid and racially tainted, picture of faceless Asian "ants" or hordes (a virulent mix of "Yellow" and "Red" Perils) that Americans had been given. (It was "fear of the unwelcome information I might be obliged to present," Snow subsequently wrote Grenville Clark, "which makes me what is called a 'controversial' writer, at least in the U.S.A.") Though Snow "leaned to one side" (in Mao's famous 1949 phrase), his report was still a valiant, if flawed, attempt to break through the rigid, stereotyped walls of antagonism between the two sides. If his book "raises more paradoxes than it answers, that may be an achievement," he told Klopfer. "It is, at any rate, China." Ironically, Snow's status as an invited (and supervised) "guest" of the regime (though paying his own way) was considerably more constricting for him as an investigative journalist than the relative freedom he had enjoyed through imperialist-imposed extraterritorial privileges under a hostile (to him) government in the old China. "The fragmented China of the 1930's could be penetrated far more easily than the mobilized totalitarian China of 1960," John K. Fairbank observed of Snow's visit.[21]

Snow's first book on China in two decades garnered (aside from predictable attacks from the right) generally mixed reviews: highly respectful of his China credentials and connections, and admiring of his reportorial talents, but critical of many of his judgments. He was best on the people, not the politics of China. In the nature of things it was not going to be another *Red Star*. Robert C. North, a Stanford specialist on Chinese communism, summed up the kinder side of this consensus: "Edgar Snow has written a powerful and engrossing book. With more discrimination and restraint and self-disciplined analyses he might have written a great one." Unfortunately for Snow, the review for the prestigious *New York Times Book Review* was considerably less admiring or charitable. It was written by Michael Lindsay, a British academic who had been an ardent champion of the wartime Red guerrillas and as a radio technician had worked for some time among them but who became an inveterate foe of the Beijing regime. "It is disappointing," Lindsay remarked, "that Mr. Snow, with his background and contacts, has added very little to accounts given by other foreign observers." And Snow's "intellectual development," Lindsay wrote (with his own political odyssey clearly in mind), "seems to have stopped in the 1930s when it was plausible to identify the conflict of political left and right with the conflict of good and evil." His review provoked an indignant (and probably ill-advised) Snow letter to the editor that gave Lindsay an opportunity, in a rejoinder to reinforce his original criticisms.[22]

Still seething over the Lindsay review, and frustrated that a months-long New York newspaper strike in the winter of 1962–1963 had put a severe crimp in Random House promotion of the book, Snow was greatly cheered by an accolade from an unexpected source. "Congratulations on your magnificent 'The Other Side of the River' which, for the first time showed the other side of Red China to me," the popular American television impresario Ed Sullivan wrote him, "and thank you for a brilliantly rendered service to the world."[23]

A major stumbling block for most reviewers was the perception that Snow had depicted the dictatorial Communist system in overly benign populist terms as a "poor man's government." This issue, as we have seen, had long preoccupied Snow's own thinking, in the interplay of his "radical" and "bourgeois" sides. He had argued in 1947 that for people in "backward" or "feudalistic" societies, it was an important "gain" if they won "a certain amount of economic democracy by exchanging one political dictatorship for another." It was a point he had tried to "explain" to Truman that same year. And Snow had simultaneously argued that "there is not now and never has been, any instance of the minority in power ruling in such a way as to help the g.n. [greatest number] at the expense of its own interests." In coming back to the Chinese revolution in 1960, Snow put his emphasis on the first half of this proposition and downplayed (but did not abandon) his caveats. The People's Republic, he argued, was an exceptional case where the interests of the "have-not" majority had been genuinely advanced and protected. "China," he wrote in a preface to the Japanese edition of *Journey*, "presents the example of a nation in which the poor collect from the rich under the auspices of the Communist Party." And pursuing his "exchange of dictatorships" thesis in *Red China Today*, he averred that in contrast to the Kuomintang's "military dictatorship" controlled by "a small have-got minority," the "Communist dictatorship has organized its bases among the have-not peasants and working people and deeply *involved* them in the revolutionary economic, social, political and administrative tasks of building a socialist society."[24]

The China scholar Benjamin Schwartz, in commenting on the above points in his review of the book (which Snow privately called "very good, but critical, or critically very good") cogently questioned Snow's "poor man's government" concept. "The fact that the ruling elite [the "800" Mao had cited to Snow] owns the power to command and to make decisions (including all the decisions involving the production and allocation of goods)—the most primordial form of ownership which has ever existed—is apparently of no consequence." Such total control of power might be necessary to the modernizing process of underdeveloped nations at a certain stage, but even in that case, Schwartz mordantly noted, there was "no need for presenting purgatory as paradise."[25]

Underlying and complicating these fundamental issues was the inauspicious timing of Snow's account. In 1936 he had met the revolution just as it was poised for its dynamic and historic wartime surge leading to ultimate victory. He now caught up with that revolution as it was beginning to falter and had already entered what would be a protracted period of political crisis, conflict, and purges, of massive upheavals, and of dramatic shifts in leadership and direction in a process still playing itself out. The years from the Hundred Flowers through the calamitous after-math of the Great Leap, combined with the growing conflict with Moscow, set the stage for a decade and more that would convulse the country and nearly shatter its ruling party structure. Needless to say, Snow could neither foresee such portentous developments nor easily discern the underlying political faults beneath the surface tremors. He thus minimized the importance of Peng Dehuai's dismissal as minister of defense, stressed the CCP's unity and stability under Mao, with the chairman "thus far" free of any "megalomania," or of Stalinist "para-noia" toward his colleagues. Snow cited, as an example of this, the in-fluential role of Liu Shaoqi, the new chairman of the republic and Mao's anointed successor as party leader. Liu, of course, would shortly be the chief target and victim of Mao's Cultural Revolution.[26]

Snow's vision was further obscured by his basic assumptions on the "dictatorship of the have-not majority." He was no longer, as in the China of the 1930s, writing as an opponent of an existing regime who had linked himself with the cultural-intellectual and student currents of dissent and protest. He now tended to picture the critics unleashed by the Hundred Flowers as at worst counterrevolutionaries, and at best lib-eral Western-educated intellectuals who hankered after a pluralistic po-litical system. The latter, Snow maintained, "had no remedy to offer ex-cept a return to the bourgeois ideology of the Kuomintang, which had already proved incapable of solving China's problems." And as for stu-dent protesters in the universities in Beijing, Snow remarked that some "demanded the right to choose their own teachers and curricula; they wanted free food for all, and no more work in the countryside." These remarks were sharply challenged in a *New Republic* review of Snow's book by René Goldman, a young China scholar of French-Polish back-ground who studied at Beijing University during these events. As one who "shared in the exultation of my Chinese fellow students," he wrote, and who "witnessed the eagerness with which they tackled national is-sues, demanding such things as respect for human rights, more learning from the West and the administration of schools by teachers who were not merely party secretaries, I find Mr. Snow's patronizing objection-able." And as for the subsequent suppression of the intellectual-acade-mic critics of the party, George Hatem, near the end of his life, privately told close friends in Beijing (among other things) that Mao's "anti-Rightist campaign took the heart out of China's intellectuals."[27]

Snow's remarks on the incapacity shown by "bourgeois ideology" to solve China's problems spoke to a key issue that continues to bedevil

Sino-American relations. As Andrew Nathan notes in his insightful study of the theory and practice of "democracy" in China over the past century, culminating in the Communist version of "people's democratic dictatorship," there are key elements of modern Chinese political culture as well as of Communist ideology involved. In contrast to Western democratic principles, such thinking views politics "as a realm of harmony rather than antagonism between the citizen and the state, of one-party leadership, of the supremacy of the public interest over citizens' rights, and of the power of the state to make any laws it deems necessary without judicial contradiction." The argument made by China's democracy advocates that "a competitive party system and an independent press are necessary to allow people to control the rulers," Nathan adds, has been a rare one for China. Thus far, Nathan concludes, China's "century-long obsession with political order and national strength had made it impossible for most other Chinese, even non-Marxists, to share [the democracy activists'] visions of change."[28]

Snow had been on both sides of the China argument. In the time of the Kuomintang, he had urged America to "push" the Generalissimo toward liberal democratic reform. Now, in dealing with his writing plans in the context of the "better" People's China he had seen, he recorded: "If anyone is looking for material to prove that the American system is the best system for China (including Taiwan!) and ought to be imposed on the Chinese people then I have nothing to say which would be helpful to the cause." It was hardly that simple, neither for Snow over the next decade of his involvement with China, nor for the Chinese and American leaders and peoples since then.[29]

In recent years, particularly with the ending of euphoria (a second "loss of China"?) that had followed the Nixon opening to Beijing, Snow came in for some especially sharp criticism for his reporting on China in the 1960s. Notably singled out for attack has been his denial in *Red China Today* of any widespread famine during the calamitous post–Great Leap years of 1959–1961. A leading Chinese dissident, the astrophysicist Fang Lizhi, later in political exile in the United States, pointed to Snow's account of the food crisis as a "telling example," in Fang's hostile view, of the American journalist as "propagandist" for the Mao regime. The American China scholar Jonathan Mirsky is also strongly critical of Snow's writings on Mao-ruled China—on the famine and much else.[30]

"I must assert," Snow wrote of the post-Leap grain crisis in *Red China Today*, "that I saw no starving people in China, nothing that looked like old-time famine," and that "I do not believe there is famine in China at this writing; and that the best Western intelligence on China is well aware of this." Snow went on, "Isolated instances of starvation due to neglect or failure of the rationing system were possible. Considerable malnutrition undoubtedly existed. Mass starvation? No."[31]

Snow's assertions were more significant for their ambiguities than as absolutes of truth or falsehood. Though Snow indeed dismissed the starvation reports coming from refugee sources in Hong Kong and widely circulated in the West, there is no evidence that during the 1960 visit he saw (or was shown) any such conditions. And given the highly exaggerated, later revised Chinese reports on grain output beginning in 1958—reflecting the frenzied, unreal, super-leftist "politics in command" syndrome affecting party cadres at all levels—perhaps even the top leadership had not yet fully recognized the true magnitude of the food crisis at local levels at the time of Snow's stay in China. Undoubtedly, great numbers of people starved to death in the most hard-hit provinces and localities, and very many millions more succumbed to the effects of sustained and severe malnutrition during what officials later called the "three bad years" of 1959 to 1961. However, there was evidently no single vast region of devastation and death such as Snow had witnessed in the northwest in 1929. As John Fairbank stated in his 1986 history of the Chinese revolution, "In 1959–60 China was better organized [than in earlier famines] and famine areas full of corpses were not seen. But the malnutrition due to thin rations made millions more susceptible to disease. The higher-than-usual mortality became obvious when the statistics were worked out." And in his careful 1984 investigation of the famine and the factors that caused it, Thomas Bernstein notes, "The extent to which famine struck China during those years, it is important to stress, has not been fully established." While "no one doubts" the serious food crisis of that time, Bernstein adds, "famine on the scale of those that struck China during the Qing and Republican periods could have taken place has long been doubted, if only because the PRC has an effective government able to organize the distribution and transportation of relief grain." It was with demographic patterns and other data available only in the early 1980s that the full impact of the calamity has to some extent emerged. Dwight Perkins, a Harvard expert on the Chinese economy, could write of the post-Leap grain crisis almost a decade after Snow's trip, that rationing and railroad construction "averted a major disaster."[32]

The intent here is not to delve into the complex web of natural and political factors that led to the disastrous consequences of those years, but to assess the claim of Snow's culpability in propagating a famine version that he either knew or should have known ("what did he know and when did he know it") was palpably false. As already noted, the magnitude and severity of the crisis of 1959–1961 remained uncertain until long after that time. It is noteworthy that the major reviews of Snow's book by China specialists (including the hostile one by Michael Lindsay) either ignored or took no particular issue with Snow's treatment of the matter. Indeed, Benjamin Schwartz in his careful 1963 review wrote, "As against Mr. Alsop's predictions of mass starvation, Mr. Snow's insistence that efficient rationing has distributed whatever malnutrition there may be seems somewhat more justified at least as of the present." The truth was evidently then more elusive than some contemporary critics assert. Like others, Snow had an a priori belief in the will and capacity of the Communist government to take effective organizational measures to avert large-scale starvation, in contrast to the massive human cost of similar crises in the past. "I read your clipping from the [Kansas City] Star about 'famine' in China," Ed wrote Mildred a few months after his return from China. "There isn't any famine there in the sense that I knew it in the past, but the Chinese are having a very tough winter" owing to crop failures brought on by natural catastrophes. "Had such a year struck China in the old days tens of millions of people would now be dying of starvation."[33]

Still, Snow was not that confident of his facts as he worked on *Look* articles and his book in the early months of 1961. In the face of a continuing barrage of famine stories, he sought to get at the truth from his foreign friends and official contacts in China. It was no doubt naive on his part to think that even if these sources were privy to state-guarded information and statistics on the national food situation, they would share data, particularly adverse data, with a Western journalist, friendly or not. Answers to most of his queries never came or consisted, as Alley's did, of blandly reassuring and generalized replies, devoid of hard facts and figures. A year later, with his book scheduled for publication in the fall, he continued to seek help from China. "I am doing my best to present the facts about the problems of China's agriculture as well as its achievements," he wrote Israel Epstein in May 1962, "but the absence of any concrete information makes it difficult to answer" the Alsops and others on the famine-starvation reports. Among other China matters on which he asked for "explanations," were the refugee exodus to Hong Kong and reports of high-level policy rifts in the CCP. "Do try to get me a few FACTS," he pleaded.[34]

Withal, Snow was not quite playing the "true believer" role. As was often the case, privately he was troubled, uncertain, and irritated at what he considered to be much stonewalling by the Chinese, not only since his departure from China but while he was there as well. In a December 1961 letter to Han Suyin, a writer friend and Red China champion, Snow expressed some of these feelings. He found it difficult to "grapple" with the wildly fluctuating agricultural and industrial output reports emanating from China since 1958—on which he complained, "I was in no way helped to understand by anyone in China." He was "terribly ignorant" when he went to China, he tellingly, if exaggeratedly, informed her. "I assumed I knew something about it. I knew nothing. I still know very little." He had spent most of the past year on research he should have done "before entering the country." Snow frankly acknowledged the barriers he had faced on his China visit. "I made the mistake of supposing that I would find a few people who would speak to me frankly and honestly about matters of the recent past as well as the present." But, he continued, he was "unable to establish any such contacts with reality." Though he acquired a "mass of material," it was "meaningless" without the "necessary background and the kind of facts no one would give me. I have done the best I can to fill in the vast void."[35]

Oh, "for the life of a novelist," he groaned to Han Suyin. *Look* (which had printed a first article of his based largely on the Zhou interviews) had paid for but rejected others as "biased," he told her. If they "had published what I wrote," he peevishly added, "much of it would have been considered 'hostile' in Peking." It is "a difficult time to emerge with a China book," he wrote Alley as his work neared publication in the fall of 1962, "but then I don't know when it hasn't been difficult to write about it for America since the revolution."[36]

A journal entry Snow made while in China in October 1960 is perhaps the most revealing exposition of the conflicts and dilemmas for him as a committed but politically independent journalist-friend of the revolution writing for a broad "bourgeois" American audience. ("Why don't you nail your flag to the mast, as I do?" Han Suyin goaded him after reading his *Look* article.)[37] Snow noted:

Mao said it is impossible to remain neutral and he is right—about China. Leaning to one side. I too have been leaning to one side. But not leaning *on* anybody. . . . To take sides but not to lean on somebody else is more difficult if one lives in an advanced capitalist society than if one lives elsewhere. Think of all the mistakes and tragedies committed by St. [Stalin] or in St's name. Who would wish to have committed himself blindly to *that* dictatorship? . . . No greater error than to suppose that one's subjective actions are not part of objective reality. If one knowingly acts in accordance with what one knows to be false one is affecting the objective situation adversely not favorably. One does not always know but when one does the first obligation is to truth.[38]

Snow's confidence in Mao, as opposed to Stalin, would be put to increasingly severe tests in the years ahead. But already, the erratic course and flawed character of the revolution in power made the "truth" he sought to discern and report dauntingly complex, ambiguous, and ultimately elusive—as his *Red China Today* amply illustrated.

By the time his book appeared (in 1962), Snow was much less sanguine about his attempts to open up genuine dialogue and ease the Sino-American deadlock. While still "leaning to one side," he was inclined to blame the Chinese as well as the Americans. Though he thought the American people were "interested and fairly openminded," he told Alley, "so far this has no impact on policy." The "USA has been on the wrong track for years," he added, "but China's policy has done little to help the American people as distinct from ye old American imperialist government find a bridge to reestablish contact. If one really believes there is a difference between the two it should find realistic expression in policy." It was a typical Snow frustration—both sides were getting in the way of his efforts to promote "a new beginning."[39]

Actually, Snow's massive book (at $10) did quite well, with American sales of over 21,000 copies. Snow was busy in the States in the early months of 1963 with lecture dates and appearances on radio talk shows and the prestigious network TV morning shows. His twelve minutes on the *Today* program, Random House sales people told him, was worth $50,000 in commercial advertising time. There were debating tussles on some shows with Michael Lindsay and others. On his American tours in 1962 and 1963, he wrote Mao in May 1963, he had spoken to audiences "in more than 50 universities and colleges, discussion forums, businessmen's clubs, teachers conventions and other organizations in more than 30 states." With the favorable reception he had been getting in these appearances, and the wide interest generated by his book as cases in point, Snow sought to impress on the chairman the value of "bourgeois" freedoms in the United States. "I doubt that it is realistic to say that freedom of speech and the press is meaningless in a country where information of this nature can be dispensed to the whole people, by those who possess it."[40]

With his visibility again on the rise in America, and with his unique China connections, Snow was then being approached to intercede with the Chinese for various prominent Americans seeking to visit the People's Republic. In particular, Grenville Clark, an eminent international lawyer and a "tireless crusader" for world peace through world law, contacted Ed on behalf of Dr. Paul Dudley White, the noted cardiologist and Eisenhower physician, and later on for himself too. Though Snow's attempts then to persuade Mao of the value to China of such contacts proved unavailing, they led to a growing friendship between Snow and Clark up to the latter's death in 1967 at age eighty-five. Snow gave warm encouragement (with important reservations in defense of the right of revolution) to Clark's goals of global federation and world disarmament.[41]

In an approach of a very different character, Snow was hit from an unanticipated, though not surprising, source. Ex-wife Helen brought a legal action against him in New York for back alimony, effectively tying up his Random House book royalties. Fortunately for him, his European earnings were unaffected. Ed's attitude toward Helen had mellowed considerably in the years since the divorce battle, helped by her forbearance on the missed alimony payments. "I suppose I should be grateful that I don't hear from her; she has been uncomplaining recently about the defaults on alimony," he wrote Bertram in 1959. Snow had contacted Peg earlier that year, acknowledging her "patience," and giving a brief "report" on his money situation. "In short, my financial status is zero," he told her. But with his evidently brightened expectations following return from China, Ed sent Peg $500 early in 1961, with apparently implied prospects of more to come. She responded with a detailed recital of her own dire financial straits and her failure thus far to place her writing commercially. "If you can send me money this year," Helen told him, "perhaps I can do a book that will sell at last." Ed was soon forced to backtrack. "I owe you an explanation because I gave you some hope that I could renew some payments to you," he wrote her in 1961. "I was too optimistic. Things have not gone as well as I had hoped." It all hinged on the book he was working on. "If it pays anything I should be able to then." Snow was inadvertently setting himself up for trouble ahead.[42]

Though Ed sent Helen a few hundred dollars more in the spring of 1962, he at the same time reiterated, "I wish you were correct in your belief that I am now in the dough but such is not the case." His only income the past year had come from some lecture engagements that netted him comparatively little after expenses and his agent's fee of 50 percent of the gross. "What a pity it is that you could not find a man to please you among all the millions here," he wistfully and transparently added. Helen acknowledged the money with a cryptic, "I was very glad to get it," and then went on in friendly enough fashion to non-personal topics of mutual interest. But with the seeming success of *Red China Today* by the spring of 1963, Helen took action.[43]

Snow morosely told Bertram in June that although his book was in a fifth printing in America, "I have made nothing at all there because your friend Peg has attached and claims all my earnings of those years and the case will presently go to court and provide ironic amusement for many and fees for the lawyers." Though the subsequent legal suits and countersuits were finally settled on terms that ended all further obligations by Ed to Helen, it sadly rekindled and intensified Snow's earlier bitterness toward Peg. (He brooded in his diary on plots for "justified homicide.") "Legally, I am paid off for quits," he unsparingly told Bertram, "but my God what a life sentence she made herself for me, not to say herself." Helen, of course, immersed in her unremunerative writing work, saw all this quite differently.[44]

Snow was back in China from October 1964 to January 1965—a clear sign that his book had been favorably viewed in Beijing. ("Your case is different [from other Americans seeking entry]," Gong Peng, a foreign ministry official and friend from Yanjing student days told him during the visit. She added, "Everyone knows you are a friend of China.") Naturally enough, he found the economy, and particularly the food supply, in much better shape than 1960. As then, his visit was highlighted by dinner and conversation with Mao, and formal interviews with Premier Zhou. (A year earlier, in January 1964, Snow had traveled to Guinea, Africa for an interview with Zhou, then visiting that continent. The text appeared in full or extract in the European press, and extract in the *New York Times*.) Snow sought interviews while in China with other top officials of the Beijing regime (including Liu Shaoqi), he told Allan Whiting of the state department, who spoke with Snow in Switzerland after Ed's return. But Premier Zhou "told me I had no need 'to bother' these 'busy men' since he could answer any questions I had, and if he couldn't, Mao could."[45]

Snow's talk with the chairman (which he was permitted to publish in unquoted form) was, as in previous Mao-Snow encounters, a fascinating example of the Chinese leader's enigmatic but purposeful style and idiosyncratic way of thinking. Snow told Whiting that the chairman "had delivered himself somewhat pontifically, more so than in 1960, reminding me of Churchill's manner in the latter part of World War II (whom I interviewed at that time)." They met on January 9, 1965, this time in a reception room of the Great Hall of the People that faced Tiananmen Square. Their conversation, in Mao's words, ranged from "south of the mountains to north of the seas."[46]

Mao's remarks, it turned out, contained a number of significant signals for the chairman's American and Soviet antagonists abroad, and his backsliding party protagonists at home. He affirmed that the Vietnam revolutionary forces could win victory on their own. He insisted that China would not go beyond its borders and would fight only if directly attacked. He did not consider such action by the United States to be likely. And China, he added, was busy enough with its internal affairs. Mao saw the Americans and Chinese eventually coming together again—"that day would surely come." He specifically cited, and accepted, official American pronouncements that the war in Vietnam would not be carried into North Vietnam. Frankly, the Red leader wryly remarked, it was "a good thing" that America had its troops in Vietnam. It gave the people there an external imperialist enemy as well as an internal target to unite against—the Maoist concept of nationalist revolutionary struggle. For the Chinese revolution to succeed, he added, "a single Chiang Kai-shek had not been enough. There had to be a Japan to overrun the country for eight and a half years." (The Chinese leaders, Snow later told Whiting, "feel certain we [United States] will lose eventually and that we will make our own situation worse in the meantime without much effort on their part.")[47]

While there would later be heavy American air strikes against North Vietnam, and Chinese economic and military assistance to Hanoi, Mao seemed to be laying out the basis of an implied understanding with the United States on the ground rules for the impending escalated conflict in Vietnam. He signaled his determination to stay clear of direct involvement; he believed that he could safely concentrate on his own domestic revolutionary agenda. He was confident that the Vietnamese revolutionaries could cope, and that in due time America would find it expedient to leave. The chairman evinced "hope" for future improvement in United States–China relations but seemed more pessimistic on prospects with Moscow despite Khrushchev's recent fall from power. The "chief difference" on that score, he whimsically commented, was that the Chinese had been deprived of "a good target for polemical articles." (On this cue, the CCP would continue to attack Soviet policies as "Khrushchevism without Khrushchev.")

Snow rather delicately raised the "personality cult" issue: the Russians had criticized Mao for it, was there "a basis for that?" Mao agreed there was "some" and, in typically allusive fashion, noted that though Stalin had been "the center" of such a cult, Khrushchev had probably fallen because he had none at all. Mao was clearly viewing the deposed Russian leader as a "negative example" in this respect also and would soon be putting even the Stalin cult in the shade. When Snow met with Mao again in December 1970, at the height of the Great Helmsman's deification, the chairman referred a bit defensively (and mildly critically) to Snow's published references to the Mao cult. "It is you Americans who go in much for the personality cult!" he told Snow, citing the name of America's capital city as an example. Though it was all "a nuisance," there was "always the need to be worshipped." Mao toyed rather fancifully with the notion of "worship": "If no one reads your [Snow's] articles and books after they come out, would you be pleased?" It was the bizarrely exaggerated mode of discourse Mao often indulged in.[48]

Paradoxically, while Snow was disturbed by the extremes of the Mao cult, he had been a significant accessory in the propagation of the Mao image from *Red Star* to his posthumous and truncated 1972 book on the Cultural Revolution. Snow summed up his assessment of Mao most strikingly in the course of their 1965 meeting. To Mao's fatalistic recital of his many close encounters with death during the revolutionary struggle, Snow responded:

Accidents of fate which spared you have made possible perhaps the most remarkable career in Chinese history. In all China's long annals I cannot recall any man who rose from rural obscurity not only to lead a successful social revolution but to write its history, to conceive the strategy of its military victory, to formulate an ideological doctrine which changed the traditional thought of China, and then to live out the practice of his philosophy in a new kind of civilization with broad implications for the whole world.[49]

Mao, the record showed, did not demur from Snow's estimate.

In further intimations of things to come, Mao told Snow that China's current youth generation had no experience of the old society, nor of revolution. Reading or hearing about it was not the same as living it. Soon his Red Guards would be stirring up a "revolutionary storm" that would become much more than enough even for the old revolutionary warrior, who would finally return them forcibly to their (Maoist) books. The seventy-one-year-old leader told Snow that he (Mao) was soon "going to see God" (another Maoism). The future was uncertain, with rapid change the order of the day. "A thousand years from now all of us," he concluded, "even Marx, Engels, and Lenin, would probably appear rather ridiculous." It was another illustration of Mao's style. Evidently he was thinking of a much shorter time-span and, with his own mortality in mind, had no intention of suffering a "ridiculous" fate. He would be charting a course aimed at keeping his revolution alive and on track.

When Snow asked if Mao had a "special message" that the American journalist might take back to President Johnson, Mao had none. It would take another six turbulent years before the Chinese leader had such a special message for Snow to transmit to another American president.

Though Snow's write-up of his Mao interview and other pieces on the trip appeared widely in Europe and Japan, he found difficulty placing them in America on terms he deemed satisfactory. For a "pittance," he finally "gave" the Mao story to the *Washington Post,* which then published it in "distorted" form, Ed grumbled to Mildred and Howard. A relatively intact version of his Mao conversation appeared only in the *New Republic.* He had concluded, he further complained to his sister, that it was "hopeless to try to deal with the U.S. press on China." (Even so, he had received "the best advance ever paid to me," from Macmillan, for a [never completed] book on the trip.) Adding to the strains, he had had health problems before, during, and after the China journey. In what would become the pattern for him, there had been surgery a few months before leaving, an attack of flu in China, and exhaustion from the pressures of work on his return. In March 1965 he was back in the hospital to clear up an infection.[50]

Compounding all this, Snow's mid-1960s China journey was soon overshadowed by the rush of events. Under the leadership of Lyndon Johnson, America plunged into its seemingly endless anti-Communist crusade in Vietnam, while Mao would soon launch his "anti-revisionist" assault on his own party, government, and intellectual establishment. Snow's reaction to the first was one of outrage and foreboding; to the second, uncertainty and some early misreading of the signals from Beijing, but continued trust in Mao-inspired socialist aims. "It is good to see the Chusi [chairman] back in form," he wrote Alley in November 1966, as Mao's Cultural Revolution escalated. A few weeks later he informed Alley of a lecture tour he was embarking on in the States "where some people fancy that I know China. I detest lecturing because I know only something about not knowing, that's all; and audiences are never pleased to be told that truth." And truly, Snow in the beginning seemed to misconstrue the Chinese upheaval. In a July 1966 letter he had seen China as gearing up for expected war with America. In splitting with the

USSR, the "go-it-alone school prevailed and the country is now committed to war." In this somber mood, he declared that "China is already at war with the U.S. in Vietnam." In time China will become "the main base" of the war as it spreads throughout Southeast Asia "and eventually NE Asia," with the Chinese fighting in the manner of the earlier Red guerrillas against Japan. "Perhaps I am too pessimistic," he closed. "I hope events prove me so." Snow amplified on these points in a *New Republic* piece at the time, in which he judged the Cultural Revolution to be the final crackdown on those who had argued against Mao's policy of confronting the rising American threat by a self-reliant, protracted people's war strategy. He dismissed the "revisionist" charges leveled at such "veteran Communists long indoctrinated by Mao's teachings, and with a lifetime of practice in the politics of the Chinese revolution," as mere "euphemisms." The escalating American involvement in Vietnam triggered a neo-isolationist mood in Ed that harked back nostalgically to his heartland youth. "I think I liked it better when we were not trying to run everybody," he told Howard in June 1965. "I remember the twenties now as a good time when we were satisfied to be ourselves without so much preaching with bombs and so on. How did we get to play god so quickly?"[51]

As the China scene became more chaotic and unpredictable, Snow delayed work on his new book commitments. He did shorter pieces for his European press outlets and the *New Republic* and spent much time (and money) putting together his China film documentary, *One Fourth of Humanity*. There were regular lecture engagements in the States, and a Japan lecture tour in 1968. ("In the U.S. my agent asks a minimum of $1000 for a lecture and usually gets it or not much less," he informed his German friend Anna Martens, in 1969.) The Japan journey was particularly successful. He flew there in April 1968 from Honolulu, after a strenuous American visit. His lectures, combined with showings of his China film documentary, attracted large audiences in all the major cities. He "interviewed and was interviewed by" editors, professors, students, and politicians, he told Howard, and was dined by the foreign minister in Tokyo. He worked on a new enlarged edition of *Red Star,* with added notes, CCP biographical data, and further extracts from his Mao interviews of 1936 and 1939. He prepared a revised and updated new edition of *Red China Today.*

His efforts to go back to China in the late 1960s were unsuccessful; in fact he too came under ultra-leftist xenophobic attack there as a "foreign agent," and those Chinese who had been associated with him were in some cases pilloried for the connection. "Indications are that I won't see you for a long time to come," he bitterly wrote Alley in July 1967. "One pays a price to remain independent in this world and it is so easy to make enemies without really trying." He wrote directly to Mao in mid-1969, complaining that "all my requests through diplomatic and other channels [to visit China] have met no response." (When Snow was finally back in China in 1970, Mao explained the delay to him, "It was a group of ultra-leftists in the *Waichiaopu* [foreign ministry] who were opposed to you.")[52]

His wish to revisit China, he wrote Han Suyin in 1969, was "simply that I am eager to replenish my scant knowledge, on which this part of the world [the West] draws to a degree not justified but hard for me to ignore, for information and interpretation." And on the consistently troubling problems for him in safeguarding his "independent" credentials in the West without undercutting his "friendly" links to the Chinese, he explained to her: "It is not easy to retain credibility as an independent writer without occasionally being misunderstood—if one is to convey any of the truth—by those one would not choose as enemies." The truth was not that simple to convey "in forums where we function, and ambiguity, sometimes necessary, may confuse friends, and ineptitude turn one into a *huai tan* [bad egg]."[53]

Snow had mounting misgivings on news of the harsh treatment of old friends in China. He commented to Anna Martens in April 1969 on a letter he received from Soong Qingling: She is "studying hard the works of the Chairman," and "mentions something about foreigners trusted for 20 yrs. who turned out to be renegades. Meaning the E's [Epstein and his wife]? Alors." Meanwhile, the Vietnam morass was causing him much anguish. On the eve of the 1968 presidential election, he wrote Mildred and Claude, condemning both Nixon and Humphrey, but with his harshest judgment directed at Johnson for "his whole immoral and stupid handling of U.S. power to waste lives and billions in senseless destruction."[54]

Snow's chronic "plumbing" problems (as he called his kidney and urinary tract troubles) were a further complicating factor for him as the 1960s decade closed and perhaps a warning of his terminal illness two years later. He was having "a general letdown, and unaccountably severe fatigue," he wrote Anna Martens in September 1969. Ordered to take a complete rest, he was forced to cancel some lectures in the States scheduled for that fall. It was the beginning of a difficult winter, with two operations and over a month in the hospital. Convalescence was impeded by a return bout of malarial fever. "Ed's illness was so up and down," Lois told the Howard Snows in July 1970, "he's had such a long drawn-out recuperation—just when he seemed out of the woods, he'd be back in bed!" Though more like himself again, Ed told Mildred in May, "I still tire easily." He would never be really fully fit again. The nearly two-hundred-year-old Swiss farmhouse and barn the Snows purchased in 1968 was also a drain, eating up a great deal of energy and cash on necessary major modernization and refurbishing projects. They worked for months fixing up the house, Lois wrote Howard and Dorothy in January 1969. Ed, she perhaps overenthused, was a "whiz with all tools—not just that typewriter." "It is a beguiling whore," Ed wrote Charles (Chuck) Hogan in October 1969 about the Eysins house, "ever demanding more money and attention." But from their new home, Lois informed the Howard Snows, "we can dip into France in ten minutes, be on top of a mountain in a jiffy, or have lunch on a lake boat going to Montreux or Geneva."[55]

In what seemed almost a replay of his thirteen-year sojourn in China, Snow looked on the Swiss location as temporary, with continued expressions to his sister and brother of his (and Lois's) intention to return to live in the United States—preferably, for Ed, to New England. "We would like to come home—we are still Americans," he told Mildred in May 1970. And in a heartfelt letter to Howard a year earlier (occasioned by the tragic death of Howard's daughter Karen), Ed reached out to his brother in terms also reminiscent of the early China years. There was a reflective sadness over the separate and separated lives of these now aging brothers. "I much need to discuss my own life with you; we have been too long too far apart," Ed wrote. "I am appalled at the short time remaining to us. How life speeds past." Yet Snow could still bounce back: "I can still do a day's work or a day's play—at tennis or swimming or skiing—with enjoyment if not with the old zest." As to thoughts of "retirement" (which he could ill afford, with two children to put through college), Ed told Howard, "I have still things to do; but I would like to be able to work fewer hours and to play more, and to enjoy—peace and quiet." The ensuing final two years would hardly fit that prescription.[56]

As the 1960s ended, Snow was reassessing his ideas on the probable course of events in Asia. The turmoil in China proved to be a much more profoundly shattering and transforming phenomenon than he had envisaged, while his apocalyptic scenario for the United States and China had been a greatly overheated one. In a preface for the new edition of *Red China Today,* Snow looked at "China in the 1970's." He laid out and seemingly endorsed the proclaimed policies and goals of Mao's new revolution—first and foremost establishing the "absolute authority" of Mao Thought. A younger generation of cadres had taken over, "albeit led by the Old Man." Mao was solidly in control, Snow insisted, and held a "new" Mandate of Heaven. The glorified Red leader had become "the personification of revolutionary creativity, independence, national self-esteem and world prestige."[57]

Snow took notice of Mao Thought as "a kind of secular religion to which organized opposition was not possible." Still, the "paradox was that Mao Tse-tung's thinking was in spirit deeply populist." As Ed summed it up, "The revolutionary purpose was human emancipation, but Mao's way left no room for heterodoxy if the Vision was to be fulfilled: that the poor (and not any Mandarin elite) should inherit the Chinese earth, marching en masse toward an egalitarian and class-free future." The "paradox" Snow noted was also at the heart of his own thinking and would shortly be sharply revealed as he in turn experienced the impact of the "new secular religion."[58]

On the prospects for Sino-American relations, Snow returned to the theme of reconciliation he had so ardently pursued in the early 1960s. China's (or Snow's?) fear of an American attack was now "reduced," with her major attention focused on what seemed the chief menace, the Soviets. A "renewal of Sino-American discourse now seemed plausible." It all brought back Snow's thesis of 1949. "As some saw it," he wrote in the 1970 preface, "China and Russia were obligingly containing each other, within the ruins of the communist monolithic." Washington could exploit the situation by favoring China as the weaker one, with moves (already being taken) toward relaxation of tension. Sooner or later, Snow noted, there would have to be a serious negotiation on the basis of the principles regarding Taiwan defined for Snow by Zhou Enlai in 1960. But, he added, perhaps letting his personal reactions color his judgments, "that time was not yet"—as evidenced by Nixon's recent "egregious political blunder" in "plunging" into Cambodia. This "amounted to repeating the tragic Vietnam miscalculation itself," he declared. Ironically, of course, the "new beginning" in America's China policy he had hoped for a decade earlier in the Kennedy years would come to pass under a president he disdained and whose motives he distrusted. It was another paradox he would soon face as a Mao-designated American symbol and emissary in this denouement.[59]

CHAPTER 16

Last Hurrah

By 1970 the most violent and chaotic phase of the Cultural Revolution had ended, the unruly and destructive Red Guards had been disbanded, ultra-leftist extremists purged, and a stage of military-dominated consolidation was in progress. Under these circumstances, and with renewed Chinese interest in détente with America, Snow was once more on his way back. This time Lois was along for her rapturous first China experience. A call had come from the Chinese embassy in Paris in June; visas issued in early July, and the two Snows were off by Swissair from Geneva to Hong Kong at the end of that month. There had been hurried arrangements for the house, children, and financing. Chris, a commuter student at the University of Geneva, remained home in Eysins with house-sitting friends of the Snows; Sian would leave later for Boston to the Howard Snows, on her way to enter Antioch College in Ohio. Ed had worked out agreements with his European journalistic outlets, and the unfulfilled Macmillan book contract had been taken over by Random House.[1]

Ed was still weak and recuperating from his surgeries; in Hong Kong he came down with a high fever and was hospitalized for a week with recurrence of a postoperative urinary infection. Illness and exhaustion would plague him throughout the six-month stay in the East. By mid-August he and Lois were in Canton, to begin a grueling round of travel and of Mao Thought–style briefings he soon found had a tedious and long-winded ritualistic sameness that lowered his spirits further. "China is a country with a single scenario," he noted shortly after arrival.[2]

In Beijing, Snow found Rewi Alley aging and alone. Foreigners were isolated now, and Rewi no longer saw his adopted Chinese sons and their families. "He spoke quietly in a mix of nostalgia and loneliness and cautious hope," Ed recorded. The Chinese diplomat Huang Hua, Snow's old Yanjing student and interpreter, was just back from a May Seventh School for "re-educating" cadres, to shepherd the Snows around. He gave Ed a euphoric picture of the "new" new China. In discussions with Huang and others, Snow was told, "We disdain money and possessions. We desire to create socialist society and a new and nobler man." He also learned that his wartime Indusco colleague Chen Hansheng (now in his seventies) had "got caught up in the same evil wind that trapped Eppy [Epstein]."[3]

Though quite fatigued, he was soon summoned one evening to see Premier Zhou during a North Korean–Chinese ping-pong match at a sports arena (only in China!). Snow had probably read reports by the Red Guards, the premier told him, "of things he [Zhou] had said and hadn't said." The Red Guards, Zhou continued, used what they wanted of his remarks, ignored the rest, or "invented things that had not been said." Zhou's statement was a telling commentary on the general level of revolutionary political discourse in China.[4]

"The extent to which Mao dominates thinking and activity here," Snow noted after a few weeks, "is greater than I thought." The largest bookstore in Beijing now offered "nothing but Mao" and a few shelves of Marxist-Leninist works. ("Very few customers incidentally," he added.) Everybody in all spheres of activity was "catechismically" reciting and memorizing Red Book phrases. Snow wondered in his diary whether Maoist "self-reliance" could be "misinterpreted" as chauvinism. "What is internationalism except sharing of tasks with foreign comrades?" Lois, Ed recorded, "thinks she had found pure, sincere, selfless people—the ideal of the convent-bred—and of course she has, they exist. But one must ask at what sacrifice of truth, self-contradiction, etc." More disquieting was a documentary Snow was shown of Zhou Enlai's May visit to North Korea. Kim Il Sung "swaggers" and was surrounded by "black-suited hoods" and a "goosestepping" honor guard. "Perfect mechanical men. The whole thing in bad taste," Ed felt. Yet he could also ponder that China's Red Guards had been "a great adventure for millions. . . . It brought out leadership in young."[5]

Snow endured four days of born-again confessional recitals at Qinghua University (a former "bastion of U.S. cultural imperialism," he was told). As he took notes on one of these evidently rehearsed group narrations, he parenthetically added of a "fast-talking" young female student, "She knows her Mao. What am I doing here, wasting my time, and I have so little left." And as one interminable account followed another, "It's like a religious service, over and over again. How many times must it be repeated." Of an exposition by a member of the People's Liberation Army propaganda team at the university, Snow recorded, "This officer speaks as if he really believes it's only a matter of studying Mao to know the answers, as convinced as any Jesuit. He looks self-righteous but thinks he is kind, reasonable."[6]

In the northwest, the Snows visited Yan'an, a May Seventh cadre school at Nanniwan, near Yan'an, and then went to Bao'an—Snow's first return there since 1936. At the cadre school, where Mao's directive on "going down to do manual labor" was being implemented, conditions seemed to Snow as hard as a prisoner's life. In Bao'an Snow saw his famous photo of Mao, taken in 1936, adorning the wall of Mao's old cave dwelling. They had arrived in Bao'an in a cavalcade of cars, not the way he came in 1936, Ed recorded. "We are receiving Vip treatment, a bit too much for my liking," he wrote editor Mary Heathcote. "What can I do?" Of his many briefings on the northwestern trip, Snow glumly noted, "Might as well stay in Peking and read Mao's works—memorize them." Back in Xi'an, Snow tried a lighter touch with his Chinese companions. "Mao Tsetung was a poet of note," he scribbled, "who lived by writing things to quote." They "did not think it was funny at all," he jotted. Snow pondered privately on all this: "All rival or complementary thought or doctrine being heresy as interpreted in the eyes of a rising new priestcraft which will soon be powerfully installed in the Party with army support." The "future bureaucrat—the product of the present ferment," will have "enormous power," he thought.[7]

The Snows were back in Beijing for the October 1 National Day celebrations, and were invited to be on the Tiananmen balcony for the big parade. As they stood watching the spectacle, there was a tug on Snow's sleeve. It was the premier, who led the two to Mao, who gave Ed a smile of welcome and (as Lois afterward remarked to Ed) turned to look Lois over appraisingly, "Up and down," a few times. The famous photo of "friendly American personage" Snow standing beside the chairman at the rostrum balustrade was perhaps meant primarily as a signal to the Chinese people that the portrayal of America as the Great Imperialist Satan might be in for some official revision. (Henry Kissinger later wrote that the signal had been "so oblique that our crude Occidental minds completely missed the point.") Mao's next signal through Snow would be much more obviously and unmistakably directed to Washington.[8]

There were many layers and complexities in Snow's attitudes and responses to the China he perceived in 1970. His extremely alienated view of Vietnam-era America played a critical part. When he had lived in opium-ridden old China, he told a veteran Red commander in Beijing, "I never thought that the U.S. would become saturated with dope [no longer a menace in China]—and that a big percentage of youths would be trying it." Snow went on: "I spoke of moral-political crisis: lack of respect for authority, breakdown in the law, lack of confidence in leaders—much of it traceable to Vietnam."[9]

On a visit to Beijing University, now situated on the original Yanjing campus where he had lectured, it was "a bit shocking" to Ed "to hear Peita [Beijing University]—Yenching history summarized as 'cultural imperialist institution' and then go on to its [new] beginnings after Liberation." Snow was alerted to await an imminent meeting with Mao and spent time preparing and "waiting for Lefty." But his get-together with the chairman was put off for over two months until mid-December. (Ed would have preferred not to spend the winter in China. "I can't conceive myself working here without being forced to join the team.")[10]

At another meeting with Zhou Enlai in the Great Hall, Snow was acutely aware of the toll on the premier of his unceasing, round-the-clock efforts to keep some sort of lid on cultural revolutionary anarchy. Zhou spoke of his aging, of heart problems, and said that he had not had a vacation in eleven years. His hand shook as he offered Snow sugar for his coffee. He had not had time for exercise and was up too many nights till three a.m. or all night, he told Ed. But the indefatigable administrator took pains to work out Snow's itinerary for his remaining time in China. Zhou even made sure the two Snows would have warm overcoats made for their travel to the northeast (Manchuria), their "Zhou coats," Lois and Ed later called them.[11]

In Beijing again in November, Alley confided to Ed on the political troubles his adopted son Allen had encountered through the years culminating in his imprisonment in the northwest on false charges after the Cultural Revolution began. He managed to escape and found haven with Alley and the Hatems in Beijing, and was finally "liberated" through the intervention of Zhou Enlai. While in prison, "all around him comrades were dying of beatings, starvation, exposure and suicide," Snow was told. Alley's other son, Mike, had been digging ditches for two years. Snow pondered on the problems China would face restoring morale among those sent down to the countryside—whether actors and musicians, writers who had stopped writing, foreigners who were sequestered, technicians (like Alley's son) digging ditches, doctors tilling the soil, or high-level bureaucrats tending pigs.[12]

As Snow ruminated on all these aspects of the China scene, he tried to take the long view, but he hardly seemed to be convincing himself. "Injustice or violence vs history may be done and be unavoidable in the struggle for power in a given situation," he jotted in his diary, but the "record cannot be erased forever," and the "balance will be redressed in time." It "is not hard to die for the revolution but what is hard is to die for the revolution or be prepared to die for the revolution," he went on, "knowing that it may be tallied as a counter-revolutionary act by those temporarily in charge of the account books. Again the only solace is the impartiality of time." It was evidently a solace Snow himself sought to find in the situation.[13]

Snow made the rounds of communes, factories, workshops, schools, hospitals, public works projects, and much else and was clearly impressed with what he observed. Alongside the numbing and all-pervasive and repetitive ideological cant he was subjected to, Snow seemed persuaded that Mao had steered the revolution back on its original peasant-populist track. In his posthumously published *Long Revolution,* Snow saw broad horizons ahead "as town and city meet to join farmer, worker, and intellectual in a one-class society," keeping "China fully occupied with peaceful works—carried out in a revolutionary way—till the year 2000." Though he was often skeptical of Lois's fresh and glowing response to China's seemingly squeaky-clean morality and proclaimed selfless devotion to the commonweal, Ed was nevertheless attracted by the possibilities (as were many others in the West at the time) of an ethical breakthrough to a new "socialist man." In writing to Mary Heathcote ostensibly on Lois's reactions but with obvious relevance to himself: "She loves the Chinese and they reciprocate. Their message gets through, she is impressed by their purity and dedication, and by the country they have scrubbed and are refurbishing—making green and great." ("For me," Lois wrote Dorothy and Howard Snow from Beijing, "it's *all* new, exciting, moving, interesting.") But contradictory realities were always intruding. Of a meeting with new revolutionary committee members in Shanghai, Snow recorded, "a sullen crowd," adding, "Few smiles. No gaiety, no joy. It's all revolution." Snow might applaud the Maoist remolding of people and society—but at arm's length.[14]

As before, what ultimately carried the day for Snow were his one-on-one interviews and conversations with the Mao-Zhou twosome, who represented for Ed the abiding revolutionary verities of the Red star he had known since 1936. And for the Red leaders, Snow remained the "friendly American" who offered the most suitable and reliable public channel for reaching out to America. In a November meeting with Zhou, the premier restated the principles he had first spelled out to Snow in 1960 for resolution of the Taiwan problem. Evidently respond-ing to feelers already emanating from Washington, Zhou told Snow, "The door is open but it depends on whether the United States is seri-ous in dealing with the Taiwan question." Mao would soon speak more bluntly to Snow on these matters.[15]

As he continued to wait for "Lefty" in December, Snow came down with his usual sinusitis, plus bronchitis, and stayed in bed for a few days. ("I still tire too easily and need too much rest," he had earlier written Heathcote.) One mid-December morning while still asleep, he was peremptorily summoned to see Mao. They met in Mao's home, had breakfast together, and talked until past noon. The Chairman was down with a cold also and was sitting clothed in a dressing gown and with a blanket over him. The Cultural Revolution, Mao told Ed with equa-nimity, was "an all-round civil war," with factional fighting everywhere and in each organization, institution, and government ministry. From the Great Helmsman's loftily and abstractly ideological perspective, this was all to the good—"it wouldn't do if you didn't have this." Counter-revolutionaries and capitalist-roaders had to be struggled against and ex-posed. Conversely, Mao complained of the widespread violence and the maltreatment of "captives," neatly absolving himself of responsibility. Foreigners had been correct, he divulged, in saying that "China was in great chaos."[16]

Snow, now more troubled than ever at the extremes of the Mao cult he had witnessed on this visit, pressed the chairman on the matter to a surprisingly frank degree. He brought up questions he had privately raised with Chinese official friends on his previous China trip regarding the "glorification" of the Red leader. It had seemed to him excessive and unnecessary. After all, he told Mao, "everybody knew that you were the main author of the revolution." Mao carefully responded with a combi-nation of personal disclaimer (as well as justification—everyone wants to be "worshipped"), political necessity, and the "nuisance" of the still-prevalent Chinese tradition of "emperor worship." (This last, of course, the Mao deification had cynically exploited and magnified.) Mao re-minded Snow of their 1965 talk, when he had linked Khrushchev's fall to the latter's lack of a personality cult. The subsequent massive propagation of the Mao cult, he now confided to his American friend, had been essential in order to recapture the political high ground from the Liu Shaoqi–led "revisionists" who had gained control of the party apparatus. Liu, a major Communist figure since the 1920s second only to Mao in party status and prestige, and president (until his downfall) of the People's Republic since 1959, was now dismissed by Mao as "a reactionary who had wormed his way into the Party." (Over a year before the time Mao related all this to Snow, Liu had died in solitary confinement of pneumonia, aggravated by ill treatment and neglect. His death and its circumstances would not be disclosed for years.) Now, Mao reassured Snow, the time had come to "cool down" Mao worship. "I don't like all this. We're going to put an end to it." He quickly added, however (in Snow's paraphrased notes), "we can't do it at once. Otherwise that would have the wrong impression too—meaning that Mao is sinking."[17]

The Chinese leader shrugged off as "overdone" the "four greats" description of himself (Great Teacher, Great Leader, Great Supreme Commander, and Great Helmsman). Only the simple "teacher" title will be retained; the rest would be got rid of "sooner or later." Mao's aspiring wise teacher role was far from a modest proposal in the Chinese cultural context. It seemed to have more in common with the place Confucius and *his* thought had held for two millennia as China's great sage and teacher. Adding to the ironies, while Mao was pointing to his schoolteacher background image as his preferred legacy, his Cultural Revolution had been reviling China's academic community in generic class-action terms as bourgeois "stinking intellectuals." On a rather similar note, in his *Life* article on the Mao conversation, Snow had cited Mao's apparent final comment to him: "he said he was not a complicated man but really very simple. He was, he said, only a lone monk walking the world with a leaky umbrella." But Snow's translator-companion in China, Yao Wei, wrote him that he had gotten this wrong. A "better translation," he told Ed, would be: "Like a monk holding an umbrella, I defy laws human and divine."[18]

Snow's query to Mao on the prospects for improvement in Sino-Soviet relations elicited a Maoist tirade against Moscow. "Those Russians," he ended, "they look down upon the Chinese, they look down upon people of many countries; they think they have only to say a word and people will all listen to them. They do not expect there are people who won't, and one of them is my humble self." His battle with the Soviets, Mao underscored, was at the root of the current Chinese political struggle. "Basically," he told the journalist, "it is a question of revisionism or anti-revisionism. Those in China who practice revisionism are bound to compromise with the Soviet Union."[19]

Turning to the United States, Mao made his open direct response to private signals coming from Washington on the possibilities of a Nixon visit. He preferred dealing with the Republicans rather than the Democrats, he averred, possibly thinking back to the (Democratic) Truman-initiated Taiwan intervention. If Nixon "wants to come to Peking, you may bring him a message," Mao told Snow. Nixon could come secretly if he wished. He "can just get on a plane and come." But Mao was also shrewdly aware of the potential political spin-off for Nixon of a China journey. The American president would likely come, he surmised, in the early part of 1972, before the next presidential elections. Nixon's journey to Beijing in February 1972 would indeed be far from a secret one. His arrival on Air Force One, covered by a vast media entourage, would be a television spectacle.[20]

In his whimsically paradoxical Taoist manner, Mao declared Nixon to be "a good fellow"—the Red leader liked those "who were the most reactionary in the world." They "helped" the world revolutionary cause much as the Japanese had earlier done for China. "You just say [to Nixon]," Mao went on in this vein, "he is a good fellow! The No. 1 good fellow in the world. That Brezhnev is no good." More to the point, the chairman noted that problems with America could not then be resolved with "the middle or the left," but only with Nixon as "the representative of the monopoly capitalists." (In his meeting with Nixon, Mao told the president, "We do not like those presidents from Truman to Johnson [but] I cast a vote for your election. . . . I like rightists.")[21]

Mao was undoubtedly also thinking of his own biological calendar in pressing an American opening. "I'm not all that well," he confided to Ed, repeating a probably exaggerated motif from his 1965 talk with the American on the eve of his political comeback. "I'm 77 and I'm soon going to heaven." It would be Snow, not Mao, for whom time ran out before the Nixon journey. On an odd, lighter note, Mao chided Snow for the latter's failure to include the two young women interpreter-secretaries present, in a toast to the chairman. This Maoist defense of women's rights resonates incongruously with the recently published account of Mao's private life by his personal physician (now living in the U.S.), with its lurid details of the older Mao's "imperial" sexual penchant for young women.[22]

When the two men parted for the last time, Mao dwelt for a moment on their mutually trustful thirty-five-year relationship. "I never lie to you and I believe you do not lie to me either." For China's supreme leader the "bourgeois" American journalist was perhaps closer to a genuinely dependable friend, and confidant of sorts than he could find among his proletarian Chinese cohorts in the conflict-ridden and often paranoid sub rosa world of Communist politics. And while their special relationship had given Snow unique and invaluable advantages as a journalist, it had placed an inevitable psychological (and political) burden on him as well. The Mao-Snow phenomenon was the ultimate example of the Chinese concept of *guanxi* (special connections), in which friendship carried its obligations. Despite Snow's reservations on the Mao cult, he remained to the end deeply conscious of and inescapably swayed by Mao's exceptional consideration for and oft-expressed confidence in him.[23]

On December 21 Lois left via Canton and Hong Kong, to be with her family in California for Christmas. She took with her material she had collected on China's new "revolutionary" opera and ballet for the book she would write, *China On Stage*. Ed had his holiday dinner at the Hatems, with Alley and other foreign friends also there. He prepared his Zhou interviews for publication, wrapped up other matters, and made the rounds of his Beijing friends. He continued to be very tired, was concerned at signs of renewed bladder infection and urinary problems. He was relying on "too much coffee, brandy, and cigarettes" to keep him going. He was anxious to finish and leave China, missed Lois, and felt "toute seule," he forlornly noted at the end of January. On top of this, at a dinner with his Chinese official hosts he raised provocative questions. "It was a bad evening. I did not have Lois to kick me under the table." There was also a disquieting conversation with Carmelita Hinton, daughter of William Hinton, who had been brought up and educated in China. She recounted the confusing experiences of students during the recent chaotic years. The youths were really working off their grievances against the system, she told him. "How can foreigners know anything about China," she quoted the Chinese students as saying, "when we don't understand it ourselves." As his China stay ended, Snow listed some of the minor and major irritations he had felt: the overfeeding, and the separation of foreign guests from the people; the retelling of the same shopworn stories to the visiting writers; the difficulties in getting information on major questions of the army, party, and economy; and the constant blare of political songs and slogans on planes and trains. Snow left by plane for Canton on February 6, 1971, and then by train to Hong Kong. He was exhausted, dispirited, and as troubled as he was inspired by his China experience, probably already in the early stages of the cancer that would end his life just a year later.[24]

Snow's tardy departure from China changed original plans for him to join Lois in California. Instead, he returned directly to their Eysins home, while Lois proceeded to New York and there handled some of Ed's publications business. (The *New York Times* offered to publish only a "bowdlerized" version of his Zhou interviews, which Snow angrily rejected.) A phone call from Chris, telling his mother that Ed had arrived "terribly tired," quickly brought Lois home. Over the next weeks, Ed worked on articles, primarily for the Italian weekly *Epoca* that had largely financed his China trip. As he labored, events were moving toward the Sino-American rapprochement Snow had so ardently advocated since the establishment of the People's Republic. During the fall of 1970 Nixon had begun secret approaches to Beijing (obliquely referred to by Mao in the December meeting with Snow), through Pakistani and Romanian go-betweens. With encouraging responses from Zhou Enlai, these private exchanges went on through the early months of 1971. In Washington this process was orchestrated in the White House through Nixon's national security adviser (later secretary of state), Henry Kissinger, thus circumventing the state department bureaucracy.[25]

In early April, in a characteristically subtle but dramatically unmistakable public signal exhibiting Zhou's diplomatic skills at its best, Beijing invited to China an American table tennis team then competing in world championships in Japan. In Beijing, the team was given a reception by the premier in the Great Hall, where Zhou stressed the friendship theme. The Americans duly invited the China team to the United States. This ping-pong diplomacy was further advanced with the publication in *Life* at the end of that month of Snow's write-up of his December conversation with Mao. The chairman had arranged for Snow to have formal notes of their talk that Ed could use for "guidance" and background, "from time to time, when needed." Evidently, the moment had now come. (Huang Hua had given an affirmative signal in response to Ed's urgent cabled query on publishing the Mao material.) "Mao would be happy to talk with [Nixon] either as tourist or President," Snow reported in the *Life* piece. He subsequently wrote the chairman that, "With the arrival of the table tennis players and other openings to Americans, the timing of the release seemed politically right." (On his own role in all this, Snow rather arrestingly wrote the Chinese consul, Xu [Hsu], in Geneva, "I hope all that I have written here and before is going to be helpful. I can only assume that there is a purpose to all interviews given to me which is not for me to judge or entirely comprehend.") Though Kissinger later downplayed the significance of the

Snow channel in the negotiations, he added, "Nevertheless, Snow's interview with Mao is interesting for what it tells us about the state of mind of China's leaders in December 1970. It shows that they were considering a Presidential visit at that early date, an idea not yet broached officially in any of our communications." In his annual report to Congress just before undertaking the China trip, Nixon gave a bit more weight to Snow's account, "which confirmed private signals we had already received of Chinese interest in my visiting China." It remained for Secretary of State William Rogers, out of the loop at the time, to react in the reflexes of the past. In a television appearance in London on April 29, he declared that the Nixon invitation, as reported by Snow in *Life,* was "fairly casually made," and he did not believe it was "a serious invitation."[26]

On July 9 Kissinger embarked on an historic secret journey to Beijing via Pakistan, for direct talks with Zhou that would finalize the Nixon visit. He spent seventeen hours with the Chinese premier over a two-day stay, the first of many lengthy encounters between these two diplomatic protagonists. The personal assessment of Zhou Enlai by this highly sophisticated, hardheaded representative of "monopoly capitalist" America was well in line with that of "friendly American" Snow. "Urbane, infinitely patient, extraordinarily intelligent, subtle," Kissinger later recounted of the premier, "he moved through our discussions with an easy grace that penetrated to the essence of our new relationship as if there were no sensible alternative." That the two nations "would seek rapprochement in the early 1970s was inherent in the world environment. That it should occur so rapidly and develop so naturally owed no little to the luminous personality and extraordinary perception of the Chinese Premier." In making his dramatic televised announcement on July 15 of his forthcoming China trip, Nixon declared, "there can be no stable and enduring peace without the participation of the People's Republic of China and its 750 million people." All this, in essence, was the message Snow had tried to deliver to other American leaders a decade earlier.[27]

In April, Lois and Ed drove to Sperlonga on the Italian Mediterranean coast above Naples for a desperately needed rest. On the way home they visited with Oliver Clubb and his family. Oliver, a political scientist, was the son of Ed's longtime friend O. Edmund Clubb, China hand and U.S. foreign service officer, and was then teaching in Syracuse University's program abroad in Florence. He remembered Snow's preoccupation with his health, and Ed's "somber" moments as well as his more typically warm, amiable, and "alive" qualities. Back in Switzerland, Ed found himself with a newly enhanced prominence in the rush of China developments. He was deluged, by phone and correspondence, with demands on his China expertise, on-the-spot experience, and unique connections—everyone, it seemed, wanted to visit China and expected (wrongly) that Ed could help them get there. (He was being bombarded by "an endless stream of people," he wrote Mao after returning home, "who think I am on the 'hot line' to the Peking visa department.") In response to Snow's pleas, his former Random House and Grove Press editor and warmly affectionate friend Mary Heathcote came over to Eysins in August to help Ed with his book. She arrived on crutches (an ankle fracture) and stayed on until December, when Snow's illness made further work on the incomplete volume impossible. Though Ed was clearly unwell, suffering from severe back pains he attributed to lumbago, the trio worked as best they could. Lois, herself incubating a severe case of hepatitis, concentrated on her book, and Mary and Ed on his. In October, Snow wrote John Simon of Random House that he had been "considerably set back in my work because of illness. I never knew what lumbago was before," he went on, "but in my case it has immobilized me." He was unable to sit at the typewriter for more than twenty minutes without resting for at least an hour, "and even that was against doctor's orders." In an effort to restore his vitality and spirits, Ed took off by himself for ten days in the sun and warmth of a beach on the Moroccan coast. He returned looking tanned, but it would be downhill for both Snows in the bleak and agonizing winter months ahead.[28]

While Snow's niche as a pioneer China bridge-builder was now being widely recognized and acclaimed, it had a bitter taste for him, underlined of course, by his grave illness. In the era of Vietnam, he felt a sense of personal betrayal at an America gone wrong. And in a final rejection of his old belief that America could be a liberating force in the world, he wrote Owen Lattimore in May 1970 that his own earlier views on American exceptionalism had been "a mirage." "American imperialism," he told Lattimore, was especially dangerous precisely "because the people, thinking themselves free, could not imagine carrying anything but freedom elsewhere." And in March 1971, after his return from China, he wrote liberal Democratic Senator George McGovern ("in *strict confidence*") on what he had learned in Beijing of Nixon's secret approaches to the Chinese on a presidential visit. "It is assumed there that, as China debate waxes hotter in the U.S., Nixon may attempt to get hold of the

China issue through some such stunt." To this future 1972 Nixon presidential opponent, Snow added, "I would like to see you get there first." In December, Snow confided to Hatem, "I never thought Nixon would invite himself to dinner with Mao." And in a press interview, evidently in Geneva, at the time he published his *Life* article on Mao's invitation to Nixon, Snow seemed to put the coming event in an oddly adversarial context. "Now some people say that because Mao offers to shake Nixon's hand he is ready to be 'taken in' by Wall Street and the Pentagon. They forget," he noted, "that Mao shook hands with Chiang Kai-shek to negotiate in 1945 and shook hands also to talk with American Ambassador Patrick Hurley. Where did that get them?" When Nixon sent Snow a brief letter two weeks before Ed's death, acknowledging the journalist's "distinguished career and achievements," Lois Snow later recounted, "We didn't answer the letter and we didn't hear again." A few weeks after Ed's passing, Lois wrote to their friend Charles Hogan, "The Nixon letter was sheerly political. I dismiss him with the contempt he deserves."[29]

As Snow reacted to the impending Nixon encounter with the Chinese, the foregoing not-unfounded political animosities and disillusionments inevitably affected his perception of the full significance and historic dimensions of these developments. In another *Life* article in July 1971 on the forthcoming presidential journey, Snow insisted that it was the Chinese who would be dealing from "a position of strength." With "a fierce domestic purge safely behind him," Mao saw "America's Vietnam venture a shambles" and believed "its political and economic position to be in trouble abroad and at home," Ed wrote. "Now, if there was a chance for China to recover Taiwan—Mao's last national goal of unification—and for China to be accepted as an equal in recognition of her great size, achievements, and potential, why not look at it?"—particularly in view of the Soviet threat from the north.[30]

Snow concluded his assessment of future Sino-American prospects on a "two-cheers" admonitory note. "The millennium seems distant and the immediate prospect is for the toughest kind of adjustment and struggle." A "more realistic world is in sight," he continued, but "popular illusions that it will consist of a sweet mix of ideologies, or an end to China's faith in revolutionary means, could only serve to deepen the abyss again when disillusionment occurs." Reaffirming his own belief in the continuing imperatives for revolutionary change in the world, with a Maoist China as its leading proponent, Snow added, "A world without change by revolutions—a world in which China's closest friends would not be revolutionary states—is inconceivable to Peking. But a world of relative peace between states is as necessary to China as to America. To hope for more is to court disenchantment."[31]

In fact the Sino-American détente ushered in both the post-Vietnam era of retreat from America's imperial interventionism in Asia, and the post-revolutionary era for China, at home and abroad. Zhou Enlai, the negotiator of the American opening, would also be the harbinger of the "four modernizations" policies that would soon mark the end of the Maoist epoch. (Zhou "is a builder, not a poet," Snow wrote in comparing him to Mao.) Perhaps Zhou was sending out some signals of his own on this, when in their July 1971 talks he rather strangely gave Kissinger an exposition on the Cultural Revolution. As Kissinger has described this singular episode: "With grace masking undoubted anguish, Chou described China as being torn between the fear of bureaucratization and the excesses of ideological zeal" which had put in jeopardy the fruits of fifty years of struggle. "He had doubted the necessity of such drastic measures, but Mao had been wiser; he had the vision to look far into the future. In retrospect," Kissinger remarked, "I doubt that Chou would have raised the point at all had he not wanted to disassociate himself from the Cultural Revolution at least to some extent and to indicate that it was over."[32]

The dilemmas that may have faced Zhou as "Mao's indispensable alter ego," in Snow's words, could well have applied also to the American journalist as Mao's admiring Boswell. Snow had first come to the revolution in its initial Maoist emergence; he had been its most effective publicist, and he had witnessed Maoism's climactic final phase on his last visit. Perhaps the strikingly different temperaments and traits of the two extraordinary Red leaders with whom Snow's entire Red star experience had been linked, mirrored (and helped resolve) the nagging doubts and conflicts that his commitment to the revolution engendered. Ed summed it all up most revealingly in the letter he wrote Mao in July 1969, at a time when his requests to return to China were being ignored and when he appeared to be under a cloud in the frenzied politics of the Cultural Revolution. In seeking the chairman's help for a China visit, Snow exhibited the aggrieved hurt of a true friend spurned while simultaneously highlighting and reaffirming his past contributions to Mao's cause and indeed his cult. "I hope that you will not forget that I have been for many years a firm supporter of your great leadership," he told the Great Helmsman. "I feel rarely fortunate to have, by chance, been privileged to know you and talk to you, and for that reason to have been able to help make known to the world the life and work of a revolutionary fully the peer of Lenin. I hope that my work has not been useless." Now, as his own life ebbed away, so did the "Snow era" of Maoist communism.[33]

In the broader perspective the Sino-American détente of 1972—looking beyond immediate political calculations, personalities, and cold war maneuverings—was clearly a triumph (if bittersweet) and vindication for Snow. He had persistently argued in the 1930s that an independent, united, and strong China was central to American strategic interests in the Pacific, at a time when Washington's neutrality policies were serving the needs of Japanese aggression against China. In bringing the Chinese Communists to the sympathetic attention of the West, in *Red Star* and much other writing, Snow consistently pictured the Reds as both patriots and revolutionaries. On the eve of full Communist victory in 1949, Snow had written (and later reiterated in *Journey* and *Red China Today*) that "in the long run the Chinese Communist Party probably cannot and will not subordinate the national interests of China to the interests of the Kremlin." If American policy "is washed clean of interventionism, history may evolve along lines for which all the necessary preconditions now exist. China will become the first Communist-run major power independent of Moscow's dictation." In line with this, during the cold war years, he urged America to make its peace with the revolution now in power. He knew that the era of viable great power intervention in China, Russian or American, was over. He insisted that it continued to be in America's (and China's) best interests for these two great nations on opposite shores of the Pacific to come to terms. ("We became friends because we had mutual interests," Nixon would later declare.) In pressing for Sino-American understanding, Snow had tended to underplay, though not ignore, ideological and political barriers. "No differences in historical experience, present social or political institutions, or conflicting national interests," he had written Mao in 1963, "could possibly justify a great war or continued great hate on both sides." But Snow believed always—if often in contradiction to his Maoist sympathies—that true human liberation ultimately demanded of all societies full economic and political empowerment of their peoples. Probably the ideals and principles of the wartime Chinese industrial cooperative movement, with its mix of individual and collective rights, interests, and responsibilities, best exemplified his notion of the good society.[34]

In late November 1971 Snow underwent diagnostic tests that revealed pancreatic cancer that had already involved the liver. Lois was herself then in the hospital with infectious hepatitis. Still weak and not entirely recovered, she returned home as Ed prepared to enter a Lausanne hospital in mid-December for major surgery. The grueling operative and postoperative ordeal did nothing to arrest the mortal course of the disease. Ed was evidently made aware of his condition but tried to deny its full implications. ("Ed knows he has cancer," Lois told the Howard Snows at the end of December, "how serious it is I don't think he knows now." He wanted no one to know it was cancer, she added.) He talked of recuperation, and of his work and plans. An assignment to go to China in advance of the Nixon media influx as a correspondent for *Life* and *Epoca* had to be postponed (then canceled). In these last months, he was thus finally once again sought after and welcomed back to center stage by a mainstream (and conservative) mass-circulation American periodical, in much the fashion of his peak years with the *Post*. "You have fans, including me," *Life*'s managing editor, Ralph Graves, wrote Snow in July 1971. "I would feel deeply disappointed," Graves told Ed in September, "if your report on the Nixon visit to China did not appear in LIFE."[35]

Ed returned home at the end of December still alluding to recovery and to further work on his book. In early January he could write John Simon of Random House that he had been operated on for "pancreatitis with complications," and that the surgeon "assures me that with proper continued rest and rebuilt resistance I should be back to relatively normal health again in a month or so." And later that month he wrote Premier Zhou, "It is of course greatly disappointing not be in China now but perhaps I can be more useful later." But Snow grew steadily weaker while enduring ineffective chemotherapy treatments.[36]

In these circumstances, the two Chinese leaders with whom his life had been so intertwined gave a valedictory expression of friendship and esteem that now rose above any further considerations of political benefit. (Snow in turn sent final poignant "Dear Friend" messages, dictated to Lois, to the chairman and the premier.) Immediately after hearing the bleak prognosis that followed Ed's surgery, Lois sent a detailed account to George Hatem in Beijing, and a transcript of the medical report. In her anguished state, and with her faith in China's health care system and "miracles," she implored, "can anything be done? I have said that if anything really serious came up I'd go to China (Oh God, we were there when this horrible thing was growing in Ed!). That is why I turn to you. What do you think?" On the basis of Lois's information and appeal, a team of medical specialists and nurses was dispatched from Peking in late January to minister to the stricken journalist.[37]

These last weeks have been movingly recorded by Lois Snow in her book on Ed's terminal illness. ("I read [the book] with tears," Soong Qingling later wrote Lois, "as the face of our dear Ed appeared on every page.") Since Snow was already too ill and weak for the original plan to transport him to Beijing for care and treatment, the Chinese team instead transformed the Snow house into an improvised hospital, greatly easing family burdens and giving Snow as comfortable and dignified an end as was medically and humanly possible. They "released Ed from care and pain," Lois wrote Charles Hogan after Snow's death. Dr. Ma (Hatem), who had trekked into Red China with Ed thirty-six years before, came as a member of the Chinese medical party. Snow slipped in and out of consciousness, rousing himself for a last time during a visit by Huang Hua, now the first ambassador of the People's Republic of China to the United Nations. As Huang and Hatem stood by his bedside, Snow quipped at this reunion of the three "bandits." Ed soon fell into a final coma and, with the Chinese medical group in attendance, died peacefully in the early morning of February 15, the first day of the Chinese lunar New Year. Less than three days later Nixon left Washington for his rendezvous with the Red leaders in Beijing. While Snow would not be among the throng covering the event, Nixon was advised by diplomatic cable from Geneva to "sample" Snow's writings, since "his name [is] likely [to] arise [in] conversation" with the Chinese leaders.[38]

Condolences came from Mao Zedong, Zhou Enlai, and Soong Qingling, and tributes and warm recollections from dignitaries and friends around the world. There were memorial services in Geneva, at the Great Hall of the People in Beijing, and at the United Nations Chapel in New York. In Sneden's Landing, where the Snows had lived for a time after their marriage, old friends gathered to remember and reminisce. Snow some time before had left a brief will and instructions for disposing of the "evidence" after his death. These oft-cited directions distilled much of the essence of his people-centered outlook, and his dual bonds to America and China:

Please cremate the "evidence," mentioned above. Then if you don't mind, someone please scatter some of the ashes over the city of Peking, and say that I loved China, I should like part of me to stay there after death as it always did during life. America fostered and nourished me. I should like part of me to be placed by the Hudson River, before it enters the Atlantic to touch Europe and all the shores of mankind of which I felt a part, as I have known good men in almost every land.

In general accord with these wishes, Snow's ashes were interred in part in the garden of a friend's home overlooking the Hudson in Sneden's Landing, and part on a rise beside No-Name Lake on the lovely campus of Beijing University. It was here, formerly the site of Yanjing, that Ed had taught for a time, and where he liked to stroll along the shores of the serene lake.[39]

Snow always reported with both heart and mind, the former state department China hand John Service wrote in remembrance. Ed recognized that "everyone of the billions of the plain people on this earth is valuable, and deserving of respect," Mary Heathcote said of him. Jim Bertram may have encapsulated his old friend's complex and contradictory makeup best: "a true liberal-democrat-radical, a rational romantic, a practical idealist," he wrote Lois and the children. Snow had given his own, more personal estimate of his life's endeavors in a 1969 letter to Howard: "All the things I thought of doing—learning, writing—increasingly seem beyond attainment and I know that I have done probably the most that I can do in this brief span."[40]

Since Ed's death, Lois Snow has continued to live in her Eysins home, with frequent visits to family and friends in the States, and some return trips to China—but none since Tiananmen. In the first years, she did lectures and articles on China and wrote her account of Ed's final travail; in 1981 she published *Edgar Snow's China,* compiled from Snow's writings on China from 1928 through 1949. Chris and Sian also live in Switzerland. They both now work as translators in Geneva.

How might Snow react to post-Mao China, shorn of its egalitarian-liberationist glow, and with a severely tarnished image of the chairman to whose revolutionary vision the American was so drawn to the end? Very likely the prospect would bring even more forcefully to the surface his skeptical turn of mind, and the troubling thoughts he so often recorded on the pitfalls of authoritarian political systems, fundamentalist thinking, and infallible superleaders. (It is a consummate irony that Snow was so closely linked with a revolutionary icon whose rule came so thoroughly and lethally to epitomize these patterns.) The pain and outrage of Lois Snow, and of Christopher and Sian, to the Tiananmen events of June 1989, may tell us something here. Still, Snow would also welcome China's greater opening to the outside world and its dynamic economic progress—though with a quizzical eye at its "capitalist road" directions and seamy social spin-offs. (Viewing the energetic accomplishments of the Hong Kong Chinese during a visit there in 1968, Snow speculated that if China itself could find a "medium" between such a "selfish" money-making drive and the Maoist preoccupation with "reforming man," then "nobody else could prevail against such a [productive] force.") He would be underscoring the importance of carefully managing the complex, mutually advantageous, but often edgy Sino-American relationship, with its risks always of stirring up cold war–like anti-Communist tendencies on the American side, and still prevalent imperialist perceptions of America on the part of the Chinese—the latter amply documented in David Shambaugh's recent study of China's professional "America Watchers." As the authors of *Sentimental Imperialists* observe, of the China "regained" after 1972, "the danger remained—as always in this relationship—that excessive [American] hopes and illusions would be followed by dangerous despair, disillusionment, and hostility." Snow would probably largely subscribe to the views expressed by former *New York Times* Beijing Bureau Chief Nicholas D. Kristof in a 1993 article: "We should be skeptical of Chinese intentions [as, he had also noted, the Chinese are of ours], without falling into hostility. We should maintain a dialogue with China, even if the tone is not always cordial." China, Kristof added, "is not a villain. It is not a renegade country like Iraq or Libya, but rather an ambitious nation that is becoming the behemoth of the neighborhood. . . . If China is able to sustain its economic miracle, then [the] readjustment of the scales will be one of the most important—and perhaps dangerous—tasks in international relations in the coming decades." For an earlier time, and in a vastly more adversarial Sino-American context, Snow had been alerting his compatriots to such realities.[41]

But beyond China, Snow was above all a master journalist who grippingly and compassionately chronicled a violent and intractable world where the have-nots immensely outnumbered the have-gots. He consistently acted on the belief that he could make a difference in changing things for the better, as he saw it. It was the essence of his commitment as a journalist and of the truths he sought to convey. "My view is that writing justifies itself," he wrote a Chinese journalist in 1964, "if its results add even a very small net contribution to man's knowledge, and I believe that that cannot be done without advancing the interests of the poor and the oppressed of this world, who are the vast majority of men."[42]

However this was never that simple, nor could it be. The revolutionary causes and liberating forces he looked to often fell disappointingly short or spawned new evils of their own. The decades of superpower contention and interventionism, of cold and hot war and nuclear-based arms races, shattered Snow's vision of a new world order—one in which an enlightened and nonimperial America could cooperate with a more benign Soviet heading an Eastern bloc of "fraternal" states, in a peaceful international environment that could accommodate necessary radical change in the have-not regions of the world. When told in China in 1970 that Mao planned to interview him rather than the other way round, Snow reflected that he was merely a "democratic personage," not "a man of power." In essence, Snow could propose, but others disposed.[43]

There was always in Snow a mix of hope and despair, of faith and disillusion—perhaps a mirror of the twentieth-century world he knew—one of unprecedented progress and unspeakable horrors, phenomenal advances and disheartening setbacks. In *Journey* Snow wrote that humankind had come to "a parting time from our pre-history, a true childhood's end when men at last have to begin behaving like Man." The world would have to mature from its "anarchy of nationalism" to "a higher concept of federated world authority," he pursued this theme in *Red China Today*. But in his darker moments he saw "childhood's end" as a distant prospect at best. It was "a childish sentiment" on his part, he confided to Jim Bertram in 1959, not "to see man universally as the ignorant, selfish, fearful and extremely primitive and pathetic creature he is—collectively capable of acting most dynamically only under compulsions of fear, and aggressively, despite individual potentials for behavior of nobility and love and reason."[44]

On a similar note, in an undated fragment Snow wrote (and preserved), probably while working on *Journey,* he reflected on a world that failed to come up to his earlier expectations:

I see that much of my disillusionment after the war was because I still had illusions that [the] war was going to start a new world, that we could relax and enjoy the fruits of hard labor, of hard work, of honest predictions fulfilled. I myself did relax. I resented the intrusion of new dilemmas, new problems. I had forgotten that a billion people still had unsatisfied wants, that oppression of myriad kinds continued. I was satisfied but the rest of the world was not. I wanted peace but other men did not. I believed it was possible to adopt a new behavior in human relationships, international affairs, but other men did not. History had so conditioned them that they could not. Who would and could ever condition them to react in my way? . . . Men do NOT have imagination; cannot be influenced by things they do not experience. See how we have forgotten Maidanek, we do not remember it and learned nothing from it.[45]

Our contemporary age, though marked by impressive strides in human advancement, is still scarred by intensified nationalisms and ethnic, tribal, and religious extremism and conflict in many parts of the globe (magnified further with the collapse of Eastern European and Soviet communism). There are human rights shortfalls, and a continuing gulf between the have-gots and the have-nots of the world. It speaks both to Snow's somber thoughts on collective humanity and on the urgency of his call for "childhood's end." The "richest billion people command 60 times the income of the poorest billion," according to the United Nations 1994 report on human development. "The world can never be at peace unless people have security in their daily lives," it warns. "The new demands of global human security," it adds, "require a more positive relationship among all nations of the world—leading to a new era of development cooperation." And as Bruce Urquhart recently remarked in regard to the problems of global policing and peacekeeping, "Sooner or later, the interdependent nature of the world we have created will pose the choice between a decline into chaos and a global society based on law." Snow's vistas of a demilitarized world of liberated nations and uplifted peoples, united in a collectively secure, equitable, and peaceful international order, remains an ongoing quest of our planet.[46]

Notes

Sources for Introduction

Theodore H. White, *In Search of History* (New York: Harper and Row, 1978), 240; Stephen R. MacKinnon and Oris Friesen, *China Reporting* (Berkeley: University of California Press, 1987), ix; Edgar Snow diaries, Book 73, October 10, 1970, Book 82, November 3, 1970, Book 73, October 1, 5, 1970 (hereafter, Diaries; see explanatory list for abbreviations of other sources used in the notes); John K. Fairbank, letter to the editors, *New York Review of Books,* April 27, 1989, 60; ES to HFS, June 9, 1937, NWC; Diaries, Book 50, November 30, 1945, Book 73, October 7, 1970; Lois Wheeler Snow, speech on tenth anniversary of Edgar Snow's death, Beijing, February 15, 1982, ESC; James C. Thomson, Jr., Peter W. Stanley, and John Curtis Perry, *Sentimental Imperialists: The American Experience in East Asia* (New York: Harper and Row, 1981); ES to James Bertram, October 25, 1952, JBP in ESC; David Wise, review of *Gentleman Spy: The Life of Allen Dulles,* by Peter Grose, *New York Times Book Review,* December 11, 1994, 9.

Chapter 1. Setting

1. Diaries, Book 5, February 21, 1931.
2. *Journey,* or *JTTB* (New York: Random House, 1958), 11.
3. ES to father, April 11, 1933, MP in ESC.
4. *JTTB,* 178; ES to Kenneth Shewmaker, September 26, 1969, ESP in ESC. As a uniquely influential reporter on the Chinese Communists, Snow's name could show up as a generic term for later (presumably favorable) firsthand journalistic accounts of the Chinese Reds. U.S. ambassador to China Clarence E. Gauss, in a February 29, 1944, dispatch to the state department on the projected visit by Chungking-based foreign correspondents to the Red areas in northwestern China, noted that according to critics of the Kuomintang, the present

trip by the correspondents to Yan'an "may result in the Kuomintang's having to face eleven Edgar Snows instead of just one" (*Foreign Relations of the United States, Diplomatic Papers, 1944*. Vol. 6, *China* [Washington, D.C.: U.S. Government Printing Office, 1967], 365–367).

5. Letter to the editors, *New York Review of Books,* April 27, 1989, 16; ES to James Bertram, April 5, 1959, JBP in ESC; ES to Rewi Alley, July 22, 1955, RAP in ESC.

6. ES to "Ross," May 8, 1971, ES to Charles White, December 27, 1954, ESP in ESC; ES to James Bertram, October 25, 1952.

7. ES to Howard Snow, May 1, 1954, HSP in ESC; ES to James Bertram, March 25, 1958, JBP in ESC. Snow could easily relate to Webb's lament that risk-taking individualism was being replaced by the growth of institutions "which take the risks and responsibilities and give in return a sense of security" to its members. The latter "constitute the army of satisfied and timid souls who are not willing to take a chance, bet on themselves, back their own ego by disputing authority or asserting leadership" (*The Great Frontier* [Austin: University of Texas Press, 1951], 116–117).

8. For an overview of the work of these historians see Richard Bernstein, "Unsettling the Old West," *New York Times Magazine,* March 18, 1990, 34, 56–59.

9. Stanley J. Kunitz and Howard Haycraft, eds., *Twentieth-Century Authors* (New York: H. H. Wilson, 1942), 1310; *JTTB,* 14–15. "I could find no record that William [Snow] the progenitor from Virginia, was any relation to this Cap. Sam. who hailed from Salem" (ES to Howard, May 1, 1953, HSP in ESC). Also, ES in Eleanor Babcock correspondence, September 1, 1951, July 3, 1952, February 1, 1953, ESC.

10. ES, Autobiographical Note (1944), RHP; ES to father, September 6, 1933, MP in ESC; "A Resolution Honoring the Late Mr. Edgar A. Snow on the Fourth Anniversary of His Death," February 13, 1976, ESC.

11. *JTTB,* 3; Nym Wales (Helen Foster Snow), Biographical Note on Edgar Snow (1938), RHP.

12. Diaries, Book 60, July 13, 1963.

13. Aunt Sallie to ES, May 13, 1951, ESP in ESC; Diaries, Book 10, January 19, 1933.

14. Kunitz and Haycraft, eds., *Twentieth-Century Authors,* 1310; ES to mother, November 22, 1929, MP in ESC; interview with Dr. Charles White, July 19, 1986.

15. Interview with Claude Mackey, July 11, 1987; ES to Mildred, May 29, 1931, ES to Mildred, November 22, 1932, MP in ESC.

16. Father to ES, March 15, 1930, MP in ESC. Progressive Republican Senator George W. Norris of Nebraska declared in 1911 that it was "in the city that we have the slum and the breeding places of anarchy, ignorance, and crime. It is there we have the mob" (quoted in Richard Lowitt, *George W. Norris: The Making of a Progressive, 1861–1912* [Syracuse: Syracuse University Press, 1963], 203); father to ES, December 4, 1933, father to Howard and ES, April 26, 1941, MP in ESC.

17. Thomas Hart Benton, *An Artist in America* (Columbia: University of Missouri Press, 1968), 262. Benton, who had resided in New York for twenty-

four years, added, "I wouldn't have missed living in New York even if I am now through with it forever" (269).

18. Interview with Claude Mackey, July 11, 1987; ES to father, March 21, 1929, MP in ESC.

19. Diaries, Book 71, August 1970; *JTTB*, 14; "The Message of Gandhi," *SEP*, March 27, 1948, 24; Autobiographical Note (1944).

20. Father to ES, May 13, 1930, ES to Mildred, February 15, 1951, MP in ESC; Autobiographical Note (1944). The hospital autopsy and medical records attributed Snow's mother's death specifically to a postoperative infection in the abdomen and urinary tract (Robert M. Farnsworth, ed., *Edgar Snow's Journey South of the Clouds* [Columbia: University of Missouri Press, 1991], introduction, 11), which did not necessarily resolve the matter of neglect or incompetence on the part of the hospital staff.

21. ES to father, November 10, 1933, MP in ESC.

22. Father to ES, November 19, 1941, MP in ESC; Diaries, Book 60, July 13, 1963. Perhaps characteristically J. Edgar had earlier inadvertently signed away to his sisters his share in an additional 280-acre inheritance from Horace Parks, resulting in much acrimony and a failed lawsuit brought by J. Edgar's heirs in the 1960s.

Chapter 2. Kansas City

1. Diaries, Book 60, July 13, 1963; Malcolm Cowley, *The Literary Situation* (New York: Viking Press, 1954), 162; Stanley J. Kunitz and Howard Haycraft, eds., *Twentieth-Century Authors* (New York: H. H. Wilson, 1942), 1310.

2. Diaries, Book 60, July 13, 1963; Interview with Edgar Snow, Armed Forces Radio, Tokyo, January 29, 1946, ESC.

3. Details on Kansas City history and politics are based on the following sources: *Missouri: A Guide to the "Show Me" State,* compiled by writers of the Works Projects Administration of Missouri (New York: Duell, Sloan and Pearce, 1941); Henry C. Haskell, Jr., and Richard B. Fowler, *City of the Future: A Narrative History of Kansas City, 1850–1950* (Kansas City: Frank Glenn Publishing, 1950); William Reddig, *Tom's Town* (Philadelphia: J. B. Lippincott, 1947); Lyle W. Dorsett, *The Pendergast Machine* (New York: Oxford University Press, 1968); William E. Parrish, Charles T. Jones, Jr., Lawrence O. Christensen, *Missouri: The Heart of the Nation* (St. Louis: Forum Press, 1980).

4. David McCullough, *Truman* (New York: Simon and Schuster, 1992), 193–252.

5. Diaries, Book 52, January 23, 1947; Edgar Snow, "Missouri Days," unpublished ms. chapter, RHP.

6. Parrish, et al., *Missouri,* 283–292; Frederick Lewis Allen, *Only Yesterday: An Informal History of the Nineteen Twenties* (New York: Harper and Brothers, 1931), 45–75.

7. Snow later wrote, "The harsh talk about British imperialism I heard in childhood from Irish relatives, strong sympathizers with the Sinn Feiners, must have helped prepare me to believe that morality always lay on the side of rebellion, and divinity as well, where Britain was the overlord" (*JTTB*, 25).

8. Diaries, Book 60, July 13, 1963; ES to Mildred, November 22, 1932, MP in ESC.

9. Diaries, Book 60, July 13, 1963; "Missouri Days."

10. *Yenching News,* Peking, October 23, 1934. In December of 1934 the two institutions formalized their relationship in a Yenching-Missouri Foundation to promote education in the profession of journalism (*Yenching News,* December 20, 1934). For details on the Missouri-China connection, see John Maxwell Hamilton, "The Missouri News Monopoly and American Altruism in China: Thomas F. F. Millard, J. B. Powell, and Edgar Snow," *Pacific Historical Review* 55 (February 1986): 28–29; and Robert Stevens, "J. B. Powell and the Missouri-China Connection," *Missouri Historical Review* 82 (April 1988): 274–275.

11. "Missouri Days."

12. Interview with Dr. Charles White, September 13, 1978, ESC.

13. ES to "Dear Tony," July 11, 1968, ESP in ESC; *JTTB,* 30; Lois Wheeler Snow, *A Death with Dignity: When the Chinese Came* (New York: Random House, 1974), 36; ES to Charles White, December 27, 1954, ESP in ESC.

14. HFS to David Barbosa, December 1, 1988, HFS files; *Westport Herald* (1923), 127, Henry Mitchell Papers in ESC.

15. "Missouri Days"; ES to mother, October 31, 1927, MP in ESC.

16. Diaries, Book 52, January 23, 1947.

Chapter 3. New York and Beyond

1. Jules Abels, *In the Time of Silent Cal* (New York: G. P. Putnam's Sons, 1969), 227, 229; Allen, *Only Yesterday,* 180–181.

2. ES to father, March 21, 1927, MP in ESC; interview with John Snow (Howard's son), November 22, 1988.

3. ES to Mildred, August 8, 1926, ES to family, January 9, 1928, MP in ESC; Interview with Edgar Snow, Tokyo, January 29, 1946; *JTTB,* 3.

4. ES to father, March 21, 1927, ES to Mildred, August 8, 1926, ES to father, October 3, 1927, MP in ESC.

5. ES to Mildred, March 6, 1927, ES to mother, May 16, 1927, ES to father, December 16, 1927, MP in ESC; ES, "They Don't Want to Play Soldier," *SEP,* October 25, 1941, 61.

6. ES to Mildred, March 6, 1927.

7. ES to father, October 3, 1927, MP in ESC; Interview with Edgar Snow, Tokyo, January 29, 1946; ES to family, January 9, 1928; ES to father, December 16, 1927; Autobiographical Note (1944).

8. Kermit Roosevelt to ES, February 23, 1928, ESP in ESC.

9. ES to parents, February 17, February 22, 1928, MP in ESC.

10. Diaries, Book 35, September 22, 1941.

11. ES to parents, February 17, 1928, ES to W. Laurence Dickey, February 22, 1928, MP in ESC; Stephen R. MacKinnon and Oris Friesen, *China Reporting* (Berkeley: University of California Press, 1987), 32–33.

12. John Maxwell Hamilton, *Edgar Snow, A Biography* (Bloomington: Indiana University Press, 1988), 11–12; William Rose Benét, ed., *The Reader's Encyclo-*

pedia (New York: Thomas Y. Crowell, 1948), 475; interview with Dr. Charles White, July 19, 1986.

13. Diaries, Book 1, February 26, 1928.

14. Ibid.

15. Ibid., ES to Howard, March 26, 1928, MP in ESC; Autobiographical Note (1944).

16. ES to Charles Hanson Towne, March 7, 1928, CHTP.

17. Charles Hanson Towne to ES, May 22, 1928, CHTP; ES to mother, July 28, 1928, MP in ESC. Ed had already rhapsodized over a "divine night" on Waikiki in a fifteen-page letter to Howard from Honolulu, April 5, 1928, MP in ESC.

18. "In Hula Land," *Harper's Bazaar* 62 (September 1928): 98–99, 136, 138, 142.

19. ES to Al Joslin, June 21, 1928, ESC; Diaries, Book 60, July 5, 1963.

20. ES to Charles Hanson Towne, June 26, 1928, CHTP.

21. Ibid; *New York Herald-Tribune Magazine,* October 21, 1928, 10–11, 14; "Kansas City Boy Stowaway," *Kansas City Journal-Post,* November 11, 1928.

22. ES to Mildred, July 31, 1928, MP in ESC.

23. ES to mother, July 28, 1928, MP in ESC.

Chapter 4. "New Influences and Ideas"

1. Cited in Emily Hahn, *The Soong Sisters* (New York: Doubleday, Doran, 1943), 139–143.

2. *JTTB,* 16.

3. *Far Eastern Front,* or *FEF* (New York: Harrison Smith and Robert Haas, 1933), 182; Interview with Edgar Snow, Tokyo, ESC.

4. Theodore H. White, *In Search of History* (New York: Harper and Row, 1978), 62, 63.

5. *JTTB,* 4; ES to Mildred, July 31, 1928, ES to mother, July 28, 1928, MP in ESC.

6. Stephen R. MacKinnon and Oris Friesen, *China Reporting* (Berkeley: University of California Press, 1987), 3 (introduction by James C. Thomson), 31–32.

7. Ibid., 26.

8. Randall Gould to Benjamin Mandel, August 29, 1954, Randall Gould Papers; John W. Powell, "Three American Reporters in China," paper presented at Smedley-Strong-Snow seminar, Shanghai, March 1987. Details on J. B. Powell and the *Review* from the following sources: John B. Powell, *My Twenty-Five Years in China* (New York: Macmillan, 1945); Robert Stevens, "J. B. Powell and the Missouri-China Connection," *Missouri Historical Review* 82 (April 1988): 267–279; Hamilton, "The Missouri News Monopoly and American Altruism in China," 30–41; interview with John W. Powell, July 6, 1987. The *Review* resumed publication in Shanghai after the war under Powell's son, John W. (Bill) Powell.

9. ES to Mildred, July 31, 1928, MP in ESC; *JTTB,* 25, 22.

10. John W. Powell, "My Father's Library," *Wilson Library Bulletin,* March 1986, 36.

11. ES to father, August 15, 1928, MP in ESC.

12. ES to mother, August 21, 1928, MP in ESC; Diaries, Book 1, undated entry.

13. ES to mother, August 21, 1928, MP in ESC.

14. ES to father, September 17, 1928, ES to Howard, September 28, 1928, MP in ESC. Snow's article was entitled "Lifting China Out of the Mud!" New China edition, *CWR,* October 10, 1928, 84–91.

15. "Adventures in Chinese Advertising," *Advertising & Selling,* May 1, 1929, 30, 32, 90, 92. (Typically, in his "Chinese Advertising" article, Snow ranged beyond the narrower confines of this topic to include an informative look at the Chinese media, literacy rates and reading habits, and a culture-sensitive view of Chinese marketing practices.) M. J. Harris to ES, December 17, 1928; Howard to father, date missing, probably October or November 1928, MP in ESC.

16. ES to Howard, October 28, 1928, MP in ESC.

17. C. Y. W. Meng, "China's Japan Policy after the Tsinan Settlement," *CWR,* April 13, 1929, 292, 294.

18. ES, "Japanese Interference at the Yellow River Bridge—and Other Aspects of Tsinanfu," *CWR,* January 19, 1929, 318.

19. ES to Howard, January 17, 1929, Howard to family, January 15, 1929, MP in ESC.

20. ES to father, March 21, 1929, MP in ESC.

21. Kenneth E. Shewmaker, *Americans and Chinese Communists, 1927–1945: A Persuading Encounter* (Ithaca: Cornell University Press, 1971), 297–319, 335–346; *JTTB,* 178; *Red Star Over China,* or *RSOC* (New York: Random House, 1938), 66–67; ES to Mildred (from Simla, India), May 29, 1951, MP in ESC.

22. ES to father, March 21, 1929, MP in ESC.

23. ES to mother, May 6, 1929, MP in ESC; *JTTB,* 5–6. In *JTTB* Snow recalled Hu's name as "something like" C. T. Washington Wu, apparently deliberately fictionalizing the name. And Harvard no longer takes any of the blame for Hu.

24. Rewi Alley, *At 90: Memoirs of My China Years* (Beijing: New World Press, 1986), 57–58; *JTTB,* 8. Snow and Alley recalled these details somewhat differently. According to Alley, after the rebuff by Hu, he returned to his refugees "and sat on the floor until we got to Salaqi in the middle of the night." Snow talks of a stopover, where he says he and Alley did some local investigating, and "next day we rode on to Saratsi." Alley makes no mention of these meetings. In an earlier account, Alley noted that while he and some student volunteers were digging telephone postholes in Saratsi, Snow came by in the company of O. J. Todd. But Alley adds, "Ed busily writing and Todd talking, they were too busy to notice us" (paper presented by Alley at Inner Mongolia symposium commemorating the eightieth birthday of Edgar Snow, July 1985, 3-S Society files, Beijing).

25. Alley, *At 90,* 59.

26. *JTTB,* 5; ES, "Saving 250,000 Lives," *New York Herald-Tribune Magazine,* September 8, 1929, 14–15, 31; *Kansas City Journal-Post,* September 12, 1929;

CWR, August 3, 1929, 418–424; mailing by "China Famine Relief, U.S.A.," September 17, 1929, MP in ESC.

27. ES, "Son of the Grand Marshal," *New York Herald-Tribune Magazine,* December 15, 1929, 14–15, 25; Barbara W. Tuchman, *Stilwell and the American Experience in China, 1911–45* (New York: Macmillan, 1970), 131; J. B. Powell, "The Truth about the Sino-Soviet Dispute in Manchuria," *CWR,* September 7, 1929, 42–43; "The Soviet Attempt to Steal 76,000 Square Miles of Chinese Territory!" *CWR,* December 28, 1929, 129–132.

28. ES, "Which Way Manchuria," *CWR,* July 20, 1929, 334.

29. ES to family, August 18, 1929; ES to mother, November 13, 1929, MP in ESC; Shewmaker, *Americans and Chinese Communists,* 20–33.

30. "The 'Middle Kingdom' from the Clouds," *CWR,* October 19, 1929, 273.

31. "Chinese Please Use Rear Entrance," *CWR,* November 9, 1929, 369; Hamilton, *Edgar Snow,* 29; John W. Powell, "Three American Reporters in China," 4.

32. ES, "Chinese Guests Now Welcome," *New York Sun,* September 25, 1930.

33. Howard to mother, July 12, 1929, Howard to family, October 27, 1929, Howard to mother, October 30, 1929, MP in ESC.

34. Howard to family, January 15, 1929, Howard to ES, February 4, 1929, ES to Howard, February 21, 1929, ES to mother, May 6, 1929, Howard to mother, undated, probably late 1929, MP in ESC.

35. ES to mother, January 7, 1930 (misdated 1929), MP in ESC.

36. ES to mother, November 22, 1929, ES to family, December 2, 1929, MP in ESC.

37. ES to mother, December 19, 1929, MP in ESC.

38. Horace Epes (Consolidated Press) to ES, April 10, 1930, ESP in ESC.

39. ES to Howard, May 17, June 3, 1930, MP in ESC.

40. ES to Howard, June 3, 1930, ES to mother, November 22, 1929, ES to Mildred, January 22, 1931, MP in ESC.

41. ES to Howard, December 7, 1931, MP in ESC. Whatever orders he might receive, Snow added parenthetically, came "from the remoteness of Washington, D.C." (the headquarters of Con Press).

42. ES to Howard, May 17 and June 3, 1930. Snow had no patience for Americans with large real estate holdings in Shanghai who, through extraterritoriality, "pay taxes neither to the American government nor to the Chinese" (ES to Horace Epes, August 26, 1930, ESP in ESC).

43. ES, "The Americans in Shanghai," *American Mercury* 20 (August 1930): 427–445.

44. Helen Foster Snow, *My China Years* (New York: William Morrow, 1984), 29, 31; *JTTB,* 85; ES to father, April 11, 1930, MP in ESC.

45. *JTTB,* 22–23.

46. ES to father, December 13, 1929, MP in ESC.

47. ES, "China Creates a New God," *New York Herald-Tribune Magazine,* March 16, 1930, 14; ES to father, April 11, 1930, MP in ESC.

48. "Helen Foster Snow," Oral History Research Office, Columbia University, New York, 1977, 13.

49. ES to father, February 15, 1930, MP in ESC.

50. Ibid. "You will never forget the experience you have had but take my suggestion and do not stay too long in that benighted country," Graham wrote Ed. Why not "come back to civilization and write a book about it" (Kelley Graham to ES, August 13, 1929, ESP in ESC).

51. Diaries, Book 1, late 1930.

Chapter 5. Travel Is Broadening

1. Horace Epes to ES, July 25, 1932, ESP in ESC. Cables should be used for specially ordered stories, "or when your own good judgment tells you that you should rush something through," Epes advised (Epes to ES, August 20, 1930, ESP in ESC).

2. ES to father, June 13, 1931, MP in ESC; ES to Horace Epes, May 28, 1931, Horace Epes to ES, June 23, September 11, 1931, ES to Horace Epes, October 25, 1931, ESP in ESC.

3. ES to Horace Epes, May 28, 1931, ESP in ESC; ES to Charles Towne, August 6, 1931, CHTP.

4. Diaries, Book 2, undated entry, probably early or mid-1930. (See Farnsworth, *Snow's Journey,* for texts of ES's World Today feature articles.)

5. Diaries, Book 1A, September 27, October 2, 1930; ES, "Some Results of 35 Years of Japanese Rule in Formosa," *CWR,* November 15, 1930, 389.

6. *JTTB,* 38.

7. *New York Sun,* April 9, 28, 1931; ES, "The Hard Lot of Women Prisoners in Hon San-so," in Farnsworth, *Snow's Journey,* 94–97; Diaries, Book 1A, November 18, 1930.

8. Diaries, Book 1, November 29, 1930, Book 3, November 23, 1930; *JTTB,* 44–45.

9. *JTTB,* 46; *New York Sun,* September 28, 1931.

10. *New York Sun,* June 30, 1931.

11. *JTTB,* 49.

12. Diaries, Book 4, January 24, 1931.

13. Diaries, Book 5, February 13, 1931.

14. Diaries, Book 6, March 9, 1931.

15. Diaries, Book 6, February 23, 1931, Book 5, February 20, 1931.

16. Diaries, Book 4, February 8, 1931, Book 5, February 21, 1931, Book 6, February 25, 1931, March 11, 1931.

17. ES to Howard, December 8, 1930, ES to Dorothy, March 20, 1931, MP in ESC.

18. Diaries, Book 6, March 12–13, 1931.

19. *JTTB,* 63–70.

20. S. B. Thomas, "Burma," in *The State of Asia,* Lawrence K. Rosinger and Associates (New York: Alfred A. Knopf, 1951), 296.

21. Diaries, Book 7, March 18–April 22, 1931.

22. Diaries, Book 7, March 15, 1931.

23. M. J. Akbar, *Nehru: The Making of India* (New York: Viking, 1988), 232–234; William L. Shirer, *Gandhi, A Memoir* (New York: Simon and Schus-

ter, 1979), 55–58; *JTTB,* 76. In hindsight, chronicles of these events tend to see the Gandhi-Irwin accord, despite its failure appreciably to advance the independence cause, as an historic breakthrough, in that the viceroy had negotiated with the Indian leader as an equal and gained him worldwide attention both in India and the world. "The psychological impact on an enslaved nation was extraordinary" (Akbar, *Nehru,* 233; also Shirer, *Gandhi,* 55). Vincent Sheean, who became an ardent disciple of Gandhi, went considerably further in declaring that "the main point" on Indian independence was gained in the Gandhi-Irwin pact, "all the rest was detail" (*Mahatma Gandhi* [New York: Alfred A. Knopf, 1955], 162).

24. ES to Horace Epes, May 28, 1931, ESP in ESC. Though coming from opposite poles, Snow's characterization echoed that of the arch-imperialist Winston Churchill, who declared that the "seditious" Gandhi was "now posing as a fakir of a type well known in the East" (cited in Akbar, *Nehru,* 233); Diaries, Book 7, May 1, 1931; ES to father, June 13, 1931.

25. ES, "The Message of Gandhi," 243; Shirer, *Gandhi,* 227.

26. *JTTB,* 403.

27. *New York Sun,* October 29, 1931.

28. Diaries, Book 7, April 29, 1931; Book 8, June 29, 1931.

29. ES, "The Trial of British Communists at Meerut, India," *CWR,* September 19, 1931, 106 (reprinted from *New York Sun*).

30. ES, "The Revolt of India's Women," *New York Herald-Tribune Magazine,* October 25, 1931, 14–15, 24–25; *JTTB,* 79; Janice R. MacKinnon and Stephen R. MacKinnon, *Agnes Smedley: The Life and Times of an American Radical* (Berkeley: University of California Press, 1988), 70–73, 290; letter to author from Ram Chattopadhyaya (nephew of Virendrenath), September 25, 1989. Chatto apparently died in a labor camp.

31. *JTTB,* 80; Diaries, Book 7, May 1931; ES to Mildred, May 29, 1931, MP in ESC.

32. *JTTB,* 81–82.

Chapter 6. Shanghai Again

1. ES to Mildred, May 29 and August 13, 1931, ES to father, June 13, 1931, MP in ESC; ES to Towne, August 6, 1931, CHTP.

2. HFS to Kenneth Shewmaker, cited in Shewmaker, *Americans and Chinese Communists,* 77; ES to Howard, June 3, 1930, MP in ESC.

3. Horace Epes to ES, September 11, 1931, ES to Epes, October 25, 1931, ESP in ESC; ES to Mildred, March 31, 1932, MP in ESC. Epes did send Snow a few hundred dollars to help defray Ed's out-of-pocket expenses on his 1930–1931 travels.

4. Horace Epes to ES, April 7, 1932, ESP in ESC; L. MacBride to Powell, February 16, 1932, ESC.

5. ES, "In the Wake of China's Flood," *CWR,* January 23, 1932, 243–245; reprinted from *New York Herald-Tribune Magazine,* December 6, 1931.

6. *FEF,* 93–95, 125–127; ES to Howard, December 7, 1931, MP in ESC.

7. ES to father, January 2, 1932, MP in ESC.

8. ES to Horace Epes, January 3, 1932, ESP in ESC.

9. ES to Howard, December 7, 1931, MP in ESC.

10. ES to father, January 2, 1932, MP in ESC.

11. ES to Dorothy, January 12, 1932, MP in ESC.

12. Howard L. Boorman, ed., *Biographical Dictionary of Republican China* (New York: Columbia University Press, 1970), 3:290–293.

13. *FEF*, 209–210; *JTTB*, 96–97. After the Shanghai "war," the station master gave a banquet for Snow (*JTTB*, 101).

14. *FEF*, 255.

15. ES to Horace Epes, March 1, 1932, ESP in ESC.

16. *FEF*, 302, 292–293.

17. ES to Horace Epes, March 1, 1932, Horace Epes to ES, April 7, 1932, ESP in ESC; ES to Dorothy, January 12, 1932, ES to Mildred, March 31, 1932, MP in ESC.

18. ES to Horace Epes, May 17, 1932, ESP in ESC; ES to Howard, May 17, 1932, MP in ESC; ES to Horace Epes, June 27, 1932, Horace Epes to ES, July 25, 1932, ESP in ESC.

19. ES to Howard and Dorothy, undated (late July 1932), MP in ESC.

20. Ibid., ES to Horace Epes, June 15, 1933, ESP in ESC; ES to Howard, September 6, 1933, ES to father, November 10, 1933, MP in ESC.

21. For the reviews specifically cited: C.H.H., "Not All Quiet on 'Far Eastern Front,'" *CWR*, November 25, 1933, 540–542; Lin Yutang, *China Critic*, December 14, 1933; Harold R. Isaacs, "Puerility in Print," *China Forum*, December 21, 1933, 16. In his final book Isaacs uncharitably summed up his view of Snow as one "who did his journalistic fellow-travelling around an orbit somewhat more distant [than Agnes Smedley and Anna Louise Strong] from the hardcore center, [but] stayed faithful in his fashion until his death in 1972" (*Re-Encounters in China* [Armonk, N.Y.: M. E. Sharpe, 1985], 74 n.).

22. *FEF*, 310–332.

23. ES, "The Strength of Communism in China, I: The Bolshevist Influence," and Reginald E. Sweetland, "The Strength of Communism in China, II: Banditry in a New Guise," *Current History* 33 (January 1931): 521–531.

24. ES, "Daughters of China's Revolution," *New York Herald-Tribune Magazine*, April 6, 1930, 2–3; *JTTB*, 82; Isaacs, *Re-Encounters in China*, 63. For a recent biography of Madame Sun, see Israel Epstein, *Woman in World History: Life and Times of Soong Ching Ling (Mme. Sun Yatsen)* (Beijing: New World Press, 1993).

25. *JTTB*, 83–84; Israel Epstein, "Strong, Smedley, Snow and Their Links with Soong Ching Ling in Shanghai" (paper presented at seminar on Anna Louise Strong, Agnes Smedley, and Edgar Snow, Shanghai, March 1988); Epstein, *Woman in World History*, 301.

26. ES, "Salute to Lu Hsun," *democracy* (Beiping), June 8, 1937, 87; Harold R. Isaacs, ed., *Straw Sandals: Chinese Short Stories, 1918–1933* (Cambridge, Mass.: MIT Press, 1974), xii; Harriet C. Mills, "Lu Xun: Literature and Revolution— From Mara to Marx," in *Modern Chinese Literature in the May Fourth Era*, ed. Merle Goldman (Cambridge, Mass.: Harvard University Press, 1977), 189, 211–220. Mills observes that Lu Xun "in his later years had shifted his hopes for China from the Guomindang at Nanking to the Communist opposition" (189).

27. *JTTB*, 132–133; Isaacs, *Re-Encounters in China*, 22; Isaacs, *Straw Sandals*, xxxiii, xxxviii; Frederic Wakeman, Jr., *Policing Shanghai, 1927–1937* (Berkeley: University of California Press, 1995), 132, 160 (*CWR* of March 28, 1936 cited on 160).

28. Isaacs, *Re-Encounters in China*, 33–36; Tsi-An Hsia, "The Enigma of the Five Martyrs," in *The Gate of Darkness* (Seattle: University of Washington Press, 1968), 163–233; *JTTB*, 87 (Snow incorrectly gives a 1932 date). Both Isaacs and Hsia voice the strong suspicion that this meeting of an opposition faction had been betrayed to the settlement police by the Communist leadership itself.

29. Hsia, "Enigma of the Five Martyrs," 232–233; John K. Fairbank, review of *Re-Encounters in China*, in *CQ* 105 (March 1986): 146–147; ES, comp. and ed., *Living China*, or *LC* (New York: John Day, 1936). Some of these translations had appeared first in *Asia*. Harold Isaacs had been making a similar collection, also with Lu Xun's help, during his *China Forum* years. Isaac's volume, *Straw Sandals*, was not published until 1977. Isaacs claimed that his break with the Stalinist left in 1934 had turned off prospective publishers in the United States, who feared they would lose a built-in (and necessary) pro-Communist market for the book. Snow "did not suffer from my handicaps," Isaacs cuttingly remarked in his introduction to *Straw Sandals* (xliv).

30. ES to Howard, March 2, 1932, MP in ESC; *JTTB*, 124, 133; ES to Mr. Henle, May 10, 1935, NWC.

31. ES, "Lu Shun, Master of Pai-Hua," *Asia* 35 (January 1935): 42 (reprinted in *LC*, 21–28); *JTTB*, 87.

32. *New York Sun*, October 18, 1932; ES, "She Fights for China's Masses," *New York Herald-Tribune Magazine*, August 6, 1933, 11.

33. ES to Horace Epes, June 27, 1932, September 11, 1932, ESP in ESC; "She Fights for China's Masses," 19.

34. *FEF*, 164–167, 328–329.

35. ES to father, April 11, 1933, MP in ESC; *JTTB*, 138; Audrey Williamson, *Bernard Shaw: Man and Writer* (New York: Crowell-Collier Press, 1963), 35–36. Williamson describes the Marxist-oriented Fabian Society, founded in 1884, as "a body of educated middle-class intelligentsia" (35); ES to Mildred, November 22, 1932, MP in ESC. Reacting to a book on eugenics he had recently read, Snow commented, "I'm almost inclined to think eugenics is perhaps the only thing that will save the next generation from being dominantly Negro, low class immigrant, or intelligence quota x or y" (ibid.).

36. ES to Howard, September 6, 1933; HFS to J. Edgar Snow, September 27, 1953, MP in ESC; "Charges of radical activities against Mr. Snow," Memorandum of Conversation with Mr. Edgar Snow, Peiping, July 5, 1933, NTJP.

37. ES to Nelson T. Johnson, February 6, 1937, ES to T. T. Li, Director, Intelligence and Publicity, Ministry of Foreign Affairs, February 4, 1937, NTJP; HFS, *My China Years*, 64; John Gunther, *Inside Asia* (New York: Harper and Brothers, 1939), 283.

38. ES to Howard, July 20, 1935, MP in ESC.

Chapter 7. Peking

1. HFS to Dick Wilson, April 17, 1988; HFS, "Self-Portrait: For Whom It May Concern" (1988), Supplementary (Autobiographical) Notes on Helen Fos-

ter Snow (Nym Wales) (1988), HFS files; Nym Wales, "Old China Hands," *New Republic,* April 1, 1967, 14.

2. Supplementary Notes on Helen Foster Snow; interview with HFS, October 13, 1987; HFS, *My China Years,* 87; *JTTB,* 102; James Bertram to author, July 30, 1989; John K. Fairbank, *Chinabound: A Fifty-Year Memoir* (New York: Harper and Row, 1982), 127; HFS, "The Snow Syndrome" (undated), HFS files.

3. Supplementary Notes on Helen Foster Snow; "My Father, John Moody Foster (1880–1948)," HFS files; Evans F. Carlson to Miss Le Hand, November 15, 1938, Franklin D. Roosevelt Library.

4. Supplementary Notes on Helen Foster Snow.

5. Ibid.; *JTTB,* 103; James Bertram to author, July 30, 1989; HFS, *My China Years,* 19–20, 47.

6. ES to Mildred and father, December 13, 1932, MP in ESC; *JTTB,* 103. A major reason for inventing her pseudonym, HFS states, was to avoid "compromising" Ed through her writings. Notes on the Nym Wales Collection (December 1990), HFS files. "Nym," Greek for "name," and "Wales," for Peg's part-Welsh ancestry. Her three poems appeared in *The Saturday Review Treasury* (New York: Simon and Schuster, 1957), 165–166.

7. Interview with HFS, March 10, 1990; ES to Horace Epes, December 11, 1932, ESP in ESC; ES, "Christmas Escapade in Japan," *Travel,* January 1935, 34–38, 47; *JTTB,* 108–109.

8. *JTTB,* 106; HFS, *My China Years,* 74–75; "Helen Foster Snow," 49; ES to Mildred and father, December 13, 1932, MP in ESC; ES to Charles Hanson Towne, March 30, 1933, CHTP.

9. HFS, *My China Years,* 74–76; Diaries, Book 10, January 14, 19, 1933. Describing the Tokyo wedding ceremony to Howard, Ed wrote that Peg said he had repeated the vows "parrotlike" (ES to Howard, December 27, 1932, MP in ESC).

10. "Helen Foster Snow," 38. On the constitutional reformist Fabian path to socialism, see Michael Holroyd, *Bernard Shaw,* vol. 2, *The Pursuit of Power* (New York: Random House, 1989), 128.

11. Diaries, Book 10, January 1–4, 1933.

12. Diaries, Book 10, January 9, 19, 1933. The Shapiros, Snow commented, had "a Jewish fondness for mimicry," and "a Jewish love of gems, of which they have made an astonishing collection—for impecunious (as they pose) school teachers" (ibid.).

13. Diaries, Book 10, January 15–18, 1933; *JTTB,* 115; ES to father, February 16, 1933, MP in ESC.

14. ES, "The Decline of Western Prestige," *SEP,* August 26, 1933, 12–14, 67–69; ES to father, April 11, 1933, MP in ESC.

15. Fairbank, *Chinabound,* 52.

16. ES to father, April 11, 1933, MP in ESC.

17. ES to Howard, May 8, 1934, MP in ESC; James Bertram, *Capes of China Slide Away: A Memoir of Peace and War, 1910–1980* (Auckland: Auckland University Press, 1993), 94; in *The Years That Were Fat: The Last of Old China* (New York: Harper, 1952), George N. Kates reminisces about "gentle Peking."

18. Stephen R. MacKinnon and Oris Friesen, *China Reporting* (Berkeley: University of California Press, 1987), 27–28, 196; Nym Wales (NW), "Notes on the Chinese Student Movement, 1935–1936," NWC, 87 (mimeographed).

19. ES to John K. Fairbank, January 25, 1957, JKFP; HFS, *My China Years,* 91; Fairbank, *Chinabound,* 40; Nym Wales, "The Modern Chinese Literary Movement," appendix A, *LC,* 335–355. Xiao Qian, then a Yanjing student and later a noted Chinese literary critic and author (one of his stories was included in *LC*), worked on the translations with Snow. He felt Snow could not read Chinese effectively, depending on his assistants to read and translate to him. He also judged Peg "pretentious" in passing judgment on Chinese writers in her essay when she herself could not read Chinese (interview with Xiao Qian, Beijing, May 19, 1987).

20. *JTTB,* 121; HFS, "Snow Syndrome"; ES to father, April 11, 1933, MP in ESC.

21. Horace Epes to ES, April 8, 1933, ESP in ESC; HFS to J. Edgar Snow, September 17, 1933, MP in ESC; *JTTB,* 125–126; HFS, *My China Years,* 122–124.

22. *JTTB,* 126–134.

23. ES to Horace Epes, December 9, 1933, Horace Epes to ES, December 18, 1933, January 12, 1934, ESP in ESC.

24. ES to Peter Dolan (*New York Sun* news editor), May 7, 1934, ESP in ESC.

25. HFS to Bai Ye, November 14, 1979, received from Bai Ye; Diaries, Book 77, October 5, 1970; ES to Horace Epes, April 25, 1935, ESP in ESC.

26. ES to father, March 3, 1934, MP in ESC.

27. ES to Henriette Herz, February 6, 1934, Henriette Herz to Harrison Smith, March 6, 1934, Harrison Smith to Henriette Herz, March 10, 1934, RHP; ES to Nelson T. Johnson, February 6, 1937, NTJP; ES to Henriette Herz, March 20, 1934, ESP in ESC.

28. ES to Henriette Herz, February 6, 1934; ES to Horace Epes, April 25, 1935, ESP in ESC. Snow's *RSOC* would give the first detailed and dramatic Western account of the Long March. The most recent study is Harrison E. Salisbury, *The Long March: The Untold Story* (New York: McGraw Hill, 1987).

29. ES to Nelson T. Johnson, February 6, 1937, NTJP; C. Walter Young to Henry Allen Moe, Guggenheim Foundation, December 20, 1934, ESC; Bennett Cerf, "A Matter of Timing," *Publisher's Weekly,* February 12, 1938, 438–439; *JTTB,* 147–148; ES to Horace Epes, April 25, 1935, ESP in ESC.

30. Bertram, *Capes of China Slide Away,* 96; John Israel, *Student Nationalism in China, 1927–1937* (Stanford: Stanford University Press, 1966), 113–114, 6; Jessie G. Lutz, "December 9, 1935: Student Nationalism and the China Christian Colleges," *Journal of Asian Studies* 26 (August 1967): 637.

31. See Lloyd Eastman, *The Abortive Revolution: China Under Nationalist Rule, 1927–1937* (Cambridge: Harvard University Press, 1974), for detailed examination of fascist influences and tendencies in Kuomintang China.

32. ES, "The Ways of the Chinese Censor," *Current History* 42 (July 1935): 386; ES to Richard Walsh, July 19, 1935, ES to George Seldes, February 13, 1954, ESP in ESC.

33. ES to Charles Hanson Towne, March 30, 1933, CHTP; ES, "Japan Builds a New Colony," *SEP,* February 24, 1934, 87.

34. ES, "Japan Imposes Her Culture," *Asia* 35 (April 1935): 218–224.

35. ES, "Weak China's Strong Man," *Current History* 39 (January 1934): 404. While stories of a "secret agreement" between Chiang and the Japanese were "most improbable," Snow wrote, "certain circumstances seem to suggest that Chiang and the Japanese general staff for some time have understood each other" (ibid.); ES to "Demaree" (Bess?), August 25, 1935, ESP in ESC.

36. ES to Kenneth Shewmaker, September 26, 1969, ESP in ESC.

37. ES to father, March 21, 1934, MP in ESC.

38. *JTTB*, 137. Snow's lecture subsequently appeared in five installments in the English-language *Peiping Chronicle:* "The Meaning of Fascism," January 8–12, 1935 (NWC).

39. William L. Shirer, *The Rise and Fall of the Third Reich* (New York: Simon and Schuster, 1960), 185. On the Social Democrats, Shirer writes, "Loyal to the Republic they were to the last, but in the end too confused, too timid to take the great risks which alone could have preserved it." As for the Communists, they had "the silly idea of first destroying the Social Democrats, the Socialist trade unions and what middle class democratic forces there were," on "the dubious theory" that while this would lead to a Nazi regime, the latter would be but a short-lived effort to save a dying capitalism—"after that, the Communist deluge!" (ibid.).

40. *History of the Communist Party of the Soviet Union,* "prepared by a group of [Soviet] authors" (Moscow: Foreign Languages Publishing House, 1960), 503.

41. HFS to Richard Walsh, apparently fall 1935 (first page of letter missing), NWC.

42. ES to Howard, July 20, 1935, MP in ESC.

43. Lutz, "December 9, 1935: Student Nationalism and the China Christian Colleges," 633.

44. Zhang Wending, "Snow on the Campus of Yanjing University," and Zhang Zhaolin, "Edgar Snow, My Good Friend and Teacher," both in *In Commemoration of Edgar Snow* (title in original, *Ji-nian Ai-de-jia Si-nuo*), ed. Liu Liqun (Beijing: Xinhua Press, 1982), 132–139, 124–128; Chen Hanbo, "Snow and His Students," in *China Remembers Edgar Snow,* ed. Wang Xing (Beijing: China Publications Centre, 1982), 39–40.

45. Interviews with Huang Hua (June 6, 1987), Xiao Qian (May 19, 1987), Chen Hanbo (June 25, 1988), Li Min (May 21, 1987), and Israel Epstein (May 16, 1987), all in Beijing; Florence Yu Liang (June 17, 1987), Shanghai. NW, "Notes on the Student Movement," 12; Nym Wales, "Old Peking," *Asia* 35 (December 1935): 794–795.

46. Interviews, see note 45 above; Hubert S. Liang, "A Profile of Peggy" (1979), 3-S Society files, Beijing; NW, "Notes on the Student Movement," 162, "Notes on the Sian Incident, 1936" (1960), NWC, 12, 32 (mimeographed).

47. NW, "Notes on the Student Movement," 87; Joseph W. Esherick and Jeffrey N. Wasserstrom, "Acting Out Democracy: Political Theater in Modern China," *Journal of Asian Studies* 49 (November 1990): 835–865. "Without a civil society, only street theater remains as a mode of political expression. No Chinese regime has ever been able to suppress it altogether" (860).

48. *JTTB*, 144; Nym Wales, "Students in Rebellion," *Asia* 36 (July 1936): 446–448. My discussion of the December Ninth movement and the Snows' part

in it is based on the following sources (in addition to my interviews in China with leading participants): *JTTB*, 139–146; HFS, *My China Years*, 154–177; NW, "Notes on the Student Movement"; Israel, *Student Nationalism*, 110–156; Wang Xing, ed., *China Remembers Edgar Snow*, 39–43; and relevant articles from three Chinese-language collections; *Si-nuo zai Zhongguo* (Snow in China) (Beijing: San-lien Bookstore, 1980); Liu Liqun, ed., *In Commemoration of Edgar Snow;* Zhao Rongsheng and Zhao Yu, eds., *The "December Ninth" Movement at No-Name Lakeside* (in original, *"I-er jiu" zai Wei-ming Lu-pan*) (Beijing: Beijing Press, 1985).

49. John Israel and Donald W. Klein, *Rebels and Bureaucrats: China's December 9ers* (Berkeley: University of California Press, 1976), 55–58; Lu Cui, "Snow and the December Ninth Movement," in *In Commemoration of Edgar Snow*, ed. Liu Liqun (Beijing: Xinhua Press, 1982), 42–43, 46; NW, "Notes on the Student Movement," 78.

50. Zhao Rongsheng, "Recollections of the December Ninth Student Movement," Beijing, *People's Daily* (Renmin ribao), December 5, 1985; *JTTB*, 139.

51. HFS, *My China Years*, 172. Helen Snow described her November 1935 letter to student Zhang Zhaolin (in which she had offered literally dozens of suggestions for action) as "the letter which started the student movement, Dec. 1935" (NW, "Notes on the Student Movement," 191). Xiao Qian thinks Helen Snow saw herself as "the mother of New China"; at the same time, he admires her devotion to and work for China (interview May 19, 1987); Chen Hanbo, "Recollections of the 'December Ninth' Movement in Yanjing," in *"December Ninth" Movement at No-Name Lakeside*, ed. Zhao Rongsheng and Zhao Yu (Beijing: Beijing Press, 1985), 36; *JTTB*, 142.

52. John Israel, "The December 9th Movement: A Case Study in Chinese Communist Historiography," *CQ* 23 (July–September 1965): 140–169; interviews with Huang Hua (1987), and Chen Hanbo (1988); HFS, *My China Years*, 165–167; Chen Hanbo, "Snow and His Students," 43.

53. ES, Notes on Conversations with Old Students, ESP in ESC. Snow reinforced these points in the notes he added to the 1968 revised edition of *RSOC* (New York: Grove Press, 1968). David Yu, he wrote, attended a secret meeting of the Yanjing Student Association on the evening of December 8, where they "planned the strategy for the daring street demonstration held on the following day" (472).

54. ES, "The December 9th Movement" (comment), *CQ* 26 (April–June 1966): 171–172; Israel, *Student Nationalism*, 157; *JTTB*, 146.

Chapter 8. Redstar-Struck

1. *JTTB*, 153–154; *RSOC*, 17–24; John Israel, *Student Nationalism* (Stanford: Stanford University Press, 1966), 169–171; John Israel and Donald W. Klein, *Rebels and Bureaucrats* (Berkeley: University of California Press, 1976), 122–124.

2. Cited in introduction to English version, Sherman Cochran and Andrew C. K. Hsieh with Janis Cochran, trans. and eds., *One Day in China: May 21, 1936* (New Haven: Yale University Press, 1983), xx; *JTTB*, 192. Mao Dun later served

as minister of culture under the People's Republic until his ouster on ideological grounds in December 1964.

3. ES, "The Japanese Juggernaut Rolls On," *SEP*, May 9, 1936, 8–9, 89–90, 92, "The Coming Conflict in the Orient," *SEP*, June 6, 1936, 14–15, 82, 84, 87; "Mr. Hirota's Third Point," *Foreign Affairs* 14 (July 1936): 598–605, "Japan Digs In," *SEP*, January 4, 1936, 8–9, 56–59.

4. "The Japanese Juggernaut Rolls On," 9, 90, 92; "The Coming Conflict in the Orient," 14–15, 84–85.

5. "The Japanese Juggernaut Rolls On," 9; "The Coming Conflict in the Orient," 82, 84–85, 87.

6. Joseph C. Goulden, *The Curtis Caper* (New York: Putnam, 1965), 39–40; "Mr. Hirota's Third Point," 598, 602, 604–605.

7. John W. Garver, "The Origins of the Second United Front: The Comintern and the Chinese Communist Party," *CQ* 113 (March 1988): 29–59; Gregor Benton, "The 'Second Wang Ming Line' (1935–38)," *CQ* 61 (March 1975): 61–94. According to the perhaps exaggerated recollections of Otto Braun (Li De), Mao in early 1936 outlined a strategy in which "he gave top priority to securing technical and military assistance from the Soviet Union" (Otto Braun, *A Comintern Agent in China, 1932–1939,* trans. Jeanne Moore [Stanford: Stanford University Press, 1982], 157).

8. Benton, "The 'Second Wang Ming Line,' " 76; "Further Interviews with Mao Tse-tung" (Bao'an, July 19, 1936, Yan'an, September 25, 1939), *RSOC* (rev. ed., 1968), 445, 447. Snow's 1939 interviews with Mao were published in *CWR,* January 13 and 20, 1940. Though the CCP greatly modified its land reform policies during the united front wartime period, the result nevertheless was "to squeeze landlording out of existence" (Tetsuya Kataoka, *Resistance and Revolution in China: The Communists and the Second United Front* [Berkeley: University of California Press, 1974], 249).

9. Garver, "Origins of the Second United Front," 49–50, 52–53. By May 1936 the CCP, under Comintern pressure, had shifted its slogan of "opposing" Chiang, to one of "compelling" him to resist Japan. The Comintern, however, called for "uniting" with Chiang, a line Mao regarded as unrealistic, in the face of the Generalissimo's demand for the virtual surrender of the Communists as the price for ending civil war (ibid., 53–54).

10. Agnes Smedley's recent biographers note that though she was "burning with envy" at Snow's opportunity, she "understood politically" that "the Communists had wanted the first journalist visitor to be someone without any association with the international left" (Janice R. MacKinnon and Stephen R. MacKinnon, *Agnes Smedley* [Berkeley: University of California Press, 1988], 73). However, the MacKinnons state further, "of course, it was Smedley who urged Snow to go to the northwest" in 1936 (167). Their apparent source is an ES letter to HFS, June 4, 1939, which seems more ambiguous. While Smedley "pretended to me, in Shanghai, that she had done everything to have me go to the NW she was actually doing her best to prevent it," Ed wrote (ES to HFS, June 4, 1939, HFS files; ES, *The Other Side of the River: Red China Today,* or *RCT* [New York: Random House, 1961, 1962], 124).

11. NW, "Notes on the Student Movement," 37, "Notes on David Yu" (December 9, 1982), David Yu to Peg and Ed, March 22, 23, and 30, 1936, NWC; *RSOC* (1968), notes, 419.

12. HFS, *My China Years*, 181.

13. Rewi Alley, *Six Americans in China* (Beijing: Intercul, 1985), 43; Alley, *At 90*, 80; interview with Alley, Beijing, May 18, 1987; Hamilton, *Edgar Snow*, 67, 304–305 n.10 (Helen Snow remembers the Polevoy visit to the Snow home, apparently in connection with her interest in leftist artists in Peking. "I do not know who he was, but seemed to be Polish or Russian and left-wing" ["Notes on NWC" (1990), HFS files]. She vehemently asserts that Polevoy had "absolutely no connection" with Snow's trip [interview with HFS, June 15, 1989]); Harrison E. Salisbury, *The Long March* (New York: McGraw Hill, 1987), 318; Braun, *Comintern Agent in China*, 251–252. According to Garver, Moscow's "endorsement of Mao's leadership . . . would not come until mid-1938" ("Origins of the Second United Front," 39). Stalin considered Mao "deficient" in Marxism-Leninism and lacking a truly "internationalist" outlook (Warren Kuo, *Analytical History of the Chinese Communist Party* [Taipei: Institute of International Relations, 1970], bk. 3, 328). *Voice of China,* a Communist-sponsored periodical published in Shanghai between March 1936 and November 1937, reflected the Moscow line on China: the push for united anti-Japanese resistance under a democratized Nanking government led by Chiang. It opposed anti-Chiang internecine conflicts (including the Xi'an Incident) as aiding and abetting the Japanese and virtually ignored the activities of the Reds in the northwest. The journal was edited by Max (Manny) Granich and his wife, Grace, sent to Shanghai for that purpose by the American Communist party (Alley, *At 90*, 82). Before they left for China, the Communist party leader Earl Browder cautioned them not to "waste their ammunition" in attacks on the Chiang regime, but to "keep your attention on Japanese imperialism" (Grace Granich, Autobiographical Typescript [1970–1971], 4, Grace and Max Granich Papers). Grace Granich's manuscript remained incomplete at her death in 1971. Bert Taube, the late Max Granich's friend, made a full run of *Voice of China* available to me.

14. ES to L. M. MacBride, April 19, 1936, June 1, 1936, December 6, 1936, "Statement of Expenses on Trip to the Chinese Soviet Areas," February 14, 1937, ESP in ESC; ES to Nelson T. Johnson, February 6, 1937, NTJP; Diaries, Book 17, September 8, 1936.

15. *RSOC*, 9–24; Diaries, Book 11, June 1936; Dong Hui Fang (daughter of Pastor Wang), speech at symposium on 50th anniversary of *RSOC*, Beijing, June 1988; interviews with Rewi Alley and Li Xue (Alley's adopted son), Beijing, May 18, 25, 1987.

16. Alley, *Six Americans*, 1–9; *RCT*, 261–263; Judy Foreman, "Doctor's Adventure Becomes His Life," *Boston Globe*, February 19, 1987. It was in *RCT* that Snow first divulged Hatem's part in their 1936 trek.

17. *RCT*, 276–281; interview with Ma Haide, May 15, 1987; Ma Haide obituary (by Walter Sullivan), *New York Times*, October 6, 1988. Hatem (Ma) apparently joined the CCP in 1937 in Yan'an (*Xinhua*, October 10, 1988, *FBIS, China*, October 1, 1988). As to Hatem's invisibility in *Red Star*, HFS says he was concerned also not to endanger his American passport (interview, August 2, 1986). Hatem may also have wished to protect his family in the U.S. from any adverse "Red" publicity.

18. *RCT*, 266; *RSOC*, 26.

19. *RSOC*, 43–45; Diaries, Book 12, July 9, 1936; ES to L. M. MacBride, December 6, 1936, ESP in ESC.

20. Interview with HFS, August 2, 1986; *Random Notes on Red China,* or *R NORC* (Cambridge, Mass.: Harvard University, 1957), 56–58. This was all "rather interesting," Snow noted in *R NORC,* "because it may indicate that at the time he spoke to me Chou did not conceive of a United Front which could include Chiang, but only of one . . . to be formed against both Chiang and Japan" (56). On arrival in Yan'an in May 1937, "everyone except Mao greeted me worriedly with the demand that I make sure my husband cut out any unfavorable words about Generalissimo Chiang Kai-shek," HFS recounted (HFS, review of *Zhou Enlai: A Biography,* by Dick Wilson, in *Washington Post,* December 3, 1984).

21. Diaries, Book 12, July 13, 1936; *RCT,* 123; letter on gift of horses, from Fourth Division of Red Army to "Dear American Comrades," August 19, 1936, 3-S Society files, Beijing.

22. *RSOC,* 66–69; Benjamin Yang, "The Zunyi Conference as One Step in Mao's Rise to Power: A Survey of Historical Studies of the Chinese Communist Party," *CQ* 106 (June 1986): 235–271; Thomas Kampen, "The Zunyi Conference and Further Steps in Mao's Rise to Power," *CQ* 117 (March 1989): 118–134. At a 1988 Beijing symposium on *RSOC* that I attended, Kampen pointed up Snow's role in augmenting Mao's image and eminence at a critical stage in the latter's political ascendancy.

23. *RSOC,* 69–72.

24. Cited in foreword, Wu Liangping, ed., *Mao Zedong's 1936 Talks with Snow* (in original, *Mao Zedong i-jiu san-liu nian tong Si-nuo de tan-hua*) (Beijing, August 1979), 3-S Society files, 5. Mao told Snow in 1939 in Yan'an that *Red Star* had "correctly reported" party policies and his own views (*R NORC,* 73).

25. Visit to Bao'an, and interview with Mr. Bei Li, Bao'an, June 10, 1987.

26. Wu, ed., *Mao's Talks with Snow,* 7; *RSOC* (1968), biographical notes, 473, 508; *R NORC,* 122.

27. Mao Zedong to ES, March 10, 1937 (copy of original letter and translation, 3-S Society files, Beijing); "Notes of Chairman Mao's Talk with Edgar Snow" (December 18, 1970), 22, 25, 31, ESP in ESC.

28. *RSOC,* 88. Otto Braun cited this interview as evidence that Mao "was indeed relying on a manipulation of the strategic situation of the soviet [CCP] base in northwestern China to draw the Soviet Union into war with Japan" (*Comintern Agent in China,* 156). See also introduction by Vladimir Petrov, "The Soviets and World Communism: Sources of the Sino-Soviet Dispute," to *Sino-Soviet Relations, 1945–1970,* O. B. Borisov and B. T. Koloskov (Bloomington: Indiana University Press, 1975), 19–20; Garver, "Origins of the Second United Front," 40–42.

29. *RSOC* (1968), notes, 426; *RSOC,* 147. In "private conversation" with Snow in 1936, "Mao blamed Russian Comintern agents for the disasters suffered by the Communist party during the counter-revolution in 1927." *JTTB,* 168–169; Diaries, Book 15, July 15, 1936; *RSOC,* 123–132, 139. Some of the diary quotations I have cited are also in *RSOC* (1968), notes, 444–445.

30. NW, "Notes on Sian Incident," 22–23, including text of ES letter to "Dear Nym," August 3, 1936.

31. Ibid., 24; Diaries, Book 12, July 9, 1936.

32. NW, "Notes on Sian Incident," 29–35; *Daily Herald* (London), October 8, 1936, NWC; *RSOC,* 396–397.

33. *RSOC,* 237–242, 248–252; Diaries, Book 17, September 10, 1936. As for the Shanghai engineer's complaint, Snow had this a bit differently in his diary: The man felt "depressed" at "the lack of effort to improve people's minds, but concentrate rather on too much singing" (ibid., September 20, 1936).

34. *RSOC,* 255–261, 280–294; Diaries, Book 17, September 17, August 27, 1936. However, desertions represented something of a problem for the Red Army. As explained to Snow, "home-sickness" among new peasant recruits was the prime factor. Fearing they would never get back home again, they "sometimes ask for leave but often take up their blanket and bowl and start over the narrow trails on foot." Brought back, they were subjected to intensive doses of "education," to understand that they had committed a crime under Red Army military law. More serious problems stemmed from infiltrators in border partisan units from the gentry-financed *min tuan*—the ubiquitous and always dangerous anti-Red local armed elements (Diaries, Book 17, September 17, 1936).

35. *RSOC,* 304–310; Diaries, Book 17, September 9, 17, 1936; Book 19, October 5, 1936.

36. *RSOC,* 262–279; Diaries, Book 16, August 16–21, 1936; Preface, *RSOC* (New York: Modern Library, Random House, 1944), ix. Peng Dehuai's "open and forthright" qualities led him courageously to criticize Mao's Great Leap Forward policies of 1958–59, for their disastrous effect on the peasantry. It resulted in his political demise and ouster as minister of defense (*The Case of Peng Teh-huai, 1959–1968* [Hong Kong: Union Research Institute, 1968]).

37. Garver, "Origins of the Second United Front," 56–57; Jerome Ch'en, "The Communist Movement 1927–1937," in *The Nationalist Era in China, 1927–1949,* Lloyd E. Eastman, Jerome Ch'en, Suzanne Pepper, and Lyman P. Van Slyke (Cambridge: Cambridge University Press, 1991), 112. See also Petrov, "The Soviets and World Communism," 20.

38. Diaries, Book 18, September 23, 1936. Mao's last statement quoted above from his diary entry did not appear in the text of the interview published in *CWR,* November 21, 1936, 420–421, or in Snow's summation of the interview in *RSOC,* 387–389.

39. Diaries, Book 18, September 23, 1936; *RSOC,* 388–389. Only the final sentence of Mao's reply appeared in *RSOC.*

40. Diaries, Book 19, September 26, 1936.

41. *RSOC,* 373, 389–390; Diaries, Book 17, September 3, 1936.

42. Interview with Gao Liang (then a Xinhua correspondent who sat with Snow on the trip), Beijing, May 28, 1987.

43. MacKinnon, *Agnes Smedley,* 173, 175; NW, "Notes on Sian Incident," 51. According to Li Min, a Yanjing student friend who was at the Snow home when Ed returned, he also carried materials hidden in his jacket lining (interview with Li Min, Beijing, May 21, 1987).

44. ES, "On Publication of Chou En-lai Interview and Other China Material" (December 4, 1960), ALSP, Beijing University. This four-page typescript memorandum, written at his home in Switzerland, was sent on by Snow to Miss Strong in Beijing (ES to Strong, December 11, 1960, ALSP).

Chapter 9. Writing and Making History

1. *JTTB*, 183; NW, "Notes on Sian Incident," 52–53.

2. ES, "Interviews with Mao Tse-tung, Communist Leader," *CWR*, November 14 and 21, 1936, 377–379, 420–421; L. M. MacBride to ES, December 15, 1936; ES to L. M. MacBride, February 7, 1937, ESP in ESC; *Life*, January 25 and February 1, 1937, 9–13, 44–49; Autobiographical Note (1944), 4; *Asia* 37 (February, July, August, September, October, November 1937); ES, "I Went to Red China," *SEP*, November 6, 1937, 9–10, 98, 100–103; a mix-up over publication rights prevented his articles from appearing in the *New York Sun* (*JTTB*, 191).

3. ES to Nelson T. Johnson, November 13, 1936, Nelson T. Johnson to ES, November 14, 1936, NTJP. Mao, Johnson remarked, "talks very much like a lot of other Chinese leaders that I have met." For the Snow-Roosevelt relationship, see chapter 14. On the foreign service officers, see E. J. Kahn, *The China Hands: America's Foreign Service Officers and What Befell Them* (New York: Viking Press, 1935); and Joseph W. Esherick, ed., *Lost Chance in China: The World War II Despatches of John S. Service* (New York: Random House, 1974).

4. *RSOC*, 407; Immanuel C. Y. Hsü, *Rise of Modern China* (New York: Oxford University Press, 1970), 662–663; Tien-wei Wu, *The Sian Incident: A Pivotal Point in Modern Chinese History* (Ann Arbor: Center for Chinese Studies, University of Michigan, 1976), 101–105.

5. *RSOC*, 405–429; *RNORC*, 1–2; James P. Harrison, *The Long March to Power: A History of the Chinese Communist Party, 1921–1972* (New York: Praeger, 1972), 268–270; Wu, *Sian Incident*, 135–153.

6. Bertram, *Capes of China Slide Away*, 101, 103, 108–116. Bertram's first book (*First Act in China, The Story of the Sian Mutiny* [New York: Viking, 1938]) was a valuable on-the-spot account of the entire Xi'an affair.

7. Interview with HFS, October 14, 1987; HFS to Randall Gould, January 26, 1937, NWC; ES to Nelson T. Johnson, February 6, 1937, NTJP. Text of Snow's January 21, 1937, talk, "The Reds and the Northwest," *Shanghai Evening Post and Mercury,* February 5, 1937, and in typescript, NWC.

8. ES, "Reds and the Northwest."

9. *Izvestia,* December 14, 1936. The *Pravda* and *Izvestia* editorials were carried in English translation by *Tass News Service,* to which the Snows subscribed in Peking; texts cited in NW, "Notes on Sian Incident," 72–74, 79.

10. *RNORC*, 1–4; NW, "Notes on Sian Incident," 77; *RSOC*, 410.

11. *RNORC*, 1–4; Diaries, Book 20, November 2, 1937; ES to Nelson T. Johnson, February 6, 1937, NTJP. In *RNORC* Snow calls Madame Sun "X".

12. Zhao Rongsheng, "Snow Led Us to Yan'an," in *China Remembers Edgar Snow,* ed. Wang Xing (Beijing: China Publications Centre, 1982), 67–69; interview with Zhao Rongsheng, Beijing, May 21, 1987.

13. Wang Fushi, "A Foreign Journalist's Impressions of the Northwest—a 'Scoop' Edition of Snow's *RSOC* in Chinese" (paper prepared for Edgar Snow symposium, Huhehot, Inner Mongolia, summer 1985); interview with Wang Fushi, Beijing, May 19, 1987; *RCT,* 5. Wang's translation (in original, "Wai Guo Ji Zhe Xi Bei Yin Xiang Ji") included a first-hand account of the Long March by a party leader, Chen Yun (under the pseudonym Lian Chen) and Mao's famous poem on the Long March.

14. Hu Youzi, "An Adventurous but Successful Experiment," in *In Commemoration of Edgar Snow,* ed. Liu Liqun (Beijing: Xinhua Press, 1982), 161–164; Zhang Xiaoding, "Si-nuo yu *Xixing Man Ji"* (Snow and *Journey to the West*), *Chang Cheng* (Great wall) (Beijing) 1 (1980): 184–191; Zhang Xiaoding, "Shan yao shijie de 'Hong Xing'" (The "Red Star" shines over the world), *Bulletin of the China Society of Library Science* (Beijing) 1 (1980): 84–89; Zhang Xiaoding, "How 'Red Star Over China' Circulated in China" (paper for symposium on fiftieth anniversary of *RSOC,* Beijing, June 1988); interview with Zhang Xiaoding, Beijing, June 24, 1988.

15. HFS, *My China Years,* 220–227; NW, "Notes on Sian Incident," 181; J. Spencer Kennard to ES, January 3, 1940, ES to Hilda Selwyn-Clarke, March 5, 1940, ESP in ESC; Hubert Liang to HFS (1974), cited in *My China Years,* 226; the journal was "a brief flash of lightning on a dark horizon," HFS added. Full run of *democracy,* 3-S Society files, Beijing.

16. ES to Nelson T. Johnson, February 6, 1937, ES to T. T. Li, February 4, 1937, NTJP.

17. Zhang Keming, "Guomindang Zhengfu dui Si-nuo zhu-zuo de cha-jin" (Regarding the banning of Snow's works by the Kuomintang government), *Shehui Ke-xue* (Social sciences) 1 (1985): 99–100 (Zhang's article in this journal from Fudan University, Shanghai, quotes a "secret" August 1941 order by Chiang Kai-shek, and earlier directives from Kuomintang files); Department of State, *Foreign Relations of the United States: Diplomatic Papers, 1944* (Washington, D.C.: U.S. Government Printing Office, 1967), 364–367. After the war, in 1945, Snow was denied an entry visa (as correspondent for the *Post*) by the Chinese government (*CWR,* December 22, 1945).

18. ES to John Leaning, April 7, 1961, ESP in ESC; HFS, *My China Years,* 224–225, 234; interview with HFS, October 14, 1987.

19. NW, "Notes on Sian Incident," 54; HFS, *My China Years,* 202–203; An Wei, "*Red Star Over China* and Helen Foster Snow" (paper for symposium on *RSOC,* Beijing, June 1988).

20. Nym Wales and Kim San, *Song of Ariran: A Korean Communist in the Chinese Revolution* (New York: John Day, 1941); HFS, *My China Years,* 203; HFS, "A Moment of Truth, Which Ruined 'My Own Work,'" HFS files; Nym Wales, "My Yenan Notebooks" (1961), NWC, 19 (mimeographed); HFS to Zhang Qi, China Literary Foundation, Beijing, November 7, 1991, HFS files.

21. Interview with HFS, October 14, 1987; NW, "My Yenan Notebooks," 1–2; ES to HFS, July 22, 1938, HFS files (Snow did urge her to go over the manuscript and "improve its style and diction—which is very rough in spots, as you know"); HFS to ES, April 24, 1937, NWC.

22. HFS to ES, April 25, 26, 27, 1937; NW, "My Yenan Notebooks," 2–4, 7–17; "F." (Kempton Fitch) to ES, May 1, 1937, NWC.

23. HFS, *My China Years,* 234–279; NW, "My Yenan Notebooks," 7–19; George Hatem to ES, December 3, 1936, Agnes Smedley to ES, April 19, 1937, ESP in ESC. The books resulting from HFS's Yan'an stay: *Inside Red China* (New York: Doubleday, Doran, 1939); *Song of Ariran*; *The Chinese Labor Movement* (New York: John Day, 1945); *Red Dust* (Stanford: Stanford University Press, 1952).

24. The text of Snow's account of this incident, translated from a 1954 Japanese version, is given in Janice R. MacKinnon and Stephen R. MacKinnon, *Agnes Smedley* (Berkeley: University of California Press, 1988), 188–192. The complete

original English typescript of Snow's account is contained in the JKFP at Harvard. Snow titled it, "The Last American Missionary to China or the Divorce of Mao Tse-tung." Helen Snow had no knowledge of all this at the time, but she did take down Lily Wu's autobiography (HFS, *The Chinese Communists: Sketches and Autobiographies of the Old Guard* [Westport, Conn.: Greenwood Publishing, 1972], 250–261). According to HFS, Smedley told her in Yan'an that she (Smedley) had been ordered by Mao to leave as soon as possible (ibid., 254). Smedley acknowledged that she "acquired a very bad reputation among the women of Yenan" because of her dance activities (Agnes Smedley, *Battle Hymn of China* [New York: Alfred A. Knopf, 1943], 170–171).

25. ES, "The Last American Missionary to China," JKFP; Smedley, *Battle Hymn of China*, 171–172; MacKinnon and MacKinnon, *Agnes Smedley*, 86.

26. James Bertram, review of *My China Years*, by HFS, in *The Dominion* (Wellington, New Zealand), March 15, 1986; ES to HFS, May 24, June 13 and 23, 1937, HFS to ES, June 23, September 6, 1937, NW, "My Yenan Notebooks," 173.

27. ES to HFS, June 9, 1937, HFS to ES, June 18, 1937, ES to HFS, July 26, 1937, HFS to ES, June 23, 1937, NWC; Gregor Benton, "'Second Wang Ming Line,'" *CQ* 61 (March 1975): 86–87; *JTTB*, 186–187. Wang was accused of "capitulationism in united front work" and of "exaggerating" the role played by the big cities and KMT troops (Benton, 86, and 86 n.24, re Zhou Enlai's "enthusiasm for the united front").

28. ES to HFS, July 26, 1937, NWC; ES, "I Went to Red China," 10, 98.

29. ES to HFS, July 26, 1937; Diaries, Book 20, August 2, 1937.

30. "I Went to Red China," 101–102. The Nationalists, Snow noted, believed oppositely that the Reds "would lose their identity in Kuomintang nationalism." With Chiang now at an all-time peak as national leader, he "believes he has nothing to fear from the National Communists who now offer the masses little more than he does" (ibid., 103). This was another indirect Snow barb at the "capitulationist" CCP line.

31. Diaries, Book 20, July 29, 30, 1937. In *Battle for Asia*, or *BFA* (New York: Random House, 1941), completed after more than three years of the China war, Snow dealt much more charitably with General Song (viewing him now as a wily fox who had managed to stall off the Japanese in northern China for a number of years) and put a positive spin on the massacre Song's troops suffered on the outskirts of Peking before the city's surrender. These sacrifices "had not been entirely futile," Snow wrote; they had stiffened "the maturing will of the nation, and made further appeasement by Nanking out of the question" (*BFA*, 21).

32. Snow's version of this incident (in *BFA*, 23; and *JTTB*, 189, in which he perhaps embellished Deng's amah role-playing ["She dropped her jaw in an idiotic grin at the sullen Japanese"]) was later denied by Deng, who claimed Snow "remembered it wrong" (interview with Lois Wheeler Snow, June 5, 1987). Bertram confirms Snow's story. "The fact was that she did travel with us, on the assumption that Ed or I would claim her as our personal *amah*," he wrote in his memoir, *Capes of China Slide Away* (126).

33. Diaries, Book 20, September 1, an undated entry (probably September 11, 1937).

34. Diaries, Book 20, September 22, 1937; NW, "My Yenan Notebooks," 176.

35. Diaries, Book 20, September 24–October 5, 1937, Book 21, December 31, 1937; ES to Francis Williams (*Daily Herald*), October 27, 1937, ESP in ESC; NW, "My Yenan Notebooks," 176–177; HFS, *My China Years,* 297–299.

Chapter 10. The Strange Life of a Classic

1. ES to HFS, May 22, July 26, 1937, NWC.

2. ES to father, September 8, 1937, January 16, 1938, MP in ESC.

3. Cerf, "A Matter of Timing," *Publisher's Weekly,* February 12, 1938, 838–839; Cerf, "News from Random House," October 22, 1937, ESC; *JTTB,* 191; Harold R. Isaacs, *Images of Asia* (New York: Harper and Row, 1972), 163 n.81; NW, "Notes on Sian Incident," 52; Diaries, Book 27, June 22, 1939; Richard O'Connor, *Heywood Broun: A Biography* (New York: Putnam's Sons, 1975), 205–224. "Now [June 1939] Broun thinks he made a mistake," Watts further told Snow (Diaries, ibid.). Looking back on *RSOC* in the late 1960s, Cerf was somewhat discomfited to think of the enthusiasm originally felt for the Red leaders who had since become America's bitter enemies ("The Reminiscences of Bennett Cerf" [Oral History Research Office, Columbia University, 1971], 373; interviews recorded in 1967 and 1968). According to Lois Snow, the Modern Library edition of *RSOC* was quietly withdrawn in the 1950s (Lois Snow to author, September 12, 1988). "It is a pity you didn't keep *RSOC* in the ML [Modern Library] as papa wanted you to do," Snow later gently chided Cerf (ES to Bennett Cerf, September 11, 1961, RHP).

4. Diaries, Book 21, November 13, 1937.

5. Isaacs, *Images of Asia,* 163 n.71, 155; Harry Price to ES and HFS, May 28, 1938, NWC; *JTTB,* 253–258; Hubert S. Liang, "Edgar Snow—The Man and His Work" (lecture at Nanjing University, May 1979, received from Florence Yu Liang; Ickes made his remarks to Liang in Washington in 1939); Diaries, Book 21, February 1938.

6. Henriette Herz to ES, November 12, 1937, ESP in ESC. While Herz (through whom the request was made) thought it "nonsense," she was nevertheless in a way "very pleased to hear of it, because we have advanced tremendously to see a commercial firm anxious to use a picture of two Soviet Chinese!" The photo appeared in ES, "The Long March," *Asia* 37 (November 1937): 746.

7. *Daily Herald,* October 11, 1937; *New York Herald-Tribune,* January 2, 1938; Pearl Buck's review in *Asia* 38 (March 1938): 202–203; Diaries, Book 26, November 26, 1938. On Evans Carlson, see *JTTB,* 196–197; and Michael Blankfort, *The Big Yankee: The Life of Carlson of the Raiders* (Boston: Little, Brown, 1947), 188–308. Though Carlson acted as one of President Roosevelt's confidants, sending reports from abroad directly to the president through his secretary, Margarite Le Hand, Carlson's unorthodox views and methods would earn him a "Red" sobriquet among the Marine Corps brass.

8. Henry Seidel Canby, "Books of the Book-of-the-Month Club," January 1938. *Red Star* was among "other books" recommended for the month. R. L.

Duffus review, in *New York Times,* January 9, 1938; *Asia* 38 (March 1938): 202; Shewmaker (*Americans and Chinese Communists,* 238–266) takes up the "agrarian reformers" thesis and refutes allegations of Snow's role in propagating it.

9. John Gunther, *Inside Asia* (New York: Harper and Brothers, 1939), 215; Diaries, Book 21, April 18, 1938.

10. Freda Utley, review, in *New Statesman and Nation* (London), November 6, 1937; Shewmaker, *Americans and Chinese Communists,* 242–243. For one of Utley's later anti-Snow tirades, see "Red Star over Independence Square: The Strange Case of Edgar Snow and the Saturday Evening Post," *Plain Talk,* September 1947, 9–20.

11. Diaries, Book 21, January 5, 1938; M. G. [Max Granich], review, in *China Today,* December 1938, 18; ES, *Geroicheskii narod Kitaya* (Heroic people of China) (Moscow: C. K. VLKSM-Molodaya Gvardiya, 1938), 108 pages. The Random House *RSOC* had 450 pages of text.

12. Harry Price to ES and HFS, May 28, 1938.

13. V. J. Jerome and Li Chuan, "Edgar Snow's 'Red Star Over China,'" *The Communist* (New York), May 1938, 457.

14. *RSOC,* 374–379, 440; Diaries, Book 22, June 26, 1938; *JTTB,* 385–386.

15. John McDermott, "Autobiographical interviews with Max Granich," Grace and Max Granich Papers, 407, 142–147. Granich, who edited *China Today* from 1938 to its demise after Pearl Harbor, also worked during that period as Earl Browder's chauffeur. Once as he drove the party leader's imperious Russian-born wife, Irena, down the West Side highway from their Yonkers home, she told Granich it would be called "Browder Road" after the Communist takeover (ibid., 7).

16. Earl Browder, "The American Communist Party in the Thirties," in *The Thirties,* ed. Rita James Simon (Urbana: University of Illinois Press, 1967), 247; Laurence Hearn (Philip Jaffe), review of *RSOC,* in *China Today,* April 1938, 17–18. Jaffe's later recollections of his relationship to Snow and to *RSOC* are in his unpublished memoir, "Odyssey," Philip J. Jaffe Papers, 72–74. The limited correspondence between the two men (from 1937–1942) in these papers contains no letters from 1938 nor any reference to *RSOC.* Snow, in a letter to his agent in New York in which he expressed his irritation at the apparent disclosure of his intended *RSOC* additions and revisions to "Those (CP) people," referred to a note he had earlier asked Herz to forward to Jaffe. She replied (testily denying any role in the leakage) that on receipt of Ed's note, Jaffe went around "foaming at the mouth." ES to Henriette Herz, October 2, 1938, Henriette Herz to ES, October 25, 1938, ESP in ESC. See Harold R. Isaacs, *The Tragedy of the Chinese Revolution* (London: Secker and Warburg, 1938), 437 n., for criticism of *RSOC* (this note was deleted from later editions of the book). On the Trotskyist review of *RSOC* and Snow's rebuttal, in *CWR,* March 26, 1938, 110–112, May 7, 1938, 271–272. The reviewer (Harry Paxton Howard), Snow noted in his reply, "so curiously interweaves his own opinions credited to me, that I fear many people may find it difficult to distinguish one from the other."

17. Diaries, Book 24, July 20, 1938.

18. Diaries, Book 21, December 19, 1937; interview with Trudy Rosenberg (widow of Shippe), Beijing, May 25, 1987; U.S. Senate Committee on the Judi-

ciary, Internal Security Subcommittee, *Institute of Pacific Relations Hearings* (Washington, D.C.: U.S. Government Printing Office, 1951, 1952), 47; "'Asiaticus' Criticizes 'Red Star Over China,'" "Edgar Snow Replies," "'Asiaticus' Holds His Ground," *Pacific Affairs* 11 (March 1938): 237–252.

19. *RSOC,* 447–448. At the same time, Snow also put a positive spin on the peaceful resolution and results of the Xi'an Incident, giving credit to the Communists, the Young Marshal, and the Generalissimo himself, concluding that "China has won, Japan has lost" (435).

20. Heinz Shippe to ES, February 27, 1938, ESP in ESC; interview with HFS, October 10, 1988; Diaries, Book 21, December 31, 1937; "Edgar Snow Replies," *Pacific Affairs,* March 1938, 247.

21. Diaries, Book 23, July 23, 1938; "The Question of Independence and Initiative Within the United Front" (November 5, 1938), *Selected Works of Mao Tsetung* (Beijing: Foreign Languages Press, 1965), 2:213–217. This concluding speech of the sixth plenary session of the party's central committee was basically Mao's counterattack against the Moscow-oriented united front line of Wang Ming. "In essence," a note accompanying the text commented, "what was involved was proletarian leadership in the united front" (213).

22. Diaries, Book 23, July 20, 1938. Shippe had close contacts with the Communist New Fourth Army, then operating under internationalist-influenced leadership in the lower Yangtze Valley near Shanghai. He was gathering material for a book on Communist guerrilla operations. Rather strangely he happened to be with a unit of the Maoist Eighth-Route Army in Shandong when he was killed in a Japanese ambush in 1941 (Asiaticus [Shippe] file [1938–1941], IPRP, University of British Columbia; interview with Trudy Rosenberg, Beijing, May 25, 1987). Excerpts from Snow's diary entries on Bo Gu and Shippe are in *R NORC,* 20–23.

23. ES to Earl Browder, March 20, 1938, ESP in ESC.

24. *RSOC,* rev. ed. (New York: Random House, 1938). The new part thirteen ("Shadows on the Rising Sun") was a six-chapter section of over fifty pages. It was replaced in the 1944 Modern Library edition by a considerably shorter epilogue Snow wrote for that edition.

25. R. Baker, "The New 'Red Star Over China,'" *Daily Worker* (New York), October 3, 1938; *China Today,* December 1938, 18.

26. *RSOC,* 107–108. These remarks remained unchanged in Snow's revised edition.

27. ES, "Will Tito's Heretics Halt Russia?" *SEP,* December 18, 1948, 109; ES, "Will China Become a Russian Satellite?" *SEP,* April 9, 1949, 148, 150.

28. Jerome and Li, "Edgar Snow's 'Red Star Over China,'" 445–457. The authors stressed, "The Soviets and the Red Army have become part of the Chinese Republic and the National Revolutionary Army" (453); Diaries, Book 25, August 29, 1938. The wartime diary of a Russian Comintern emissary to Yan'an, published posthumously and in abridged form by Moscow in the 1970s, noted in a June 1942 entry that Mao "pursues a policy that runs counter to the line and principles of the Comintern" regarding the anti-Japanese national front (Peter Vladimirov, *The Vladimirov Diaries: Yenan: 1942–1945* [New York: Doubleday, 1975], 31–32). Vladimirov served as a liaison officer of the Comintern with the central committee of the CCP from

1942 to 1945. He "doubled" as (or used the cover of) a *Tass* correspondent. The Doubleday volume was edited from a translation supplied by the Novosti Press Agency publishing house in Moscow. As the publishers observe, this book should be read "as both a historical and contemporary document."

29. Twenty-five thousand copies of *Heroic People of China* were printed. As for Snow, the introduction (by "A. Lin") noted that though his experience in the Soviet regions of China "opened his eyes to many things, he was unable to overcome his petty-bourgeois philistinism and his narrow-mindedness, reflected in many places in his book" (5–6). The lengthy introduction makes only a single cursory reference to Mao, in listing the names of those whose histories were included in the volume.

30. The reports on and review of *Red Star* I have cited appeared in *Knizhnye Novosti* (Book news) 12, no. 17–18 (1938). I am indebted to Grant Harris, senior reference librarian, Library of Congress, and Eugene Beshankovsky, Slavic bibliographer, Lehman Library, Columbia University, for information on both the publication history and the reviews of *Red Star* in the Soviet media. I am also indebted to the staff of the Labour Library of Foreign Literature, Moscow, for a list of all Snow writings translated into Russian. The biographical accounts of the Chinese Red leaders included in the Soviet edition of *RSOC* also appeared in the literary journal, *Novyi Mir* no. 1 (1938): 250–283. Four wartime pieces by Snow were included in a volume called *Doroga na Smolyensk* (Road to Smolensk) (Moscow, 1985).

31. Diaries, Book 21, February 2, 1938; Book 40, April 27, 1941, December 24, 1942, October 17, 1942, March 20, 1943. In his 1957 Harvard monograph, however, Snow showed some familiarity with the Russian version published "without my knowledge, in which all reference to Sian, the Comintern, Russia, and any and all 'controversial' matters was omitted" (*RNORC*, 3). In the preface to the Modern Library edition of *RSOC*, Snow elaborated on his brief diary entry on the Smolensk partisan fighter. He referred to three girls he spoke to from a guerrilla unit who told him, "'We got some ideas from a book called *Red Star Over China*,' they said—not knowing who I was" (ix). Of course, they could not have used that title in Russian (unless briefed), though it may have been so translated to Snow.

32. Israel Epstein, "Fooling the People," *China Monthly Review* (Shanghai), January 1952, 38–39. Bill Powell continued to publish the *Review*, finally as a monthly, until its demise in 1953. Epstein has had a notable China journalistic and writing career as a lifelong supporter of the CCP. He had been and, as the political tides shifted, would again be a Snow friend and admirer. Snow reacted acidly to Epstein's attack and referred to the latter's "reverent and devout" adherence to the party line (ES to Mildred, February 18, 1952, ESP in ESC).

33. Zhang Xiaoding, "The 'Red Star' shines over the world," 84. Bibliographical information on *RSOC* in China from 1949 on, received from the Museum of the Chinese Revolution, and interviews with Zhang Xiaoding and Dong Leshan, Beijing, June 1987 (Zhang has written extensively on the publishing history of *RSOC*, and Dong did the new translation for the first publicly

available Chinese edition in 1979). ES, "Notes on meeting with Mao Tse-tung" (Beijing, October 22, 1960), ESP in ESC.

34. *RCT,* 736, 4–7; interview with Dong Leshan, Beijing, June 1, 1987. Dong, who is a member of the Institute of American Studies of the Chinese Academy of Social Sciences, noted that only "some copies" of the 1960 edition were distributed internally.

35. Interview with Dong Leshan, June 1, 1987; according to him, there were only a few "minor deletions" from the English text.

36. ES to Theodore Herman, September 2, 1971, Herman file, ESC; E. Pashchenko, "Edgar Snow and the 'China Card,'" *Far Eastern Affairs* (Moscow) 1 (1981): 160.

37. Vaclav Oplustil, *The Epicenter of Disaster,* trans. Ivo Dvorak (Prague: Orbis Press Agency, 1980), 38.

38. The discussion of the 1970s context is based on the following Soviet sources: A. S. Titov, "O polititcheskikh kontaktakh Mao Tsze-duna s Edgarom Snow" (Political contacts of Mao Zedong with Edgar Snow), *Problemy Dalnego Vostoka* (Problems of the Far East [Moscow]) 2 (1972): 119–127; L. A. Bereznyi, "Zarozhdenie promaoiskoy kontseptsii kitaiskoy revolutsii v amerikanskoy istoriografii" (Emergence of the pro-Maoist conception of the Chinese revolution in U.S. historiography), *Istoriografia i istochnikovedenie istorii stran Asii i Afriki* (Historiography and bibliography of history of countries of Asia and Africa), part 4, Leningrad State University, 1975, 12–23. Copies of these articles received from State Library of Foreign Literature, Moscow.

39. Ibid.; "Notes of Chairman Mao's Talk with Edgar Snow" (December 18, 1970), 15.

40. See Robert P. Newman's major study, *Owen Lattimore and the "Loss" of China* (Berkeley: University of California Press, 1989).

41. *RSOC,* 140; HFS, "*Red Star Over China* and Me" (paper submitted to symposium on *RSOC,* Beijing, June 1988).

Chapter 11. Gung Ho for a Wartime China

1. Diaries, Book 21, January 1938; *BFA,* 84–91.

2. *BFA,* 79, 86.

3. Rewi Alley to Edward C. Carter, March 7, 1939, IPRP; ES to James Bertram, November 15, 1938, ESP in ESC.

4. Preface to Nym Wales, *China Builds for Democracy* (Hong Kong: Kelly and Walsh, 1940).

5. Nym Wales, "Notes on the Beginnings of the Industrial Cooperatives in China" (1961), NWC, 1 (mimeographed). ES, *BFA,* 97; Rewi Alley, "Two Years of Indusco," cited in NW, "Notes on CIC," 4; and in Alley, *At 90,* 104. Snow sought at the last moment to heighten his reference in *BFA* to Helen's seminal role in the Indusco movement, by inserting the phrase, "It was Nym Wales who first conceived the idea of workers' cooperatives," but the book was already in print (Henriette Herz to Belle Becker [Random House], undated, late January 1941, RHP). Herz quoted from a letter she had received from Snow.

6. NW, "Notes on CIC," 4; Alley, *At 90*, 105; Nym Wales, *China Builds for Democracy* (New York: Modern Age Books, 1941), vi, 32 (hereafter *CBFD*); *BFA*, 97.

7. Diaries, Book 25, August 23 and 27, 1938; ES to J. B. Powell, August 28, 1938, ESP in ESC.

8. Diaries, Book 22, July 7, 1938; *JTTB*, 199.

9. *JTTB*, 199–202; Alley, *At 90*, 106–107; Douglas R. Reynolds, "The Chinese Industrial Cooperative Movement and the Political Polarization of Wartime China, 1938–1945" (Ph.D. diss., Columbia University, 1975), 116.

10. *JTTB*, 42; *CBFD*, 43–44; Alley, *At 90*, 105–109; ES to J. B. Powell, August 28, 1938, ES to Bertram, November 15, 1938, ESP in ESC.

11. Bertram, *Capes of China Slide Away*, 142. On the 1938 Hankou scene, which attracted mostly from the left an international coterie of journalists, writers, and political figures, Stephen R. MacKinnon, "Agnes Smedley's Hankow, 1938" (paper for Snow symposium, Huhehot, Inner Mongolia, July 1985); Stephen R. MacKinnon and Oris Friesen, *China Reporting* (Berkeley: University of California Press, 1987), 37–47.

12. Victoria W. Bailie, *Bailie's Activities in China* (Palo Alto: Pacific Books, 1964), 100, 171, 174; NW, "Notes on CIC," 49.

13. *Bailie's Activities in China*, 99–100, 188, 226; Joseph Bailie to Mr. Liebold (Ford Company), January 22, 1923, Henry Ford office correspondence, Henry Ford Museum.

14. *Bailie's Activities in China*, 485, 494, 511; *CBFD*, 45–50; Alley letter cited in NW, "Notes on CIC," 49–50.

15. *CBFD*, 45–49, 17 (note); *Bailie's Activities in China*, 485–486.

16. Reynolds, "CIC Movement," 179, 213–220; ES, "China's New Industrial Army," *Left News* (London), July 1939, 1346; *JTTB*, 202, 214; *CBFD*, 1, 129–134. In order to meet production quotas and schedules for the army blanket program, various exploitative practices and other deviations from cooperative principles crept into the work. Thus despite the money and prestige the blanket project brought CIC, "it distorted the real size and character of the grass roots industrial cooperative movement" (Reynolds, "CIC Movement," 218–220).

17. Reynolds, "CIC Movement," 204–205; ES, "China's New Industrial Army," 1346; *CBFD*, 199, and appendix 2, 266–279, for text of the CIC constitution.

18. *BFA*, 230; Jawaharlal Nehru, foreword to *CBFD* (Allahabad, 1942), 5–9. Rewi Alley, defending both CIC and himself during the xenophobic Cultural Revolution in 1968, asserted that the appeal of Gung Ho to "the big names" in the U.S. and Britain had been "direct encouragement [to the KMT] not to give in" to the Japanese ("Some Notes on Gung Ho," Beijing, June 17, 1968, RAP in ESC).

19. *JTTB*, 203–208; HFS to Ida Pruitt, January 13, 1939, Indusco files; Diaries, Book 27, June 23, 1939.

20. *JTTB*, 212–219; Diaries, Book 27, July 7, 11, 1939; Reynolds, "CIC Movement," 133–134. Madame Chiang Kai-shek noted her sister's special interest in CIC, and that she had "financially helped some of the Mining Co-operatives and is now planning to enlist co-operative zeal and competency in the development of the ramie fibre [China linen] industry" (Madame Chiang to Polly Babcock, April 10, 1940, NWC).

21. Reynolds, "CIC Movement," 123–126; ES to James Bertram, March 1, 1939, ESP in ESC; *CBFD,* 44; Boorman, ed., *Biographical Dictionary,* 2:263–269.

22. Reported by Snow in Diaries, Book 27, May 7, 1939; Pruitt replied, "It has no color." On Alley's suggestions for the CIC board of directors, Reynolds, "CIC Movement," 126, citing a 1955 Alley book, *Yo Banfa!*

23. Alley, *At 90,* 107–108. Bo Gu, a leader of the internationalist wing of the party, told Alley that "the main task of Gung Ho had to be to help keep Chiang Kai-shek in the war" (ibid., 108).

24. Reynolds notes: "As a political and economic 'middle way,' however, CIC failed. CIC was not by itself unified or powerful enough as an organization, nor by itself persuasive enough as an idea, to bind together two hostile forces, the controlling KMT right-wing and the Communists, whose social and political ideologies and whose political ambitions were in the long run fundamentally opposed—even though the cooperatives received personal endorsements from both Chiang Kai-shek and Mao Tse-tung" ("CIC Movement," 182).

25. "The Three Soong Sisters" (typescript dated November 2, 1940, evidently written for *Who* magazine), HFS files; *JTTB,* 213. Even when Snow "finally decided in 1941, to report some of the facts about the Kungs' operations," he in the end killed the story, chiefly because he "thought it might ruin Indusco" (*JTTB,* 218).

26. ES, "China's Fighting Generalissimo," *Foreign Affairs,* 16 (July 1938): 612–625; Diaries, Book 23, July 12, 1938, Book 25, August 1, 1938; ES, "The Sun Also Sets," *SEP,* June 14, 1938, 30; ES, "The Generalissimo," *Asia* 40 (December 1940): 646–648 (the *Asia* article was virtually identical to the chapter on Chiang in *BFA,* 115–119); ES, "The Dragon Licks His Wounds," *SEP,* April 13, 1940, 9–11, 155, 157–158, 160; Hollington K. Tong to ES, March 19, 1940, ESP in ESC. (Tong had read an advance copy of the April article.) At the beginning of 1940, a time when KMT-CCP tensions had appeared more heated, Snow had written more pessimistically on united front prospects: see "China's Precarious Unity," *New Republic,* January 8, 1940, 44–45. Snow's more sharply leftist pieces tended then to appear in smaller-circulation liberal journals such as *Asia* and *New Republic.*

27. ES to Bertram, November 15, 1938; Diaries, Book 27, July 13 and 14, 1939.

28. ES to Bertram, November 15, 1938; ES to Harry Price, November 23, 1939, NWC; ES to Richard Walsh, April 2, 1940, ESP in ESC.

29. Diaries, Book 30, September 23, 1939; ES to Mao, September 30, 1939, ESP in ESC; "Recommendations to the International Committee" (October 21, 1939), NWC.

30. HFS to Epstein, February 24, 1939, Indusco files; Epstein to HFS and ES, March 15, 1939, ES to Epstein, February 25, 1939, March 29, 1939, ESP in ESC.

31. ES to Israel Epstein, March 29, 1939, ESP in ESC; ES to HFS, August 4, 1938, HFS files.

32. Reynolds, "CIC Movement," 233–236; Alley to Ida Pruitt, August 17, 1940, Indusco files.

33. ES to "friend" (Madame Sun), March 13, 1939, ESP in ESC; Alley, *At 90,* 146–147; Hugh Deane, "How Americans Learned 'Gung Ho'," *U.S.–China Review,* September–October 1985, in *The Gung Ho Papers,* comp. Helen Foster

Snow and Margaret Stanley, ed. Dennis Gendell (Madison, Conn.: Bookmark Ltd. Press, 1985), A-1–A-4; Reynolds, "CIC Movement," 236–237.

34. Alley, *At 90*, 125–127; NW, "Notes on CIC," 64, 69–72. However, Snow was obliged to reassure one such overseas Chinese contributor that "There is no ground whatever for the suspicion that CIC 'is not supported by the Central Government and that the purpose is only to help the 8th Route Army and a New Fourth Route Army'" (ES to Mr. Dee, June 17, 1939, ESP in ESC).

35. ES to Ida Pruitt, February 5, 1940, Indusco files; NW, "Notes on CIC," 64, 74–77; Mark Selden, *The Yenan Way in Revolutionary China* (Cambridge, Mass.: Harvard University Press, 1971), 208–276; ES to Alley, December 3, 1941, Victor Hicks to Ida Pruitt, May 11, 1945, Victor Hicks to Lucy Pierce, May 14, 1945, Indusco files. Hicks, apparently working with CIC, reported on meetings with Chinese Communist representatives at the United Nations founding conference in San Francisco in the spring of 1945. Senior Communist party leader Dong Biwu told Hicks that though the CIC "had been good at the beginning," it had come under the control of the Kuomintang and could do very little. Monies raised in America, he added, did not reach cooperatives in the field. According to an October 1939 report by the Yan'an CIC office, "there are 137 productive cooperatives organized by the Construction Department of the Government, in addition to the 15 C.I.C.s . . . these 137 cooperatives are to be incorporated into the C.I.C. units" (report cited in NW, "Notes on CIC," 77). Snow's assertion in *JTTB* (233) that "By 1942 the Yenan depot came to be much the largest regional headquarters in the country, with as many workers as all the others in China combined," would seem to reflect the fact that, according to the above report, "the number of members in the government cooperatives reached 28,000" before becoming part of CIC. Peter Schran, in his study of the border region's wartime economy, notes that CIC membership "did not assume large proportions." Financial support from outside decreased sharply by 1941; during the 1939–1943 years, the border region government supplied 88 percent of the funds for the CIC branches there (*Guerrilla Economy: The Development of the Shensi-Kansu-Ninghsia Border Region, 1937–1945* [Albany: State University of New York Press, 1976], 71 [tb. 4.1], 74 n.30, 278).

36. Diaries, Book 25, September 21, 22, 23, and 30, 1938; ES to HFS, August 28, 1938, HFS files.

37. ES to Bertram, March 1, 1939, ESP in ESC; Robert Haas to Henriette Herz, February 3, 1939, RHP; HFS to Hubert Liang, December 15, 1938, NWC.

38. *JTTB*, 208–210, 257; *Gung Ho Papers*, B-17–B-20, for text of petition to Roosevelt (July 22, 1940); Nym Wales to President Roosevelt, February 24, 1942, Roosevelt Presidential Papers, Franklin D. Roosevelt Library.

39. ES to Pruitt, May 1, 1940, ES to Pruitt, July 25, 1941, Indusco files.

40. HFS to Alley, November 9, continued December 5, 1938, Indusco files.

41. ES to Madame Sun, March 13, 1939; ES to Pruitt, June 2, 1940, Indusco files.

42. Rewi Alley, "Edgar Snow and Indusco" (February 15, 1982 commemorative remarks), *Gung Ho Papers*, B-24; ES to Ma Haide, October 31, 1939, ESP in ESC; HFS to Snows, September 17, 1939, MP in ESC; ES to father, March 6,

1940, ES to "Roy," July 25, 1940, ESP in ESC; ES to Richard Walsh, July 25, 1941, Indusco files.

43. ES to Pruitt, May 1, 1940, ES to Richard Walsh, July 25, 1941, Indusco files.

44. ES to Robert Haas, May 24, 1940, RHP; ES, "China's Blitzbuilder, Rewi Alley," *SEP*, February 8, 1941, 12–13, 36, 38, 40; Alley, *At 90*, 159.

45. ES, "China's Blitzbuilder," 40.

46. Reynolds, "CIC Movement," 40; Olga Lang Wittfogel to Ida Pruitt, February 18, 1942, Indusco files, cited in Reynolds, ibid., 52–53.

47. ES to Richard Walsh, July 25, 1941; Graham Peck, *Two Kinds of Time* (Boston: Houghton Mifflin, 1967), 170; Alley to Ida Pruitt, June 4, 1939, cited in NW, "Notes on CIC," 48; Rewi Alley, probably to CIC in Hong Kong, October 6, 1940, Evans Carlson to ES and HFS, August 22, 1940, NWC.

48. Peck, *Two Kinds of Time*, 164.

49. Diaries, Book 27, July 13, 1939; Rewi Alley, probably to Helen Snow, June 18, 1939, NWC; ES to Ida Pruitt, February 26, 1939, HFS to ES, May 23, 1939, Indusco files; Chen Han-seng to HFS, August 7, 1940, NWC. "Just had a note from the elusive Alley, the Blind Alley, from Kweilin, Kwangsi, who still gives no indication that he has ever received a note of mine," Ed acerbically wrote Pruitt (January 3, 1939, Indusco files).

50. ES to Ida Pruitt, February 26, 1939, HFS to Ida Pruitt, January 13, 1939, HFS to Ida Pruitt, February 25, 1939, HFS to ES, May 23, 1939, ES to Rewi Alley, August 6, 1940, Indusco files; Alley, "Some Notes on Gung Ho," 2, 3; Peck, *Two Kinds of Time*, 176; *CBFD*, 18, 50.

51. *JTTB*, 203, 220; Diaries, Book 27, May 31, 1939; Rewi Alley to Lewis Smythe, April 25, 1943, Indusco files.

52. Reynolds, "CIC Movement," 333–363; Alley, *At 90*, 185–217. On the CIC situation after 1941, Reynolds writes: "The complex of developments with IC [international committee] further represents a partial realization of Ida Pruitt's fear of 1941: the fear that Indusco, Inc. and the International Committee might be overwhelmed by UCR [United China Relief] elements 'trying to control all China aid and get it into the hands of missionaries and of the Kuomintang,' with a resulting stultifying effect on the movement" ("CIC Movement," 362–363).

53. Reynolds, "CIC Movement," 430; Alley, *At 90*, 213, 224–228; Alley, "The New Bailie School Project in Shandan" (Beijing, December 25, 1984), NWC; interview with Alley, Beijing, May 18, 1987. In "Some Notes on Gung Ho" (1968), Alley tried to counter revived "imperialist" charges against CIC and himself.

54. ES, "How Rural China Is Being Re-made," *CWR*, December 16, 1933, 98–101, December 30, 1933, 202–203; James C. Thomson, Jr., *While China Faced West: American Reformers in Nationalist China, 1928–1937* (Cambridge, Mass.: Harvard University Press, 1969), 234–244.

55. Rewi Alley to ES, November 16, 1955, Rewi Alley to ES, September 1, 1968, RAP in ESC.

56. Alley, *At 90*, 231–232; interview with Alley, Beijing, May 28, 1987.

57. ES to Rewi Alley, December 3, 1941, Indusco files.

Chapter 12. Final China Years

1. Diaries, Book 26, October 18, 1938; *JTTB*, 209–210.

2. Diaries, Book 26, October 18, 1938.

3. Diaries, Book 26, October 27 and 30, 1938.

4. ES to Clark-Kerr, January 11, 1939, ESP in ESC.

5. ES, "They Love Us, They Love Us Not," *SEP*, April 29, 1939, 25, 62, 64, 69.

6. ES, "Filipinos Change Their Minds," *Asia* 39 (September 1939): 493–496; "Japan's 'Peaceful' Invasion," *Asia* 39 (October 1939): 590–592; "Filipinos Want a Guarantee," *Asia* 39 (November 1939): 659–661. The figures on Japanese imports from the U.S. are cited in Waldo Heinrichs, *Threshold of War: Franklin D. Roosevelt and American Entry into World War II* (New York: Oxford University Press, 1988), 7.

7. Diaries, Book 27, July 18, 1939.

8. Diaries, Book 28, July 30, 1939; Peggy Durdin talk at Snow symposium, Beijing, June 1988; ES to father, December 18, 1939, ESP in ESC. Chungking description in Hugh Deane, *Good Deeds & Gunboats* (San Francisco: China Books & Periodicals, 1990), 220–221.

9. Diaries, Book 28, August 3, 5, 1939.

10. Diaries, Book 29, August 20, 1939; ES to father, December 18, 1939.

11. Diaries, Book 28, September 21, 1939, Book 30, September 23, 1939; ES to father, December 18, 1939.

12. Mao interview, Diaries, Book 30, September 23, 1939. On Yan'an-era rectification and purges, see Dai Qing, *Wang Shiwei and 'Wild Lilies': Rectification and Purges in the Chinese Communist Party, 1942–1944* (Armonk, N.Y.: M. E. Sharpe, 1994).

13. Diaries, Book 30, September 23, 1939; ES, "Notes on Mao Interview," Hong Kong, November 4, 1939, ESP in ESC.

14. ES to Mao, September 30, 1939, ESP in ESC; ES to HFS, undated excerpts, ESP in ESC. Though the initial and final pages of this letter are missing, the context clearly shows it to be written to Helen, and in the same time-frame as the above letter to Mao.

15. *BFA*, 288–290, 294; Mark Selden, *The Yenan Way in Revolutionary China* (Cambridge, Mass.: Harvard University Press, 1971), 177–181.

16. *BFA*, 287–291.

17. Diaries, Book 27, June 24, 1939.

18. Stephen R. MacKinnon and Oris Friesen, *China Reporting* (Berkeley: University of California Press, 1987), 154–155 (A. T. Steele comments); Harrison Forman, *Report from Red China* (New York: Henry Holt, 1945), 177.

19. John Service's memorandum of October 9, 1944, cited in Joseph W. Esherick, ed., *Lost Chance in China* (New York: Random House, 1974), 248–249. On the Dixie mission, Michael Schaller, *The U.S. Crusade in China, 1938–1945* (New York: Columbia University Press, 1979), 177–200; David D. Barrett, *Dixie Mission: The United States Army Observer Group in Yenan, 1944* (Berkeley: Center for Chinese Studies, University of California, 1970).

20. Diaries, Book 26, January 2, 1939.

21. Ibid.; ES, "Aftermath of the Cultural Revolution," *New Republic*, April 10, 1971, 18–19.

22. ES to HFS (undated), ES to James Bertram, November 15, 1938, ESP in ESC; Diaries, Book 27, May 23, 1939, Book 30, October 9, 1939.

23. "The Dragon Licks His Wounds," 158.

24. *BFA*, 298; Bertram, *Capes of China Slide Away*, 160–161, 162–241.

25. HFS to Mildred and J. Edgar Snow, September 17, 1939, MP in ESC.

26. ES to Will Babcock, November 18, 1939, ES to HFS (undated), ESP in ESC; Polly Babcock Feustel to author, August 15, 1989.

27. ES to Will Babcock, November 18, 1939.

28. Ibid., ES to HFS (undated), ESP in ESC.

29. ES to Will Babcock, November 18, 1939, ES to James Bertram, December 13, 1939, ESP in ESC.

30. ES, "Will Stalin Sell Out China?," *Foreign Affairs* 18 (April 1940): 450–455.

31. Ibid., 457–463; ES to J.B. Powell, December 19, 1939, ESP in ESC.

32. "Will Stalin Sell Out China?" 461–463; Snow had not precluded the possibility of a "simple non-aggression pact" between Tokyo and Moscow, which would exclude "the question of either nation's policy toward the Chinese Government" (461).

33. Ibid., 463; ES to Hall, February 25, 1940, ESP in ESC.

34. ES, "Things That Could Happen," *Asia* 41 (January 1941): 7–16. The article was subtitled, "If America Enters the War? If America Stays Out?"

35. Ibid.

36. *JTTB*, 238–239; ES, "Chiang's Armies," *Asia* 40 (November 1940): 582; Bertram, *Capes of China Slide Away*, 177; Diaries, Book 32, January 1, 1941, for ES confirming notes on the Bertram get-together; *New York Herald-Tribune*, December 26, 1940.

37. Diaries, Book 26, November 11, 1940; *JTTB*, 240.

38. Diaries, Book 32, November 16, 20–26, 1940.

39. Diaries, Book 32, November 29, December 3, 1940, June 26, 1941; *JTTB*, 235–236; ES, "Reds Fought Off Chiang Troops 9 Days in China," *New York Herald-Tribune*, January 22, 1941. Snow's dispatch had a January 21, Hong Kong dateline, though he of course had left there two weeks earlier. An addendum to Snow's report noted that "The official account given out by Chiang's military council at Chungking on Jan. 17 differs in important respects from the account received from Mr. Snow." For a recent in-depth scholarly account of the incident, see Gregor Benton, "The South Anhui [New Fourth Army] Incident, January 1941" (paper for the International Symposium on the History of the Chinese Anti-Japanese Bases during World War II, Tianjin, Nankai University, August 1984).

40. ES to Mr. Chen, January 4, 1964, ESP in ESC; Diaries, Book 32, December 7, 20, 25, 1940, January 1, 1941.

41. Diaries, Book 32, December 25, 1940, January 1, 1941. To a friend who knew the Snows well after the couple's return to the States, Ed's personality "was just the opposite of Peg's" (interview with Susan B. Anthony, II, June 10, 1989).

42. James Bertram, *In the Shadow of a War* (London: Victor Gollancz, 1947), 82, for description of Bertram's New Year meeting with Snow; James Bertram to author, July 30, 1989; Hamilton, *Edgar Snow*, 123; interview with Polly Babcock Feustel, July 22, 1989; interview with HFS, October 14, 1987; Polly Babcock to HFS, January 13, 1941, NWC.

43. ES diary page, dated January 13 (1941), HFS files; interview with HFS, October 14, 1987; ES to "Tony," July 11, 1968, ESP in ESC.

44. Diaries, Book 33, January 13, 17, 23, 1941.

45. Diaries, Book 32, March 2, 18, 1941; *JTTB*, 241.

46. Interview with John Snow, November 22, 1988; HFS to ES, July 7, 1939; interview with HFS, October 14, 1987; HFS, "Four Years," HFS files.

47. Diaries, Book 33, January 16, 1941; ES to HFS, October 14, 1946, HFS files. On their wartime separation, "He (Ed) has been away from home . . . most of the time since 1941, and I have lived alone in the house in Connecticut nearly all the time he was away," Helen wrote her lawyer in 1946 (HFS to "Dear Sir" [Mr. Rothenberg], December 11, 1946, HFS files).

Chapter 13. After China

1. *JTTB*, 246–247. Snow's *Journey* account of the Dreiser episode may have benefited from hindsight. His diary entry (Diaries, Book 33, February 4, 1941), was noncommittal on Dreiser's statements but more interested in the author's great concern and sympathy for China's cause.

2. Carl W. McCardle, "Edgar Snow, Back from Orient, Thinks We'll Fight Japan Soon," *Philadelphia Evening Bulletin,* June 4, 1941; ES to Bennett Cerf, December 10, 1941, RHP.

3. Diaries, Book 32, February 23, 1941 (Snow noted that *BFA* had lost out to Jan Valtin's *Out of the Night*). *BFA* had sold 9,700 copies by early December 1941 (Bennett Cerf to ES, December 10, 1941, RHP).

4. *BFA,* 66; ES to Robert Haas (Random House), May 24, 1940; Dorothy Woodman, review of *Scorched Earth* [*BFA*'s English edition, published by Victor Gollancz in 1941], *New Statesman and Nation,* April 19, 1941.

5. *BFA,* 364; Henry Luce to ES, February 25, 1941, ESP in ESC.

6. John F. Davidson, review of *BFA,* in *Canadian Forum,* April 1941, 25; *BFA,* 199–238, 327–359.

7. *BFA,* 58–61, 66–69, 187–195. See also John W. Dower, *War Without Mercy* (New York: Pantheon Books, 1986), 133. Dower cites Snow's *BFA* remarks on Japanese "inferiority," in support of his thesis on the significant role of racism in the Pacific War.

8. *BFA,* 385, 415.

9. *BFA,* 413, 416; Diaries, Book 34, August 11, 1941, Book 32, June 25–27, 1941. Wilson's fourteen points, Michael H. Hunt has written, "carried to new limits the old American commitment to an active international policy in the name of national greatness and liberty for all men" (*Ideology and U.S. Foreign Policy* [New Haven: Yale University Press, 1987], 134).

10. *BFA,* 416–417.

11. Hunt, *Ideology and U.S. Foreign Policy,* 11.

12. *BFA,* 417–423.

13. *JTTB*, 258; "Reminiscences of Bennett Cerf," 372.

14. Henry A. Kissinger, "Clinton and the World," *Newsweek,* February 1, 1993, 45; ES, "The Political Battle of Asia," in *Smash Hitler's International: The*

Strategy of an Offensive Against the Axis (New York: Keystone Press, 1941), 57; *BFA,* 422. Snow's contribution to the *Smash Hitler's International* volume was identical with his article, "How America Can Take the Offensive: II," *Fortune* 23 (June 1941): 69, 175–180; James C. Thomson, Jr., Peter W. Stanley, and John Curtis Perry, *Sentimental Imperialists* (New York: Harper and Row, 1981), 311.

15. *New Statesman and Nation,* April 19, 1941.

16. Freda Utley, review of *BFA,* in *New York Times Book Review,* April 9, 1941, 9; Diaries, Book 32, January 1, 1941.

17. Utley, review of *BFA.*

18. ES, "Is It Civil War in China?," *Asia* 41 (April 1941): 169–170.

19. *BFA,* 299; Snow added, perhaps a bit condescendingly, that his comments did "not mean that I might not personally prefer Mr. Ford [the Communist candidate] to Mr. Garner, of course."

20. Diaries, Book 33, February 4, 1941; Henriette Herz to Belle Becker (undated, evidently late January or early February 1941), in which she quotes from the letter received from Snow; ES to Belle Becker, February 6, 1941, RHP.

21. *JTTB,* 248–249; Franklin Folsom (national executive secretary, American Writers Congress) to ES, June 4, 1941, ESP in ESC.

22. Franklin Folsom to ES, June 4, 1941, ES to Franklin Folsom, June 6, 1941, ESP in ESC. The resolutions adopted by the Writers Congress "in general followed the Communist party line," the *New York Times* reported, June 9, 1941. According to American Communist party leader William Z. Foster, the American Writers Congress in those years "was a powerful force in cultural circles, not the least in Hollywood." The Communists "were most active in this development," he added (William Z. Foster, *History of the Communist Party of the United States* [Westport, Conn.: Greenwood Press, 1968], 319–320).

23. ES, "China, America and the World War" (typescript, May 31, 1941), ESP in ESC; *Philadelphia Evening Bulletin,* June 4, 1941. The quotation from the *Bulletin* is given as reported by the newspaper.

24. "China, America and the World War"; *JTTB,* 224. Snow's article ("China and the World War," *Asia* 41 [July 1941]: 341–343) contained much the same points as the China portions of the congress talk, including the conditions Snow had laid down for American aid to Chungking.

25. ES, "The Political Battle of Asia," 61, 66–67; ES, "Things That Could Happen," 12; ES, "Showdown in the Pacific," *SEP,* May 31, 1941, 47.

26. Diaries, Book 33, June 15, 1941, Book 34, August 11, 1941, Book 35, August 22, 1941, December 7, 1941; "The Political Battle of Asia," 62–63; ES to Rewi Alley, December 3, 1941.

27. Diaries, Book 32, June 26, 1941, Book 35, December 16, 1941; ES to Edward C. Carter, January 16, 1942, IPRP. There were apparently no contemporary diary entries on the Roosevelt meeting, which Snow recounts in *JTTB,* 253–258.

28. Diaries, Book 35, September 22, November 24, December 5, 1941.

29. ES to Rewi Alley, December 3, 1941; Diaries, Book 32, June 27, 1941, Book 35, October 31, 1941. "I have long and consistently been known in this country as a friend of the Soviet Union," Snow wrote Carter of the Institute of Pacific Relations regarding his Soviet visa problem. "It would seem to me a tragedy for Russia to reject this opportunity to get a fair hearing in the columns

of so influential a journal" as the *Post* (ES to Edward C. Carter [confidential], March 28, 1942, IPRP). It took another six months, with pressure from the U.S. government, for Snow's visa finally to come through (*JTTB*, 259–260).

30. ES, "They Don't Want to Play Soldier," *SEP,* October 25, 1941, 14–15, 61–67; "What Is Morale?" *SEP,* November 15, 1941, 16–17, 119–120, 122–123; Diaries, Book 35, November 12, 1941.

31. "They Don't Want to Play Soldier," 65; "What Is Morale?" 120–122.

32. ES to Rewi Alley, December 3, 1941; *JTTB*, 258–260. Snow's wartime volumes were *People on Our Side,* or *POOS* (New York: Random House, 1944), and *The Pattern of Soviet Power,* or *TPOSP* (New York: Random House, 1945).

33. Diaries, Book 37, April 19, 1942; Michael Schaller, *U.S. Crusade in China* (New York: Columbia University Press, 1979), 231–250; Hugh Deane, *Good Deeds & Gunboats* (San Francisco: China Books & Periodicals, 1990), 116–125. According to Schaller, "Miles increasingly defined SACO's mission in terms not only of the struggle against Chinese Communism, but also of America's future global position" (ibid., 245).

Chapter 14. Global War, and Cold War Blues

1. ES to "Ross," May 8, 1971, ESP in ESC; Diaries, Book 38, May 8, July 10, 1942.

2. *POOS,* 25; Diaries, Book 38, September 2, 1942.

3. Diaries, Book 39, June 1, 1942.

4. Diaries, Book 38, June 13, May 16, 1942.

5. ES, "How Russia Upset Hitler," *SEP,* January 30, 1943, 20; *POOS,* 215–216.

6. "How Russia Upset Hitler," 20–21, 87, 89–90; "I Saw It with My Own Eyes," *SEP,* May 29, 1943, 12–13, 86–88; "The Ukraine Pays the Bill," *SEP,* January 27, 1945, 18–19, 82–84; "What Kind of a Man Is a Russian General?" *SEP,* April 17, 1943, 20–21, 105–106; "Is Red Marriage Turning Blue?" *SEP,* January 13, 1945, 28–29, 36; "Meet Mr. and Mrs. Russia at Home," *SEP,* December 22, 1945, 14–15, 65; *TPOSP,* 142–147; *POOS,* 71–72. On Snow's projections of Communist-led "popular front" regimes in eastern Europe, functioning in "fraternal" cooperation and alliance with Moscow, see *TPOSP,* 58–72. On Stalin glorification, Snow typically recorded while in Moscow that Stalin "takes up 2 pages of the 4-page paper quite often." In Tsarist times, "no one would have toasted the Tsar on every occasion." The "Infallibility thing is built up re leadership and regime, and maintained at all cost of logic or consistency" (Diaries, Book 40, January 26, 1943).

7. *POOS,* 255.

8. *POOS,* 131.

9. Diaries, Book 40, January 31, February 28, 1943.

10. Diaries, Book 42, May 15, 1943.

11. Ibid., May 30, 1943, Book 43, June 2, 1943.

12. *POOS,* 279.

13. Diaries, Book 44, May 26, 1944.

14. Ibid., July 19, 1944; *JTTB*, 335–341.

15. Diaries, Book 46, August 6, 1944, Book 48, May 1945; ES, "Eastern Europe Swings Left," *SEP,* November 11, 1944, 71; ES, "The Nazi Butchers Wasted Nothing," *SEP,* October 28, 1944, 18–19, 96; *TPOSP,* 47–53.

16. Diaries, Book 45, March 2, 1945; "Interviews with Major-General William A. Worton (Marine Corps, ret.)," Oral History Research Office, Columbia University, 1969, 154. In a eulogy at a memorial meeting for Carlson in New York in January 1948, Smedley said that Snow had helped change Carlson from a reactionary to "a fighter for the people" during the mid-1930s in Peking (Janice R. MacKinnon and Stephen R. MacKinnon, *Agnes Smedley* [Berkeley: University of California Press, 1988], 317).

17. Diaries, Book 45, March 2, 1945.

18. *TPOSP,* 140; ES, "Must China Go Red?," *SEP,* May 12, 1945, 9–10, 67–68, 70.

19. Cited by ES, *TPOSP,* 127; Michael Schaller, *U.S. Crusade in China* (New York: Columbia University Press, 1979), 89, 174. In commenting on Roosevelt's remarks to Snow, Schaller notes, "nowhere did Roosevelt give any indication that he understood the nature of the real problems in China, nor did he indicate any displeasure with Hurley or Wedemeyer" (ibid., 217).

20. Schaller, *U.S. Crusade in China,* 305.

21. Diaries, Book 50, July 30, 1945.

22. Ibid., August 22, 1945.

23. O. Edmund Clubb, *Twentieth-Century China* (New York: Columbia University Press, 1964), 244–246; Schaller, *U.S. Crusade in China,* 260; Diaries, Book 50, August 30, 1945.

24. ES to Saxe Cummins, November 10, 1945, ESP in ESC.

25. Diaries, Book 50, November 30, 1945.

26. Ben Hibbs's cable to President Harry S. Truman, December 4, 1945, and Truman memorandum to Secretary of State James F. Byrnes, December 8, 1945, Truman Presidential Papers, Harry S. Truman Library ("It seems to me that the Chinese are making a mistake in this matter," Truman told Byrnes. "Suggest that you investigate it").

27. Diaries, Book 51, December 19, 1945, and December 1945–January 1946 entries from Korea; Bertram, *Capes of China Slide Away,* 252.

28. Lois Wheeler Snow, *Edgar Snow's China* (New York: Random House, 1981), xi–xii; Lois Snow, *Death with Dignity,* 20; Lois Snow to author, February 19, 1995.

29. Diaries, Book 52, June 1946—May 1947; ES to Martin Sommers, September 14, 17, 1947, ESP in ESC.

30. ES to Natalie and Jerry Crouter, ESP in ESC. The first page is missing and thus undated; the letter is continued on December 2, 1947, evidently the following day.

31. Ibid. For an insightful analysis of the theory and practice of democracy in twentieth-century China, see Andrew J. Nathan, *Chinese Democracy* (Berkeley: University of California Press, 1985).

32. ES to Saxe Cummins, July 21, 1945, ESP in ESC; Diaries, Book 54, July 18, 1947, February 10, 1948.

33. "Notes on Edgar Snow conversation with Maxim Litvinov," Moscow, October 8, 1944, 5, Roosevelt Presidential Papers. Snow had transmitted these notes

directly to Roosevelt, who wrote Snow that he was "tremendously interested" in them (Franklin D. Roosevelt to ES, January 2, 1945, Roosevelt Presidential Papers).

34. Diaries, Book 52, September 17, December 25, 1946; MacKinnon and MacKinnon, *Agnes Smedley*, 265–67; ES, *Stalin Must Have Peace*, or *SMHP* (New York: Random House, 1947); ES to Raymond A. de Groat, September 26, 1949, ESP in ESC; ES to Natalie and Jerry Crouter. President Bill Clinton would declare in Moscow in May 1995, on the fiftieth anniversary of Allied victory in Europe, "The Cold War obscured our ability fully to appreciate what your people suffered and how your extraordinary courage helped hasten the victory we all celebrate today (*Detroit Free Press,* May 10, 1995).

35. Basilio Raymundo Hanago, "The Saturday Evening Post under Ben Hibbs, 1942–1961" (Ph.D. diss., Northwestern University, 1968), 106; Diaries, Book 52, February 1, 1947; ES to Martin Sommers, June 25, 1947, ESP in ESC.

36. ES to Charles G. Ross (White House), January 21, 1947, Truman Presidential Papers. "As I left [the meeting with Truman]," Snow recorded, "I told him I would send him news of anything of interest I ran into along the way." Snow, incidentally, identified himself politically as a Democrat. Diaries, Book 52, January 23, 1947.

37. Diaries, Book 54, February 9, 13, 1948. On the issue of "camps," Snow rather petulantly added, "I wasn't a Russian and I didn't have to live in one, thank goodness!" (Diaries, February 13, 1948).

38. Diaries, Book 52, December 4, 1946; interviews with HFS, October 14, 1987, June 1, 1989; ES to James Bertram, October 25, 1952.

39. ES, "Will Tito's Heretics Halt Russia?" *SEP,* December 18, 1948, 23, 108–110.

40. Ibid., 109–110.

41. ES to Raymond A. de Groat, September 26, 1949.

42. ES, "Will China Become a Russian Satellite?," *SEP,* April 9, 1949, 30–31, 147–150; Sergei N. Goncharov, John W. Lewis, and Xue Litai, *Uncertain Partners: Stalin, Mao, and the Korean War* (Stanford: Stanford University Press, 1993), 206.

43. ES to Natalie ("Pete") Crouter, July 3, 1954, ESP in ESC; ES to James Bertram, April 5, 1959. The CCP had earlier issued a careful endorsement of Stalin's break with Tito. As for the onset of the Korean War, North Korean leader Kim Il Sung "proposed it, fought for it, and with a Soviet army battle plan to guide him, executed it. The invasion of June 25, 1950, was pre-planned, blessed, and directly assisted by Stalin and his generals, and reluctantly backed by Mao at Stalin's insistence" (Goncharov, et al., *Uncertain Partners,* 213). The authors note further, of China's entrance into the war, that "Mao knew that the decision to go to war immeasurably strengthened Stalin's trust in him and dispelled his suspicions" (217).

44. ES, "The New Phase—Undeclared War," *Nation,* March 10, 1951, 220–223; ES, review of *Moscow and Chinese Communists,* by Robert C. North, in *Nation,* November 14, 1953, 407.

45. ES to Ben Hibbs, December 11, 1950, ESP in ESC.

46. ES, "The Message of Gandhi," 145; ES to Ben Hibbs, March 18, 1948, ES to Ben Hibbs and Martin Sommers, March 29, 1948, ES to Martin Sommers, March 24, 1950, ESP in ESC.

47. Ben Hibbs to ES, March 26, 1948 (only first page has survived), Ben Hibbs to ES, April 12, 1948, ESP in ESC.

48. ES, "The Venomous Doctor Vyshinsky," *SEP,* October 21, 1950, 19–21, 143–144, 146.

49. Martin Sommers to ES, February 3, March 7, April 4, August 16, October 30, 1950, ES to Martin Sommers, March 24, April 5, July 23, 1950, ESP in ESC.

50. ES to Martin Sommers, March 24, 1950; ES to James Bertram, October 25, 1952.

51. ES, "Red China's Gentleman Hatchet Man," *SEP,* March 27, 1954, 24–25, 116, 118–119; ES to Mildred (undated, probably 1954), ES to father, November 21, 1956, MP in ESC.

52. MacKinnon and MacKinnon, *Agnes Smedley,* 337, 347; ES to Marshal Chu Teh (Zhu De), August 26, 1960, ES to Hilda Selwyn-Clarke, May 22, 1950, ESP in ESC.

53. ES to Mildred, July 14, 1953, MP in ESC; ES to father, October 20, 1953, ES to Lois Snow, July 3, 1959, ES to Darryl Berrigan, October 2, 1954, ESP in ESC; Lois Snow, *Death with Dignity,* 23–24; ES to James Bertram, October 25, 1952.

54. ES to father, November 21, 1956, MP in ESC; report to director, FBI, June 29, 1953, Snow FBI file, ESC.

55. ES to Natalie Crouter, July 3, 1954; ES to Darryl Berrigan, October 2, 1954, ESP in ESC.

56. Interview with Seiko Matsuoka, Tokyo, June 28, 1987; Yoko Matsuoka, postscript to Japanese edition of *JTTB* (Tokyo, 1988). This was a slightly revised edition of a translation published in 1963 by Kinokuniya, Tokyo. Copy of the 1988 edition received from the late Yoko Matsuoka's daughter Seiko. Yoko Matsuoka also wrote an autobiography in English, *Daughter of the Pacific* (New York: Harper and Brothers, 1952).

57. ES to James Bertram, April 5, 1959; ES to Rewi Alley, January 27, 1959, RAP in ESC.

58. *JTTB,* 95; ES to Rewi Alley, January 27, 29, 1959, Alley to ES, January 18, 1959, RAP in ESC.

59. *JTTB,* 413–419.

60. Ibid., 385–386.

61. Ibid., 386–389.

62. Ibid., 422–423; see also ES, "Point IV for America," *Nation,* May 12, 1956, 394–397.

63. Karl Jaeger (International School of America) to ES, July 17, 1959, ES to Karl Jaeger, September 8, 9, 1959, ES to Allan Dreyfuss, July 17, 1959, ESP in ESC; Lois Snow, *Death with Dignity,* 44; Lois Snow to Mildred Snow, May 1, 1968, MP in ESC. The Snows' New Jersey home was sold in 1962.

64. Diaries, Book 58, November 27–29, 1959.

Chapter 15. Return to China

1. ES to Rewi Alley, January 27, 1959, RAP in ESC.

2. ES to Alley, September 28, 1955, RAP in ESC.

3. ES to Mao, September 15, 1955, ESP in ESC.

4. Alley to ES, January 30, 1957, ES to Yang Han-seng and Lao She, March 1, 1957, RAP in ESC. The letter of invitation to Snow, dated January 25, 1957, is not available. Lao She is the pen name of Shu She-yu, a novelist known in the U.S. for the best-selling English version of *Rickshaw Boy* (1945; written in 1936); he reportedly committed suicide in 1966 during the Cultural Revolution.

5. ES to Alley, March 1, 1957, Alley to ES, March 19, 1957, December 24, 1957, RAP in ESC; ES to Yang Han-seng and Lao She, January 6, 1958, ESP in ESC.

6. ES to Alley, February 25, June 14, 1958, Alley to ES, June 30, 1958, ES to Alley, January 27, 1959, RAP in ESC.

7. ES to Alley, June 14, 1958.

8. ES to James Bertram, April 5, 1959.

9. Bertram to ES, March 9, 1960, ES cable to Bertram, March 26, 1960, JBP in ESC.

10. ES to Bertram, March 23, 1960, Bertram to ES, March 30, 1960, JBP in ESC; *RCT,* 4–10; Andrew H. Berding to Richard Wilson (Cowles Publications), June 23, 1960 (draft), Harris Huston to "Andy" (Berding), June 23, 1960, Department of State files (received under Freedom of Information Act).

11. "On Publication of Chou En-lai Interview"; ES to Mao, May 10, 1963, Grenville Clark Papers; Soong Qingling to ES, November 3, 1960, ESC; Anna Louise Strong to ES, January 1, 1961, ALSP; ES to Bennett Cerf (via Lois Snow), July 5, 1960, RHP.

12. ES to Anna Louise Strong, June 17, 1963, ALSP; Donald Klopfer to ES, June 27, 1961, RHP.

13. *RCT,* 736.

14. ES to Anna Louise Strong, May 27, 1960, ALSP; *RCT,* 15; ES, notebooks, Beijing, July 9–18, Harbin and Changchun, July 25–30, 1960, ESP in ESC.

15. *RCT,* 22.

16. The following account of Snow's two meetings with Mao are based on Snow's typescript "Notes on Meeting with Mao Tse-tung," Beijing, October 22, 27, 1960, ESP in ESC. Though these conversations were off the record, Mao did later agree to some paraphrasing of his remarks.

17. "Notes on Edgar Snow's Interviews with Premier Chou En-lai," Beijing, August 30, October 18, 1960, ESP in ESC; *Shanghai Communique, New China News Agency (Xinhua),* February 28, 1972; Warren I. Cohen, *America's Response to China* (New York: John Wiley and Sons, 1971), 211–225.

18. "Notes on Edgar Snow's Interview with Premier Chou En-lai," October 18, 1960; *RCT,* 763–764.

19. "On Publication of Chou En-lai Interview."

20. *RCT,* 727–728; ES to Donald Klopfer, October 15, 1961, RHP. Before leaving for China, Snow had planned to write "a short book (200–250 pages)," he told Klopfer (ES to Donald Klopfer, April 16, 1960, RHP).

21. ES to Donald Klopfer, December 19, 1961, RHP; ES to Grenville Clark, August 21, 1964, Grenville Clark Papers; John K. Fairbank, letter to the editor, *New York Review of Books,* April 27, 1989, 61. The China historian Benjamin Schwartz observed in his review of *RCT,* regarding the "Asian hordes" image, that "Mr. Snow has some cogent things to say about the whole 'blue ant' cliché

which in my view he correctly associates with the old 'Yellow Peril' image" (*CQ* 14 [April–June 1963]: 246).

22. Robert C. North, review of *RCT,* in *Nation,* February 23, 1963, 162–163; Michael Lindsay, review of *RCT,* in *New York Times Book Review,* December 9, 1962, 6, 30; ES and Lindsay letters to the book review editor, April 17, 1963.

23. Ed Sullivan to ES, December 27, 1962, RHP.

24. See chapter 14; ES, preface to *JTTB* (Tokyo, 1988); *RCT,* 326.

25. Benjamin Schwartz, review of *RCT,* 248–249; Diaries, Book 60, March 20, 1963.

26. *RCT,* 336–337, 641–642.

27. Ibid., 393–398; René Goldman, review of *RCT,* in *New Republic,* April 27, 1963, 23–24; Hatem's remarks quoted in Sidney Shapiro, *Ma Haide: The Saga of American Doctor George Hatem in China* (San Francisco: Cypress Press, 1993), 206. A "Democracy Wall" and a "Democracy Square" had been established by students at Beijing University in May 1957 (Merle Goldman, "Mao's Obsession with the Political Role of Literature and the Intellectuals," in *The Secret Speeches of Chairman Mao: From the Hundred Flowers to the Great Leap Forward,* ed. Roderick MacFarquhar, Timothy Cheek, and Eugene Wu [Cambridge, Mass.: Council on East Asian Studies, Harvard University, 1989], 57).

28. Andrew J. Nathan, *Chinese Democracy* (Berkeley: University of California Press, 1985), ix, xii, 232.

29. ES, "On Publication of Chou En-lai Interview." A recent study of contemporary China's "America Watchers" concludes that it "seems that Chinese perceptions of the United States are fundamentally confounded by the strong American commitment to pluralism in politics, economic organization, and social structure." The author ends, "Fluctuating Sino-American relations reflect the continuing ambivalent images that the United States and China hold of each other. For the Chinese, the United States remains a Beautiful Imperialist" (David Shambaugh, *Beautiful Imperialist: China Perceives America, 1972–1990* [Princeton: Princeton University Press, 1991], 299, 303).

30. Fang Lizhi, "The Chinese Amnesia," *New York Review of Books,* September 27, 1990, 30–31. See also Jonathan Mirsky, review of *Edgar Snow,* by John Hamilton, in *New York Review of Books,* February 16, 1989, 15–17; and exchange of letters with John K. Fairbank, *New York Review of Books,* April 27, 1989, 60, and Jonathan Mirsky, review of *China Misperceived: American Illusion and Chinese Realities,* by Steven Mosher, *New York Review of Books,* May 30, 1991, 19–27.

31. *RCT,* 619–620.

32. John K. Fairbank, *The Great Chinese Revolution, 1800–1985* (New York: Harper and Row, 1986), 303; Thomas P. Bernstein, "Stalinism, Famine, and Chinese Peasants," *Theory and Society* 13 (May 1984): 393; Dwight Perkins cited in Bernstein, ibid., 372 n.20.

33. Benjamin Schwartz, review of *RCT,* 246; ES to Mildred, February 5, 1961, MP in ESC.

34. ES to Sol Adler (an expatriate American economist working for the Chinese government), January 29, 1961, ES to Kung (Gong) Peng, February 24, 1961, Henry Mitchell Collection in ESC; Alley to ES, August 26, 1961, RAP in ESC; ES to Israel Epstein ("Eppy"), May 22, 1962, ES to Epstein, June 17, 1963,

Israel Epstein Papers in ESC. There is no record of any immediate response by Epstein; he apparently wrote Snow in the spring of 1963, with his comments on *RCT*. Snow had sent a copy of *RCT* to Alley, who passed it along to Epstein. According to Alley, Epstein "thinks it the best thing you have done since *Red Star*" (Alley to ES, February 6, 1963, RAP in ESC).

35. ES to Han Suyin, December 21, 1961, Han Suyin Papers in ESC.

36. ES to Han Suyin, December 21, 1961; ES to Alley, September 22, 1962, RAP in ESC.

37. Han Suyin to ES, February 2, 1961, Han Suyin Papers in ESC.

38. ES memorandum, Beijing, October 4, 1961, ESP in ESC.

39. ES to Alley, September 22, 1952.

40. A. T. Steele, *The American People and China* (New York: McGraw-Hill, 1966), 172 n.11; ES to Mao, May 10, 1963.

41. ES–Grenville Clark Correspondence, 1963–1966, Grenville Clark Papers; copies in ESC. See also Kenneth E. Shewmaker, "The Grenville Clark–Edgar Snow Correspondence," *Pacific Historical Review* 45 (November 1976): 598–601. Snow argued the case for three U.S. senators (Democrats Ed Muskie, Frank Moss, and Warren Magnuson), who were hoping to investigate hydroelectric developments in China (ES to Mao, May 10, 1963). Dr. White did ultimately visit China in 1971 and was then accompanied by Clark's daughter, Mary Clark Dimond (Shewmaker, "Clark-Snow Correspondence," 600).

42. Diaries, Book 60, May 13, 1963; ES to Charles and Nina Hogan, July 25, 1963, Hogan files. ES to Bertram, April 5, 1959; ES to HFS, March 10, 1959, HFS to ES, February 12, 1961, ES to HFS, August 6, 1961, HFS files.

43. ES to HFS, April 4, 1962, HFS to ES, April 16, 1962, HFS files.

44. Diaries, Book 60, May 13, 1963; ES to Bertram, June 23, 1963, July 19, 1965, JBP in ESC.

45. ES to Bertram, July 19, 1965; ES, "An African Interview with Chou En-lai," *Arts and Sciences* (London) 2 (April–May 1964): 2–7; Allan S. Whiting, Department of State, "Memorandum of Conversation" (with Edgar Snow), St.-Cerque, Switzerland, April 2, 1965, 1, Snow FBI file in ESC.

46. Whiting, "Memorandum of Conversation," 2; ES, "Interview with Mao," *New Republic,* February 17, 1965, 17–23; more complete version in *The Long Revolution,* or *TLR* (New York: Random House, 1972), appendix, 197–223.

47. Whiting, "Memorandum of Conversation," 2. My discussion of the Mao-Snow exchange is based on the text in *TLR,* 197–223.

48. "Notes of Chairman Mao's Talk with Edgar Snow," December 18, 1970.

49. *TLR,* 220–221.

50. ES to Howard, April 13, 1965, HSP in ESC; ES to Mildred, April 13, 1965, MP in ESC.

51. ES to Alley, November 12, 30, 1966, RAP in ESC; ES to "Dick," July 4, 1966, ESP in ESC; ES, "China and Vietnam," *New Republic,* July 30, 1966, 12–14; ES to Howard, June 1, 1965, HSP in ESC.

52. ES to Anna Wang Martens (the former wife of Chinese Communist diplomat Wang Bingnan), September 26, 1969, ESC; ES to Howard, July 15, 1968, HSP in ESC; ES to Alley, July 22, 1967; interviews with Chen Hanbo, Beijing, June 25, 1988, and Lo Xinyao, Beijing, June 8, 1987; ES to Mao, July 30, 1969, ESP in ESC; Diaries, Book 73, Beijing, October 1, 1970.

53. ES to Han Suyin, August 4, 1969, Han Suyin Papers in ESC.

54. ES to Anna Wang Martens, April 7, 1969, ESC; ES to "Mildred and Co.," November 3, 1968, MP in ESC.

55. ES to Anna Wang Martens, September 26, 1969; ES to Yoko Matsuoka, May 19, 1970, ESP in ESC; Lois Snow to Howard and Dorothy, July 16, 1970, HSP in ESC; ES to Mildred, May 17, 1970, MP in ESC; Lois Snow to Howard and Dorothy, January 11, 1969, HSP in ESC; ES to Charles Hogan, October 9, 1969, Hogan files; Lois Snow to Howard and Dorothy, May 28, 1969, HSP in ESC.

56. ES to Mildred, May 17, 1970, MP in ESC; ES to Howard, May 22, 1969, HSP in ESC.

57. *Red China Today* (New York: Random House, 1971), 33–40.

58. Ibid., 40.

59. Ibid., 38–40.

Chapter 16. Last Hurrah

1. Diaries, Book 71, Hong Kong, July 31, 1970; Robert Mills to ES, July 20, 1970, RHP. Lois also received a Random House contract for a book on the Chinese theater (Robert Mills to Lois Snow, July 20, 1970, RHP).

2. Diaries, Book 71, Hong Kong, August 11, Canton, August 14–15, 1970.

3. Ibid., Beijing, August 16, 1970.

4. Ibid.

5. Ibid., August 23 and 27, September 5, 1970.

6. Diaries, Book 72, Beijing, August 31–September 3, 1970.

7. Diaries, Book 73, Xi'an, Yan'an, Bao'an, September 20–26, 1970; Book 75, Bao'an, Xi'an, September 22 and 24, 1970; ES to Mary Heathcote, November 27, 1970, ESP in ESC.

8. Diaries, Book 73, October 1, 1970; Henry A. Kissinger, *White House Years* (Boston: Little, Brown), 698. Nixon floated a much blunter signal at that time in the course of a *Time* interview, Kissinger noted. "If there is anything I want to do before I die," Nixon remarked, "it is to go to China. If I don't, I want my children to" (699).

9. Diaries, Book 73, October 1, 1970.

10. Ibid., October 9, 1970.

11. Ibid., October 19, 1970; Lois Snow, *Death with Dignity*, 111.

12. Diaries, Book 82, November 8, December 7, 1970.

13. Ibid., November 19, 1970.

14. *TLR*, 150; ES to Mary Heathcote, August 30, 1970, ESP in ESC; Lois Snow to Dorothy and Howard, September 4, 1970, HSP in ESC; Diaries, Book 82, November 20, 1970.

15. *TLR*, 160.

16. ES to Mary Heathcote, August 30, 1970; *TLR*, 168; "Notes of Chairman Mao's Talk with Edgar Snow," December 18, 1970, 1–2, ESP in ESC.

17. This description of the Mao-Snow conversation is based on both the more formally transcribed notes cited in note 16 above, and on the informal draft notes of the talk, as recounted by Ed to Lois immediately after the interview ("Mao Tse-tung Interview," December 18, 1970, Beijing, ESP in ESC.)

18. "Notes of Mao's Talk," 19; ES, "A Conversation with Mao Tse-tung," *Life,* April 30, 1971, 48; Yao Wei to ES, August 21, 1971, ESP in ESC. Yao Wei's interpretation is corroborated in the recent account by Mao's physician, Li Zhisui, *The Private Life of Chairman Mao* (New York: Random House, 1994), 120. "Mao's interpreter that day," Li writes, "was a young woman without a classical education" who misunderstood and mistranslated Mao's allusion to a "lone monk."

19. "Notes of Mao's Talk," 25–28.

20. Ibid., 6–7, 12. Though Mao also evinced some skepticism as to whether Nixon would really come, the Red leader was clearly both prodding and expecting the president to make the trip. (This seems more evident in Snow's original recollections of the conversation, "Mao Tse-tung Interview," 5–6.)

21. Mao's remarks to Nixon cited (from CCP documentary sources) in He Di, "The Most Respected Enemy: Mao Zedong's Perception of the United States," *CQ* 137 (March 1994): 145.

22. Li, *Private Life of Chairman Mao,* 105.

23. "Mao Tse-tung Interview," 2; "Notes on Mao's Talk," 31. "More and more people," Snow wrote Mao just weeks before his (Snow's) death "see how necessary, wise, and difficult have been these steps of your leadership which have brought China's revolutionary achievements into brilliant illumination of the world" (ES to Mao, December [no day], 1971, Beijing, Museum of the Chinese Revolution). Yet he could also record in his diary while in China the year before that "Mao is a mixture of Hollywood star and god" (Diaries, Book 73, September 7, 1970). Li Zhisui seems on shaky ground in reporting that in 1970 Mao thought Snow to be a CIA agent (*Private Life of Chairman Mao,* 532). If accurate, it would appear more likely to have been an example of Mao's often eccentric and exaggerated rhetorical style — in this case, in connection with his use of Snow as an informal and indirect channel of communication with Washington. Li himself is quite wide of the mark in stating that Snow was "a pariah in his own country" in 1970 (ibid.).

24. Lois Wheeler Snow, *China on Stage* (New York: Random House, 1972); Diaries, Book 82, December 21 and 22, 1970, January 15, 25, and 30, February 6 and 7, 1971.

25. Lois Snow, *Death with Dignity,* 26–31; ES to Senator George McGovern, March 8, 1971, ESP in ESC; Kissinger, *White House Years,* 698–718.

26. "Mao Tse-tung Interview," 12; ES to Mao, May 16, 1971, ES to Hsu Ching-wei (Chinese consul general, Geneva), April 26, 1971, ESP in ESC; ES, "A Conversation with Mao Tse-tung," 47; *New York Times,* February 20, 1972, Week in Review; Kissinger, *White House Years,* 703, 708–720; Secretary Rogers's statement, 720.

27. Kissinger, *White House Years,* 745–746, 759.

28. Lois Snow, *Death with Dignity,* 35–46; interview with Oliver Clubb, Syracuse, February 24, 1987; ES to Mao ("Dear Friend"), February 6, 1971, ES to Mary Heathcote, May 29, June 26, July 2, 1971, ES to John Simon (Random House), October 13, 1971, ESP in ESC.

29. ES to Owen Lattimore, May 19, 1970, ES to Senator George McGovern, March 8, 1971, ES to "Shag" (Hatem), December 6, 1971, "Interview with Edgar Snow, 1971," ESP in ESC; Lois Snow, *Death with Dignity,* 67; Lois Snow to Charles Hogan, March 13, 1972, Hogan files.

30. ES, "What China Wants from Nixon's Visit," *Life,* July 30, 1971, 22–26; also the final chapter in *TLR,* 179–188.

31. "What China Wants from Nixon's Visit," 26; *TLR,* 188.

32. Kissinger, *White House Years,* 750–751.

33. ES to Mao, July 30, 1969, ESP in ESC.

34. *JTTB,* 417; *RCT,* 6–7 (here Snow removed the qualifier "probably"); Beijing, November 1, 1989, report (*Foreign Broadcast Information Service Daily Report: China* [National Technical Information Service, U.S. Department of Commerce, Springfield, Va.]); ES to Mao, May 10, 1963.

35. Lois Snow, *Death with Dignity,* 47–63; Lois Snow to "Shag," December 17, 1971, Beijing, foreign ministry files, Museum of the Chinese Revolution; Lois Snow to Dorothy and Howard, December 27, 1971, HSP in ESC; Ralph Graves (*Life*) to ES, July 22, September 17, 1971, ESP in ESC.

36. ES to John Simon, January 4, 1972, ESP in ESC; ES to Zhou Enlai ("Dear Friend"), January 19, 1972, foreign ministry files, Museum of the Chinese Revolution.

37. Lois Snow to "Shag," December 15 and 22, 1971, Ma Haide (Hatem) to Zhang Wenjin (ministry of foreign affairs), December 24, 1971, January 2, 1972, foreign ministry files, Museum of the Chinese Revolution; ES to Zhou, December (no day) 1971, and to Mao, December (no day) 1971, Museum of the Chinese Revolution; ES to Zhou, January 19, 1972, ESP in ESC. Hatem asked Zhang Wenjin to forward Lois Snow's letter to Mao and Zhou and suggested that Ed be invited to China for care in his final illness.

38. Lois Snow, *Death with Dignity,* 87–133; Lois Snow to Charles Hogan, March 13, 1972; Huang Hua, speech at tenth anniversary Snow memorial meeting, Beijing, February 15, 1982, Hugh Deane Papers, ESC; interview with Dr. Huang Huojun, Beijing, June 3, 1987; John Roots to Henry Kissinger, February 19, 1972, Nixon Presidential Materials, National Archives, Washington, D.C.

39. Edgar Snow's will (October 1965), typed copy from Museum of the Chinese Revolution; Lois Wheeler Snow, "The Burial of Edgar Snow," *New Republic,* January 26, 1974, 9–11.

40. John S. Service, "Edgar Snow: Some Personal Reminiscences," *CQ* 50 (April–June 1972): 218; Mary Heathcote, talk at memorial meeting for Snow, New York, March 27, 1972, James Bertram to Lois, Sian, and Christopher Snow, February 20, 1972, ESP in ESC; ES to Howard, May 22, 1969.

41. Lois Snow to author, June 30, 1989; ES to Howard, July 15, 1968; David Shambaugh, *Beautiful Imperialist* (Princeton: Princeton University Press, 1991); James C. Thomson, Jr., Peter W. Stanley, and John Curtis Perry, *Sentimental Imperialists* (New York: Harper and Row, 1981), 293; Nicholas D. Kristof, "The Rise of China," *Foreign Affairs* 72 (November/December 1993): 73–74.

42. ES to Mr. Chen, January 4, 1964, ESP in ESC.

43. Diaries, Book 73, October 10, 1970.

44. *JTTB,* 423; *RCT,* 737–738; ES to James Bertram, April 5, 1959.

45. ES, "The Last Chapter" (note fragment, undated), ESP in ESC.

46. United Nations Development Programme, *Human Development Report 1994* (New York: Oxford University Press, 1994), 1–4; Brian Urquhart, "Who Can Police the World?" *New York Review of Books,* May 12, 1994, 33.

Select Bibliography

Primary Sources

See chapter notes for the full range of secondary sources used.

EDGAR SNOW'S WORKS

Books

Far Eastern Front. New York: Harrison Smith and Robert Haas, 1933.
Living China: Modern Chinese Short Stories. Compiled and edited by Edgar
   Snow. New York: John Day, in association with Reynal and Hitchcock,
   1936.
Red Star Over China. New York: Random House, 1938. Modern Library
   edition, Random House, 1944.
Battle for Asia. New York: Random House, 1941.
People on Our Side. New York: Random House, 1944.
The Pattern of Soviet Power. New York: Random House, 1945.
Stalin Must Have Peace. New York: Random House, 1947.
Random Notes on Red China, 1936–1945. Harvard East Asian Monographs, no. 5.
   Cambridge, Mass.: Harvard University, 1957.
Journey to the Beginning. New York: Random House, 1958.
The Other Side of the River: Red China Today. New York: Random House, 1962.
   Revised edition published as *Red China Today* (New York: Random House,
   1970).
Red Star Over China. Revised and enlarged edition. New York: Grove Press,
   1968.
The Long Revolution. New York: Random House, 1972.

Articles

"In Hula Land." *Harper's Bazaar* 62 (September 1928): 98–99, 136, 138, 142.

"Lifting China Out of the Mud!" *China Weekly Review,* October 10, 1928, 84–91.

"A *First Class* Stowaway." *New York Herald-Tribune Magazine,* October 21, 1928, 10–11, 14.

"Kansas City Boy Stowaway." *Kansas City Journal-Post,* November 11, 1928.

"Japanese Interference at the Yellow River Bridge—and Other Aspects of Tsinanfu." *China Weekly Review,* January 19, 1929, 315–318.

"Adventures in Chinese Advertising." *Advertising & Selling,* May 1, 1929, 30, 32, 90, 92.

"Which Way Manchuria." *China Weekly Review,* July 20, 1929, 333–339.

"Saving 250,000 Lives." *New York Herald-Tribune Magazine,* September 8, 1929, 14–15, 31.

"The 'Middle Kingdom' from the Clouds." *China Weekly Review,* October 19, 1929, 273–276, 278.

"Chinese Please Use Rear Entrance." *China Weekly Review,* November 9, 1929, 369–370.

"Son of the Grand Marshal." *New York Herald-Tribune Magazine,* December 15, 1929, 14–15, 25.

"China Creates a New God." *New York Herald-Tribune Magazine,* March 16, 1930, 4–5, 14.

"Daughters of China's Revolution." *New York Herald-Tribune Magazine,* April 6, 1930, 1–3.

"The Americans in Shanghai." *American Mercury* 20 (August 1930): 427–445.

"Chinese Guests Now Welcome." *New York Sun,* September 25, 1930.

"Some Results of 35 Years of Japanese Rule in Formosa." *China Weekly Review,* November 15, 1930, 389–391.

"The Strength of Communism in China, I: The Bolshevist Influence." *Current History* 33 (January 1931): 521–526.

"En Route from Taihoku to Hong Kong via the Subsidized D.S.K.—a Second-Class Passage with Two Chinese Ladies, a Japanese Girl and Three Japanese Men." *New York Sun,* April 28, 1931.

"The Railroad Journey to Yunnanfu Is Filled with Scenic Thrills." *New York Sun,* June 30, 1931.

"Canton, Metropolis of South China, Where the Feverish Rush of Occidental Cities Is Noted—Much of the Old Has Made Way for Modern Progress." *New York Sun,* April 9, 1931. Reprinted as "Canton—Home of Rebels and Revolutions" (*China Weekly Review,* August 1, 1931, 344, 346–347).

"The Trial of British Communists at Meerut, India." *China Weekly Review,* September 19, 1931, 106.

"The Revolt of India's Women." *New York Herald-Tribune Magazine,* October 25, 1931, 14–15, 24–25.

"Calcutta, India, City of Contrasting Beauty and Squalor—The Hindu Rituals on the Banks of the Sacred Ganges River." *New York Sun,* October 29, 1931.

"In the Wake of China's Flood." *China Weekly Review,* January 23, 1932, 243–245.

"Says Reds Will Rule China." *New York Sun*, October 18, 1932.

"She Fights for China's Masses." *New York Herald-Tribune Magazine*, August 6, 1933, 10–11, 19.

"The Decline of Western Prestige." *Saturday Evening Post*, August 26, 1933, 12–14, 67–69.

"How Rural China Is Being Re-made." *China Weekly Review*, December 16 and 30, 1933, 98–101, 202–203.

"Weak China's Strong Man." *Current History* 39 (January 1934): 402–408.

"Japan Builds a New Colony." *Saturday Evening Post*, February 24, 1934, 12–13, 80–81, 84–87.

"Lu Shun, Master of Pai-Hua." *Asia* 35 (January 1935): 40–43.

"Christmas Escapade in Japan." *Travel*, January 1935, 34–38, 47.

"Japan Imposes Her Culture." *Asia* 35 (April 1935): 218–224.

"The Ways of the Chinese Censor." *Current History* 42 (July 1935): 381–386.

"Japan Digs In." *Saturday Evening Post* , January 4, 1936, 8–9, 56–58.

"The Japanese Juggernaut Rolls On." *Saturday Evening Post* , May 9, 1936, 8–9, 89–90, 92.

"The Coming Conflict in the Orient." *Saturday Evening Post*, June 6, 1936, 14–15, 82, 84–85, 87.

"Mr. Hirota's Third Point." *Foreign Affairs* 14 (July 1936): 596–605.

"Interviews with Mao Tse-tung, Communist Leader." *China Weekly Review*, November 14 and 21, 1936, 377–379, 420–421.

"An Army of Fighting Chinese Communists Takes Possession of China's Northwest." *Life*, February 1, 1937, 44–49.

"Autobiography of Mao Tse-tung." *Asia* 37 (July 1937): 480–488; 37 (August 1937): 570–578; 37 (September 1937): 619–623; 37 (October 1937): 682–686.

"Soviet China." *New Republic*, August 4, 1937, 351–354; August 11, 1937, 9–11; August 18, 1937, 42–44; September 8, 1937, 124–125.

"The Long March." *Asia* 37 (October 1937): 687–692; 37 (November 1937): 741–747.

"I Went to Red China." *Saturday Evening Post*, November 6, 1937, 9–10, 98, 100–103.

"The Sun Also Sets." *Saturday Evening Post*, June 14, 1938, 5–6, 30, 33–34, 37.

"China's Fighting Generalissimo." *Foreign Affairs* 16 (July 1938): 613–625.

"They Love Us, They Love Us Not." *Saturday Evening Post*, April 29, 1939, 25, 62, 64, 69.

"China's New Industrial Army." *Left News* (London), July 1939, 1346–1347.

"Filipinos Change Their Minds." *Asia* 39 (September 1939): 493–496.

"Japan's 'Peaceful' Invasion." *Asia* 39 (October 1939): 590–592.

"Filipinos Want a Guarantee." *Asia* 39 (November 1939): 659–661.

"China's Precarious Unity." *New Republic*, January 8, 1940, 44–45.

"Chinese Communists and Wars on Two Continents: Interviews with Mao Tse-tung." *China Weekly Review*, January 13, 20, 1940, 244–246, 277–280.

"The Dragon Licks His Wounds." *Saturday Evening Post*, April 13, 1940, 9–11, 155, 157–158, 160.

"Will Stalin Sell Out China?" *Foreign Affairs* 18 (April 1940): 450–463.

"Chiang's Armies." *Asia* 40 (November 1940): 579–582.

"The Generalissimo." *Asia* 40 (December 1940): 646–648.

"Break Is Feared as Chiang-Red Split Deepens." *New York Herald-Tribune,* December 26, 1940.

"Reds Fought Off Chiang's Troops 9 Days in China." *New York Herald-Tribune,* January 22, 1941.

"Things That Could Happen." *Asia* 41 (January 1941): 7–16.

"China's Blitzbuilder, Rewi Alley." *Saturday Evening Post,* February 8, 1941, 12–13, 36, 38, 40.

"Is It Civil War in China?" *Asia* 41 (April 1941): 166–170.

"Showdown in the Pacific." *Saturday Evening Post,* May 31, 1941, 27, 40, 43–44, 47.

"How America Can Take the Offensive: II." *Fortune* 23 (June 1941): 69, 175–180. Also published as "The Political Battle of Asia" in Edmund Taylor, et al., *Smash Hitler's International: The Strategy of a Political Offensive Against the Axis.* New York: Keystone Press, 1941, 49–71.

"China and the World War." *Asia* 41 (July 1941): 341–343.

"They Don't Want to Play Soldier." *Saturday Evening Post,* October 25, 1941, 14–15, 61, 63–67.

"What Is Morale?" *Saturday Evening Post,* November 15, 1941, 16–17, 117–120, 122–123.

"How Russia Upset Hitler." *Saturday Evening Post,* January 30, 1943, 20–21, 87, 89–90.

"What Kind of a Man Is a Russian General?" *Saturday Evening Post,* April 17, 1943, 20–21, 105–106.

"I Saw It with My Own Eyes." *Saturday Evening Post,* May 29, 1943, 12–13, 86, 88.

"The Nazi Butchers Wasted Nothing." *Saturday Evening Post,* October 28, 1944, 18–19, 96.

"Eastern Europe Swings Left." *Saturday Evening Post,* November 11, 1944, 9–11, 69–71.

"Is Red Marriage Turning Blue?" *Saturday Evening Post,* January 13, 1945, 28–29, 36.

"The Ukraine Pays the Bill." *Saturday Evening Post,* January 27, 1945, 18–19, 82–84.

"Must China Go Red?" *Saturday Evening Post,* May 12, 1945, 9–10, 67–68, 70.

"The Stalin Truman Faces." *Saturday Evening Post,* June 30, 1945, 20–21, 63–64.

"Meet Mr. and Mrs. Russia at Home." *Saturday Evening Post,* December 22, 1945, 14–15, 65.

"The Message of Gandhi." *Saturday Evening Post,* March 27, 1948, 24–25, 143–144.

"Will Tito's Heretics Halt Russia?" *Saturday Evening Post,* December 18, 1948, 23, 108–110.

"Will China Become a Russian Satellite?" *Saturday Evening Post,* April 9, 1949, 30–31, 147–150.

"The Venomous Doctor Vyshinsky." *Saturday Evening Post,* October 21, 1950, 19–21, 143–144, 146.

"The New Phase—Undeclared War." *Nation,* March 10, 1951, 220–223.

"Red China's Gentleman Hatchet Man." *Saturday Evening Post,* March 27, 1954, 24–25, 116, 118–119.

"Point IV for America." *Nation*, May 12, 1956, 394–397.
"A Report from Red China." *Look*, January 31, 1961, 85–88, 91–94, 97–98, 103–104.
"An African Interview with Chou En-lai." *Arts and Sciences* (London) 2
    (April–May 1964): 2–7.
"Interview with Mao." *New Republic*, February 17, 1965, 17–23.
"China and Vietnam." *New Republic*, July 30, 1966, 12–14.
"Mao and the New Mandate." *New Republic*, May 10, 1969, 17–21.
"Aftermath of the Cultural Revolution." *New Republic*, April 10, 1971, 18–21.
"A Conversation with Mao Tse-tung." *Life*, April 30, 1971, 46–48.
"What China Wants from Nixon's Visit." *Life*, July 30, 1971, 22–26.

Miscellaneous Items

"The Meaning of Fascism." Yanjing University lecture, December 1934.
    Published in *Peiping Chronicle*, January 8–12, 1935.
"First Pictures of China's Roving Communists." *Life*, January 25, 1937, 9–13.
"The Reds and the Northwest." Peking Men's Forum talk, January 21, 1937.
    Published in *Shanghai Evening Post and Mercury*, February 5, 1937.
"Notes on Mao Interview." Hong Kong, November 4, 1939. Edgar Snow
    Papers–Edgar Snow Collection.
"The Three Soong Sisters." November 2, 1940. Nym Wales Collection.
Nym Wales. Preface to *China Builds for Democracy*. Hong Kong: Kelly and
    Walsh, 1940.
"China, America, and the World War." May 31, 1941. Undelivered speech
    prepared for American Writers Congress, June 1941. Edgar Snow
    Papers–Edgar Snow Collection.
Autobiographical Note (1944). Random House Papers.
"Notes on Edgar Snow Conversation with Maxim Litvinov, Vice-Commissar
    of Foreign Affairs of the USSR." October 8, 1944. Presidential Papers.
    Franklin D. Roosevelt Library.
Interview with Edgar Snow. Tokyo, Armed Forces Radio, January 29, 1946.
    Edgar Snow Collection.
"Missouri Days." Unpublished chapter for *Journey to the Beginning*. Random
    House Papers.
"The Last American Missionary to China or the Divorce of Mao Tse-tung."
    July 1956. John King Fairbank Papers.
"Notes on Conversations with Old Students (1960)." Edgar Snow
    Papers–Edgar Snow Collection.
"Notes on Mr. Edgar Snow's Interviews with Premier Chou En-lai." Beijing,
    August 30, October 18, 1960. Edgar Snow Papers–Edgar Snow Collection.
"Notes on Meeting with Mao Tse-tung." Beijing, October 22, 27, 1960. Edgar
    Snow Papers–Edgar Snow Collection.
"On Publication of Chou En-lai Interview and Other China Material."
    December 4, 1960. Anna Louise Strong Papers, Beijing University.
Edgar Snow's Will. October 1965. Typed copy, Museum of the Chinese
    Revolution, Beijing.
"The December Ninth Movement." Comment, *China Quarterly* 26
    (April–June 1966): 171–172.

"Notes of Chairman Mao's Talk with Edgar Snow." Beijing, December 18, 1970. Edgar Snow Papers–Edgar Snow Collection.

Diaries

Transcripts of Snow's diary notebooks, received from Lois Wheeler Snow

Books 1–8, 1A	February 1928–January 1931
Book 10	January–February 1933
Books 11–19	June–October 1936
Books 20–35	July 1937–January 1942
Books 37–54	February 1942–November 1948
Book 58	October 1959–January 1960
Book 60	October 1962–January 1964
Book 66	December 1964–January 1965
Books 71–75, 77	July–October 1970
Book 82	November 1970–February 1971 (directly follows Book 77)

Edited Collections

Dimond, E. Grey. *Ed Snow Before Paoan: The Shanghai Years*. Kansas City: Edgar Snow Memorial Fund, undated. Excerpts of Snow letters in the Edgar Snow Collection.

Farnsworth, Robert M. *Edgar Snow's Journey South of the Clouds*. Columbia: University of Missouri Press, 1991. A compilation, with commentary, of Snow's articles written during his 1930–1931 travels in southern China, Indochina, Burma, and India.

Snow, Lois Wheeler. *Edgar Snow's China: A Personal Account of the Chinese Revolution Compiled from the Writings of Edgar Snow*. New York: Random House, 1981.

Archival Collections and Papers

Edgar Snow Collection

Major holdings in the collection in University Archives, University of Missouri–Kansas City

Edgar Snow Papers
Mildred and Claude Mackey Papers
Howard Snow Papers

Rewi Alley Papers
Mary Clark Dimond Papers
Henry Mitchell Collection

The collection also includes correspondence files acquired from many other individuals with a Snow connection, including James Bertram, Israel Epstein, Han Suyin, and Kenneth Shewmaker, and Snow materials from China sources.

For complete contents of the Edgar Snow Papers, see *A Guide to the Edgar Snow Papers*. Kansas City: University of Missouri–Kansas City Archives, July 1994.

Other Archival Sources

Asiaticus [Heinz Shippe] file, Institute of Pacific Relations Papers, University of British Columbia, Vancouver
Grenville Clark Papers, Baker Library, Dartmouth College. Copies of the Snow-Clark correspondence from these papers are also in the Edgar Snow Collection
John King Fairbank Papers, Pusey Library, Harvard University
Henry Ford Office Correspondence, Henry Ford Papers, Henry Ford Museum, Dearborn, Michigan
J. William Fulbright Papers, Special Collections Department, University of Arkansas Libraries
Randall Gould Papers, Hoover Library, Stanford University
Grace and Max Granich Papers, Tamiment Library, New York University
Ben Hibbs Papers, Spencer Research Library, University of Kansas
Indusco Files, Rare Book and Manuscript Library, Columbia University
Institute of Pacific Relations Papers, Rare Book and Manuscript Library, Columbia University
Philip J. Jaffe Papers, Woodruff Library, Emory University
Nelson T. Johnson Papers, Manuscript Division, Library of Congress
Random House Papers, Rare Book and Manuscript Library, Columbia University
Snow files, Smedley-Strong-Snow Society of China, Beijing
Snow files, Museum of the Chinese Revolution, Beijing
Anna Louise Strong Papers, Manuscript Section, University of Washington Library
Anna Louise Strong Papers, Library, Beijing University
Charles Hanson Towne Papers, Rare Books and Manuscripts Division, New York Public Library
Nym Wales Collection, Hoover Library, Stanford University

U.S. GOVERNMENT SOURCES AND PRESIDENTIAL ARCHIVES

Department of State. *Foreign Relations of the United States: Diplomatic Papers, 1944.* Vol. 6, *China.* Washington, D.C.: U.S. Government Printing Office, 1967.
———. Snow documents (obtained through Freedom of Information Act).
Federal Bureau of Investigation. Edgar Snow file (copy in Edgar Snow Collection).

Lyndon B. Johnson Library. Presidential Papers. Austin, Texas.
National Archives. Files of Nixon Presidential Materials.
Franklin D. Roosevelt Library. Presidential Papers. Hyde Park, New York.
Harry S. Truman Library. Presidential Papers. Independence, Missouri.
U.S. Senate Committee on the Judiciary. Internal Security Subcommittee.
    Institute of Pacific Relations Hearings, 1951–1952. Washington, D.C.: U.S.
    Government Printing Office, 1952.

Privately Held Personal Files

Polly Babcock Feustel files
Dr. Charles and Nina Hogan files
Helen Foster Snow files

Personal Memoirs

Alley, Rewi. *At 90: Memoirs of My China Years*. Beijing: New World Press,
    1987.
Bertram, James. *Capes of China Slide Away: A Memoir of Peace and War,
    1910–1980*. Auckland: Auckland University Press, 1993.
Braun, Otto. *A Comintern Agent in China, 1932–1939*. Translated from the
    German by Jeanne Moore. Stanford: Stanford University Press, 1982.
Fairbank, John K. *Chinabound: A Fifty-Year Memoir*. New York: Harper and
    Row, 1982.
Jaffe, Philip J. "Odyssey." Philip J. Jaffe Papers, Emory University, Atlanta,
    Georgia.
Kissinger, Henry A. *White House Years*. Boston: Little, Brown and Company,
    1979.
Service, John S. "Edgar Snow: Some Personal Reminiscences." *China
    Quarterly* 50 (April–June 1972): 209–219.
Snow, Helen Foster. *My China Years*. New York: William Morrow, 1984.
Snow, Lois Wheeler. *A Death with Dignity: When the Chinese Came*. New
    York: Random House, 1974.
"Reminiscences of Anna Louise Strong." Anna Louise Strong Papers, Beijing
    University.
Vladimirov, Peter. *The Vladimirov Diaries: Yenan: 1942–1945*. New York:
    Doubleday, 1975. Edited from a translation supplied by the Novosti Press
    Agency Publishing House, Moscow.
Wales, Nym. "My Yenan Notebooks." Nym Wales Collection, 1961.
    Mimeographed.
"The Reminiscences of Bennet Cerf." Oral History Research Office, Columbia
    University, 1967–1968.
"Helen Foster Snow." Oral History Research Office, Columbia University,
    1977.
"Interview with Major-General William H. Worton, U.S. Marine Corps
    (ret.)." Oral History Research Office, Columbia University, 1969.

Persons Interviewed

United States (1986–1990)

Susan B. Anthony, II
O. Edmund Clubb (by correspondence)
Oliver Clubb
Harry Davis
Peggy Durdin
John K. Fairbank
Polly Babcock Feustel
Dr. Charles Hogan and Nina Hogan
Owen Lattimore (by correspondence)
Claude Mackey
William Powell
Trudie Schafer
Helen Foster Snow
John Snow
Lois Wheeler Snow
Margaret Stanley
Leland Stowe
Dr. Charles White

China (1987 and 1988)

Rewi Alley (Beijing)
An Wei (Xi'an)
Bai Li (Bao'an)
Chen Hanbo (Beijing)
Chen Hansheng (Han-seng) (Beijing)
Chen Hoheng (Beijing)
Chen Hui (Beijing)
Chen Xiuxia (Beijing)
Dong Leshan (Beijing)
Dong Weifang (Beijing)
Du Jiangguo (Yan'an)
Israel Epstein (Beijing)
Gao Liang (Beijing)
Talitha Gerlach (Shanghai)
Guo Da (Beijing)
Dr. Huang Guojun (Beijing)
Huang Hua (Wang Rumei) (Beijing)
Li Min (Beijing)
Li Xue ("Mike"—Alley's son) (Beijing)
Florence Yu Liang (Shanghai)
Liu Liqun (Beijing)
Liu Zunqi (Beijing)

Lu Guangmian (Beijing)
Lu Wanru (Beijing)
Lo Xinyao (Beijing)
Dr. Ma Haide (George Hatem) (Beijing)
Meng Bo (Shanghai)
Trudy Rosenberg (Beijing)
Sidney Shapiro (Beijing)
Wang Fushi (Beijing)
Ruth Weiss (Beijing)
Xiao Qian (Beijing)
Yang Xiaofo (Shanghai)
Yu Janting (Beijing)
Zhang Xiaoding (Beijing)
Zhang Yifang (Beijing)
Zhao Rongsheng (Beijing)
Zhou Shenlin (Shanghai)

Japan (1987 and 1988)

Reiko Matsuoka (Tokyo)
Seiko Matsuoka (Tokyo)

New Zealand (1989)

James Bertram (by correspondence)

India (1989)

Ram Chattopadhyaya (by correspondence)

OTHER SOURCES

Chinese Sources

Alley, Rewi. "Edgar Snow." In *Six Americans in China,* 43–70. Beijing:
    Intercul, 1985.
Liang, Hubert S. "Edgar Snow—the Man and His Work." Nanjing University
    lecture, May 1979. Received from Florence Yu Liang.
Liu Liqun, ed. *Ji-nian Ai-de-jia Si-nuo* (In commemoration of Edgar Snow).
    Beijing: Xinhua Press, 1982.
Qiu Ke'an, ed. *Si-nuo zai Zhongguo* (Snow in China). Beijing: San-lian
    Bookstore, 1980.
Wang Fushi, ed. "Wai Guo Ji Zhe Xi Bei Yin Xiang Ji" (A foreign journalist's
    impressions of the northwest). Beiping, 1937. Translation of portions of
    Snow's *Red Star Over China.*
Wang Xing, ed. *China Remembers Edgar Snow.* Beijing: China Publications
    Centre, 1982.

Wu Liangping, ed. *Mao Zedong i-jiu san-liu nian tong Si-nuo de tan-hua* (Mao Zedong's 1936 talks with Edgar Snow). Beijing, August 1979. 3-S Society files.

Xixing Man Ji (Journey to the west). Beijing: Xinhua Press, 1979. Translation by Don Leshan of *Red Star Over China.*

Zhang Keming. "Guomindang Zhengfu dui Si-nuo Zhu-zuo de Cha-jin" (Regarding the banning of Snow's works by the Kuomintang government). *She-hui Ke-xue* (Social sciences) (Fudan University, Shanghai) 1 (1985): 99–100.

Zhang Xiaoding. "Shan yao Shijie de 'Hong Xing'" (The "Red Star" shines over the world). *Bulletin of the China Society of Library Science* (Beijing) 1 (1980): 84–89.

———. "Si-nuo yu *Xixing Man Ji*" (Snow and *Journey to the West*). *Chang Cheng* (Great wall) (Beijing) 1 (1980): 184–191.

Zhao Rongsheng and Zhao Yu, eds. "*I-er-jiu*" *zai Wei-ming Lu-pan* (The "December Ninth" movement at No-Name lakeside). Beijing: Beijing Press, 1985.

RUSSIAN SOURCES

Bereznyi, L. A. "Zarozhdenie promaoiskoy kontseptsii kitaiskoy revolutsii v amerikanskoy istoriografii" (Emergence of the pro-Maoist conception of the Chinese revolution in U.S. historiography). In *Istoriografia i istochnikovedenie istorii stran Asii i Afriki* (Historiography and bibliography of history of countries of Asia and Africa), part 4, 12–23. Leningrad State University, 1975.

Borisov, O. B., and B. T. Koloskov. *Sino-Soviet Relations, 1945–1970.* Bloomington: Indiana University Press, 1975. Translated from the Russian "by machine," and edited, with an introductory essay, by Vladimir Petrov.

Pashchenko, E. "Edgar Snow and the 'China Card.'" *Far Eastern Affairs* (Moscow) 1 (1981): 151–160.

Reviews of *Red Star Over China. Knizhnye Novosti* (Book news) (Moscow), nos. 12, 17–18 (1938).

Snow, E. *Geroicheskii narod Kitaya* (Heroic people of China). Moscow: C. K. VLKSM–Molodaya Gvardiya, 1938. Abridged translation of *Red Star Over China.*

Titov, A. S. "O polititcheskikh kontaktakh Mao Tsze-duna s Edgarom Snow" (Political contacts of Mao Zedong with Edgar Snow). *Problemy Dalnego Vostoka* (Problems of the Far East) (Moscow) 2 (1972): 119–127.

OTHER WRITINGS ON EDGAR SNOW

Boorstin, Robert O. "Edgar Snow and America's Search for a Better China: The Making of *Red Star Over China,* 1928–1938." B.A. thesis, Harvard University, 1981.

Dimond, Mary Clark. *Edgar Snow, 1905–1972.* Kansas City: Edgar Snow Memorial Fund, University of Missouri–Kansas City, 1982.

Erickson, Bruce R. "The Reporting of Edgar Snow." M.S. thesis, University of Kansas, 1976.

Hamilton, John Maxwell. "The Missouri News Monopoly and American Altruism in China: Thomas F. F. Millard, J. B. Powell, and Edgar Snow." *Pacific Historical Review* 55 (February 1986): 27–48.

———. "Edgar Snow: China Hand from Missouri." *Missouri Historical Review* 81 (April 1987): 253–274.

———. *Edgar Snow: A Biography.* Bloomington: Indiana University Press, 1988.

Israel, Jerry. "Mao's Mr. America: Edgar Snow's Images of China." *Pacific Historical Review* 47 (February 1978): 107–122.

Shewmaker, Kenneth E. *Americans and Chinese Communists, 1927–1945: A Persuading Encounter.* Ithaca: Cornell University Press, 1971. Includes material on Edgar Snow and Helen Foster Snow.

Snow, Lois Wheeler. "The Burial of Edgar Snow." *New Republic*, January 26, 1974, 9–11.

Index

Compositor:	Impressions Book and Journal Services, Inc.
Text:	10/13 Galliard
Display:	Galliard
Printer and Binder:	Edwards Brothers, Inc.